SEEKING WISDOM'S DEPTHS AND TORAH'S HEIGHTS

Smyth & Helwys Publishing, Inc.
6316 Peake Road
Macon, Georgia 31210-3960
1-800-747-3016
©2020 by Barry R. Huff and Patricia Vesely
All rights reserved.

Cover photograph: Petra, Jordan, by Barry R. Huff

Library of Congress Cataloging-in-Publication Data

Names: Balentine, Samuel E. (Samuel Eugene), 1950- honoree. | Huff, Barry R., editor. | Vesely, Patricia, 1975- editor.
Title: Seeking wisdom's depths and Torah's heights : essays in honor of Samuel E. Balentine / edited by Barry R. Huff and Patricia Vesely.
Description: First. | Macon : Smyth & Helwys, 2020. | Includes bibliographical references and index.
Identifiers: LCCN 2020027850 | ISBN 9781641732314 (paperback)
Subjects: LCSH: Bible. Old Testament--Criticism, interpretation, etc. | Wisdom literature--Criticism, interpretation, etc.
Classification: LCC BS1171.3 .S4339 2020 | DDC 221.6--dc23
LC record available at https://lccn.loc.gov/2020027850

Disclaimer of Liability: With respect to statements of opinion or fact available in this work of nonfiction, Smyth & Helwys Publishing Inc. nor any of its employees, makes any warranty, express or implied, or assumes any legal liability or responsibility for the accuracy or completeness of any information disclosed, or represents that its use would not infringe privately-owned rights.

Edited by Barry R. Huff and Patricia Vesely

Seeking Wisdom's Depths and Torah's Heights

Essays in Honor of Samuel E. Balentine

Samuel E. Balentine

Acknowledgments

Samuel E. Balentine is an internationally acclaimed biblical scholar known for his detailed and theologically innovative work in wisdom and Torah. Sam's lasting impact on his colleagues, students, mentees, and friends is not just a result of his academic achievements, however, but also of his character. This was clearly demonstrated in the outpouring of enthusiastic responses from authors and publishers when we shared our plan to honor Sam with a Festschrift. We are grateful to the authors for their outstanding contributions to this volume. The expertise, insight, and time they have graciously given to this Festschrift are a wonderful tribute to Sam. Their groundbreaking essays resonate with Sam's publications in shedding new light on Torah, wisdom, and the human capacity to know God further. Due to Balentine's vast impact in biblical studies, these authors represent just a fraction of those who have been enriched by his scholarship and friendship. For the contributors to this volume, the endorsers, and the many authors to whom we were not able to extend invitations, we and Sam are truly thankful for the role you have played in his life.

We deeply appreciate Smyth & Helwys's wholehearted support for this project, from our initial conversation with Keith Gammons to the diligent work of Leslie Andres, Chelsea Madden, Dave Jones, Kelley Land, and all who were involved in bringing this volume to publication. Smyth & Helwys is a fitting home for Balentine's Festschrift in light of the over twenty-five years he has served as Old Testament General Editor for the Smyth & Helwys Bible Commentary series. The meaningful theological interpretation of biblical texts and insightful analysis of the Bible's reception history found throughout this series also are key features of this book.

We are grateful to the Fitzwilliam Museum for granting permission to access manuscripts in its collection and to the Harvard Art Museums, Museo Nacional del Prado, Princeton University's Scheide Library, The Frick Collection, Union Presbyterian Seminary's William Smith Morton Library, the Victoria and Albert Museum, and KIK-IRPA, Brussels, for granting permissions to use photographs of the items from their collections detailed in the List of Figures. Furthermore, we thank Amy Torbert and Betty Balentine for their photographs of Sam featured in the opening and closing of this book as well as Betty, Graham, and Lauren—Sam's beloved wife and children—for their heartfelt messages in Sam's biography.

While we have much to be thankful for, it was with great sadness that we learned of the passing of S. Dean McBride, Jr., one of the contributors, just prior to the publication of this volume. We are honored that Dean's voice is a part of the chorus of voices expressing their admiration of Sam. We are deeply grateful for the excellence of Dean's essay and the profound impact that his scholarship and character have had on all who were fortunate to know him.

Contents

Contributors	xv
List of Figures	xix
Abbreviations	xxiii
Introduction *Patricia Vesely and Barry R. Huff*	1
Biography: "Have You Considered My Servant, Samuel E. Balentine?" *E. Carson Brisson*	13
Bibliography of Samuel E. Balentine's Publications	25

Part I: Torah's Heights

1. There's a Wildness in God's Mercy: God's Sovereignty, Quantum Probability, and a Biblical Worldview *Mark E. Biddle*	39
2. The Primeval History as an Etiology of Torah *Andreas Schuele*	59
3. Why Moses Was Barred from the Land of Israel: A Reassessment of Numbers 20 in Literary Context *Marvin A. Sweeney*	75

4. Interpretive Reception of the Book of Exodus in the   89
    English Geneva Bible of 1560
      S. Dean McBride, Jr.

5. Finoglio's *Joseph and Potiphar's Wife* at Harvard: 127
    Biblical Reception Meets Art Historical Methodology
      Heidi J. Hornik with Mikeal Joseph Parsons

Part II: Wisdom's Depths

6. Practicality in a World of Hubris   157
      Walter Brueggemann

7. "God Set Infinity into Their Minds": Qohelet's Quest   179
    to Comprehend the Incomprehensible
      Heather Woodworth Brannon

8. Wisdom through Symbolic Objects: The Second   199
    Temple Intellectual Context of Symbolic Bodies in and
    beyond Proverbs 1–9
      Phillip Michael Lasater

9. Ethics and Character Formation in Biblical Wisdom Texts   233
      John Barton

10. Job and the "Comforting" Chaos   247
      William P. Brown

11. When Eternal Questions "Dance" within the Human   267
    Imagination: The Making of the Ballet *Job: A Masque
    for Dancing*
      Patricia Vesely

Part III: Torah in Wisdom and Wisdom as Torah

12. Woman Wisdom and Her Afterlife   295
      Katharine J. Dell

13. Sacred Recitation as Commentary in Ben Sira's Praise of   311
    the Ancestors
    Samuel L. Adams

14. Job the Priest: From Scripture to Sculpture   327
    Barry R. Huff

Scripture Index   355

Contributors

Samuel L. Adams is the Mary Jane and John F. McNair Chair in Biblical Studies and Professor of Old Testament at Union Presbyterian Seminary. He received his PhD from Yale University in 2006. He is the author of *Social and Economic Life in Second Temple Judea* (Westminster John Knox) and *Wisdom in Transition: Act and Consequence in Second Temple Instructions* (Brill), and he is editor of the journal *Interpretation*.

John Barton is Emeritus Oriel & Laing Professor of the Interpretation of Holy Scripture at University of Oxford, UK, and is a Senior Research Fellow at Campion Hall, Oxford. His most recent publication is *A History of the Bible: The Book and Its Faiths* (Allen Lane), also published as *A History of the Bible: The Story of the World's Most Influential Book* (Viking).

Mark E. Biddle, DTheol, served as Dr. Balentine's junior colleague at the Baptist Theological Seminary at Richmond until succeeding him as Russell T. Cherry Professor of Old Testament there. Even before that relationship, Biddle joined the editorial board of the Smyth & Helwys Bible Commentary series, of which Balentine is the Old Testament General Editor. Along with the volume on Deuteronomy in that series, Biddle's publications include a commentary on Judges, monographs on Jeremiah, *Missing the Mark: Sin and Its Consequences in Biblical Theology* (Abingdon), *A Time to Laugh: Humor in the Bible* (Smyth & Helwys), and numerous articles and reviews.

Heather Woodworth Brannon is currently a PhD candidate in Hebrew Bible at Emory University and a candidate for ordination in the Presbyterian Church (USA). She previously studied at Union Presbyterian Seminary with Samuel E. Balentine and at Johns Hopkins University. Her primary interests include epistemology, theodicy, and the reception history of wisdom literature, especially Job and Ecclesiastes.

E. Carson Brisson is Associate Professor of Bible and Biblical Languages at Union Presbyterian Seminary and Faculty Essayist for *Sharon & Brook* magazine, a publication of Union Presbyterian Seminary. Sam and Carson have been friends for many years. In addition to their years at the Baptist seminary in Wake Forest, North Carolina, they have served together since 2004 on the faculty of Union Presbyterian Seminary.

William P. Brown is an ordained minister of the Presbyterian Church (USA) and the William Marcellus McPheeters Professor of Old Testament at Columbia Theological Seminary. Bill has also taught at Union Presbyterian Seminary in Richmond and at Emory University. He is the author of several books and numerous essays, including *A Handbook to Old Testament Exegesis* (Westminster John Knox), *Sacred Sense* (Eerdmans), *Wisdom's Wonder* (Eerdmans), *The Seven Pillars of Creation* (Oxford University Press), and *Seeing the Psalms* (Westminster John Knox), and is editor of *Engaging Biblical Authority* (Westminster John Knox).

Walter Brueggemann is William Marcellus McPheeters Professor Emeritus of Old Testament at Columbia Theological Seminary. He is the author of over one hundred books and numerous scholarly articles. Some of his most recent monographs include *From Judgment to Hope: A Study on the Prophets* (Westminster John Knox), *Preaching from the Old Testament* (Fortress), and *Tenacious Solidarity: Biblical Provocations on Race, Religion, Climate, and the Economy* (Fortress).

Katharine J. Dell is Reader in Old Testament Literature and Theology at the Faculty of Divinity in the University of Cambridge and is a Fellow of St. Catharine's College, Cambridge. She is an expert on the wisdom literature of the Old Testament/Hebrew Bible and has written many books and articles, including *Job: An Introduction and Study Guide: Where Shall Wisdom Be Found* (Bloomsbury), *Opening the Old Testament* (Wiley-Blackwell), and *"Get Wisdom, Get Insight": An Introduction to Israel's Wisdom Literature* (Darton, Longman & Todd).

Heidi J. Hornik is Professor of Italian Renaissance and Baroque Art History at Baylor University. This paper is Hornik's first collaboration with her oldest son, **Mikeal Joseph Parsons** (Harvard, A.B., 2019), who studied the Finoglio painting while completing a secondary (minor) in the History of Art and Architecture. Hornik's book, *Michele Tosini and the Ghirlandaio Workshop in Cinquecento Florence* (Sussex Academic Press), is the first biography on the Mannerist painter. Hornik and Mikeal C. Parsons co-authored the three-volume *Illuminating Luke* series (Bloomsbury) and *The Acts of the Apostles through the Centuries* (Wiley-Blackwell), and they co-edited *Interpreting Christian Art: Reflections on Christian Art* (Mercer University Press). Hornik's most recent solo-authored book is *The Art of Christian Reflection* (Baylor University Press).

Barry R. Huff is Associate Professor of Biblical Studies and Religious Studies Department Chair at Principia College, where the student body selected him as Principia's Teacher of the Year in 2013 and 2019. He received his PhD from Union Presbyterian Seminary in 2017. His dissertation, advised by Samuel E. Balentine, analyzes the use and transformation of the Torah's priestly terms, themes, texts, and theologies in the book of Job. Huff's essays, primarily on wisdom literature and reception history, appear in multiple books and journals.

Phillip Michael Lasater is currently a postdoctoral researcher and lecturer at the University of Zurich, where he completed his PhD after studying under Samuel E. Balentine as an MDiv student at Union Presbyterian Seminary. He is the author of the monograph *Facets of Fear: The Fear of God in Exilic and Post-exilic Contexts* (Mohr Siebeck). Some of his other publications are in *Zeitschrift für die* *alttestamentliche Wissenschaft, Harvard Theological Review, Journal of Religion,* and *Journal of the Bible and Its Reception.*

S. Dean McBride, Jr. was Cyrus H. McCormick Professor Emeritus of Hebrew and Old Testament Interpretation at Union Presbyterian Seminary. He was a member of the translation committee that produced the New Revised Standard Version of the Bible. McBride was also a member of the editorial board of Hermeneia: A Critical and Historical Commentary on the Bible.

Andreas Schuele is Professor of Old Testament and Dean of the School of Theology at University of Leipzig. Prior to that, Schuele served on the faculty at Union Presbyterian Seminary as Aubrey Lee Brooks Professor of Biblical Theology. His publications include *Der Prolog der hebräischen Bibel: Der literar- und theologiegeschichtliche Diskurs der Urgeschichte (Genesis 1-11)* (Theologischer Verlag Zürich), *Theology from the Beginning: Essays on the Primeval History and Its Canonical Context* (Mohr Siebeck), *An Introduction to Biblical Aramaic* (Westminster John Knox), and *Die neuen alttestamentlichen Perikopentexte: Exegetische und homiletisch-liturgische Zugänge* with Alexander Deeg (Evangelische Verlagsanstalt).

Marvin A. Sweeney is Professor of Hebrew Bible at Claremont School of Theology, c/o Williamette University, Salem, Oregon. He is the author of numerous works on the Hebrew Bible and Jewish studies, most recently *Jewish Mysticism: From Ancient Times until Today* (Eerdmans) and *The Pentateuch* (Abingdon).

Patricia Vesely is Assistant Professor of Hebrew Bible and Christian Ethics at Memphis Theological Seminary. She earned her PhD under Samuel E. Balentine at Union Presbyterian Seminary in 2017. Vesely is the author of *Friendship and Virtue Ethics in the Book of Job* (Cambridge University Press).

List of Figures

Figure 4.1. Leaf 22 obverse [beginning of Exodus], Great Bible, 1539. Photo Credit: Special Collections, William Smith Morton Library, Union Presbyterian Seminary.

Figure 4.2. Title page, Geneva Bible, 1560. Photo Credit: Special Collections, Scheide Library, Princeton University.

Figure 4.3. Leaf 24 obverse [beginning of Exodus], Geneva Bible, 1560. Photo Credit: Special Collections, Scheide Library, Princeton University.

Figure 4.4. Leaf 30 reverse [Exodus 14:10-26 with woodcut illustration of Red Sea Event], Geneva Bible, 1560. Photo Credit: Special Collections, Scheide Library, Princeton University.

Figure 4.5. Leaf 20 obverse [beginning of Exodus], Robert Estienne French Bible, 1553. Photo Credit: Special Collections, Scheide Library, Princeton University.

Figure 4.6. Initial leaf of Exodus in S. Münster, *Hebraica biblia*, 1534. Photo Credit: Special Collections, William Smith Morton Library, Union Presbyterian Seminary.

Figure 5.1. Paolo Finoglio, *Joseph and Potiphar's Wife*, ca. 1634. Oil on canvas. 232.7 x 193.7 cm. Harvard Art Museums/Fogg Museum, Cambridge, MA. Gift of Samuel H. Kress Foundation. Photo Credit: President and Fellows of Harvard College.

Figure 5.2. Paolo Finoglio, *Circumcision of Christ*, 1626. Oil on canvas. 255 x 170 cm. Sala Capitolare, Certosa di S. Martino, Naples. Photo Credit: Public Domain.

Figure 5.3. Caravaggio, *Seven Works of the Misericordia*, 1606–1607. Oil on canvas. 390 x 260 cm. Church of Pio Monte della Misericordia, Naples. Photo Credit: Public Domain.

Figure 5.4. Artemisia Gentileschi, *Esther before Ahaseurus*, ca. 1628–1630. Oil on canvas. 208.3 x 273.7 cm. Metropolitan Museum of Art, New York. Photo Credit: Public Domain.

Figure 5.5. Paolo Finoglio, *Christ and the Adulterous Woman*, ca. 1634. Oil on canvas. 120 x 149 cm. Museo Provinciale Sigismondo, Lecce. Photo Credit: Public Domain.

Figure 5.6. Taddeo Zuccaro, *Joseph and Potiphar's Wife*, ca. 1550. Pen and brown ink, brush and brown wash, heightened with white gouache over traces of black chalk, on blue paper. 13.2 x 11.2 cm. Metropolitan Museum of Art, New York. Bequest of John and Alice Steiner, 2003. Photo Credit: Public Domain.

Figure 5.7. Marcantonio Raimondi (after Raphael), *Joseph Fleeing from Potiphar's Wife*, ca. 1515–1525. Engraving. 20.7 x 124.1 cm. Metropolitan Museum of Art, New York, Harris Brisbane Dick Fund, 1941. Photo Credit: Public Domain.

Figure 5.8. Sebald Beham, *Joseph and Potiphar's Wife*, 1544. Engraving. 8.1 x 5.6 cm. National Gallery of Art, Washington, D.C., Rosenwald Collection. Photo Credit: NGA Images Open Access.

Figure 11.1. William Blake, "So the Lord Blessed the Latter End of Job More than the Beginning," Plate XXI of William Blake, *Illustrations of the Book of Job*, 1823–1825. Engraving. 40.6 x 27.3 cm. Yale Center for British Art, New Haven, CT. Gift of J. T. Johnston Coe in memory of Henry E. Coe, Yale BA 1878; Henry E. Coe Jr., Yale BA 1917; and Henry E. Coe III, Yale BA 1946. Photo Credit: Public Domain.

LIST OF FIGURES   xxi

Figure 11.2. William Blake, "Thus Job Did Continually," Plate I of William Blake, *Illustrations of the Book of Job*, 1823–1825. Engraving. 40.6 x 27.3 cm. Yale Center for British Art, New Haven, CT. Gift of J. T. Johnston Coe in memory of Henry E. Coe, Yale BA 1878; Henry E. Coe Jr., Yale BA 1917; and Henry E. Coe III, Yale BA 1946. Photo Credit: Public Domain.

Figure 11.3. William Blake, "Then Went Satan Forth from the Presence of the Lord," Plate V of William Blake, *Illustrations of the Book of Job*, 1823–1825. Engraving. 40.6 x 27.3 cm. Yale Center for British Art, New Haven, CT. Gift of J. T. Johnston Coe in memory of Henry E. Coe, Yale BA 1878; Henry E. Coe Jr., Yale BA 1917; and Henry E. Coe III, Yale BA 1946. Photo Credit: Public Domain.

Figure 11.4. J.W. Debenham, *Job: A Masque for Dancing*, 1931. Photograph. The Old Vic/Cambridge Theatre London. Victoria and Albert Museum, London. Photo Credit: J.W. Debenham/Victoria and Albert Museum, London.

Figure 11.5. William Blake, "When the Morning Stars Sang Together and All the Sons of God Shouted for Joy," Plate XIV of William Blake, *Illustrations of the Book of Job*, 1823–1825. Engraving. 40.6 x 27.3 cm. Yale Center for British Art, New Haven, CT. Gift of J. T. Johnston Coe in memory of Henry E. Coe, Yale BA 1878; Henry E. Coe Jr., Yale BA 1917; and Henry E. Coe III, Yale BA 1946. Photo Credit: Public Domain.

Figure 12.1. Paolo Veronese, *Allegory of Wisdom and Strength*, ca. 1565. Oil on canvas. 214.6 x 167 cm. The Frick Collection, New York, Henry Clay Frick Bequest. Photo Credit: The Frick Collection, New York.

Figure 14.1. *Sint-Job (Saint Job)*, ca. 1390–1430. Polychromed wooden sculpture. 70 cm. tall. Kerk Sint-Martinus, Wezemaal, Belgium. Photo Credit: KIK-IRPA, Brussels.

Figure 14.2. *Job op de Mesthoop (Job on the Dung Heap)*, 1510–1520. Wooden sculpture. 79.5 cm. tall. Museum Mayer van den Bergh, Antwerp, Belgium. Photo Credit: KIK-IRPA, Brussels.

Figure 14.3. Bernard Van Orley, *Retable de la Passion (Passion Altarpiece)*, detail, 1500–1510. Oil on oak. Church, Nordingra, Sweden. Photo Credit: KIK-IRPA, Brussels.

Figure 14.4. Bernard Van Orley, *Retable de la Passion (Passion Altarpiece)*, closed, 1500–1510. Oil on oak. Church, Nordingra, Sweden. Photo Credit: KIK-IRPA, Brussels.

Figure 14.5. Bernard Van Orley, *Retable de la Passion (Passion Altarpiece)*, open, 1500–1510. Oil on oak. 185 x 221 x 20.5 cm. Church, Nordingra, Sweden. Photo Credit: KIK-IRPA, Brussels.

Figure 14.6. Jan Wynants, *Cilindermonstrans (Cylinder Monstrance)*, 1601–1650. Silver. 64 cm. tall. Kerk Sint-Martinus, Wezemaal, Belgium. Photo Credit: KIK-IRPA, Brussels.

Figure 14.7. Jan Wynants, *Cilindermonstrans (Cylinder Monstrance)*, detail, 1601–1650. Kerk Sint-Martinus, Wezemaal, Belgium. Photo Credit: KIK-IRPA, Brussels.

Figure 14.8. *Snijsporen op Gevelsteen (Cut Marks on Brick)*, ca. 1401–1500. Kerk Sint-Martinus, Wezemaal, Belgium. Photo Credit: KIK-IRPA, Brussels.

Figure 14.9. *Sint-Job (Saint Job)*, ca. 1500. Stone. 177 x 87 x 43 cm. Kerk Sint-Martinus, Wezemaal, Belgium. Photo Credit: KIK-IRPA, Brussels.

Abbreviations

AB	Anchor Bible
ABRL	Anchor Bible Reference Library
AFCHAB	*Actes des VIIe Congrès de l'Association des Cercles Francophones d'Histoire et d'Archéologie de Belgique*
AIL	Ancient Israel and Its Literature
ATANT	Abhandlungen zur Theologie des Alten und Neuen Testaments
BETL	Bibliotheca Ephemeridum Theologicarum Lovaniensium
BEvT	Beiträge zur evangelischen Theologie
BI	*Biblical Illustrator*
BibInt	*Biblical Interpretation*
BRLA	Brill Reference Library of Judaism
BZAW	Beihefte zur Zeitschrift für die alttestamentliche Wissenschaft
CBET	Contributions to Biblical Exegesis and Theology
CBQ	*Catholic Biblical Quarterly*
CBS	Core Biblical Series
CRBR	*Critical Review of Books in Religion*
EBR	*Encyclopedia of the Bible and Its Reception.* Edited by Hans-Josef Klauck et al. Berlin: de Gruyter, 2009–.
ECC	Eerdmans Critical Commentary

EDB	*Eerdmans Dictionary of the Bible.* Edited by David Noel Freedman. Grand Rapids: Eerdmans, 2000.
EGB	English Geneva Bible
EJL	Early Judaism and Its Literature
ExAud	*Ex Auditu*
FAT	Forschungen zum Alten Testament
FOTL	Forms of the Old Testament Literature
FRLANT	Forschungen zur Religion und Literatur des Alten und Neuen Testaments
HACL	History, Archaeology, and Culture of the Levant
HALOT	*The Hebrew and Aramaic Lexicon of the Old Testament.* Ludwig Koehler, Walter Baumgarner, and Johann J. Stamm. Translated and edited under the supervision of Mervyn E. J. Richardson. 4 vols. Leiden: Brill, 1994–1999.
HAR	*Hebrew Annual Review*
HBS	Herders Biblische Studien
HBT	*Horizons in Biblical Theology*
HeBAI	*Hebrew Bible and Ancient Israel*
Hor	*Horizons*
HS	*Hebrew Studies*
HThKAT	Herders Theologischer Kommentar zum Alten Testament
HTR	*Harvard Theological Review*
HUCA	*Hebrew Union College Annual*
IBC	Interpretation: A Bible Commentary for Teaching and Preaching
Int	*Interpretation*
IOSOT	International Organization for the Study of the Old Testament
JBL	*Journal of Biblical Literature*
JBRec	*Journal of the Bible and Its Reception*
JPS	Jewish Publication Society
JSJ	*Journal for the Study of Judaism in the Persian, Hellenistic, and Roman Periods*

JSJSup	Supplements to the Journal for the Study of Judaism
JSOT	*Journal for the Study of the Old Testament*
JSOTSup	Journal for the Study of the Old Testament Supplement Series
JSP	*Journal for the Study of the Pseudepigrapha*
JTS	*Journal of Theological Studies*
KIK-IRPA	Koninklijk Instituut voor het Kunstpatrimonium - Institut Royal du Patrimoine Artistique (The Royal Institute for Cultural Heritage, Belgium)
KJV	King James Version
LCL	Loeb Classical Library
LHBOTS	The Library of Hebrew Bible/Old Testament Studies
LTQ	*Lexington Theological Quarterly*
LXX	Septuagint
MDB	*Mercer Dictionary of the Bible*. Edited by Watson E. Mills. Macon, GA: Mercer University Press, 1990.
NIB	*The New Interpreter's Bible*. Edited by Leander E. Keck. 12 vols. Nashville: Abingdon, 1994–2004.
NIDB	*New Interpreter's Dictionary of the Bible*. Edited by Katharine Doob Sakenfeld. 5 vols. Nashville: Abingdon, 2006–2009.
NRSV	New Revised Standard Version
OBT	Overtures to Biblical Theology
OG	Old Greek
OTP	*Old Testament Pseudepigrapha*. Edited by James H. Charlesworth. 2 vols. New York: Doubleday, 1983, 1995.
OtSt	*Oudtestamentische Studiën*
PRSt	*Perspectives in Religious Studies*
PSB	*Princeton Seminary Bulletin*
RBS	Resources for Biblical Study
RevExp	*Review and Expositor*
SBL	Society of Biblical Literature

SBLDS	Society of Biblical Literature Dissertation Series
SBS	Stuttgarter Bibelstudien
SHBC	Smyth & Helwys Bible Commentary
SJT	*Scottish Journal of Theology*
STDJ	Studies on the Texts of the Desert of Judah
SwJT	*Southwestern Journal of Theology*
SymS	Symposium Series
ThTo	*Theology Today*
TJ	*Trinity Journal*
TTE	*The Theological Educator*
VT	*Vetus Testamentum*
WBC	Word Biblical Commentary
WMANT	Wissenschaftliche Monographien zum Alten und Neuen Testament
WUNT	Wissenschaftliche Untersuchungen zum Neuen Testament

Introduction

Patricia Vesely and Barry R. Huff

This Festschrift celebrates the illustrious career of Samuel E. Balentine, Professor of Old Testament and Director of Graduate Studies Emeritus at Union Presbyterian Seminary, on the occasions of his seventieth birthday and retirement. Balentine's impact in the field of biblical studies is monumental. He is the author of seven books to date, including *The Hidden God: The Hiding of the Face of God in the Old Testament* (1983), *Prayer in the Hebrew Bible: The Drama of Divine-Human Dialogue* (1993), *The Torah's Vision of Worship* (1999), *Have You Considered My Servant Job?: Understanding the Biblical Archetype of Patience* (2015)—a text that was awarded Outstanding Academic Title for 2015 by *Choice*—and *Wisdom Literature* (2018). Balentine authored commentaries on Leviticus in the Interpretation series (2002) and Job in the Smyth & Helwys Bible Commentary series (2006). He is currently working on the following forthcoming books: Ecce Homo*: Behold the Man. Ethical Imperatives of the Lenten Journey* as well as *"Look at Me and Be Appalled": Essays on Job, Theology, and Ethics*. In addition, he is the Old Testament General Editor for the Smyth & Helwys Bible Commentary series and the Series Editor for Interpretation: Resources for the Use of Scripture in the Church. His extensive contributions as an editor also include serving as Editor-in-Chief of *The Oxford Encyclopedia of the Bible and Theology* (2015), Editor-in-Chief of *The Oxford Handbook of Ritual and Theology in the Hebrew Bible* (2020), and Co-Editor (2005–2009) and Editor (2010–2013) of the periodical *Interpretation: A Journal of Bible and Theology*.

In addition to the more than one hundred works detailed in this Festschrift's bibliography of Samuel E. Balentine's publications, his dedication to the profession includes serving as Chair of the Steering Committee for the Israelite Prophetic Literature Section of the Society of Biblical Literature (SBL) (1997–2003), President of SBL's Southeast Region (1999–2000), Member of the Steering Committee for SBL's Theology of the Hebrew Scriptures Section (2004–2010), Chair of the Steering Committee for the Carl Howie Center for Science, Art, and Theology (2006–2013), and Director of Graduate Studies at Union Presbyterian Seminary (2014–2019). Sam's teaching career spans over thirty-five years, including eleven years as Professor of Old Testament at Baptist Theological Seminary of Richmond and fifteen years as Professor of Old Testament at Union Presbyterian Seminary.

The inspiration for this Festschrift comes from Balentine's groundbreaking publications on Torah and wisdom literature. Our contributors were asked to write either on Torah or wisdom literature in a way that resonates with at least one of the following three aspects of Balentine's scholarship: (1) his innovative theological and vital ethical interpretations of biblical texts; (2) his interest in the relationship of biblical studies with other fields, such as science, philosophy, and psychology; or (3) his pioneering work on the history of the Bible's reception in visual arts, literature, theater, and other cultural expressions.

We are pleased that the essays we received reflect aspects of Sam's scholarship from the span of his career. Several articles, including those by Heather Woodworth Brannon and Phillip Michael Lasater, pay tribute to Sam's careful, lexical work undertaken in his PhD program at Oxford under James Barr and exhibited in his first monograph, *The Hidden God: The Hiding of the Face of God in the Old Testament* (1983). Two of Sam's subsequent books, *The Torah's Vision of Worship* (1999) and *Leviticus* (2002), illumine the Torah's priestly texts, themes, and theologies. The essays by Samuel L. Adams, Mark E. Biddle, Barry R. Huff, Andreas Schuele, and Marvin A. Sweeney highlight these aspects of Sam's scholarship.

A number of our authors, including John Barton, Mark E. Biddle, William P. Brown, Walter Brueggemann, and Andreas Schuele, offer innovative theological and ethical interpretations of the Bible.

These emphases are reflected throughout Balentine's publications, including his commentaries on Leviticus (2002) and Job (2006) and his monographs *Prayer in the Hebrew Bible: The Drama of Divine-Human Dialogue* (1993) and *Wisdom Literature* (2018). In addition, several authors bring the Bible into conversation with other fields, including psychology (Brown) and quantum physics (Biddle), resonating with Balentine's interdisciplinary approach in multiple works. Likewise, Balentine's commentary on Job in the Smyth & Helwys Bible Commentary series and his monograph *Have You Considered My Servant Job?: Understanding the Biblical Archetype of Patience* (2015) showcase his pioneering work in the reception history of the Bible. The essays by Samuel L. Adams, Katharine J. Dell, Heidi J. Hornik and Mikeal Joseph Parsons, Barry R. Huff, S. Dean McBride, Jr., and Patricia Vesely display this aspect of Balentine's scholarship in their exploration of the reception history of Torah or wisdom literature in literary works, sculptures, paintings, and the performing arts. Finally, Balentine's most recent interests in epistemology and imagination play a central role in the essays by Heather Woodworth Brannon, Phillip Michael Lasater, and Patricia Vesely.

The essays included in this Festschrift cover a wide range of topics and approaches within Torah and wisdom literature, including careful textual analyses, theological interpretations, cross-disciplinary studies, and explorations of the reception history of the Bible in works of literature and art. This Festschrift includes voices both of scholars who are well established and of Balentine's students who are up-and-coming in the field. All of our contributors, though representing diverse areas of expertise, are unanimous in their desire to express their gratitude to Sam Balentine for his expansive, detailed, and inspiring work in the field of biblical studies.

Summary of Contents

This Festschrift begins with a biography of Balentine's life and work written by his longtime friend and colleague, E. Carson Brisson. A bibliography of publications by Balentine follows. Then, the remaining essays are organized into three sections. The first section includes five essays that focus on portions of Torah. The next section features six essays dealing with wisdom in the Bible and related texts. The final section includes three more essays that bridge the gap between Torah and wisdom, exploring the relationship and potentially fluid boundary between these two genres.

Torah's Heights

The Torah section begins with an essay by Mark E. Biddle titled "There's a Wildness in God's Mercy: God's Sovereignty, Quantum Probability, and a Biblical Worldview." Using quantum physics as a reading lens through which to interpret portions of the Hebrew Bible, Biddle argues that Genesis 1 and the divine speeches of Job 38–41 depict a world that is not a closed system of physical causality—as classical, Newtonian physics once imagined—but rather, in keeping with quantum theory, a world that is open both to God's involvement and to creaturely independence. As Biddle demonstrates through his examination of these two texts, God's creativity is highlighted not so much as divine determinism but as actualizing potentiality through observation.

In the next essay, "The Primeval History as an Etiology of Torah," Andreas Schuele argues that Genesis 1–11 provides the necessary foundations for the establishment of Torah. As Pentateuchal scholars are increasingly recognizing, Genesis 1–11 does not function in isolation from the rest of Genesis. Schuele convincingly argues that this is so, in large part, because of its role in depicting a world order that cannot persist without *command* and *covenant*. As Schuele's title indicates, one of the primary functions of Genesis 1–11 is to provide an *etiology of Torah*.

Next, Marvin A. Sweeney explores the perplexing question of why Moses and Aaron were excluded from the promised land in "Why Moses Was Barred from the Land of Israel: A Reassessment of Numbers 20 in Literary Context." Sweeney argues that the literary context provided by Numbers 17–19, in particular, provides a justification for YHWH's decision in 20:12. Numbers 17–19 focuses on the appointment of the tribe of Levi as holy priests for YHWH and the requirements for purification following corpse contamination. The narrative placement of Miriam's death just prior to the episode of Moses' obtaining water from the rock offers the explanation: the regulations for purification were not met by Moses and Aaron in the burial of their sister. As Sweeney demonstrates, the narrative sequencing found in Numbers 17–20 thus emphasizes the seriousness of the priestly role: even the most celebrated leaders of the nation cannot set aside their priestly identities and sacred obligations to YHWH.

In "Interpretive Reception of the Book of Exodus in the English Geneva Bible of 1560," S. Dean McBride, Jr., assesses the scholarly and hermeneutical significance of the Geneva Bible, first produced in 1560, with a particular focus on its treatment of the book of Exodus. Through detailed historical and textual analyses, McBride shows how this annotated translation of the Bible, undertaken by a group of English-speaking refugees living in Geneva during the Reformation period, continued the translative and interpretive legacy begun by William Tyndale decades earlier. The result was a monumental work that—in its translation, instructions, and invitations to audiences to participate in the interpretive process—has deeply impacted biblical scholarship in the Reformed Tradition for nearly five centuries.

In the final essay of this section, Heidi J. Hornik and Mikeal Joseph Parsons offer a careful analysis of the painting *Joseph and Potiphar's Wife* by Italian Baroque painter Paolo Finoglio (ca. 1590–1645). Their essay, "Finoglio's *Joseph and Potiphar's Wife* at Harvard: Biblical Reception Meets Art Historical Methodology," situates Finoglio in the apex of the Italian Baroque period and details how the painter distinguished himself through techniques that are vividly illustrated in his portrayal of the failed seduction of Joseph by Potiphar's wife (Gen 39). Hornik and Parsons demonstrate how Finoglio's use of light, facial expression, body language, and, in particular, the selection of cloth as a key subject in the artwork, enable Finoglio to tell a complex, multidimensional narrative over and above simply depicting a single scene from the biblical tale.

Wisdom's Depths

The next section focusing on wisdom literature begins with Walter Brueggemann's "Practicality in a World of Hubris." In this essay, Brueggemann probes the question "Where shall wisdom be found?" (Job 28:12) through the landscape of the books of Kings. Brueggemann contrasts the biblical narrator's ironic portrayal of royal wisdom—embodied by the monarchs of Jerusalem and characterized by self-deception and hubris—with "wisdom from below"—embodied by the prophetic figures of Elijah and Elisha.

Brueggemann links these prophets' demonstration of wisdom with Balentine's description of biblical wisdom, which Balentine identifies as practical, attuned to justice, and opposed to selfishness and pride.[1]

In the next essay, "'God Set Infinity into Their Minds': Qohelet's Quest to Comprehend the Incomprehensible," Heather Woodworth Brannon continues the theme of the human quest for wisdom by examining closely Ecclesiastes 3:11b and what it means for God to "set infinity" in the human mind (ʾet- hāʿ ōlām nātan bĕlibbām). Through careful textual analysis, Brannon argues that this initiative by God serves as a catalyst for Qohelet to continue his efforts to investigate the unknown further and results in an increased perception of the world around him and his place within it.

Next, Phillip Michael Lasater investigates the means by which wisdom is acquired according to Proverbs 1–9 in "Wisdom through Symbolic Objects: The Second Temple Intellectual Context of Symbolic Bodies in and beyond Proverbs 1–9" through a detailed examination of the term *lēb* ("heart") in these texts. Lasater observes that the "heart" functions as the key instrument for acquiring knowledge in Proverbs 2 and 4 but stresses that the meaning of *lēb* in these passages is something other than a bodily organ. Asking why the term was used this way, Lasater traces the interpretive move away from allegorical to literal meanings of words in the early-modern period and concludes that an allegorical understanding of "meanings of objects" helps explain what the ancient scribes were doing when they used the term *lēb* in their depiction of the human search for wisdom.

In "Ethics and Character Formation in Biblical Wisdom Texts," John Barton investigates the question of whether the wisdom books of the Bible demonstrate an interest in character or virtue ethics. Against an earlier thesis in which Barton denied such an approach to ethics in the Hebrew Bible,[2] he argues here that ancient Israel's wisdom texts do, in fact, bear witness to a concern for character and moral formation. Barton's essay dialogues both with Anne

---

1. Samuel E. Balentine, *Job*, SHBC (Macon, GA: Smyth & Helwys, 2006), 431–32.

2. John Barton, "Virtue in the Bible," *Studies in Christian Ethics* 12/1 (1999): 12–22.

W. Stewart's *Poetic Ethics in Proverbs: Wisdom Literature and the Shaping of the Moral Self* (Cambridge University Press, 2016) and Patricia Vesely's *Friendship and Virtue Ethics in the Book of Job* (Cambridge University Press, 2019). He expands the discussion through a close examination of ethics in several psalms and texts from the Second Temple period, including Ben Sira and the Wisdom of Solomon.

Following Barton's essay, William P. Brown offers an innovative reading of Job's enigmatic response to YHWH in Job 42:6 in his piece "Job and the 'Comforting' Chaos." Brown suggests that the verb *nāḥam* in Job 42:6 may appropriately be translated "to find comfort," in keeping with its use throughout the book of Job. Brown then asks how Job can profess to be "comforted" by YHWH's response in Job 38–41. Brown draws from psychological studies on "awe," exploring how this human experience of vastness, decenteredness, and accommodation might help readers better understand both the meaning of the divine speeches and Job's declaration that he is "comforted over dust and ashes" (42:6).

In "When Eternal Questions 'Dance' within the Human Imagination: The Making of the Ballet, *Job: A Masque for Dancing*," Patricia Vesely explores the collaborative efforts involved in the making of the Joban ballet *A Masque for Dancing*, first performed in London in 1931. Vesely traces the development of the production from the Joban illustrations by William Blake that served as the inspiration for the project to the final production on stage. Like the biblical story itself, the collaborators—including Geoffrey Keynes, Gwendolyn Raverat, and Ralph Vaughan Williams—wrestled with questions of Job's guilt, God's role in Job's suffering, and the nature of Job's restoration. Vesely notes that while marked by disharmony and disagreement in its creation, the finished product achieved Blake's desired aim of the revival of the human spirit through art, as *A Masque for Dancing* paved the way for the creation of The Royal Ballet of London, one of the most widely acclaimed ballet companies in the world.

Torah in Wisdom and Wisdom as Torah

The Festschrift's final section includes pieces that explore the relationship between Torah and wisdom, suggesting that the boundaries between these two genres are not immobile. In the first essay, "Woman Wisdom and Her Afterlife," Katharine J. Dell returns to the question of Job 28:12, "Where shall wisdom be found?," by tracing the development and location of Woman Wisdom among biblical and extrabiblical texts. Dell begins with a comparison of Wisdom's portrayal in several biblical texts (Prov 1:20-33; 3:13-20; 8; Job 28), noting Wisdom's dual identity as both immanent and transcendent, both present in creation and yet hidden in full from humanity. Dell then follows Wisdom's path throughout Ben Sira, Baruch, the Wisdom of Solomon, and the New Testament, demonstrating that this peculiar identity is "resolved," in part, through the allocation of Wisdom among the community of the faithful (as Torah or *Logos*). Wisdom's hiddenness remains for humanity at large, but for those who have access to such treasures, she is present.

In "Sacred Recitation as Commentary in Ben Sira's Praise of the Ancestors," Samuel L. Adams details Ben Sira's development of Israel's sapiential and priestly traditions through the intertwining of Torah and wisdom. In his essay, Adams examines the "Praise of the Ancestors" found in Sirach 44–50 and articulates the possible reasons for the author's abundant praise and frequent focus on priestly figures, such as Aaron and the high priest Simon II. Adams's essay demonstrates the reception history of Torah in its early phases, as sapiential writers in the late Second Temple period were incorporating and recasting key figures from Israel's past in new ways and identifying Torah as an essential component of wisdom.

The role of the Torah's priestly themes in wisdom literature, analyzed in Adams's essay and in several of Balentine's publications, also is addressed by Barry R. Huff in the final essay, "Job the Priest: From Scripture to Sculpture." Huff draws on his dissertation and on his research in Belgium of Job sculptures to build on Balentine's groundbreaking scholarship on the theological implications of priestly themes in the book of Job and its reception history. Huff analyzes depictions of burnt offerings and fire in Job, the Testament of Job, and Gregory the Great's *Moralia in Job* to illuminate a sculpture of Job holding a flame that drew thousands of diseased pilgrims to St. Martin's Church in Wezemaal. This church and the Bible juxtapose depictions of Job as both a priest and an unclean sufferer in need of a priest.³ This juxtaposition empathetically attunes priests to the voices of sufferers and inspires sufferers with a model of faith forged in the fire and holiness embodied even by those labeled unclean.

Exegesis for the World: A Tribute to Samuel E. Balentine

All of these essays pay tribute to Balentine's innovative studies in which he has courageously pushed the boundaries of previous scholarship. We close this introduction by paying tribute to Balentine's character, as exemplified through the larger purpose of his exegesis and through his transformative impact on our lives.

Both Barry and I (Tricia) had the privilege of studying under Professor Balentine in the PhD program at Union Presbyterian Seminary in Richmond, Virginia. I vividly remember the first class I took with him. I had recently completed an MTS degree at another theological institution and was uncertain whether continued academic training was in my near future or if biblical studies would remain something I pursued on the side. I enrolled as an auditor in Balentine's Old Testament class to see if I might gain some clarity with respect to my uncertain future. As I heard over and over again from students at Union, Balentine's classes are life-changing, or maybe I should say life-*jolting*. I experienced that firsthand as I listened to the opening lecture in which Sam spoke about "the ministry of exegesis." He specifically stressed that biblical exegesis is not something we do for our own enjoyment or edification, although it certainly could include those benefits; rather, he told us, biblical exegesis is a calling undertaken *for the sake of others*. That day, I knew that I would not be satisfied relegating my interests in biblical studies to a mere "pastime." I wanted to embark on the exciting journey reflected by Dr. Balentine's teaching and to seek out the depths and riches that I sensed were a part of his own experiences as a seasoned traveler on this road.

From that day forward and throughout the course of my work with Sam, as both a ThM student and a PhD student, he continued to impress upon me the notion that academic study and the journey of life are not two "separate disciplines." My essay, "When Eternal

---

3. Cf. Samuel E. Balentine, "Job as Priest to the Priests," *ExAud* 18 (2002): 38.

Questions 'Dance' within the Human Imagination: The Making of the Ballet *Job: A Masque for Dancing*," is an attempt to pay tribute to this aspect of Balentine's teaching. He was the first person to bring to my attention that the ballet existed. I have worked as a pianist for professional ballet companies and the schools attached to them for over twenty years, first in Grand Rapids, Michigan, and then in Richmond, Virginia, and Sam was well aware of my outside interests in the performing arts. He first suggested that I research the ballet for a final paper in one of my ThM classes. Though I looked into it briefly, at the time I found too little information to complete the piece, so I selected another topic. I filed the subject and our conversation away for later, not knowing if or when the opportunity to explore this matter further would resurface. Now, over ten years later and with more experience and tools at hand, I have been able to return to the subject of the ballet on Job. Alongside fruitful conversations with fellow biblical scholars, my work on this piece has brought me into conversations with musicians, artists, and dancers, including many of my coworkers at the School of the Richmond Ballet. As Sam has so wonderfully instilled from his own experience, biblical interpretation is a dance that finds its way into all corners of life. My essay is a way of saying "thank you" to him, not only for igniting my curiosity on this subject many years ago but also for introducing me to a discipline that is able to traverse so many diverse stages. As Sam frequently attests, it is often in the interplay between those diverse stages that new and deeper meaning is to be found.

Sam's emphasis on the essential intersection of biblical interpretation and life also profoundly moved me (Barry). Before I ever met Sam, his bold biblical exegesis, detailed analysis of texts, vital ethical applications, and invigorating theological conclusions grasped and transformed my theological and moral imagination. While researching my MTS thesis on Job, I felt the heart of Scripture beat through Sam's innovative and empowering proclamation that God's response to Job "may be interpreted not as a rebuke or a denial of Job, but rather as a radical summons to a new understanding of what it means for humankind to be created in the image of God. In this view, it is not silence and submission that God requires; it is steadfast lament and relentless opposition to injustice and innocent suffering, wherever it appears."[4] Inspired by Sam's publications, I applied to Union Presbyterian Seminary's PhD program with the hope of studying with him.

At Union, I was delighted to discover that Sam is as wonderful a professor, adviser, scholar, human, mentor, and friend as he is an author. In one of our first conversations, Sam planted the seed that would blossom into my dissertation through years of his thoughtful nourishment. Like Tricia's experience, Sam also inspired the topic of my essay through his vast knowledge of and passion for the reception history of Job. Thanks to Sam's facilitation, I was at the University of Oxford for a term conducting dissertation research when I heard from him about an email he had received from the leading historian of the devotion to Job at St. Martin's Church in Wezemaal, Belgium. With Sam's encouragement, weeks later I was in Wezemaal meeting with this historian and viewing a sculpture of Job visited by pilgrims for centuries. These examples illustrate Sam's extraordinary support of his students, their research, and their lives.

While I first encountered Sam as a theologically invigorating author, I have since been blessed to experience him also in many other roles: as an engaging lecturer who leaves students on the edges of their seats; a dissertation adviser who empowers PhD candidates to reach their full potential and steadfastly supports them each step of the way; an eagle-eyed editor whose thoughtful comments inspire authors to new discoveries; a Renaissance man who effortlessly weaves literature, art, and science into a brilliant tapestry of biblical interpretation; an attentive shepherd who graciously guides a lost sheep back to the group on a travel seminar; a professor who ignites in his students a love for and understanding of the Bible; a caring mentor who supports others regardless of whether they follow his wise advice; a friend who cares deeply about one's health and well-being; an ally whose bold exegesis inspires readers to embrace more fully their identity as the image of God; an advocate who opens doors to exciting possibilities; and a loving father, grandfather, and husband

---

4. Samuel E. Balentine, "'What Are Human Beings, That You Make So Much of Them?' Divine Disclosure from the Whirlwind: 'Look at Behemoth,'" in *God in the Fray: A Tribute to Walter Brueggemann*, ed. Tod Linafelt and Timothy K. Beal (Minneapolis: Fortress, 1998), 260.

whose face lights up when talking about his beloved children, grandchildren, and wife. Sam has deeply blessed countless lives, including mine, and I will always be grateful for the wonderful opportunity to learn from his sterling scholarship, example, and character.

The two of us—Tricia and Barry—sensed early on in our PhD work that we had been given the rare opportunity to be guided under the mentorship of someone who possesses not only a keen intellect, expansive curiosity, and extraordinary range of knowledge—encompassing the Bible, literature, philosophy, art, and other cultural expressions—but also a one-of-a-kind, exemplary character. Sam lives the ethics about which he writes: he embodies the virtue of integrity in all that he does; he is able to see the best in each person; he is unquestionably loyal, truthful, and compassionate; and he willingly chooses the difficult road to aid those who are struggling.

Throughout his career, Balentine has scaled the heights of Torah and probed the depths of wisdom. In this journey, he has guided countless others nearer to these treasures, enabling those who are willing to accompany him into these far-reaching realms to understand further what it means to be made in God's image and to glimpse, where least expected, the hidden face of God.

Biography
"Have You Considered My Servant, Samuel E. Balentine?"[1]

E. Carson Brisson

More than thirty-five years ago at this writing, in the gray predawn of an August morning, my wife and I stumbled into a glittering emergency room in a hospital in Raleigh, North Carolina. The outer bands of wind and rain from a hurricane hovering off the coast of the state were encroaching on the fringes of the sleeping city.

We had hoped to be in that hospital's maternity ward a few weeks later that very month in order to bring home, in the eleventh year of our marriage, our firstborn. We had not expected to be there any sooner. But, by the late afternoon of that long, rainy, and unexpected day, after trauma endured with immeasurable courage and integrity by my wife, she was being discharged. We were leaving childless, no longer parents-to-be.

As my wife waited quietly in a wheelchair within a covered drive-through area attended by a soft-spoken hospital staff member, I ran to get our car. During the day, the threatening hurricane had turned away from the city back toward its mother, the sea. Even so, a dark, cold rain plunged down from where the blue summer sky should have been. All horizons were temporarily missing. I wandered in

---

1. See Job 1:8.

the parking lot completely disoriented for some time. My thoughts turned to the silence or, worse, the disordered heavens.

When I finally found our car and started the short drive up the slight slope to where my wife and her kind attendant waited, I began to make out through the indifferent rain a silhouetted form kneeling slightly in front and to the left of my wife's wheelchair. The figure was soaked. It was leaning forward and had embraced my wife in her stillness and anguish.

It was Samuel E. Balentine.

Sam, whom we had met over a decade before, had taught Hebrew all that day in the intensive summer session at the seminary where he and I worked, approximately twenty miles away. He had learned that my wife had been admitted to the hospital for an emergency, and, after that long, long day of classes, he had driven through the weather to be with her and with us. Out of every place on earth to be on that lost, late August afternoon, Sam was there with her, with us, in the place where for us the world did not work. In that forsaken space at that broken moment, Samuel E. Balentine was *with* us.

May I never forget. May I never fail to remember.

Samuel Eugene Balentine was born to Elizabeth Abrams Balentine and David W. Balentine on August 12, 1950, in Greenville, South Carolina. Elizabeth worked occasionally outside the home but was primarily a homemaker, known for the strength, peace, and hospitality with which she greeted all who came to her door. David was a well-known and respected local home builder. Sam, his name chosen by his mother because of her identification with the biblical story of Hannah and Elkanah, would be the first of two children born to the Balentines. The second, Michael, arrived four years later. The Balentines remained in the Greenville area during Sam and his brother Michael's childhood, where they were active in the community and attended Laurel Road Baptist Church.

Upon graduation from high school, Sam entered Furman University. He graduated with a bachelor of arts degree in 1972, having excelled at his studies. It was during his college years that Sam became deeply concerned with the human cost and ethical implications of the Vietnam War—a conflict he opposed—and sought opportunities to contribute his voice to communities and movements that were praying, calling, and working for peace. This period of his life would foreshadow Sam's lifelong commitment, which is reflected in his scholarship and in his affiliations, to seeking with heart, mind, and soul to understand the relationship between suffering and loss and the possibility and nature of a virtuous life, a life of integrity, lived *corum deo*, "east of Eden."

After he completed college studies, Sam's sense of vocation and academic abilities, as well as the support of his family and faith community, helped lead him to the Baptist seminary located one state away in the village of Wake Forest, North Carolina. The seminary there, founded in the year of Sam's birth and on the original campus of what had later become Wake Forest University in Winston-Salem, North Carolina, had begun to earn a reputation for its academic excellence in equipping ministers for all vocations of the church. Sam enrolled in the Master of Divinity degree program at the seminary and soon displayed an aptitude and interest in biblical studies and languages. His work came to the attention of faculty members, particularly in the field of Old Testament, who encouraged Sam to pursue further graduate work as his senior year approached.

Sam matriculated at Regent's Park College, University of Oxford, in fall 1975. His student sojourn and work at Oxford would initiate a lifelong love for the school and for the town and would plant the seeds of his subsequent love and study of English poetry, especially the verse of Coleridge, Tennyson, and Wordsworth. Sam would return to Oxford many times over the years for academic and personal reasons.

During his Oxford years, Sam's studies and dissertation were guided by James Barr, a leading biblical scholar and Semitist who served at the time as the Regius Professor of Hebrew. Barr's scholarship focused in part on the theological challenges confronting all attempts to render biblical languages into other languages, an endeavor Barr critiqued as having come to rely too heavily on comparative semantics and without adequate attention to underlying theological assumptions. His work was widely received as a needed corrective in the field of biblical scholarship. Barr's scholarship deeply influenced Sam's own work, which would come to be characterized by a fearless intellectual probing wedded to a relentless pursuit of the theological and ethical implications arising from the text. An abiding friendship grew between Professor Barr and Sam, which would be replicated in future years with students and peers during Sam's subsequent decades of teaching. In Sam's own teaching, Barr's influence would come to be felt, among other ways, in Sam's signature contribution to travel seminars, wherein it became his practice, at the end of packed days of discovery highlighted by convivial evening meals, to gather students in plenary session to address among themselves two questions: "What did you learn today? What difference does it make?"

After completing the Doctor of Philosophy at Oxford in 1979, Sam's first full-time teaching assignment brought him to the biblical department at Midwestern Baptist Theological Seminary in Kansas City, Missouri. Employed on a yearly contract basis, Sam taught Hebrew and introductory courses in Old Testament. While at Midwestern, two of Sam's deepest friendships and most formative collegial relationships were forged. In his department, Sam became close to William H. Morton, who taught in the field of Old Testament with an emphasis in archaeology. Sam also became friends with Morris Ashcraft. Ashcraft taught in the theology department at Midwestern and would later serve as Dean of the seminary in Wake Forest, North Carolina, where years earlier Sam had earned his Master of Divinity degree. In addition to their character, scholarship, and teaching, Sam was drawn to these colleagues for their understanding that seminary faculty bore heavy and, if need be, costly responsibility not just for their classroom and research but for the overall direction and ethos of their school. In years to come, Sam would remember his time at Midwestern and the influence of these two individuals as the source of his understanding that such responsibility must be included in "what it means to be a member of a seminary faculty."

Joyfully eclipsing all other developments at Midwestern, however, was Sam's meeting, courtship of, and marriage to Betty Ann McDonald of Lebanon, Tennessee. That courtship began in the fall of Sam's first semester of teaching. Betty and Sam were married on July 12, 1980, in the First Baptist Church of Lebanon, Tennessee, chosen by Betty for its interior and exterior beauty. Recently reflecting on that time and the years since, Betty writes,

> Sam has been my friend since the day we first met. It was just by accident that our paths crossed at all. But we have made the most of our nearly 40 years together. We have shared many good times, been blessed with two thoughtful and amazing children,

and now soon to be four grandchildren. We have explored the world together and shared many extraordinary moments. Our love for theater and music has been a constant source of enjoyment on all of our trips. Second-row seats have been a major joy for us in London and in New York. . . . We have also had to work through some hard times. Having a good and patient friend helps you come out the other side a stronger person. Sam has been that kind of friend to me.[2]

On November 5, 1982, while Sam was serving in his fourth one-year contract at Midwestern, Betty and Sam welcomed their first child into their home, David Graham Balentine. Young Graham would eventually share in his father's tall physical height and would become a gifted athlete, particularly in basketball. He and Sam, who is an avid fan of University of North Carolina basketball and of the coaching philosophy of the late University of North Carolina coach Dean Smith, bonded especially during their time enjoying sports events together. Of several summer trips to professional baseball parks from Baltimore to Los Angeles and of the meaning of these excursions for their relationship, Graham, now a father himself, writes, addressing his father directly:

> I remember those trips fondly, even if time has eroded some of the distinct facts and blurred them into an overarching friendship that only a son and a dad can share. For that, and so many other things, I say "Thank you." I can only hope that I can be half the dad to [my children] that you are to me. I love you.

In 1983, Sam returned to his seminary alma mater in Wake Forest, North Carolina, to a tenure-track appointment in the biblical faculty. In so doing, he rejoined his former Midwestern colleague and friend, Morris Ashcraft, who had by that time become the dean of the seminary there after twenty-two years on the Midwestern faculty. The depth of the relationship between "Ash" and Sam perhaps is best revealed in Sam's words at Morris Ashcraft's memorial service in

---

2. All citations from Sam's family members are taken from notes received in August 2019, and they are used with permission.

January 2011: "In an age often characterized by attempts to recover its integrity, Morris Ashcraft never lost his."

While in Wake Forest, Sam and Betty welcomed their second child, a daughter, Lauren Ashley Balentine, born on June 12, 1988. Lauren, now serving as a public schoolteacher in Virginia and a mother of two, writes of her father (who is called "Opa" by Lauren's young daughter):

> When I think of my father's role in his daughter's life, many things come to mind: protector, mentor, nurturer, care-taker, disciplinarian, and role model just to name a few. When I was younger, my dad was there to guide and support me as I grew into a young woman. . . . While he will always be there to guide and support me, he now has become more of a friend and someone I truly enjoy spending time with. . . . I never thought that my love for my father could get any stronger, that is, until I saw the relationship he is building with my daughter. . . . He will also become "Opa" to my son soon. I am proud to call Dr. Balentine my dad, but also my friend.

Over the years at the seminary in Wake Forest, Sam's work and publishing progressed, and he earned tenure. His focus on prayer and worship in the Old Testament and his in-depth study of the Wisdom tradition made important contributions to scholarship and to the church. Among Sam's notable publications during this period are *The Hidden God: The Hiding of the Face of God in the Old Testament* (Oxford University Press, 1983) and *Prayer in the Hebrew Bible: The Drama of Divine-Human Dialogue* (Fortress, 1993).

In 1987, Sam received a prestigious Humboldt Research Award. He and his family were able to spend a sabbatical year in Germany through the resources afforded by the Humboldt at a time when the infamous Berlin Wall was still a tragic reality. Sam's understanding of suffering, separation, and loss on a systemic level was deepened by an unexpected event during this period of study. On one occasion while Sam and his family were legally crossing the infamous wall at a checkpoint, he was temporarily separated from his family and detained in complete darkness and isolation for several hours. No explanation was ever given. The experience, and particularly not knowing what had happened to his family in the meantime, was a searing example and reminder of the system of domination, separation, and fear that the wall epitomized for countless lives.

In 1993, Sam, having resigned his tenured position at the seminary in Wake Forest, joined the faculty of the newly established Baptist Theological Seminary at Richmond, Virginia (BTSR). The school had been founded several years earlier by moderate Baptists after a conservative majority on the Board of Trustees at the seminary in Wake Forest—in sympathy with cultural currents inimical to the academic and conscientious freedom that was sweeping across much of the Southern Baptist denomination—adopted policies designed to ensure a future in which only faculty members who affirmed biblical inerrancy would be allowed to teach. Sam's colleague and close friend, Morris Ashcraft, from whom Sam states he learned "not to speak until you have something to say," served for one year as the acting president of BTSR until its trustees elected the school's first, long-term president. Sam, while enjoying the leadership provided by BTSR dean and American church historian G. Thomas Halbrooks, would go on to serve many productive years at the Baptist seminary in Richmond, teaching required and elective courses in Old Testament, until in 2004 he accepted a call to Union Presbyterian Seminary (at that time Union Theological Seminary & Presbyterian School of Christian Education), also located in Richmond.

Sam joined the Union faculty as Professor of Old Testament. As he noted at his faculty interview with Union, by this juncture of his work in teaching, research, and publishing, his academic and personal interests had begun to draw him toward the role of the arts in biblical interpretation, an interest abundantly and beautifully clear in his commentary on Job (Smyth & Helwys, 2006), which contains, in addition to discussions of art and literature in the text itself, nearly 400 sidebars and illustrations referencing works from artists and writers from diverse cultural settings and philosophical perspectives.

Sam's work at Union Presbyterian Seminary ranged across a wide spectrum of duties and areas of expertise. In addition to his courses in Old Testament/Hebrew Bible, which have included co-leadership of Travel Seminars to the Middle East, Sam has been involved in the leadership of Union's Howie Center, a continuing education entity dedicated to exploring the intersections of science, art, and theology. For many years, Sam edited the seminary's internationally recognized journal *Interpretation* and helped lead it to a successful and financially sound relationship with SAGE Publishing. Sam has served as Director of Graduate Studies at Union since 2014 and has guided his own PhD students to completion of their degrees for more than a decade. During his Union tenure, he also has edited the two-volume *Oxford Encyclopedia of the Bible and Theology* (Oxford University Press, 2015) and has continued to serve as the Old Testament General Editor of the well-received Smyth & Helwys commentary series. The list could go on.

If one project were to be held up as exemplary among the teaching, editing, and publishing contributions for which Sam is noted, his commentary *Job* would be a leading candidate (Smyth & Helwys, 2006). Dedicated to his family, *Job* has been hailed as the kind of commentary "Job must have been created for" (Patrick Miller), a work in which Sam has "thought profoundly, written elegantly, and empathized fully with" the protagonist who is the "object of a gratuitous divine test" (James L. Crenshaw), and "a breath-taking commentary" (Walter Brueggemann).[3]

In *Job*, in addition to investigating the story's prose and poetry in its original language and cultural setting, Sam weaves into his exegesis at nearly every point, as the Smyth & Helwys series intended its commentaries to do, rich conversations between the ancient text and urgent theological questions faced by contemporary faith communities. These conversations are amplified over and over again by scholarly, philosophical, ecclesiastical, and artistic voices and artifacts that frame the commentary's discussion. Collectively, these "friends of the text" function as a virtual choir assembled by Sam from across the ages and four corners of the earth. They accompany Job in his suffering and loss, his protest and questioning, and, finally, his faith and integrity. They irresistibly offer the reader engagement with the world.

Near the end of this magisterial commentary, Sam turns to consider Job and the quandaries his sufferings raise through the lens of the pericope of Ancestor Jacob at the Jabbok (Gen 32:22-31). Sam's discussion here offers a revealing moment with respect to his

---

3. These statements may be found in Samuel E. Balentine, *Job*, SHBC (Macon, GA: Smyth & Helwys, 2006).

intense and unflinching exploration of the possibility and nature of a virtuous life.

Sam begins by noting that in both the story of Jacob and the story of Job, the first character trait attributed to each individual—despite Jacob's later lucrative career in deception contrasted to Job's legendary life of blamelessness—is the same: integrity (*tām*; Gen 25:27; Job 1:1).[4] Sam discerns in Jacob's life and journeys lessons indispensably related to this virtue. The question of integrity reaches a climax for Ancestor Jacob in his nocturnal combat on the banks of the Jabbok where stubborn brokenness and elusive wholeness wrestle, while, one might add in addition to Sam's remarks, the proverbial dawn approaches as both threat *and* promise. Of Jacob's definitive and revelatory night, Sam writes,

> For all his careful planning, [Jacob] finds himself confronting a mysterious opponent he had not expected (Gen 32:22-32). Through the night he wrestles with this assailant, both physically and rhetorically, trying to secure a victory and if not at least a blessing. With respect to the physical contest, he learns that he cannot overpower his opponent. He cannot win this match, but he will not give up the fight, and in the end, surprisingly, he manages to secure a crippling draw. With respect to the blessing, he discovers, also to his surprise, that what he had tried to secure by force, he receives as a gift. On the other side of this encounter, he is changed. His name is no longer "Jacob"—"heel/trickster/supplanter"—but "Israel"—"the one who fights with God." His last words in this pericope summarize the outcome: "I have seen God face to face, and yet my life is preserved" (Gen 32:30).[5]

Sam, referencing Frederick Buechner, goes on to ponder whether or not it is precisely in such struggles and encounters with God, veiled and unplanned as is Jacob's divine confrontation, that defeated "brokenness" becomes "the source and sustenance of blessing" for "all whose faith is shaped by the *roguish integrity* of the people called Israel," and the "*scandalous integrity*" of the One who says to his

---

4. Balentine, *Job*, 702.

5. Ibid.

disciples, "[All] who want to save their life will lose it, and those who lose their life for my sake will find it" (Matt 16:25).[6]

Of the lessons Sam's scholarship and life put before us, his reflections on the possibility of a faithful "roguish" and "scandalous" integrity that emerges from life-and-death struggles in pre-dawn crossroads where conflict with God and blessing from God modulate one into the other as completely unexpected "gift" may be the most important. Sam's discoveries, hard won, graciously invite us to our own Jabboks and urge us to spend the night precisely there, wrestling *with* all diligence and *in* all hope, *as* the dawn approaches.

In his study in the beautiful and welcoming home Betty and Sam have created in Chesterfield, Virginia, on bookshelves custom crafted by the love and skill of a friend and colleague at Union Presbyterian Seminary, Sam displays in a prominent location a plaque given to him by a former student (and contributor to this Festschrift). That individual, like no few of Sam's students, has now gone on to advanced degree work in biblical studies and cites Sam's mentorship as indispensable in that decision.[7] The plaque reads in Hebrew, "Have you considered my servant Job?" More literally of course, in the poetic image employed by the Hebrew text, one might render this query, "Have you placed your heart upon my servant Job?"

Though he would surely disapprove, probably through a still and piercing gaze and a redolent silence rather than by *wasting* a single word, one might well imagine substituting the name "Sam" for the name Job in this engaging biblical question, a question Sam ranks as among the most searing in Scripture, one that ignites a probing of the human condition not unrelated to Jesus' question from the agony and loneliness of his cross.[8]

"Have you placed your heart upon my servant Sam?" So might we put this query, at least for a moment. And, in lives lived in the presence of the Hidden/Revealed God, in lives, Sam might argue and celebrate, that more often limp than sprint toward the hope,

---

6. Ibid.

7. Union Presbyterian Seminary, "Graduation Tributes," *Sharon & Brook*, Summer 2019, https://www.upsem.edu/wp-content/uploads/2019/07/July19SB.pdf.

8. Balentine, *Job*, 724.

mystery, and beauty of divine gifts temporal and divine promises eternal, more than a few of us have done just that. Sam's beloved family, Sam's friends, and many of Sam's students, colleagues, and peers—to cite an incomplete list—have indeed considered, "placed [our] heart upon," Samuel Eugene Balentine. So have we found ourselves, through Sam's profound erudition and equally through his inspiring friendship, challenged and moved in mind, in heart, and finally in soul, "twice blest," beyond measure, beyond words.

Laus deo.

Bibliography of Samuel E. Balentine's Publications

This bibliography contains three sections: books; editorial work; and articles, chapters, entries, and reviews. Each section is arranged chronologically.

Books

The Hidden God: The Hiding of the Face of God in the Old Testament. Oxford Theological Monographs. Oxford: Oxford University Press, 1983.

Prayer in the Hebrew Bible: The Drama of Divine-Human Dialogue. OBT. Minneapolis: Fortress, 1993.

The Torah's Vision of Worship. OBT. Minneapolis: Fortress, 1999.

Leviticus. IBC. Louisville: John Knox, 2002.

Job. SHBC. Macon, GA: Smyth & Helwys, 2006.

Have You Considered My Servant Job?: Understanding the Biblical Archetype of Patience. Studies on Personalities of the Old Testament. Columbia: University of South Carolina Press, 2015. (Outstanding Academic Title, 2015, awarded by *Choice*.)

Wisdom Literature. CBS. Nashville: Abingdon, 2018.

Ecce Homo*: Behold the Man. Ethical Imperatives of the Lenten Journey.* Macon, GA: Smyth & Helwys, 2020.

"Look at Me and Be Appalled": Essays on Job, Theology, and Ethics. Leiden: Brill, forthcoming.

Made in the Image—and Imagination—of God. Leiden: Brill, forthcoming.

Editorial Work

Old Testament General Editor, SHBC, 1993–Present.

Language, Theology, and the Bible: Essays in Honor of James Barr. Edited with John Barton. Oxford: Oxford University Press, 1994.

Editorial Board, *PRSt*, 1996–1999.

"Festschrift for J. Morris Ashcraft." *PRSt* 25/2 (1998): 133–208.

"Theodicy at the Turn of Another Century." *PRSt* 26/3 (1999): 241–330.

Editorial Council and Executive Committee, *Int*, 2001–2005.

Co-Editor, *Int*, 2005–2009.

Editor, *Int*, 2010–2013.

Editorial Board, *NIDB*, 2005–2010.

Series Editor, *Interpretation: Resources for the Use of Scripture in the Church*, 2014–Present.

The Oxford Encyclopedia of the Bible and Theology. Editor-in-Chief. 2 vols. Oxford: Oxford University Press, 2015.

The Oxford Handbook of Ritual and Theology in the Hebrew Bible. Editor-in-Chief. Oxford: Oxford University Press, 2020.

Articles, Chapters, Entries, and Reviews

1980

"A Description of the Semantic Field of Hebrew Words for 'Hide.'" *VT* 30 (1980): 137–53.

1981

"The Interpretation of The Old Testament in the New Testament." *SwJT* 23 (1981): 41–57.

"Jeremiah: His Life and Ministry." *TTE* 12 (1981): 13–21.

"Jeremiah, Prophet of Prayer." *RevExp* 78 (1981): 331–44.

1984

"The Prophet as Intercessor: A Reassessment." *JBL* 103 (1984): 161–73.

"The Royal Psalms and the New Testament: From 'messiah' to 'Messiah.'" *TTE* 29 (1984): 56–62.

1985

"Prayer in the Wilderness Traditions: In Pursuit of Divine Justice." *HAR* 9 (1985): 53–74.

1987

Review of *Die Verheissung des neuen Bundes in ihrem theologieges-chichtlichem Zusammenhang ausgelegt*, by Christoph Levin. *JBL* 106 (1987): 708–709.

"Torah: The Promise and Mystery of the Presence of God." *TTE* 35 (1987): 25–40.

1988

"Jethro: All We Know." *BI* 14 (1988): 24–25.

Review of *Gebet im Alten Testament*, by Henning Graf Reventlow. *JBL* 107 (1988): 299–301.

1989

"Prayers for Justice in the Old Testament: Theodicy and Theology." *CBQ* 51 (1989): 587–616.

"The Prophetic Message: Its Origin, Setting and Significance." *Faith and Mission* 6 (1989): 3–17.

Review of *Holiness in Israel*, by John G. Gammie. *HBT* 11 (1989): 107–108.

1990

"The Book of Job." Pages 455–56 in *MDB*.

"Justice/Judgment in the Old Testament." Pages 482–83 in *MDB*.

"Prayer in the Old Testament." Pages 706–707 in *MDB*.

Review of *The Cry to God in the Old Testament*, by Richard Nelson Boyce. *JBL* 109 (1990): 119–21.

1992

"Enthroned on the Praises and Laments of Israel." *PSB* Supplementary Issue 2 (1992): 20–35.

Review of *Ṣôm-Fasten: Kollektive Trauer um den verborgenen Gott im Alten Testament*, by Thomas Podella. *JBL* 111 (1992): 513–15.

1993

"Enthroned on the Praises and Laments of Israel." Pages 20–36 in *The Lord's Prayer: Perspectives for Reclaiming Christian Prayer*. Edited by Daniel L. Migliore. Grand Rapids: Eerdmans, 1993. Repr., *PSB* Supplementary Issue 2 (1992): 20–35.

Review of *Biblical Criticism in Crisis?: The Impact of the Canonical Approach on Old Testament Studies*, by Mark G. Brett. *HS* 34 (1993): 106–109.

1994

"Isaiah 45: God's 'I Am,' Israel's 'You Are.'" *HBT* 16 (1994): 103–20.

"James Barr's 'Quest for Sound and Adequate Biblical Interpretation.'" Pages 5–15 in *Language, Theology, and the Bible: Essays in Honour of James Barr*. Edited by Samuel E. Balentine and John Barton. Oxford: Oxford University Press, 1994.

"Preaching the Prayers of the Old Testament." *Journal for Preachers* 17 (1994): 12–17.

Review of "*And You Shall Tell Your Son . . .": The Concept of the Exodus in the Bible*, by Yair Zakovitch. *CRBR* 6 (1994): 193–94.

1995

"Job." Pages 405–30 in *Mercer Commentary on the Bible*. Edited by Watson E. Mills and Richard F. Wilson. Macon, GA: Mercer University Press, 1995.

1996

"The Politics of Religion in the Persian Period." Pages 129–46 in *After the Exile: Essays in Honour of Rex Mason*. Edited by John Barton and David J. Reimer. Macon, GA: Mercer University Press, 1996.

Review of *The Life of Moses: The Yahwist as Historian in Exodus–Numbers*, by John Van Seters. *Int* 50 (1996): 295–97.

1997

Review of *They Cried to the Lord: The Form and Theology of Biblical Prayer*, by Patrick D. Miller. *Int* 51 (1997): 77–79.

"'You Can't Pray a Lie': Truth and Fiction in the Prayers of Chronicles." Pages 246–67 in *The Chronicler as Historian*. Edited by Patrick M. Graham, Kenneth G. Hoglund, and Steven L. McKenzie. JSOTSup 238. Sheffield: Sheffield Academic, 1997.

1998

"'What Are Human Beings, That You Make So Much of Them?' Divine Disclosure from the Whirlwind: 'Look at Behemoth.'" Pages 259–78 in *God in the Fray: A Tribute to Walter Brueggemann*. Edited by Tod Linafelt and Timothy K. Beal. Minneapolis: Fortress, 1998.

1999

"Between Text and Sermon: Job 23:1–9, 16–17." *Int* 53 (1999): 290–93.

"The Church of Saint Job." *RevExp* 96 (1999): 501–18.

Reviews of *Education in Ancient Israel: Across the Deadening Silence*, by James L. Crenshaw, and *Scribes and Schools: The Canonization of the Hebrew Scriptures*, by Philip R. Davies. *Int* 53 (1999): 410–12.

"Who Will Be Job's Redeemer?" *PRSt* 26 (1999): 269–89.

2000

"Holy Week." Pages 199–266 in *New Proclamation: Year C, 1999–2000*. Edited by Marshall D. Johnson. Minneapolis: Fortress, 2000.

"Prayer." Pages 1077–79 in *EDB*.

Review of *The Book of Job: A Short Reading*, by Roland E. Murphy. *CBQ* 62 (2000): 732.

Reviews of *A Poetics of Jonah: Art in the Service of Ideology*, by Kenneth M. Craig; *Job*, by James A. Wharton; and *The Bible and the Comic Vision*, by J. William Whedbee. *PRSt* 27 (2000): 207–10.

2001

Review of *The Biblical Jubilee, After Fifty Years*, by Robert North. *CBQ* 63 (2001): 729–30.

Review of *Penitential Prayer in Second Temple Judaism: The Development of a Religious Institution*, by Rodney Alan Werline. *JBL* 120 (2001): 550–52.

2002

"Have You Considered My Servant Job?" *RevExp* 99 (2002): 495–501.

"Job's 'Struggle for the Last Truth about God.'" *RevExp* 99 (2002): 579–80.

"My Servant Job Will Pray for You." *ThTo* 58 (2002): 502–18.

2003

"For No Reason." *Int* 57 (2003): 349–69.

"'It Is Not Too Late to Seek a Newer World.' A Tribute to Phyllis Trible." *LTQ* 38 (2003): 3–9.

"Job as Priest to the Priests." *ExAud* 18 (2003): 29–52.

"Let Love Clasp Grief Lest Both Be Drowned." *PRSt* 30 (2003): 381–97.

"Passover." Pages 350–53 in *The Westminster Theological Wordbook of the Bible*. Edited by Donald E. Gowan. Louisville: Westminster John Knox, 2003.

"Praise." Pages 378–80 in *The Westminster Theological Wordbook of the Bible*. Edited by Donald E. Gowan. Louisville: Westminster John Knox, 2003.

"Pray, Prayer, Intercede." Pages 380–86 in *The Westminster Theological Wordbook of the Bible*. Edited by Donald E. Gowan. Louisville: Westminster John Knox, 2003.

Review of *Holiness to the Lord: A Guide to the Exposition of the Book of Leviticus*, by Allen P. Ross. *CBQ* 65 (2003): 453–54.

"Sabbath." Pages 439–41 in *The Westminster Theological Wordbook of the Bible*. Edited by Donald E. Gowan. Louisville: Westminster John Knox, 2003.

"Sacrifice, Offer, Offering." Pages 441–47 in *The Westminster Theological Wordbook of the Bible*. Edited by Donald E. Gowan. Louisville: Westminster John Knox, 2003.

"Turn, O Lord! How Long?" *RevExp* 100 (2003): 465–81.

2004

Review of *Reverberations of Faith: A Theological Handbook of Old Testament Themes*, by Walter Brueggemann. *Int* 58 (2004): 68–69.

2005

"The Emergence of Scripture." Pages 53–78 in *Judaism From Moses to Muhammed: An Interpretation*. Edited by Jacob Neusner, William Scott Green, and Alan Jeffrey Avery-Peck. BRLA 23. Leiden: Brill, 2005.

2006

"Afterword." Pages 193–204 in *The Origins of Penitential Prayer in Second Temple Judaism*. Vol. 1 of *Seeking the Favor of God*. Edited by Mark J. Boda, Daniel K. Falk, and Rodney A. Werline. EJL 21. Atlanta: Society of Biblical Literature, 2006.

"Ask the Animals, and They Will Teach You." Pages 3–11 in *"And God Saw That It Was Good": Essays on Creation and God in Honor of Terence E. Fretheim*. Edited by Frederick J. Gaiser. Word and World Supplement Series 5. Saint Paul, MN: Luther Seminary, 2006.

"I Was Ready to Be Sought Out by Those Who Did Not Ask." Pages 1–20 in *The Origins of Penitential Prayer in Second Temple Judaism*. Vol. 1 of *Seeking the Favor of God*. Edited by Mark J. Boda, Daniel K. Falk, and Rodney A. Werline. EJL 21. Atlanta: Society of Biblical Literature, 2006.

2007

"Day of Atonement." *NIDB* 2:42–45.

"Inside the 'Sanctuary of Silence': The Moral-Ethical Demands of Suffering." Pages 63–80 in *Character Ethics and the Old Testament: Moral Dimensions of Scripture*. Edited by M. Daniel Carroll R. and Jacqueline E. Lapsley. Louisville: Westminster John Knox, 2007.

2008

"The Book of Job." Pages 71–124 in vol. 5 of *The Pastor's Bible Study: A New Interpreter's Bible Study*. Edited by David Albert Farmer. Nashville: Abingdon, 2008.

"Easter Day, Isaiah 25:6–9, Exegetical Perspective." Pages 359, 361, 363 in *Feasting on the Word: Preaching the Revised Common Lectionary, Year B, Volume 2*. Edited by David L. Bartlett and Barbara Brown Taylor. Louisville: Westminster John Knox, 2008.

"Easter Vigil, Exodus 14:10–31, Exegetical Perspective." Pages 335, 337, 339 in *Feasting on the Word: Preaching the Revised Common Lectionary, Year B, Volume 2*. Edited by David L. Bartlett and Barbara Brown Taylor. Louisville: Westminster John Knox, 2008.

"Job, Book of." *NIDB* 3:319–36.

"Second Sunday of Easter, Acts 4:32–35, Exegetical Perspective." Pages 383, 385, 387 in *Feasting on the Word: Preaching the Revised Common Lectionary, Year B, Volume 2*. Edited by David L. Bartlett and Barbara Brown Taylor. Louisville: Westminster John Knox, 2008.

"Traumatizing Job." *RevExp* 105 (2008): 213–28.

2009

"Epiphany of the Lord, Isaiah 60:1–6, Exegetical Perspective." Pages 195, 197, 199 in *Feasting on the Word: Preaching the Revised Common Lectionary, Year C, Volume 1*. Edited by David L. Bartlett and Barbara Brown Taylor. Louisville: Westminster John Knox, 2009.

"First Sunday After Christmas Day, 1 Samuel 2:18–20, 26, Exegetical Perspective." Pages 147, 149, 151 in *Feasting on the Word: Preaching the Revised Common Lectionary, Year C, Volume 1.* Edited by David L. Bartlett and Barbara Brown Taylor. Louisville: Westminster John Knox, 2009.

"He Unrolled the Scroll . . . and He Rolled Up the Scroll and Gave It Back." *CrossCurrents* 59 (2009): 154–75.

"Numbers." Pages 51–62 in *Theological Bible Commentary.* Editors Gail R. O'Day and David L. Petersen. Louisville: Westminster John Knox, 2009.

"Second Sunday After Christmas Day, Sirach 24:1–12, Exegetical Perspective." Pages 171, 173, 175 in *Feasting on the Word: Preaching the Revised Common Lectionary, Year C, Volume 1.* Edited by David L. Bartlett and Barbara Brown Taylor. Louisville: Westminster John Knox, 2009.

"Suffering and Evil." *NIDB* 5:390–94.

2011

"Barr, James." *EBR* 3:543–46.

"The Prose and Poetry of Exile." Pages 345–64 in *Interpreting Exile: Displacement and Deportation in Biblical and Modern Contexts.* Edited by Brad E. Kelle, Frank Richtel Ames, and Jacob L. Wright. AIL 10. Atlanta: Society of Biblical Literature, 2011.

2013

"Foreword" and contribution to "Arguing with the Text." Pages ix–xi and 1–42 in *Living Countertestimony: Conversations with Walter Brueggemann.* Edited by Carolyn J. Sharp. Louisville: Westminster John Knox, 2013.

"Job and the Priests: 'He Leads Priests Away Stripped' (Job 12:19)." Pages 42–53 in *Reading Job Intertextually.* Edited by Katharine J. Dell and Will Kynes. LHBOTS 574. New York: Bloomsbury T&T Clark, 2013.

"Preaching Job's God." *Journal for Preachers* 36 (2013): 22–27.

2016

"The Future Beyond the End: Lessons from History by Herodotus and Daniel." *PRSt* 43 (2016): 145–59.

"Legislating Divine Trauma." Pages 161–76 in *Bible through the Lens of Trauma*. Edited by Elizabeth Boase and Christopher G. Frechette. SemeiaSt 86. Atlanta: SBL Press, 2016.

"Wisdom." Pages 274–91 in *The Cambridge Companion to the Hebrew Bible/Old Testament*. Edited by Stephen B. Chapman and Marvin A. Sweeney. Cambridge: Cambridge University Press, 2016.

2017

"God and the 'Happiness Formula': The Ethos and Ethics of Happiness." Pages 197–216 in *Mixed Feelings and Vexed Passions: Exploring Emotions in Biblical Literature*. Editor F. Scott Spencer. RBS 90. Atlanta: SBL Press, 2017.

"'I Am a God and Not a Human Being': The Divine Dilemma in Hosea." Pages 54–69 in *Torah and Tradition: Papers Read at the Sixteenth Joint Meeting of the Society for Old Testament Study and the Oudtestamentisch Werkgezelschap, Edinburgh, 2015*. Edited by Klaas Spronk and Hans M. Barstad. *OtSt* 70. Leiden: Brill, 2017.

2018

"Sagacious Divine Judgment: Jeremiah's Use of Proverbs to Construct an Ethos and Ethics of Divine Epistemology." Pages 113–25 in *The Book of Jeremiah: Composition, Reception, and Interpretation*. Edited by Jack R. Lundbom, Craig A. Evans, and Bradford A. Anderson. VTSup 178. Leiden: Brill, 2018.

2019

"Foreword." Pages 8–10 in *Postcolonial Commentary and the Old Testament*. Edited by Hemchand Gossai. London: Bloomsbury T&T Clark, 2019.

Review of *Dictionary of the Bible and Western Culture*, edited by Mary Ann Beavis and Michael J. Gilmour. *JTS* 70 (2019): 733–34.

Forthcoming

"Galileo Reading Qohelet: Seeing the World with 'Curiosity's Eye.'" *BibInt*, forthcoming.

"'Get Away! Impure! Get Away!': Defiled and Defiling Priests in Lamentations." In *Reading Lamentations Intertextually*. Edited by Brittany Melton and Heath Thomas. LHBOTS. London: Bloomsbury, forthcoming.

"The Joban Theophany and the Education of God." In *Texts, Theological Readers, and Their Worlds*. Vol. 2 of *Theology of the Hebrew Bible*. Edited by Soo J. Kim Sweeney, David Frankel, and Marvin A. Sweeney. RBS. Atlanta: SBL Press, forthcoming.

"Prayer in the Hebrew Bible: Retrospect and Prospect." In *Studies on Prayer in the Deuterocanonical Books*. Edited by Kristin De Troyer and A. K. Sims. Leuven: Peeters, forthcoming.

"Proverbs." In *The Oxford Handbook of Wisdom and the Bible*. Edited by Will Kynes. Oxford: Oxford University Press, forthcoming.

"Written on the Heart, Erased from the Mind: Rewriting Moral Agency in Jeremiah." In *The Oxford Handbook of Jeremiah*. Edited by Louis Stulman. Oxford: Oxford University Press, forthcoming.

Part I
Torah's Heights

There's a Wildness in God's Mercy
God's Sovereignty, Quantum Probability, and a Biblical Worldview

Mark E. Biddle

Sam and I became acquaintances some thirty-five years ago through mutual friends and a common academic discipline. In the meantime, I joined the editorial board of the Smyth & Helwys Commentary under his leadership, came to be his junior colleague at the Baptist Theological Seminary at Richmond, and succeeded him as the Russell T. Cherry Professor of Old Testament there when he moved, literally, across the street to Union Presbyterian Seminary. Throughout, Sam has been an example, a counselor, a champion, and, above all, a dear and valued friend. I offer this modest contribution as an inadequate token of my gratitude to him.

Introduction

The problem of the relationship between science and religion first arose when biblical interpretation confronted the conflict between the worldview of ancient Israel and the emerging consensus around material/mechanical causation as a sufficient explanation for the cosmos. The body of scientific knowledge amassed post-Newton but pre-quantum theory pointed to a materially deterministic, *causally closed* world with room neither for God's activity nor human free will.[1] Biblical scholarship largely resorted then to differentiating biblical mythopoeism from the empirically verifiable claims of science. Since, by definition, *myth* involves divine intervention in the "material" world, this interpretive strategy effectively removed the biblical witness from any dialogue with modern science. If theology and science have absolutely no interrelation, believers must bifurcate their worldview in an untenable metaphysical dualism.[2]

The advent of quantum physics and relativity revolutionized science. Unfortunately, this revolution only widened the chasm between an empirical worldview and the classical Christian worldview. Recently, however, theologians and philosophers of religion have employed quantum mechanics to recast the traditional theological view of God's sovereign control over and in the world and, thereby, to bridge the chasm between science and religion. To date, biblical scholarship has played only a minor role in this discussion.[3]

This paper will explore whether portions of the Hebrew Bible assume a perspective on God's relationship to creation that is compatible with quantum mechanics. To be clear, this paper makes

---

1. Stephen M. Barr, *Modern Physics and Ancient Faith* (Notre Dame: University of Notre Dame, 2003), 175–76.

2. Cf. Cornelius Willem du Toit, "The Higgs Boson, Creation and 'Truth'," *R&T* 21 (2014): 390; John F. Haught, "Teilhard de Chardin: Theology for an Unfinished Universe," in *From Teilhard to Omega: Co-creating an Unfinished Universe*, ed. Ilia Delio (Maryknoll, NY: Orbis, 2014), 9; K. Nürnberger, "Theology in the Light of Universal Evolution: Can Biblical Faith Be Described Adequately in Terms of a Radically Inductive Approach to Reality?" in *Reading the Universe through Science, Religion and Ethics: The Evolving Science and Religion Debate*, ed. C. W. du Toit (Pretoria, SA: Research Institute for Theology and Religion, 1999), 87; Ilia Delio, "Introduction," in *From Teilhard to Omega: Co-creating an Unfinished Universe*, ed. Ilia Delio (Maryknoll, NY: Orbis, 2014), 2.

3. Exceptions include Christopher Southgate, "Re-reading Genesis, John, and Job: A Christian Response to Darwinism," *Zygon* 46 (2011): 370–95; John Polkinghorne, "Scripture and an Evolving Creation," *Science & Christian Belief* 21 (2009): 163–73; and, notably, William P. Brown, *The Seven Pillars of Creation: The Bible, Science, and the Ecology of Wonder* (Oxford: Oxford University Press, 2010).

no claim that ancient Israel anticipated modern quantum physics, and certainly not that a proper interpretation of the Bible would necessarily disclose a quantum view of creation. Rather, it utilizes quantum insights as a lens through which to read portions of the Hebrew Bible in ways that might otherwise go unnoticed.[4] It will reveal the outlines of a biblical theology of God's creating, sustaining, and influencing work that accommodates contemporary scientific understanding surprisingly well.

A Brief Quantum Primer

First, it will be helpful to distinguish between classical and quantum physics.[5] William E. Brown summarizes the four basic assumptions of classical physics as (1) "objective realism"—the physical world exists apart from human observation; (2) "physical sufficiency"—physical causation can explain every event; (3) "inductive validity"—inferences drawn from empirical observation are valid; and (4) "upper limit"—nothing can travel faster than the universal constant, the speed of light.[6] Quantum physics overturns classical causality. Beginning with the observation that light behaves simultaneously as a wave and a particle, it soon became apparent that this phenomenon of *wave-particle duality* pertains not just to light but generally at the subatomic level.

---

4. Dean Fowler, "Quantum Physics and Christian Anthropology," *Hor* 7 (1980): 214. Cf. the approach that Philip Jay Bentley employs in "Uncertainty and Unity: Paradox and Truth," *Judaism* 33 (1984): 191–201.

5. This discussion relies heavily on Robert John Russell, "The Physics of David Bohm and Its Relevance to Philosophy and Theology," *Zygon* 20 (1985): 165–58; William E. Brown, "Quantum Theology: Christianity and the New Physics," *JETS* 33 (1990): 477–87; Gennaro Auletta, "How Quantum Mechanics Suggests New Insights in Metaphysics and Natural Theology," *Anton* 78 (2003): 705–10; Ian G. Barbour, "Theology and Physics Forty Years Later," *Zygon* 40 (2005): 507–11; Ross H. McKenzie and Benjamin Myers, "Dialectical Critical Realism in Science and Theology: Quantum Physics and Karl Barth," *Science & Christian Belief* 20 (2008): 49–66; Dillard W. Faries, "A Personal God, Chance, and Randomness in Quantum Physics," *Perspectives on Science and Christian Faith* 66 (2014): 13–22; and Denis Edwards, "Toward a Theology of Divine Action: William R. Stoeger, S.J., on the Laws of Nature," *Theological Studies* 76 (2015): 485–502.

6. Brown, "Quantum Theology," 479.

Classical physics requires two factors in order to describe completely a physical system: its coordinates in space-time and its dynamic function.[7] In a quantum system, however, these *conjugate qualities* (position/momentum, time/energy, etc.) cannot be determined simultaneously (*complementarity*). Indeed, measuring a quantum system for one of these conjugate qualities renders its partner indeterminate (*quantum indeterminacy*). Measurement disturbs the system. If one looks at the system in terms of its location, one finds a particle; if one looks at the system in terms of its energy, one finds a wave. Measurement causes the wave function of a quantum system to "collapse" into the observed state. Consequently, quantum theory can say nothing about reality if someone is not observing it (the *Heisenberg Uncertainty Principle*) because the system exhibits *quantum superposition*. That is, it is in both states until it is measured for one (*Schrödinger's cat*). All of this means that quantum systems are *probabilistic*. In mathematical terms, one cannot predict which of the many possible solutions of a *wave function* will actualize. Newtonian physics predicts that a cue ball directed at another billiard ball at a given angle and with a given momentum will set the target ball into motion at a predictable angle and momentum: there is only one solution. In stark contrast, quantum physics understands "an event" to be "a selection of one among a huge number of possibilities 'encapsulated' in the initial state of the system."[8] Consequently, any condition A can result in any of $B^1, B^2, B^3 \ldots B^n$, while any condition B^1 may have resulted from any of $A^1, A^2, A^3 \ldots A^n$. Quantum physics excludes causation understood as a linear, predictable relationship.

Another phenomenon, *quantum entanglement*, also contradicts the logic of mechanical causation. Physicists have observed that if two quantum particles interact, they are thereafter linked to one another in such a way that a change in the condition of particle A coincides instantaneously with a change in particle B *even if at a distance from*

---

7. Neils Bohr, "The Quantum Postulate and the Recent Development of Atom Theory," *Nature* 121 (1928): 580–90.

8. Auletta, "How Quantum Mechanics," 707. Auletta (709) calls attention to the similarities between the probabilistic nature of reality as revealed by quantum physics and Alfred Whitehead's process metaphysics.

one another. The "information" instantaneously exchanged between the two particles, therefore, travels faster than the speed of light, the universal constant. No causal mechanism or force is evident.[9]

Similarly, classical causality does not apply in *emergence* or *top-down causality*. Emergence is the phenomenon in which properties arise at a higher or more complex level that cannot be anticipated from the properties of the lower-level, less complex constitutive components. Examples of emergence include any number of chemical compounds (carbon and oxygen are basics for life, but they are lethal in the compound carbon monoxide), the rise of life from carbon compounds (self-organizing chemistry), the emergence of mind (which, in turn, exerts top-down influence on the body), fractals, and thermodynamic systems.

Evolutionary processes manifest probabilistic and emergent characteristics. Every organism manifests the realization of instructions encoded in its genes, its DNA (deoxyribonucleic acid). Remarkably, all DNA has the same chemical composition: two intertwined chains of alternating deoxyribose (a sugar) and a phosphate, each sugar linked to one of four bases (adenine, cytosine, guanine, and thymine). These four bases form pairs in only two possibilities—an adenine/thymine pair or a cytosine/guanine pair. The genetic instructions for every aspect of life, therefore, consists of long strings of A-T and C-G pairs. The difference in the mental capacities of a human being and a scorpion emerge from differences in the sequencing of these two pairs in the genes of the respective organisms. Rearrangements in this sequence produce mutations. Thus, even minor changes in this chemistry produce properties at the higher level of the organism that cannot be anticipated from the properties of the arrangement of A-T and G-C pairs. Furthermore, these mutations appear not in linear fashion but in probabilistic distributions. In other words, while the mutation of a particular gene in a particular individual cannot be predicted, "in a large population of many thousands of individuals the occurrence of that mutation at least once may be very likely."[10]

---

9. Einstein, who considered this effect an indication of the inadequacy of quantum theory, referred to it as *spukhafte Fernwirkung* ("spooky action at a distance"). Meanwhile, it has been demonstrated experimentally.

10. Barrie Britton, "Evolution by Blind Chance," *SJT* 39 (1986): 344–45.

Similarly, the evolutionary principle of natural selection, or survival of the fittest, operates in a probabilistic manner. A given individual genetically disadvantaged in comparison to another in the same population may, indeed, survive. Yet, in terms of the entire population of the species, the "fittest" will survive in greater proportion than the "weakest," driving the evolution of the species toward the advantageous trait.

Physics, Metaphysics, and Theology

Pre-Newtonian theological formulations stressed God's active, causal engagement with the natural order and in human history. Newtonian physics describes nature as governed by a set of laws that could, in theory, explain all natural events in terms of material causation. Strict materialists extend that model to include human behavior and thus human history. This scheme threatened to relegate God to the role of the watchmaker God of the deists. Some found room for God's continued engagement in nature and history in the areas where science had not *yet* discovered the laws that adequately accounted for certain phenomena—the so-called "God of the gaps" argument. Of course, as science progressed, these "gaps" diminished, threatening to exclude the possibility of divine involvement altogether. The notion of a watchmaker God also undermines any idea of human free will. Everything that happens in the present is the only possible result of the chain of material causation that preceded it.

Quantum physics represents a revolution in the scientific understanding of reality that its proponents recognize as having metaphysical (and therefore theological) ramifications. What does it mean that the foundations of the real world rest on dualities that resolve into waves or particles only when an observer measures the system? Bohr and Heisenberg advocated the so-called "Copenhagen interpretation" of quantum physics: the potentials inherent in a wave function only become actual through observation. Without an observer, the system is only potential; observation essentially brings about the quantum event. Eugene P. Wigner's interpretation takes this position to its radical extreme. In his view, reality requires consciousness coupled with quantum processes; without the mind of a conscious observer, wave functions would never collapse, and, consequently, nothing would ever happen in the universe. Hugh

Everett argues for the diametrically opposite interpretation, namely that every potential in a system is actualized in some reality so that "many worlds" exist in parallel realities. Whichever interpretation of quantum phenomena proves to be correct, their counter-intuitive, even apparently irrational nature confirms "(J. B. S.) Haldane's Law": "The Universe is not only queerer than we suppose, but queerer than we can suppose."

Correspondences with Scripture

As William P. Brown has demonstrated clearly and systematically, the probabilistic character of quantum physics and evolutionary biology provide powerful instruments with which to read the Bible.[11] Such a reading reveals a wide range of "consonances" between the Bible and contemporary science. It remains to integrate Brown's insights and others gained by this comparative method into the ongoing discussion involving systematic and constructive theology, science, and metaphysics.

That discussion centers on whether and how one can say that God "acts" in the world, both in creating and within creation. The desired description will avoid an interventionist deity violating the deity's own laws of nature yet actually influential on/in the world. The new understanding of causation in terms of probabilities and "top-down" influences, on the other hand, challenges the traditional theological conception of God's sovereignty. While the demise of strict Newtonian determinism and its theological counterparts, the clockwork deity and the deterministic world, restores the credibility of freedom even for the material universe, and at all levels, quantum indeterminacy and probability distributions post the problem of harmonizing sovereignty and chance. Curiously, in many cases, the biblical view exhibits greater "consonance" with probabilistic science than with the classical formulation of divine sovereignty and suggests directions for a theology that can equip contemporary believers with a coherent worldview.

The trajectory from the Genesis 1 account of creation to Job's account of the encounter between God and Job, for example, provides rich resources for theological reflection on these issues. The

---

11. Brown, *Seven Pillars*.

comparison sheds light on the sophistication of the Bible's treatment, at points, of the idea of a transcendent deity who stands *beyond* creation instead of being a cause *within* it. As depicted in Geneis 1 and Job 38–41, God does not reach into the world in the *deus ex machina* of mythology. Instead, God authorizes, undergirds, and delights in the world, including *the natural processes that transpire in and produce it.*

Potential Actualized

Genesis 1:2 describes the initial state of the created order as *tōhû wābōhû*. The phrase occurs elsewhere in the Hebrew Bible only in Jer 4:23. Notably, Jeremiah continues, "and there was no light." As a broken pair, the two terms appear in Isa 34:11 where, together, they connote emptiness and futility. These three occurrences exhaust the biblical usage of *bōhû*. On the other hand, *tōhû* appears alone in reference to desert wastelands (Deut 32:10; Job 6:18; 12:24; Ps 107:40; Isa 29:21; 34:11, an image poorly suited to the watery chaos of Gen 1), as the antonym of "inhabited" and thus "empty" (Isa 45:18), and, most often, to denote "nothingness"/"nothing" (1 Sam 12:21; Job 26:7; Isa 24:10; 40:17, 23; 41:29; 44:9; 45:19; 49:4; 59:4). English translations usually render the expression in Gen 1:2 with some version of KJV's "without form and void." William P. Brown, crediting Mark S. Smith, offers "void and vacuum,"[12] which preserves the poetic quality of the Hebrew nicely but seems to suggest the vast, "empty" expanses of interstellar space. Something like "without substance or structure" emphasizes the notions of nothingness and disorder more clearly associated with the terms as used elsewhere in the Hebrew Bible. In any case, the Genesis account of creation begins with the world in an indeterminate state of pure potential, with nothing yet actualized like a wave function yet to "collapse."

Remarkably, Genesis 1 describes God's role in creation without reference to any physical act of God. Instead, in a series of phases, God wills elements of the world to be, observes that they have become, and evaluates them. According to Gen 1, this state of *nothing except potential* becomes something through God's *performative word*. In stark contrast to the creator gods of the world's mythologies, the

---

12. Ibid., 34.

biblical God *does* nothing in this account except to express volition. As William P. Brown and others have remarked, the backbone of the Genesis account consists of a series of statements God makes about the components of the universe, in each case *before* these components have come into existence (vv. 3, 6, 9, 11, 14, 20, 24, 26). All but the last employ the peculiar Hebrew verb form, with no counterpart in English, known as a "jussive," which expresses the speaker's will in the third person. They do not, however, indicate the strength of the speaker's will *per se*. Instead, they may indicate that the speaker desires, is willing to grant permission, or demands an action. The context of Gen 1 accommodates any of these possibilities. Significantly, in any case, Gen 1 reports that the components of the cosmos came into being, not because God *caused* them in any physical manner but because God willed, authorized, enabled, or required them to come into being. God did not participate in the physical process as the first cause and, thus, from within existence. Rather, to use Paul Tillich's phrase, God was and is "the Ground of Being," the will on which beings can exist.

Actualized through Observation

Genesis records that, after each component of creation came into being, God "saw" it. According to the "Copenhagen Interpretation," reality is not real unless and until observed, a concept raising the specter that, to cite only one example, the fossil remains that testify to earth's paleo-history have not existed throughout the eons but only come into existence when unearthed by a paleologist observer. In order to evade such an apparent absurdity, the nineteenth-century British Empiricist George Berkeley, arguing from philosophical and not quantum premises, maintained that the stable existence of everything rests on the fact that, even when no human consciousness perceives a reality, God perceives it:

> [A]ll the choir of heaven and furniture of the earth, in a word all those bodies which compose the mighty frame of the world, have not any subsistence without a mind— . . . their *being* is *to be perceived or known*; . . . consequently so long as they are not actually perceived by me, or do not exist in my mind or that of any

other created spirit, they must either have no existence at all, or else subsist in the mind of some Eternal Spirit.[13]

It does no violence to the text of Gen 1 to paraphrase it in quantum terms as saying that the universe exists because, having willed it, God observed it—and maintains it in existence by continuing to perceive it.

Creation: A Design Executed or a Dynamic Process?

Together, several elements of the Genesis 1 account suggest that, rather than executing a precise plan for creation, God engaged with creation in the process of its unfolding. By allowing creation a degree of independent agency, God took into account that aspects of the world might emerge that God may not have wished. Human sin is a clear example. Viruses that mutate into pathogens are another. "God achieves the divine purposes through the undirected unfolding of the potentialities built into the initial framework of creation."[14] The openness exhibited here, throughout biblical history and beyond, implies the importance of human cooperation with God as God moves history toward the completion God intends.[15]

Having perceived, God expressed an assessment of the result. In each case, God pronounced the created thing "good" (vv. 4, 10, 12, 18, 21, 25) and once "very good" (v. 31). Significantly in the context of contemporary scientific understanding, God did not, however, pronounce creation "perfect."[16] Western theology's typical concept of God in conjunction with the doctrine of the "Fall" requires "perfection" as a category applicable both to the deity and to the original

---

13. George Berkeley, "The Principles of Human Knowledge," in *The Principles of Human Knowledge and Three Dialogues Between Hylas and Philonous*, ed. Geoffrey J. Warnock (Cleveland: World Publishing, 1963), 67–68; cf. Brown, *Seven Pillars*, 59 and 72 ("God's sight carries creation to its completion").

14. Stephen J. Pope, "Does Evolution Have a Purpose? The Theological Significance of William Stoeger's Account of 'Nested Directionality'," *Theological Studies* 78 (2017): 464.

15. Cf. Edward Schillebeeckx, *God, the Future of Man* (New York: Sheed and Ward, 1968), 36.

16. Cf. Brown, *Seven Pillars*, 61.

state of creation. Of course, it is difficult to see how the category of perfection applies to creatures lacking moral awareness or to imagine a vegetarian tiger. While parts of Gen 1–11 seem to envision an original creation absent the violence associated with animal predation, including human consumption of meat (cf. Gen 6:13; 9:3-4), a conception that conforms to the notion that creation lost an original innocence, Gen 1 (and 2) do(es) not explicitly depict a perfect world. Furthermore, apart from the difficulties associated with defining human perfection and with asserting divine immutability, the paleontological record does not attest to a period in which nature was not "red in tooth and claw."

In contrast to the creation of light, in which case God occasioned its existence merely by expressing the wish that it exist, five moments of creation involve *creaturely agency* as the direct means of creation through the emergence of higher order from lower.[17] The waters under the firmament "gather themselves together" (*yiqqāwû*)[18] and the dry land "appears" (*tērā'eh*) in response to God's wish (v. 9). God authorizes the earth to cause (*tadšē'*) the herbage and trees to sprout (v. 11). Similarly, the waters are to "teem" (*yišrĕṣû*) with life (v. 20),[19] and the earth is to "bring forth" (*tôṣē'*) land life in its various kinds (v. 24). John Polkinghorne calls attention to the descriptions of the creative agency of natural processes in parallel with statements that God "made" components of the world (vv. 11, 20-21, and 24-25).[20] Taken together, vv. 20-21 offer an instructive amplification of the process. The author of Gen 1 has God first express the will for the existence of aquatic and avian life (v. 20), then specifies that God created (*bārā'*) the giant sea creatures (v. 21), and finally "blessed" all of this life by endowing them with the capacity for pro-*creation* and enjoining them to fill their habitats with life (v. 22). This capacity extends creaturely agency to subsequent generations of living things. Summarizing his wonder at this cooperation between God and God's creation, Polkinghorne cites the nineteenth-century theologians

---

17. Cf. Ibid., 44–45, 69–70.

18. Brown's translation in *Seven Pillars*, 34.

19. Like the light, birds simply appear directly in response to God's wish.

20. Polkinghorne, "Scripture and an Evolving Creation," 165.

Charles Kingsley and Frederick Temple who reacted to Darwin by observing that God cleverly created a world in which "creatures would make themselves."[21]

Wild Potential

For the most part, the Genesis account follows this pattern: expression of will, observation, and evaluation of the result. The accounts of God's creation of the "great sea monsters" (*hattannînim haggĕdōlîm*) in v. 21 and of humankind in vv. 26-30 depart from this pattern significantly. In both, God's expression of will issues in another statement that God "created" (*brʾ*) in accordance with God's will. Thereafter, the account of the creation of humankind includes the blessing of fecundity and the grant of seed-bearing vegetation as sustenance for humankind and herbage as sustenance for animal life. Only then comes the standard announcement that "it was so" (v. 30). The observation and assessment of creation in v. 31 applies not merely to the creation of humankind but to "everything [God] had done." Similarly, after God's expression of the will for sea and avian life to come into being, the account specifies that God created the *tannînim*. There is no typical assertion that "it was so," and, in the reverse of the sequence in vv. 26-31, the fecundity blessing appears last. This departure from the symmetry of the rest of the account leads scholars to ask source questions, of course, but its significance for this paper lies in the fact that, whereas the account identifies all the other components of God's creation in broad categories "after their kind," v. 21 specifies the *tannînim* and, paralleling vv. 26-31, elevates them in comparison to humankind (*brʾ*). What are the implications?

Outside Gen 1:21, *tannîn* appears thirteen times in the Hebrew Bible. In twelve of the fourteen instances, LXX translates with *drakōn*, "dragon." Genesis 1:21 LXX offers *kētos*, "sea monster." In a few texts, the Hebrew term seems to refer simply to poisonous terrestrial snakes. In Deut 32:33, where the Hebrew parallels *peten*, "venomous serpent," LXX recognizes this and translates *aspis*, "asp," although, despite the same parallel with *peten* in the Hebrew (lion/adder// young lion/serpent), Ps 91:13 LXX repeats the *drakōn* translation.

---

21. Ibid., 169.

In contrast, including Gen 1:21, eight of the fourteen occurrences refer to sea creatures and seem to involve some association with the *Chaoskampf* tradition of ANE mythology.[22] In Job 7:12, Job asks whether he represents to God the kind of chaotic threat posed by Yam and Tannîn.[23] The tradition of violent conflict is self-evident in Ps 74:13. Isaiah 27:1 projects the battle between God and the great aquatic monsters into the future and, significantly, equates Leviathan, *nāḥāš* ("serpent"), and Tannîn. Similarly, Isa 51:9, which refers to an ancient conflict, parallels Rahab and Tannîn. Jeremiah and Ezekiel compare Nebuchadnezzar (Jer 51:34) and Pharaoh (Ezek 29:3; 32:2) to the voracious dragon. Ezekiel explicitly associates it with water.[24]

Scholarship has long recognized that Gen 1 "demythologizes" the components of creation. According to Genesis, God did not create the world by defeating and repurposing enemy deities. Here, even the mythological sea dragon is nothing more than a creature. Yet the explicit statement that God created the *tannîn*, like the description of God setting the boundaries between the waters above and below the firmament and between the waters below the firmament and the dry

---

22. René A. López ("The Meaning of 'Behemoth' and 'Leviathan' in Job," *Biblia Sacra* 173 [2016]: 401–24) has recently catalogued an impressive body of evidence that Tanin, Leviathan (= Lotan), Rahab, Yamm (Sea), Tehom (Ti'amat), Orion, Zaphon, etc. represent mythological figures, "demythologized" by biblical authors, before concluding, seemingly on dogmatic grounds, that they constitute emblems for evil powers; cf. Eric Ortlund, "The Identity of Leviathan and the Meaning of the Book of Job," *TJ* 34 (2013): 17–23. Ortlund argues that elsewhere in the Bible and ANE literature the name Leviathan refers to the mythic sea monster of the *Chaoskampf* tradition. David J. A. Clines's survey of scholarship on the question finds this mythological interpretation of Leviathan and Behemoth to be the current consensus (*Job 38–42*, WBC [Nashville: Thomas Nelson, 2011], 148–57).

23. Cf. J. Gerald Janzen, "Another Look at God's Watch Over Job (7:12)," *JBL* 108 (1989): 113.

24. The two remaining usages are somewhat ambiguous. Although the competition between Moses and Aaron on the one side and the priests/magicians of Pharaoh on the other—both serving as proxies for their deities—suggests a mythological context, Exod 7:9, 10, 12 seem to refer to terrestrial "serpents." Psalm 148:7, where *tannîn* may serve as a "pivot" element functioning in both the preceding ("from the earth") and succeeding ("all deeps") clauses, appears in the context of the psalmist's invocation of all creation to offer God praise.

land, implicitly acknowledges that God does not tame watery chaos. Indeed, God *created* the monstrous sea serpent (and the poisonous terrestrial serpents, too).

What Gen 1 implies, God proclaims in the divine response to Job's challenge. Interestingly, God calls the attention of the wisdom teacher, Job, to certain wild, even ferocious aspects of natural order as evidence of the character of God's creation. Wisdom typically reflects on nonthreatening components of creation, as a survey of the book of Proverbs testifies (cf. 5:19; 6:5, 6; 7:22-23; 11:22; 14:1; 15:17; passim).[25] God's response to Job, however, concentrates on natural phenomena whose mechanisms were unknown and, for Job, unknowable (39:2; 39:13-18) or that stand out for their wildness and ferocity (39:5-12).

Remarkable in the latter category are, of course, Behemoth (40:15-24) and Leviathan (41:1-34), quintessential representatives of the wild power manifest in God's created order. As does Gen 1, the deity's description of nature to Job at times "demythologizes." Yam, the sea, is no god but a creation (38:8-11); even though borrowed from ancient Near Eastern mythology and although no actual creatures fit the descriptions, Job 40–41 in effect hyperbolizes characterizations of mythic figures.[26] The theme of "untamed/untamable might" throughout God's speeches in Job emphasizes the notions that these majestically powerful components of creation enjoy freedom limited only by the boundaries and restrictions established by God. Job 38:8-11 demythologizes Yam, the sea, but continues to emphasize its power and freedom, restrained only by the limits God places on it. God set the wild ass free (39:5), but only to enjoy that freedom in the steppes that God determined for its home. God makes it clear in these speeches that, rather than resulting from the corruption of nature occasioned by the Fall, ferocity, even predation (38:29-41), actualizes potentialities in elements of creation. God can impose

---

25. This is not to say that proverbial wisdom averts its eyes entirely from the thornier aspects of creation. In Proverbs, see references to thorns (15:19; 22:5; 26:9), the desert (21:19), a she-bear robbed of her cubs (17:11), the lion (19:12; 22:13; 26:13; 30:30), and the roaring lion or charging bear (28:15).

26. For the debate concerning the identity of Behemoth and Leviathan, see note 34 above and Robert Moses, "'The *satan*' in Light of the Creation Theology of Job," *HBT* 34 (2012): 29; cf. Ortlund, "Identity of Leviathan," 23–30.

limits on these creatures, but their might prevents human beings from domesticating them (cf. the wild ox, 39:9-12). Behemoth and Leviathan represent the apex of this mighty freedom subject only to God's restraints.

Significantly, however, God not only claims credit for creating and restricting Tannîn, Behemoth, and Leviathan but also *delights* in their ferocity. God is *proud* of them. God enjoins Job to consider Behemoth, which, God says, "I made as I made you" (40:15). Regarding Leviathan, God remarks that everything "under all of heaven is mine" (41:3), including this incomparable monster (41:33).

Another correspondence between Gen 1 and Job involves the agency God grants components of creation to act within divinely established bounds, although not in the fulfillment of specifically defined design. Earlier in the book of Job, the idea of creaturely agency appears in the descriptions of the means by which the *śāṭān* subjects Job to horrible misery: human agency in the form of Sabean and Chaldean marauders (Job 1:15, 17), who were presumably only doing what marauders do, unaware that they were playing any role in the wager of the *śāṭān* with God; and natural agency in the form of fire, wind, and illness (Job 1:16, 19; 2:7).

Theological Implications

Everyday experience, the biblical witness, and, now, the contemporary scientific understanding of reality join to attest that the world does not follow the direct path of God's determining will, not on the subatomic level of quantum indeterminacy, not in the processes of evolution,[27] and not in the course of human affairs. If the contrary were true, of course, God's sovereignty would effectively be tyranny. This assertion does not, however, exclude God from the role of creator,

---

27. "When we read the account of Creation in Genesis we risk imagining that God was a magician, complete with an all-powerful magic wand. But that was not so. He [sic] created beings and let them develop according to the internal laws with which He endowed each one, that they might develop, and reach their fullness" (Pope Francis, "Address of His Holiness Pope Francis on the Occasion of the Inauguration of the Bust in Honour of Pope Benedict XVI," lecture at the Pontifical Academy of Sciences, Vatican City, 27 October 2014, http://www.vatican.va/content/francesco/en/speeches/2014/october/documents/papa-francesco_20141027_plenaria-accademia-scienze.html).

sustainer, and guide.[28] Rather, it suggests the need for new metaphors to describe God's relationship with creation. Other portions of the biblical narrative provide clues. Genesis 17 indicates that God had not "directed" the birth of Ishmael. Nonetheless, God incorporated the initiative of Abraham and Sarah into God's overall intention. As Joseph eventually recognized, the series of misadventures he had experienced ironically positioned him to deliver his family from starvation. On Easter, God corrected the horror of "Good" Friday. As Paul stated it, "God works all things together for good" (Rom 8:28). God's relationship to the world is more like that of a jazz band leader to the band. God calls the tune, but the musicians play it, including the improvisational solos.

A theological position concerning God's relationship with the world as its creator and sustainer that does not require denying the insights of quantum theory will include reappraisals of (1) divine intervention, not as the contravention or suspension of the immutable laws of nature but as an influence that does not alter the probability distribution;[29] (2) divine sovereignty in relation to the probabilistic quality fundamental to nature; (3) creation as a cooperative action;[30] (4) the emergent character of the universe, i.e., that God is "the Lord of becoming, as well as being";[31] and (5) the openness of nature toward the future, i.e., that God's purposes for creation were only potentialities at the start. The result will be an understanding of God as one who does not "cause" but who is the Ground of Being, immanent in the quantum potentials, granting the world is own creativity, delighting in emergent phenomena while, at the same time, exerting *top-down* influence through the call to become that will culminate in de Chardin's *omega* point.

---

28. Polkinghorne, "Scripture and an Evolving Creation," 171–72.

29. Barbour, "Theology and Physics," 510.

30. See Thomas Aquinas, *Summa theologiae* (London: Blackfriars, 1964–1980), q. 22, a. 3 (as cited in Edwards, "Toward a Theology," 499).

31. Faries, "A Personal God," 21.

Bibliography

Aquinas, Thomas. *Summa Theologiae*. London: Blackfriars, 1964–1980.

Auletta, Gennaro. "How Quantum Mechanics Suggests New Insights in Metaphysics and Natural Theology." *Anton* 78 (2003): 705–10.

Barbour, Ian G. "Theology and Physics Forty Years Later." *Zygon* 40 (2005): 507–11.

Barr, Stephen M. *Modern Physics and Ancient Faith*. Notre Dame: University of Notre Dame, 2003.

Bentley, Philip Jay. "Uncertainty and Unity: Paradox and Truth." *Judaism* 33 (1984): 191–201.

Berkeley, George. "The Principles of Human Knowledge." Pages 45–146 in *The Principles of Human Knowledge and Three Dialogues Between Hylas and Philonous*. Edited by Geoffrey J. Warnock. Cleveland: World Publishing, 1963.

Bohr, Neils. "The Quantum Postulate and the Recent Development of Atom Theory." *Nature* 121 (1928): 580–90.

Britton, Barrie. "Evolution by Blind Chance." *SJT* 39 (1986): 344–45.

Brown, William E. "Quantum Theology: Christianity and the New Physics." *JETS* 33 (1990): 477–87.

Brown, William P. *The Seven Pillars of Creation: The Bible, Science, and the Ecology of Wonder*. Oxford: Oxford University Press, 2010.

Clines, D. J. A. *Job 38–42*. WBC. Nashville: Thomas Nelson, 2011.

Delio, Ilia. "Introductio." Pages 1–3 in *From Teilhard to Omega: Co-creating an Unfinished Universe*. Edited by Ilia Delio. Maryknoll, NY: Orbis, 2014.

du Toit, Cornelius Willem. "The Higgs Boson, Creation and 'Truth.'" *R&T* 21 (2014): 380–90.

Edwards, Denis. "Toward a Theology of Divine Action: William R. Stoeger, S.J., on the Laws of Nature." *Theological Studies* 76 (2015): 485–502.

Ellis, G. F. R. "Science and the Spiritual Quest: The Limits of Science and the Nature of Transcendence." Pages 1–26 in *Reading the Universe through Science, Religion and Ethics: The Evolving Science and Religion Debate*. Edited by C. W. du Toit. Pretoria: Research Institute for Theology and Religion, 1999.

Faries, Dillard W. "A Personal God, Chance, and Randomness in Quantum Physics." *Perspectives on Science and Christian Faith* 66 (2014): 13–22.

Fowler, Dean. "Quantum Physics and Christian Anthropology." *Hor* 7 (1980): 205–17.

Haught, John F. "Teilhard de Chardin: Theology for an Unfinished Universe." Pages 1–3 in *From Teilhard to Omega: Co-creating an Unfinished Universe*. Edited by Ilia Delio. Maryknoll, NY: Orbis, 2014.

Janzen, J. Gerald. "Another Look at God's Watch Over Job (7:12)." *JBL* 108 (1989): 109–14.

López, René A. "The Meaning of 'Behemoth' and 'Leviathan' in Job." *Biblia Sacra* 173 (2016): 401–24.

McKenzie, Ross H., and Benjamin Myers, "Dialectical Critical Realism in Science and Theology: Quantum Physics and Karl Barth." *Science & Christian Belief* 20 (2008): 49–66.

Moses, Robert. "'The *satan*' in Light of the Creation Theology of Job." *HBT* 34 (2012): 29.

Nürnberger, K. "Theology in the Light of Universal Evolution: Can Biblical Faith be Described Adequately in Terms of a Radically Inductive Approach to Reality?" Pages 87–103 in *Reading the Universe through Science, Religion and Ethics: The Evolving Science and Religion Debate*. Edited by C. W. du Toit. Pretoria: Research Institute for Theology and Religion, 1999.

Ortlund, Eric. "The Identity of Leviathan and the Meaning of the Book of Job." *TJ* 34 (2013): 17–23.

Polkinghorne, John. "Scripture and an Evolving Creation." *Science & Christian Belief* 21 (2009): 163–73.

Pope Francis. "Address of His Holiness Pope Francis on the Occasion of the Inauguration of the Bust in Honor of Pope Benedict XVI." Lecture presented at the Pontifical Academy of Sciences. Vatican City, 27 October 2014. http://www.vatican.va/content/francesco/en/speeches/2014/october/documents/papa-francesco_20141027_plenaria-accademia-scienze.html.

Pope, Stephen J. "Does Evolution Have a Purpose? The Theological Significance of William Stoeger's Account of 'Nested Directionality.'" *Theological Studies* 78 (2017): 462–82.

Russell, Robert John. "The Physics of David Bohm and its Relevance to Philosophy and Theology." *Zygon* 20 (1985): 165–58.

Schillebeeckx, Edward. *God, the Future of Man.* New York: Sheed and Ward, 1968.

Southgate, Christopher. "Re-reading Genesis, John, and Job: A Christian Response to Darwinism." *Zygon* 46 (2011): 370–95.

The Primeval History as an Etiology of Torah[1]

Andreas Schuele

Introduction: Creation and Flood in the Priestly Primeval History

It is one of Sam Balentine's many academic achievements to have developed both a concise and inspiring interpretation of Priestly theology in the Pentateuch/the Torah. This includes the account of creation in Genesis 1:1–2:3 that Balentine connects with the Priestly vision of worship. Worship is "the goal of creation,"[2] Balentine submits, or, as he also puts it, "the Torah's vision begins with the liturgy of creation."[3] There is an intrinsic connection between what God creates and what creation is meant to be. In a similar vein, other recent contributions to Genesis 1–11 have highlighted the significance of Gen 1:1–2:3 (Gen 1) as the prologue not only of the Primeval History but also of the entire Priestly and, arguably,

---

1. Originally published in Andreas Schüle, *Theology from the Beginning: Essays on the Primeval History and its Canonical Context*, FAT 113 (Tübingen: Mohr Siebeck, 2017), 165–75.

2. Samuel E. Balentine, *The Torah's Vision of Worship* (Minneapolis: Fortress, 1999), 63.

3. Ibid., 81.

also non-Priestly Pentateuch.[4] There are good reasons why Gen 1 deserves particular attention. It is part of an overarching framework that links the Priestly account of creation to the building and consecration of the tabernacle in Exodus 25–31 and 35–40.[5] Creation and temple, cosmology and cult,[6] are the elliptical poles around which Priestly theology is organized, although it remains debated whether the Priestly version of the Sinai legislation complements, completes, or, as I would prefer to say, deepens the creation account in Gen 1.

In this perspective, however, one may bypass the detail that the Priestly code (P) does not employ the creation narrative to give the reader the depiction of a perfect world. Rather, as P's Primeval History unfolds, it becomes clear that the world of Gen 1, despite God's best intentions and the blessings that God bestows on living beings, does not prosper in the way God had intended. Rather, according to Gen 5, it takes only ten generations for this very good creation to deteriorate and fill with violence (Gen 6:13). P does not give us any graphic details of what had happened, but the term *ḥāmās* suggests that "all flesh" was drowning in violence, bloodshed, and killing. God looks at the world and realizes that it is beyond repair. In P the flood is not so much a means of divine punishment as it is the unavoidable consequence of the creatures' proneness to violence. Put in different terms, the flood finishes off a world that had already self-destructed.[7]

---

4. S. Dean McBride, "Divine Protocol: Genesis 1:1–2:3 as Prologue to the Pentateuch," in *God Who Creates*, ed. William P. Brown and S. Dean McBride (Grand Rapids: Eerdmans, 2000), 3–41; Matthias Millard, *Die Genesis als Eröffnung der Tora. Kompositions- und auslegungsgeschichtliche Annäherungen an das erste Buch Mose*, WMANT 90 (Neukirchen-Vluyn: Neukirchener Verlag, 2001); Andreas Schüle, *Der Prolog der hebräischen Bibel. Der literar- und theologiegeschichtliche Diskurs der Urgeschichte (Genesis 1–11)*, ATANT 86 (Zürich: TVZ, 2006), 425–30.

5. Erich Zenger, *Gottes Bogen in den Wolken. Untersuchungen zu Komposition und Theologie der priesterschriftlichen Urgeschichte*, SBS 112 (Stuttgart: Katholisches Bibelwerk, 1983), 170–75; Millard, *Genesis*, 124–37.

6. Bernd Janowski, "Tempel und Schöpfung. Schöpfungstheologische Aspekte der priesterschriftlichen Heiligtumskonzeption," in *Gottes Gegenwart in Israel. Beiträge zur Theologie des Alten Testaments*, ed. Bernd Janowski (Neukirchen-Vluyn: Neukirchener Verlag, 1993), 222–40.

7. Schüle, *Der Prolog der hebräischen Bibel*, 260–68.

This is what P indicates by using the term *šḥt* for both the corruption of "all flesh"[8] and God's decision to destroy all flesh.[9]

If one looks at Gen 1 in the larger context of P's Primeval History, it becomes clear that Gen 1 depicts a world that is "very good" as far as God's own work is concerned. However, this world is also quintessentially flawed: while it can bring forth living beings, it appears to be incapable of sustaining and protecting life. Thus there is a peculiar tension between the language of completion and divine rest at the end of the creation narrative (Gen 2:2-3) and the negative account that one finds at the beginning of the flood narrative (Gen 6:9-13). One is reminded of the logic of prophetic parables like Isaiah's vineyard song (Isa 5:1-7) where the vineyard that God made with great care and consideration turns bad for no apparent reason. The song then affirms that God has no choice but to tear down the vineyard. The fact that there is no explanation for this unfortunate outcome suggests to the reader that there is no guarantee that good intentions turn into positive outcomes—not even with regard to God's own work.

The Priestly flood narrative displays the same logic: there is no apparent reason why the world fills with violence. Nonetheless, the occurrence of evil calls for God's intervention, which, again, is reminiscent of words from the prophetic tradition, specifically the prophetic message of doom. The expression (literally) "the end of all flesh has come before me" (Gen 6:13) seems to allude either to Amos 8:2 and Ezek 7:2-6 directly or, at least, to the judgment message contained in these texts.[10] These parallels are instructive regarding the meaning of the "end" that "has come before God" in this verse. Some

---

8. *šḥt*, hitp. "to become corrupt."

9. *šḥt*, hif. "to destroy." Norbert C. Baumgart, *Die Umkehr des Schöpfergottes. Zu Komposition und religionsgeschichtlichem Hintergrund von Gen 5–9*, HBS 22 (Freiburg: Herder, 1999), 210–12.

10. Rudolf Smend, "'Das Ende ist gekommen' Ein Amoswort in der Priesterschrift," in *Die Mitte des Alten Testaments. Gesammelte Studien*, ed. Rudolf Smend, BEvT 99 (München: Beck, 1986), 155–59; Robert Oberforcher, *Die Flutprologe als Kompositionsschlüssel der biblischen Urgeschichte. Ein Beitrag zur Rekationsgeschichte* (Innsbruck: Tyrolia, 1981), 438–40; Erich Bosshard-Nepustil, *Vor uns die Sintflut. Studien zu Text, Kontexten und Rezeption der Fluterzählung Genesis 6–9* (Stuttgart: Kohlhammer, 2005), 170–73.

versions of the Bible translate the phrase, "the end of the world is already decided as far as I am concerned." Such a translation suggests that the "end" refers to a situation when God will have obliterated the world—an idea one finds in Ezekiel:[11]

> You, O mortal, thus says YHWH God to the land of Israel: An end! The end has come upon the four corners of the land. Now the end is upon you, I will let loose my anger upon you; I will judge you according to your ways, I will punish you for all your abominations. My eye will not spare you, I will have no pity. I will punish you for your ways, while your abominations are among you. Then you shall know that I am YHWH. (Ezek 7:2-6)

Clearly, here, the "end" is the punishment that God is about to bring upon Israel for all the abominations that they have committed. And yet this "end" has a purpose, which is apparently not to erase Israel from the face of the earth altogether but to force them finally to accept what they had been avoiding all along: "Then you shall know that I am YHWH." So the purpose of God's punishment extends even beyond what Ezekiel calls the "end." The notion seems to be that at point zero Israel will come to recognize YHWH as their God, although, at least at this point in Ezekiel, it is not clear if there is going to be a new future for Israel as God's people.

The Priestly flood narrative, likewise, suggests that God's decision to put an end to the world is God's response to a world that has drowned in violence. However, the Priestly narrative shifts the emphasis of God's judgment on "all flesh." In Gen 6:13, the end receives a dual connotation: the world filled with violence and, simultaneously, the world inundated with the floodwaters. It seems as though the Priestly text was interested in demonstrating a parallel between the state of the world and God's activity. The demise of the world is not so much a punishment as the maturation of a fatal dynamic that is already at work. If one wishes to preserve the Hebrew play on words, one could translate the gist of the matter as follows: God ruins what is already ruined.

It is important to realize that the unresolved but intentional tension between Gen 1 and Gen 6 is part and parcel of the Priestly

---

11. Moshe Greenberg, *Ezechiel 1–20*, HThKAT (Freiburg: Herder, 2001), 180.

view of creation. There is something missing, something incomplete about the world that God made in the beginning. Christian exegetes sometimes overlook or downplay this programmatic tension in the Priestly text because, according to traditional Christian doctrine, God's creation in Gen 1 would have been perfect had humans not allowed sin to enter the world (Gen 2–4). It is for lack of human morals, not of divine design, that the created world deteriorates.

One of the reasons that traditional historical-critical scholarship viewed Gen 1 as a text that presupposes Gen 2–3 may have something to do with the centrality of the doctrine of sin in Christian theology. If one reads Gen 2–3 as a story of the "fall," it becomes clear that the cause of evil in the world is that initial misdeed of humankind and, perhaps even more important, the inherent human disposition to disobey God's command. As the supposedly later text,[12] P would have presupposed this view and built its cosmology to match this

---

12. The literary history of the Primeval History has been under much discussion lately, which cannot be reviewed here in any detail. However, it may be worth pointing out one misunderstanding that seems to have muddied that discussion. Proponents of the view that the non-Priestly texts of Gen 1–11 are younger than P typically do not claim that this should be a model for the rest of Pentateuch as well (with the exception perhaps of Joseph Blenkinsopp, *The Pentateuch: An Introduction to the First Five Books of the Bible* [New York: Doubleday, 1992], 31–53). Given the complexity of the transmission history of the Pentateuch, any one-size-fits-all approach runs the risk of oversimplifying the case. However, if one limits one's perspective to the Primeval History, it is an agreed-upon fact that only P offers a self-standing narrative. Traditional source criticism, therefore, has to explain why the supposedly older, non-Priestly source ("J") was fragmented at some point, which of course requires a largely hypothetical argument with no direct evidence to support it. The position, however, that the non-Priestly texts (independent of when they were written down for the first time) never formed a continuous narrative but were either inserted in the Priestly text or written to complement P ("Fortschreibung") does not have to resort to any fragmentation theories. Thus, even David Carr, in an unnecessarily polemical review of contributions in favor of P as the oldest layer in Gen 1–11, has to admit that these theories typically offer more sophisticated interpretations of the layered text than approaches that follow the traditional documentary hypothesis (David M. Carr, "Strong and Weak Cases and Criteria for Establishing the Post-Priestly Character of Hexateuchal Material," in *The Post-Priestly Pentateuch: New Perspectives on Its Redactional Development and Theological Profiles*, ed. Federico Giuntoli and Konrad Schmid [Tübingen: Mohr Siebeck, 2015], 33).

negative view of humankind: God's initial world was perfect; sin, through human doing, came later.

The quintessential flaw of this interpretation is that, according to P, evil in the world is not at all a problem of human will, or desire, or humans' susceptibility to temptation. P locates the origin of evil at a much more basic level. It is the proneness to violence as a "genetic defect" in *all* living beings ("all flesh") that, for reasons that P does not explain, endangers the created world.[13] P's subtle use of the term "good" and even "very good" in Gen 1 as words from God's mouth leaves the reader wondering when and where the opposite of "good" will enter the picture in P's cosmology. Interestingly, the opposite term is not "evil" in P, as in the Eden story (Gen 2:17) and the non-Priestly evaluation of the human heart in the flood narrative (Gen 6:5; 8:21); rather, the opposite of "goodness" is "violence" (Gen 6:11-13). This is the most basic danger in the created world, according to P.[14]

It is safe to say that one of P's main interests with regard to creation is how it was possible that living beings could occur in a world that used to be *tōhû wābōhû*, "a formless void" (Gen 1:2, NRSV). Precisely because of this emphasis, it is of key significance that P does not consider the world at the stage of Gen 1:1–2:3 ready and able to protect life and, by the same token, to keep the destructive potentials inherent in all flesh at bay.

The Divine Speech after the Flood (Gen 9:1-17)

This takes us to the end of the flood narrative and, more specifically, to the divine speech after the flood, in which God establishes new rules for all life in the postdiluvian world. The flood in the most literal sense is a watershed that separates the world that failed from the one that prevailed, which raises questions such as these: What is different between the prediluvian and postdiluvian worlds? What makes the postdiluvian world more stable and less susceptible to self-destruction and decay? Initially, the divine speech picks up

---

13. For a conversation between evolutionary biology and the Primeval History cf. R. Walter L. Moberly, *The Theology of the Book of Genesis* (Cambridge: Cambridge University Press, 2009), 57–65.

14. Bosshard-Nepustil, *Sintflut*, 266.

where the creation narrative left off: God blesses the survivors of the flood and commissions them to be fruitful and multiply (Gen 9:1). There is no indication, however, that the flood survivors will be any different from their prediluvian ancestors and that they will be less violent or more morally refined than the generations before them. There is no sense of *telos* in the Priestly Primeval History, no expectation that creatures in general and human beings in particular will fundamentally alter their behavioral patterns.

What does change, however, is God's attention to the created world. Interesting in this regard is the motif of God "remembering" in Gen 8:1 and 9:15. This motif echoes certain mythic understandings that God must actually be reminded not to exterminate the world. The notion that gods are moody and (sometimes deliberately) forgetful beings who would rather not be bothered with human concerns is a motif that pervades the myths of both Greek and Mesopotamian origins. And it seem that, at its surface, the flood narrative, too, depicts God as someone who needs to remind himself to refrain from something that he perhaps might have done otherwise. At least this seems to be the meaning behind Gen 9:13-15. Whenever in the future God will bring about clouds (and rain), the rainbow will appear and stop God from taking things too far, as it were. Yet underneath the mythic surface hides a more profound theological insight. The notion that God is "reminded" of the covenant implies that God is not always and everywhere "present," but approaches the world from a certain distance and then withdraws from it again. Starting with the creation account, the Priestly document develops a worldview in which God has no particular place. To be sure, the world is God's creation and follows the rhythms and orders that God instituted. This does not also automatically imply the idea of God's continuous personal presence in the world, however.

This basic motif of the God who acts from a distance also accompanies the Priestly narrative of the postdiluvian period, although with an important alteration: there are events in the world that, in fact, "automatically" call God to action. These include, for one, uncontrolled bloodshed (the first part of the divine speech; Gen 9:1-7) and, second, the potential destruction of the world by another flood (the second part of the divine speech; Gen 9:8-17). God's role is, above all, to actively combat and restrain everything that threatens the existence of the world, both internally and externally. Consequently, the commandments and the covenant instituted in this divine speech have the same objective. The covenant addresses threats to the world that are not created or influenced by human beings, while the commandments concern the reality lived and shaped by creatures.

With commandment and covenant, the Priestly document introduces categories into the Primeval History that gain significance in subsequent portions of the Pentateuch. The covenant with Abraham in Gen 17 follows the Noahide covenant,[15] which includes all living beings. The covenant theme in Priestly tradition finally concludes with the Sinai revelation, which addresses the one people exclusively chosen by God. The fact that the Priestly document already anchors the category of covenant in the Primeval History indicates once more that the Primeval History does not intend to be understood alone but as part of an overall composition that extends from the first day of creation to the encounter between God and Israel at Sinai. Within this narrative arc, God becomes more concretely present in the world,[16] although God is never "absorbed" in this world. Even at Sinai and the tabernacle consecrated there—in which the glory of God sometimes resides but from which, however, it also frequently withdraws—there continue to be temporary encounters with God and an immovable boundary between divine and human realities.

The Laws to Protect Life (Gen 9:4-6)

The Priestly document intentionally draws a contrast between the world at the beginning and the world after the flood. In between lies a phase of uncontrolled and excessive spreading of violence, which P views as the reason for the demise of the world. The theme of violence and dominion deals with the tendency toward destruction and self-destructiveness embodied in the world, and it seems as though the Priestly document associates this tendency with the chaotic state of the world before creation.[17] Accordingly, the blood commandments that follow in Gen 9:4-6 are not "orders of creation"

---

15. Millard, *Genesis*, 107–109.

16. Walther Zimmerli, *Grundriß der alttestamentlichen Theologie* (Stuttgart: Kohlhammer, 1972), 12–15.

17. Schüle, *Prolog*, 260–68.

in the same manner as in Gen 1.[18] One may speak rather of "orders of preservation" that prevent the world from repeatedly ending in self-destruction. To this end, killing and bloodshed are now permissible only under "controlled" conditions. Human life is essentially exempted from this regime because humans stand under the protection of "godlikeness." Wherever the blood of God's image is shed, God will require this blood of the perpetrator.

Interestingly, this threat also applies to animals as possible perpetrators. Like a human, an animal that attacks and kills a person is subject to divine retribution. Naturally, this situation raises the question of how one should conceive of God's role in the execution of the *ius talionis*, life for life. Is the idea that God personally intervenes and brings the perpetrator to account through natural or supernatural means? The legal corpora of the Pentateuch that follow later and that deal with crimes of manslaughter offer some guidelines. Along the lines of Priestly theology and with regard to animals as possible "perpetrators," Exod 21:12-32 is especially relevant. According to the text, when a goring ox kills a human being, the ox should be stoned (v. 28). This legislation is a preventative measure to avoid further harm to people. In addition, however, Exod 21:28 prohibits the butchering of the animal, which indicates that the killing of the ox was not understood as slaughter but, in fact, as retribution (in the sense of Gen 9:5) for the shedding of human blood.

The casuistic regulations for homicides among humans are, as might be expected, more nuanced than the simple principle "blood for blood." Thus they distinguish between intentional, malicious murder and actions that result in the inadvertent death of a person (Exod 21:12-14) and capital crimes that do not necessarily involve bloodshed, such as bodily injury of parents or kidnapping (21:15-16). Even in the latter cases, however, one can surmise that the integrity of humans as God's image is fundamentally questioned or negated. The prohibition against harming one's parents has a direct parallel in Gen 5:1-3, for example, which mentions the likeness of children to their parents in relation to the *imago dei*.

One need not understand the commandments of Gen 9:4-6 too strictly as "casuistic" since more nuanced legal corpora follow in

---

18. Millard, *Genesis*, 137–38.

the Pentateuch. They do involve, however, a "foundation" of casuistic law linked in the Priestly document with the *imago dei* and the protection of life. One should note in this regard that P's understanding of the commandments in Gen 9:4-6 involves a *universal* principle. As the Priestly document emphasizes in Gen 10, the Table of Nations, the world consists of many nations, clans, and languages. This may include an awareness that there is a corresponding multiplicity of potentially divergent legal and moral codes. While one must be cautious against the application of modern categories to ancient cultures, one can still say that the Priestly document thinks in "pluralistic" dimensions. For this very reason, the establishment of the inviolability of human life and the respect for life in general as universally normative stands out in the Priestly text. Every law and every morality must do justice to this principle. Furthermore, this establishment means that the protection of life does not end at the border of one's respective cultural realm. The godlikeness of all human beings requires regard not just for the life of the near neighbor but also for the life of the foreigner. As varied as "all the others" may be, the Priestly document regards this one legal principle as anchored in the order of the creation of the world itself.

This takes us to another layer of this new legal system that goes beyond the world order of Gen 1. For this system to work, individual entities have to be more than just species or "all flesh"; rather, they have to be viewed as moral agents who can be held accountable if they violate the laws that God implements in 9:4-6.

Individual Responsibility

Scholars typically view the principle of individual responsibility as occurring relatively late in the Old Testament history of ideas. It is unclear when exactly this principle assumed theological significance and became a part of texts such as Gen 9. It appears that in the environment of the Priestly document and contemporary traditions such as the books of Ezekiel and Jeremiah, an intensified awareness of human beings as irreducible individuals with corresponding legal status and responsibilities is present. Thus, it is not humanity overall but every individual human being who is the "image of God," a notion complemented by the emphasis on the integrity of the life of every individual in Gen 9:4-6. In the book of Ezekiel, one finds a related argument in which God will no longer call his people to account on the principle of collective liability, but henceforth individuals must bear the consequences (only) for their own transgressions:

> The word of the YHWH came to me again: "What do you mean by repeating this proverb concerning the land of Israel, 'The fathers have eaten sour grapes, and the children's teeth are set on edge'? As I live, says the YHWH God, this proverb shall no more be used by you in Israel. Behold, all souls are mine; the soul of the father as well as the soul of the son is mine: the soul that sins shall die." (Ezek 18:1-9; cf. Jer 31:19-20)

In a substantive analogy to the Priestly document in Gen 9:5, Ezekiel also operates with the notion of the "life substance," which is a characteristic not just of the species but of every individual human being. This means that the life of every individual human being has unconditional integrity; it also means, however, that all individual human beings must bear responsibility for themselves and their deeds.

The significantly older Mesopotamian Flood mythology demonstrates that this idea is by no means a peculiarity of the Old Testament. There, too, the resolutions after the end of the flood include the notion that henceforth moral responsibility will fall on the individual instead of collective retribution. Thus, in the flood account of the Gilgamesh epic, the goddess Ea complains to the god Enlil who was responsible for the flood: "You wisest of the gods, hero! How could you send the Flood without deliberating? Lay sins to the account of the sinner, evil to the evil-doer!"[19] The intention here is that "only the sinner" or "every individual sinner" must account for his or her transgression.

With both the laws concerning the protection of life and the principle of individual responsibility in place, it appears that the postdiluvian world is equipped with a system of order and of divine surveillance that, in and of itself, is already sufficient to avoid the kind of uncontrolled spreading and accumulation of violence that characterized the world before the flood. This raises a question that surfaces

---

19. Otto Kaiser, Bernd Janowski, Gernot Wilhelm, and Daniel Schwemer, eds., *Texte aus der Umwelt des Alten Testaments* III/4 (Gütersloh: Gütersloh Verlagshaus, 1982–2001), 374.

only occasionally in the scholarly debate about Gen 1–9: whatever happened to the *dominium terrae* as the idea that humans should rule the world? In place of the commission to exercise dominion, one now finds the formulation that "the fear and dread of you will fall on every beast of the earth" and that the animals have been "given into the hands" of human beings (9:2). Is this essentially a paraphrase of the *dominium terrae*? Perhaps, to the extent that the Hebrew terminology in Gen 1:26, 28 also has overtones of violent subjugation. However, the perspective in Gen 9 differs from that in Gen 1.[20] The theme in Gen 9 is not whether human beings have a duty in relation to the animals and, if so, what that duty is. Instead, Gen 9 conveys that the presence of humans in the world provokes terror.[21] In modern terms, there is now a food chain, with humankind standing at the top. In contrast to the ideal of a world of humans and animals that live as vegetarians (Gen 1:30), after the flood, God legitimates the killing of animals for food. Although this legitimization does not receive separate treatment, one may assume that this statement also implements the food chain within the animal world itself. In other words, God changes the world order after the flood into the state every reader knows: humans eat animals and animals eat animals.

Covenant and Law

To this point, the divine speech in Gen 9:1-17 deals with the (altered) conditions under which life in the postdiluvian world is to regenerate, while the commandment of 9:4-6 represents the essential contrast in relation to the antediluvian world. The relationship between this commandment and the subsequent covenant with Noah must further be examined. In essence, the Noahide covenant is a guarantee of the continuation of life after the flood. No bilateral components are envisioned. Consequently, God will no more employ the collective

---

20. Baumgart, *Umkehr*, 358: "Indem Gott nach der Flut dem Menschen die alleinige Antwort auf die menschliche Gewalt aus der Hand nimmt und dabei sich definitiv als die Rechtsinstanz im Falle der Verletzungen des menschlichen Lebens einsetzt, schützt Gott den Menschen vor solchen Menschen, die auf die Gewalt am Menschen antworten."

21. Annette Schellenberg, *Der Mensch, das Bild Gottes? Zum Gedanken einer Sonderstellung des Menschen im Alten Testament und in weiteren altorientalischen Quellen*, ATANT 101 (Zürich: Theologischer Verlag, 2011), 60–68.

eradication of all creatures as a means for restricting the spread of violence. It does not claim or even expect that the violent disposition of creatures will be less pronounced than before the flood, however. Postdiluvian creation does not differ and is certainly no better than antediluvian creation.

The content of the Noahide covenant is essentially twofold: (1) Verses 9-11 depict the covenant as an event that includes all living beings. It is no less a covenant with the animals than with humanity, as v. 10 confirms by referring back to the taxonomy of living beings from Gen 1. The covenant includes all "living beings," i.e., all the inhabitants of heaven and earth. Neither the totality of creation nor the individual species shall ever again be annihilated by a flood or, literally, be "cut off (from life)." (2) In vv. 12-16, God chooses the rainbow as a sign that will function to remind God of his covenant. The significance of the rainbow is self-evident: it traces the heavenly vault that protects the world from the waters of chaos and, thus, serves as a "signal" for God to stop the rain and the floodwaters before they cause damage.

While this is called a covenant, it is not immediately clear why. What we have here is essentially God's personal sticky note reminder not to destroy the world again. This covenant does not include any particular rights, privileges, or obligations on the part of living beings. As a matter of fact, they do not even have to be aware of the existence of this covenant. Living beings are supposed to be fruitful and multiply in the same way as in Gen 1 where there was no covenant. As Walther Zimmerli demonstrated, in order to appreciate the Priestly notion of covenant one needs to realize how it unfolds, becomes more specific, and increasingly involves human agents as one moves from Gen 9 to Gen 17 and eventually Exod 31.[22] As already mentioned above, while this covenant, at the stage of Gen 9, includes a negative promise of what God will refrain from doing, this is not the reason that creation will be safe from *self*-destruction and the spreading of violence. To put it pointedly, what the world needs after the flood is certainly God's covenant but, even more so, God's

---

22. Walther Zimmerli, *Grundriß der alttestamentlichen Theologie* (Stuttgart: Kohlhammer, 1972), 45–47.

law,²³ understood as that which protects and sustains life in the postdiluvian world.²⁴ In this perspective, the Priestly Primeval History demonstrates how and why God's law, including the notion of divine presence and individual responsibility, are built into the very fabric of life. According to P, we live in a moral universe precisely because it is anchored in the moral principles and legal mechanisms that God establishes in the early days of the world.²⁵

As mentioned at the outset of this paper, recent work on Gen 1–11 has highlighted the cultic significance of the Priestly account of creation and the way in which it anticipates and provides a foundation for the building of the tabernacle in Exodus. While this overarching frame is certainly part of the Priestly agenda, I submit that there is yet another etiological layer in the Priestly Primeval History, which is equally significant. It is important not to limit one's perspective to the account of creation in Gen 1 but to consider also the whole drama of creation as it unfolds in Gen 1–9 and culminates in the giving of the first and most elementary laws to the postdiluvian world. In this perspective, it becomes clear that, at its most profound level, the Priestly Primeval History presents itself as an etiology of the law or, as one might also say with regard to what follows in later parts of the Pentateuch, as an etiology of *Torah*.

---

23. Millard, *Genesis*, 106–107.

24. Cf. Patrick D. Miller's assessment of the significance of the Deuteronomic laws: "At every point the existence and effective enactment of these laws is seen as a positive force, what is necessary to make human life work. Without these laws operating, the world falls apart and life disintegrates" (Patrick D. Miller, "'That You May Live': Dimensions of Law in Deuteronomy," in *Concepts of Law in the Sciences, Legal Studies, and Theology*, ed. Michael Welker and Gregor Etzelmüller [Tübingen: Mohr Siebeck, 2013], 157).

25. Hartmut Gese, "Das Gesetz," in *Zur Biblischen Theologie*, ed. Hartmut Gese (Tübingen: Mohr Siebeck, 1983), 63–66.

Bibliography

Balentine, Samuel E. *The Torah's Vision of Worship*. Minneapolis: Fortress, 1999.

Baumgart, Norman C. *Die Umkehr des Schöpfergottes. Zu Komposition und religionsgeschichtlichem Hintergrund von Gen 5–9*. HBS 22. Freiburg: Herder, 1999.

Blenkinsopp, Joseph. *The Pentateuch: An Introduction to the First Five Books of the Bible*. New York: Doubleday, 1992.

Bosshard-Nepustil, Erich. *Vor uns die Sintflut. Studien zu Text, Kontexten und Rezeption der Fluterzählung Genesis 6–9*. Stuttgart: Kohlhammer, 2005.

Carr, David M. "Strong and Weak Cases and Criteria for Establishing the Post-Priestly Character of Hexateuchal Material." Pages 19–34 in *The Post-Priestly Pentateuch: New Perspectives on Its Redactional Development and Theological Profiles*. Edited by Federico Giuntoli and Konrad Schmid. Tübingen: Mohr Siebeck, 2015.

Gese, Hartmut. "Das Gesetz." Pages 63–66 in *Zur Biblischen Theologie*. Edited by Hartmut Gese. Tübingen: Mohr Siebeck, 1983.

Greenberg, Moshe. *Ezechiel 1–20*. HThKAT. Freiburg i.B.: Herder, 2001.

Janowski, Bernd. "Tempel und Schöpfung. Schöpfungstheologische Aspekte der priesterschriftlichen Heitligtumskonzeption." Pages 222–40 in *Gottes Gegenwart in Israel. Beiträge zur Theologie des Alten Testaments*. Edited by Bernd Janowski. Neukirchen-Vluyn: Neukirchener Verlag, 1993.

Kaiser, Otto, Bernd Janowski, Gernot Wilhelm, and Daniel Schwemer, editors. *Texte aus der Umwelt des Alten Testaments*. Gütersloh: Gütersloh Verlagshaus, 1982–2001.

McBride, S. Dean. "Genesis 1:1–2:3 Prologue to the Pentateuch." Pages 3–41 in *God Who Creates*. Edited by William P. Brown and S. Dean McBride. Grand Rapids: Eerdmans, 2000.

Millard, Matthias. *Die Genesis als Eröffnung der Tora. Kompositions- und auslegungsgeshichtliche Annäherungen an das erste Buch Mose.* WMANT 90. Neukirchen- Vluyn: Neukirchener Verlag, 2001.

Miller, Patrick D. "'That You May Live': Dimensions of Law in Deuteronomy." Pages 137–57 in *Concepts of Law in the Sciences, Legal Studies, and Theology.* Edited by Michael Welker and Gregor Etzelmüller. Tübingen: Mohr Siebeck, 2013.

Moberly, R. Walter L. *The Theology of the Book of Genesis.* Cambridge: Cambridge University Press, 2009.

Oberforcher, Robert. *Die Flutprologue als Kompositionsschlüssel der biblischen Urgeschichte. Ein Beitrag zur Rekationsgeschichte.* Innsbruck: Tyrolia, 1981.

Schellenberg, Annette. *Der Mensch, das Bild Gottes? Zum Gedanken einer Sonderstellung des Menschen im Alten Testament und in weiteren altorientalischen Quellen.* ATANT 101. Zürich: Theologischer Verlag, 2011.

Schüle, Andreas. *Der Prolog der hebräischen Bible. Der literar- und theologiegeschichtliche Diskurs der Urgeschichte (Genesis 1–11).* ATANT 86. Zürich: Theologische Verlag Zürich, 2006.

———. *Theology from the Beginning: Essays on the Primeval History and Its Canonical Context.* FAT 113. Tübingen: Mohr Siebeck, 2017.

Smend, Rudolf. "'Das Ende ist gekommen' Ein Amoswort in der Priesterschrift." Pages 155–59 in *Die Mitte des Alten Testaments. Gesammelte Studien.* BEvT 99. Edited by Rudolf Smend. München: Beck, 1986.

Zenger, Erich. *Gottes Bogen in den Wolken. Untersuchungen zu Komposition und Theologie der priesterschriftlichen Urgeschichte.* SBS 112. Stuttgart: Katholisches Bibelwerk, 1983.

Zimmerli, Walther. *Grundriß der alttestamentlichen Theologie.* Stuttgart: Kohlhammer, 1972.

Why Moses Was Barred from the Land of Israel
A Reassessment of Numbers 20 in Literary Context

Marvin A. Sweeney

It is my pleasure to honor Sam Balentine for his distinguished career as a biblical scholar and his contributions to the field!

I.

Samuel E. Balentine's study, *The Torah's Vision of Worship*, presents an insightful examination of key Pentateuchal texts relevant to the study of worship in ancient Israel and Judah.[1] It does much to call scholarly attention to the study of worship and liturgy in the Bible, which is particularly important given the decline in interest in the topic that is evident in the field prior to the publication of his book. With a focus on Exodus, Leviticus, and Deuteronomy, Balentine covers key texts that have been in the forefront of Pentateuchal study, i.e., Exod 19–24; 25–40; Lev 17–26; and Deuteronomy at large. But he pays relatively little attention to Numbers, like many in the field, only noting the concentric circles of holiness with the Levites and

---

1. Samuel E. Balentine, *The Torah's Vision of Worship*, OBT (Minneapolis: Fortress, 1999).

the holy tabernacle in the center as the people journeyed through the Wilderness to the promised land of Israel.² Biblical scholars have struggled to understand Numbers, although recent advances have been made in the field with commentaries by Levine, Milgrom, and Knierim and Coats as well as studies by Lee, Leveen, and Roskop, among others.³

A particularly insightful proposal appears in a recent Claremont dissertation by Matthew A. Thomas, *These Are the Generations*, who built on earlier work by Frank M. Cross, Jr., and others to recognize that the "Toledoth" formulae that play a key role in the formal structure of Genesis also appear in Num 3:1, "And these are the generations of Aaron and Moses, on the day that YHWH spoke with Moses on Mt. Sinai," which extends the formal structure of Genesis to encompass the entire text of the Pentateuch.⁴ Within the formal structure of Numbers 3–Deuteronomy 34, it becomes clear that the Numbers narrative focuses on Aaron and Moses in an effort to highlight the role of the Levites in ancient Israel. YHWH states to Moses three times in Num 3:11-13; 3:44-51; and 8:13-19 that the Levites will replace the firstborn sons of Israel to assist the sons of Aaron in

---

2. Ibid., 177–78.

3. Jacob Milgrom, *Numbers*, JPS Torah Commentary (Philadelphia: Jewish Publication Society, 5750/1990); Baruch A. Levine, *Numbers 1–20*, AB 4 (New York: Doubleday, 1993); idem, *Numbers 21–36*, AB 4A (New York: Doubleday, 2000); Rolf P. Knierim and George W. Coats, *Numbers*, FOTL 4 (Grand Rapids: Eerdmans, 2005); Won W. Lee, *Punishment and Forgiveness in Israel's Migratory Campaign* (Grand Rapids: Eerdmans, 2003); Adriane Leveen, *Memory and Tradition in the Book of Numbers* (Cambridge, UK: Cambridge University Press, 2008); Angela R. Roskop, *The Wilderness Itineraries: Genre, Geography, and the Growth of Torah*, HACL 3 (Winona Lake, IN: Eisenbrauns, 2011). See also Thomas B. Dozeman, *The Pentateuch: Introducing the Torah* (Minneapolis: Fortress, 2017), 417–73; Marvin A. Sweeney, *The Pentateuch*, CBS (Nashville: Abingdon, 2017), 71–91.

4. Matthew A. Thomas, *These Are the Generations: Identity, Covenant, and the Toledoth Formulae* (New York: T&T Clark, 2011); Frank Moore Cross, Jr., "The Priestly Work," *Canaanite Myth and Hebrew Epic: Essay in the History of the Religion of Israel* (Cambridge, MA: Harvard University Press, 1973), 293–325; cf. Sweeney, *The Pentateuch*, xvii–xxix.

the holy service of the sanctuary.[5] The Levites are consecrated for such service in Num 8, and they are confirmed for holy service in Num 17–18. It is therefore striking that apart from Lev 25:32, 33, which refer to their property rights, the Levites are not mentioned in the book of Leviticus. Leviticus focuses instead on Aaron and his sons, but the Levites appear constantly in Numbers.[6]

Insofar as Numbers is especially concerned with the Levites and their role in ancient Israelite and Judean worship, it is appropriate to examine Numbers for insight into the Torah's vision of worship. It would be impossible to include the purview of the entire book of Numbers on worship within the space of a brief Festschrift paper, but a focus on the account of YHWH's decision to bar Moses and Aaron from the promised land would be an appropriate place to begin, particularly because the divine decision is based in large measure on considerations relevant to worship. The passage has presented major difficulties to interpreters from the very outset of biblical interpretation, but Balentine's focus on worship provides a perspective that might help to understand the reasons for YHWH's decision.

Numbers 20:1-13 describes YHWH's decision to bar Moses and Aaron from the promised land of Israel. YHWH's decision is a consequence of their actions before YHWH in supplying the people of Israel with water while encamped at Kadesh in the Wilderness of Zin during their journey from Egypt to the promised land. When the people complain to Moses and Aaron, they turn to YHWH, who instructs them to take the rod, assemble the people, and strike the rock before them to produce water for the people to drink. When they do so, Moses says to the people, "Hear now, you rebels, shall water come out for you from this rock?" (v. 10). He then strikes the rock two times and water comes out for the people. But in the aftermath of Moses' action, YHWH informs Moses and Aaron, "Because you did not trust in me to sanctify me before the eyes of the people

---

5. See Marvin A. Sweeney, "The Literary-Historical Dimensions of Intertextuality in Exodus–Numbers," in *Second Wave Intertextuality and the Hebrew Bible*, ed. Marianne Grohmann and Hyun Chul Paul Kim, RBS 93 (Atlanta: Society of Biblical Literature, 2019), 41–52.

6. Gerhard Lisowky, *Konkordanz zum Hebräischen Alten Testament*, 2nd ed. (Stuttgart: Württembergische Bibelantalt, 1966), 1635.

of Israel, therefore you shall not bring this congregation into the land which I have given to them" (v. 12). Aaron dies later in Num 20 at Mount Hor, and Moses dies in Moab in Deut 34, immediately prior to Israel's entry into the promised land of Israel.

Jacob Milgrom in his JPS commentary on the book of Numbers describes YHWH's decision to forbid Moses' entry into the promised land as one of the Gordian Knots of biblical exegesis.[7] He arranges the numerous attempts to explain why YHWH forbade Moses to enter Israel under three aspects: (1) Moses' improper actions in striking the rock; (2) deficiencies in Moses' character; and (3) deficiencies in Moses' words before striking the rock, suggesting that somehow Moses had misrepresented G-d. Milgrom's survey of these various attempts demonstrates that none constitutes an adequate explanation. But his own attempt to explain YHWH's decision by claiming that Moses did not keep silent as expected of priests while serving before YHWH also is inadequate, largely because Moses speaks before YHWH and before the people frequently throughout the Exodus and Wilderness narratives. Most notably, YHWH commands Moses and Aaron to speak to the rock in Num 20:8.

But Milgrom and other interpreters have overlooked one major factor: Miriam's death in Num 20:1 and her burial immediately prior to the incident at the rock. Moses and Aaron are Miriam's closest relatives, and they would have been responsible for her burial. They are also priests, and priests are required to purify themselves prior to engaging in holy service before YHWH. But Moses and Aaron did not do so. Their impurity in standing before YHWH as priests then would explain YHWH's judgment. This paper therefore examines the literary context of the narrative concerning the rock in Num 20:1-13 in an effort to demonstrate that Moses' and Aaron's burial of Miriam prior to the incident at the rock rendered them impure, thereby disqualifying them to serve before YHWH until they repurified themselves. This paper treats several aspects of the issue, including Aaron's designation by YHWH as Moses' mouthpiece in Exod 3; the early role of firstborn sons as priests in the Pentateuch; YHWH's choice of Aaron and the tribe of Levi as priests for holy service before YHWH in Num 17–18; the laws of purification from the pollution

---

7. Milgrom, *Numbers*, 448–56.

of death in Num 19; and the culminating role of YHWH's decision to bar Moses and Aaron from the land of Israel in Num 20.

II.

The status of Moses and Aaron as priests must first be qualified. From the outset of the Exodus narrative, the status of Moses and Aaron as Levites is clear. Exodus 2 relates how Moses was born to a man of the House of Levi and his wife, who was also a Levite. The narrative describes the birth of Moses and the need to protect him as Pharaoh had decreed that sons born to a Hebrew mother would be put to death in an effort to protect Egypt from the deliverer promised to the Hebrews by YHWH. So baby Moses was placed in an ark, sealed with bitumen, and set adrift on the Nile River under the watchful eyes of his older sister, Miriam. Ironically, Moses was discovered by the daughter of Pharaoh, whose servants fished baby Moses from the water so that she might raise him in the house of her father as her own son. Equally ironic is the fact that Moses' mother was engaged as a wet nurse for baby Moses. Although Exod 2 has generally been recognized as a J narrative in the past, the recent redating of J to the late monarchic period and the recognition of E as the foundational source of the Pentateuch from the ninth to eighth centuries BCE indicate that the accounts of the birth of Moses are relatively early.[8] The later P material in Exod 6:20 identifies Moses' father as Amram, his mother as Jochebed, and his brother as Aaron.

When we turn to the narrative concerning the burning bush in Exod 3–4, we see an account that is typically analyzed as a combined E and J narrative.[9] The narrative depicts Moses' encounter with YHWH on Mount Horeb, here identified as the Mountain of G-d, a clear indication of the E provenance of this account, a typical prophetic call narrative. Moses sees a vision of a bush that burns but is not consumed. Such a bush is known in the Sinai Wilderness

---

8. Antony F. Campbell and Mark A. O'Brien, *Sources of the Pentateuch: Texts, Introductions, Annotations* (Minneapolis: Fortress, 1993), 92–93; see the essays in Thomas B. Dozeman and Konrad Schmid, *A Farewell to the Y-hwist? The Composition of the Pentateuch in Recent European Interpretation*, SymS 34 (Atlanta: Society of Biblical Literature, 2006); Sweeney, *The Pentateuch*; idem, "The Jacob Narratives: An Ephraimitic Text?" *CBQ* 78 (2016): 236–55.

9. Campbell and O'Brien, *Sources of the Pentateuch*, 132–35, 184–85.

as the *rubus sanctus*, which blossoms in the spring with red flowers that make the bush appear aflame when viewed from a distance.[10] Such a motif aids in building the case that YHWH is the true G-d of creation as well as the G-d of Israel and all the nations of the world. In the present instance, Moses approaches the bush and hears the voice of G-d instructing him to remove his shoes as he is standing on holy ground. The narrative goes on with YHWH's self-identification as the G-d of Moses' ancestors, Abraham, Isaac, and Jacob; YHWH's account to Moses of Israel's suffering under Egyptian oppression; and YHWH's commission to Moses to return to Pharaoh to demand that Israel be freed from Egyptian control. When Moses asks YHWH who is sending him so that he may identify YHWH to the people, YHWH responds with the idem per idem rhetorical device, "I am who I am." The response delays announcing YHWH's name because it is holy. The response also presents a pun that suggests that YHWH's name means "he is/he exists" and that demonstrates YHWH's intention to be free from human control.[11]

As scholars have long recognized, the burning bush episode represents the well-known prophetic call narrative or vocation account, which includes a number of typical elements: a divine confrontation, an introductory word, a commission, an objection by the prophet, a reassurance, and a sign.[12] All of these elements are apparent in Exod 3–4. Analogous accounts of prophetic commissioning appear in Judg 6, Jer 1, and Ezek 2–3. Indeed, Moses appears to act as an oracular prophet who serves as a mouthpiece for YHWH. Aaron also is included in the narrative, where he is assigned by YHWH to interpret YHWH's words through Moses and announce them to the audience at hand. In this respect, Aaron might be considered to function in priestly terms, although it is not clear that he has direct access to YHWH.

---

10. Nahum Sarna, *Exodus*, JPS Torah Commentary (Philadelphia: Jewish Publication Society, 5751/1991), 14.

11. Thomas B. Dozeman, *Exodus*, ECC (Grand Rapids: Eerdmans, 2009), 134–36.

12. George W. Coats, *Exodus 1–18*, FOTL 2A (Grand Rapids: Eerdmans, 1999), 34–42.

Jeffrey Stackert has noted that Moses functions throughout the Exodus narratives as an oracular spokesman for YHWH.[13] YHWH speaks directly to him, and Moses, sometimes with the aid of Aaron and sometimes not, communicates YHWH's instructions to the people of Israel, Pharaoh, and anyone else who needs to be addressed. It is not clear that his status as prophet is dependent on his Levitical identity.

As for Aaron, his quasi-priestly status also does not appear to be dependent on his Levitical identity. Throughout the narrative, Exodus stresses that an important element of the exodus event is not only the redemption of the people of Israel but also the redemption of the firstborn of the flock, herd, asses, and human beings as well. But whereas animals born to the flock or herd are designated for offerings at the altar, the firstborn of asses and of human beings are to be redeemed for sacred service to G-d. This provision is made clear in Exod 13:2: "Consecrate to Me every firstborn, who breaks the womb among the sons of Israel, among humans and animals." This instruction is further clarified in Exod 34:19-20: "all that break the womb are mine including all your cattle that produce a male as the firstborn among cattle and sheep. The firstborn of an ass you shall redeem with a sheep, and if you do not redeem it, you shall break its neck. All the firstborn of your sons, you shall redeem." Although Exodus does not specify that consecration of the firstborn is for holy service as priests, the following material in the book of Numbers makes this clear.

III.

Most interpreters read the introductory material of the book of Numbers in Num 1:1–10:10 diachronically as the P conclusion to the Sinai narrative in Exod 19–Num 10:10.[14] As such, it is considered to focus on preparations for the journey through the Wilderness to the promised land of Israel. But there is a very telling concern in the first chapters of Numbers that appears in YHWH's speeches to Moses in Num 3:11; 3:40-51; and 8:5-19, namely, the consecration of the Levites to serve as priests in place of the firstborn sons of

---

13. Jeffrey Stackert, *A Prophet Like Moses: Prophecy, Law, and Israelite Religion* (Oxford: Oxford University Press, 2014).

14. Campbell and O'Brien, *Sources of the Pentateuch*, 67–80.

Israel. Although the reason for YHWH's decision is not made clear in these texts, it appears to be based on the zeal for YHWH shown by the Levites in the golden calf episode of Exod 32–34. YHWH refers repeatedly to the previous practice of employing the firstborn sons of Israel as priests, but YHWH instructs Moses to consecrate the Levites for holy service as priests before YHWH. Indeed, Num 8 presents a lengthy instruction as to how the Levites are to be consecrated for priestly service much like Aaron and his sons in Exod 29 and Lev 8. Insofar as Aaron is the firstborn son of Amram and Jochebed, he served as a priest in this capacity. But Aaron is also a Levite, and so his priestly status is reinforced by YHWH's decision to appoint the Levites as consecrated priests.

Thus, a major agenda of the book of Numbers is to justify the appointment of the tribe of Levi as holy priests for YHWH in place of the firstborn sons of Israel who had previously served in this capacity. As for Moses, his status as a prophet is now augmented by his newly recognized status as a Levitical priest. The recognition of the interest of Numbers in consecrating the Levites for holy service as priests before YHWH aids in understanding YHWH's decision to bar Moses and Aaron from the land of Israel.

When read in its final, synchronic literary form, the notice of Miriam's death and burial in the Wilderness of Zin in Num 20:1 is not a random notice. The notice includes no indication that Moses and Aaron purified themselves in any way following the burial of Miriam and their subsequent appearance before YHWH to bring water from the rock. Although some might object that the notice includes no direct statement that Moses and Aaron actually performed the burial, particularly since all Israel is noted as arriving at the Wilderness of Zin and could presumably have performed the burial, Moses and Aaron must be recognized as the likely candidates for those who would have buried Miriam. Miriam is the older sister of Aaron and Moses, and there is no account of her marriage or her giving birth to any children. Because Aaron and Moses are her brothers, they are her closest relatives and would therefore have borne primary responsibility for her burial at the Wilderness of Zin.

In his analysis of the instructional character of Lev 1:1-9, Rolf P. Knierim notes that the instructions concerning the preparation of the *ōlâ* or "whole burnt offering" do not include detailed accounts of what to do at every point in the procedure. Rather, they only present the conceptualization of the prescribed procedure and outline the key points, leaving those that are presumably obvious unstated.[15] The same principle applies here, i.e., because Aaron and Moses are Miriam's closest relatives, they bear primary responsibility for her burial, including the preparation of her body for burial and their role in any service that might take place. Leviticus 21:1-4 makes it clear that priests may not defile themselves for the dead with the exception of their closest blood relatives, including a parent, a child, or a sibling. In the case of a sister, the text stipulates that she would be a virgin sister who has never married a man (v. 3). Miriam is presumably a virgin sister who has never married, and therefore her brothers—but not her nephews or nieces—would have been able to perform her burial despite the fact that they are Levitical priests.

It is therefore noteworthy that the notice of Miriam's burial is deliberately placed before the account of the episode of water from the rock in Num 20:2-13 in order to signal the reason why Moses and Aaron were barred from the land of Israel. The underlying reason for their ban was that they became impure due to contact with the dead, and they failed to purify themselves prior to serving before YHWH and the people as Levitical priests.

The literary context of the passage in Num 17–18, which recounts YHWH's selection of Aaron and the tribe of Levi to serve as holy priests before YHWH, and Num 19, which specifies the means by which one is purified from corpse contamination, makes this clear. Both of these texts are generally assigned to the P stratum of the Pentateuch much like Num 20:1-13.[16]

Numbers 17–18 follows immediately upon the account of the punishment of Korah and his supporters in Num 16 in which they had attempted to revolt against the leadership of Moses and Aaron by improperly offering incense before YHWH. Korah and his supporters were punished with death for their attempt to offer incense before YHWH because they were not authorized to do so. Numbers 16–18

---

15. Rolf P. Knierim, *Text and Concept in Leviticus 1:1-9*, FAT 2 (Tübingen: Mohr Siebeck, 1992), esp. 17–22.

16. Campbell and O'Brien, *Sources of the Pentateuch*, 84–87, although Num 19 is often seen as a non-source text due to its legal character (ibid., 200).

recounts how YHWH commanded Moses to instruct Eleazar ben Aaron to remove the firepans used by Korah and company because they had become sacred to YHWH due to their use in the attempted offering. The removal was to remind the people that no one who was not a descendant of Aaron was authorized to offer incense before YHWH. When the people objected to such removal, arguing that Moses and Aaron had brought death upon the people for their transgression of sacred boundaries, YHWH announced the intention to kill the people for their transgression, but Moses ordered Aaron to make expiation for the people in an effort to save their lives. To protect the people, Aaron stood between the living and the dead to demarcate the sacred boundary between the presence of YHWH and the people of Israel.[17]

YHWH then commanded Moses to gather the chieftains of the twelve tribes of Israel together with their staffs. Moses deposited the staffs before YHWH in the Tent of the Pact. In the morning, Moses found that the staff of Aaron, chieftain of the tribe of Levi, had blossomed and produced almonds, indicating that Aaron and the tribe of Levi had been chosen by YHWH for holy service. Moses announced to them their charge: that Aaron and the tribe of Levi had been designated to bear the sin of the sanctuary. The Levites are attached (Hebrew, *nilwû*, derived from the root *lwh/lwy*) to Aaron for holy service before YHWH; that is, they are chosen to serve as Levitical priests alongside Aaron and his sons. The Levites are assigned to do the work of the Tent of Meeting, whereas Aaron and his sons are assigned to perform the priestly duties of the altar and the holy of holies of the sanctuary that are hidden behind the curtain.

YHWH then instructs Aaron in the gifts that he and his Levitical tribesmen are to receive for their sacred service. Aaron and his sons are assigned the *minḥâ* (grain), the *ḥaṭṭāʾt* (sin), and the *ʾāshām* (guilt) offerings of the people as well as the *tĕrûmâ* (gift) offering of the *tĕnûpâ* (elevation) offerings of the people in return for their sacred service (Num 18:9, 11). Also included are the first fruits of the oil, wine, and grain offerings as well as the firstborn of the womb, although firstborn human beings and non-kosher animals are redeemed and

---

17. See James D. Findlay, *From Prophet to Priest: The Characterization of Aaron in the Pentateuch*, CBET 76 (Leuven: Peeters, 2017).

exempted from the offerings given to Aaron and his sons (vv. 12-17). These gifts are designated by YHWH as an everlasting covenant of salt for the support of the priesthood. The Levites are then granted tithes of Israel in return for their sacred service, although they are restricted from service in the Tent of Meeting. The Levitical gift is then designated as an eternal statute for all generations. Nevertheless, the Levites are required to present an offering of one-tenth of their gifts to YHWH to support the priesthood.

Here we must note that, although Aaron had already been performing priestly functions in the Pentateuchal narratives, Moses—as a Levite—was just designated for sacred service in the temple together with the rest of his Levitical tribesmen. Moses the prophet was just designated as a Levitical priest.

Numbers 19 then follows with a presentation of laws pertaining to purification for the Tent of Meeting and persons subject to corpse contamination. These laws are frequently read separately from their literary context in modern scholarship because laws and narratives are considered to come from different sources.[18] But given the role of the priests in the purification of the sanctuary just mentioned in Num 18 and the circumstances of Moses' and Aaron's burial of their dead sister, Miriam, purification becomes a matter of paramount importance in the Numbers narrative.

The first law in Num 19:2-10 presents the law of the red heifer and its use in purifying the Tent of Meeting and later the sanctuary. The red heifer must be an ideal animal that has only red hair with no trace of white hair whatsoever, no yoke laid upon it, and no blemish or defect. It is brought to Eleazar the priest who takes it outside the camp for slaughter. Eleazar uses his finger to take blood from the slaughtered red heifer to sprinkle the front of the Tent of Meeting. Afterwards, the heifer is burned in its entirety with cedar wood, hyssop, and crimson. Eleazar, the man performing the slaughter, and the man gathering the ashes of the red heifer shall then bathe in water, although they will remain impure until evening. The ashes are to be deposited in a clean place for use by the people to purify themselves. This law becomes an eternal statute in Israel.

---

18. Campbell and O'Brien, *Sources of the Pentateuch*, 200.

Numbers 19:11-22 then follows with instruction concerning the purification of a person who suffers corpse contamination due to contact with a dead body. The person will remain unclean for seven days, although he must cleanse himself with the water of lustration on the third and seventh days following his contact with the corpse. The waters of lustration are made by mixing ashes from the fire of cleansing with water and hyssop, to be sprinkled on the defiled person on the third and seventh days. He then washes himself and his clothing so that at nightfall he will be considered as clean. This is an eternal statute for the purification of those rendered impure due to contact with the dead. Such a ritual is of utmost importance for anyone who has had to prepare a body for burial.

The placement of the laws of purification, particularly from corpse contamination, prior to the notice of the death and burial of Miriam in Num 20:1 and the incident concerning water at the rock in Num 20:2-13 must be considered a deliberate move to explain why Moses and Aaron are barred from the promised land of Israel. They were banned for appearing before YHWH without having purified themselves as required.

IV.

The above considerations indicate that YHWH's decision to ban Moses and Aaron from the promised land of Israel was due to their failure to purify themselves from corpse contamination caused by their handling of the corpse of their sister, Miriam, for burial prior to their appearance before YHWH in the account of YHWH's bringing water from the rock in Num 20:2-13. As the laws of purification in Num 19 make clear immediately prior to the account of Miriam's death and burial in Num 20:1 and the account of the incident at the rock in Num 20:2-13, Moses and Aaron were required to purify themselves from corpse contamination due to the burial of their sister, Miriam, before undertaking any holy service before YHWH. The purpose of the account in Num 20:2-13 would have been to make clear that such a failure must be taken seriously and to remind its audience that this provision applies to all, including figures as highly placed as Moses and Aaron, who led Israel out of Egypt. Despite their celebrated status, even Moses and Aaron, the leaders of the nation of Israel in the Wilderness period, nevertheless could not ignore or set aside their priestly identities and the sacred obligation that their holy identities entailed. As a result of their failure, both Moses and Aaron were barred from entering the land of Israel. Aaron reportedly dies in Num 20:22-29 at the border of the land of Edom. Moses continues to lead the people through the Wilderness to Moab and the Jordan River, but the account in Deut 34 makes it clear that he dies and is buried in Moab before Israel crosses the Jordan to enter the promised land.[19]

Bibliography

Balentine, Samuel E. *The Torah's Vision of Worship*. OBT. Minneapolis: Fortress, 1999.

Campbell, Antony F., and Mark A. O'Brien. *Sources of the Pentateuch: Texts, Introductions, Annotations*. Minneapolis: Fortress, 1993.

Coats, George W. *Exodus 1–18*. FOTL 2A. Grand Rapids: Eerdmans, 1999.

Cross, Frank Moore, Jr. "The Priestly Work." Pages 293–325 in *Canaanite Myth and Hebrew Epic: Essays in the History of the Religion of Israel*. Cambridge: Harvard University Press, 1973.

Dozeman, Thomas B. *Exodus*. ECC. Grand Rapids: Eerdmans, 2009.

———. *The Pentateuch: Introducing the Torah*. Minneapolis: Fortress, 2017.

———, and Konrad Schmid, editors. *A Farewell to the Y-hwist? The Composition of the Pentateuch in Recent European Interpretation*. SymS 34. Atlanta: Society of Biblical Literature, 2006.

Findlay, James D. *From Prophet to Priest: The Characterization of Aaron in the Pentateuch*. CBET 76. Leuven: Peeters, 2017.

---

19. This is a revised version of a paper presented at the Annual Meeting of the Western Association for Jewish Studies, Claremont, CA, March 26, 2017, and at the International Meeting of the Society of Biblical Literature, Rome, Italy, July 3, 2019. I would like to thank the organizers of both events for including my paper in their respective programs.

Knierim, Rolf P. *Text and Concept in Leviticus 1:1-9*. FAT 2. Tübingen: Mohr Siebeck, 1992.

———, and George W. Coats. *Numbers*. FOTL 4. Grand Rapids: Eerdmans, 2005.

Lee, Won W. *Punishment and Forgiveness in Israel's Migratory Campaign*. Grand Rapids: Eerdmans, 2003.

Leveen, Adriane. *Memory and Tradition in the Book of Numbers*. Cambridge, UK: Cambridge University Press, 2008.

Levine, Baruch A. *Numbers 1–20*. AB 4. New York: Doubleday, 1993.

———. *Numbers 21–36*. AB 4A. New York: Doubleday, 2000.

Lisowky, Gerhard. *Konkordanz zum Hebräischen Alten Testament*. 2nd ed. Stuttgart: Würtembergische Bibelanstalt, 1966.

Milgrom, Jacob. *Numbers*. JPS Torah Commentary. Philadelphia: Jewish Publication Society, 5750/1990.

Roskop, Angela R. *The Wilderness Itineraries: Genre, Geography, and the Growth of Torah*. HACL 3. Winona Lake, IN: Eisenbrauns, 2011.

Sarna, Nahum. *Exodus*. JPS Torah Commentary. Philadelphia: Jewish Publication Society, 5751/1991.

Stackert, Jeffrey. *A Prophet Like Moses: Prophecy, Law, and Israelite Religion*. Oxford: Oxford University Press, 2014.

Sweeney, Marvin A. "The Jacob Narratives: An Ephraimitic Text?" *CBQ* 78 (2016): 236–55.

———. "The Literary-Historical Dimensions of Intertextuality in Exodus–Numbers." Pages 41–52 in *Second Wave Intertextuality and the Hebrew Bible*. Edited by Marianne Grohmann and Hyun Chul Paul Kim. RBS 93. Atlanta: Society of Biblical Literature, 2019.

———. *The Pentateuch*. CBS. Nashville: Abingdon, 2017.

Thomas, Matthew A. *These are the Generations: Identity, Covenant, and the Toledoth Formulae*. New York: T&T Clark, 2011.

Interpretive Reception of the Book of Exodus in the English Geneva Bible of 1560[1]

S. Dean McBride, Jr.

There is ample indication in recent decades that the field of biblical scholarship is beginning to explore new directions. A salient example is the magnificent commentary of Samuel E. Balentine on the book of Job, which attends insightfully not only to what the ancient drama "meant" in its generative context but also to what it was interpreted to "mean" in

---

1. Thanks are due also to a number of people who have aided me in the preparation of this essay. Mengistu Lemma diligently assisted in the later stages of the work by checking resources in the William Smith Morton Library of Union Presbyterian Seminary and gaining access to others through interlibrary loan. Paula Skreslet, also of Morton Library, Alan Cooper of Jewish Theological Seminary, and Chip Dobbs-Allsopp and Mark S. Smith of Princeton Theological Seminary provided help and encouragement when needed. Paul S. Needham (Special Collections librarian, Scheide Library, Princeton University) enthusiastically made available to me digitized portions of the Estienne French Bible of 1553, as well as the 1560 English Geneva Bible, and granted permission to display selected leafs in the published essay.

the history of its theological and wider cultural "reception." In celebrating Balentine's scholarship, I want also to express my personal gratitude and delight that he was willing, literally, to move "across the street" and to become a colleague at Union Presbyterian Seminary during my final years of active teaching. He has since provided the skilled, mature leadership needed to maintain the seminary's tradition of biblical exegesis as a "learned" critical and theologically engaged discipline in the service of Christian ministry.

The Reformation of the sixteenth century was profoundly shaped and sustained by a brilliant flourishing of biblical scholarship, rooted in the humanist "new learning" associated with the Renaissance. For Johannes Reuchlin, Desiderius Erasmus, and other humanist scholars, the principal aim was to recover and exposit the major literary works of classical antiquity, including Jewish and Christian Scriptures, through informed philological study of textual sources in their languages of origin.[2] These humanist efforts created a trilingual academic curriculum that featured Hebrew and Greek alongside the traditional Latin cherished by medieval Scholasticism. A foundational outcome was the production of scholarly editions of classical literature and the language tools needed for their critical interpretation. But the most immediately impactful as well as enduring achievement of Reformation philology and hermeneutics was the translation of Hebrew-Aramaic and Greek scriptural traditions into the vernacular languages of western Europe.

Among the other English versions of the Bible published during the sixteenth and seventeenth centuries, none had such a remarkable conception or auspicious reception as the multi-faceted "study edition" of 1560, produced by a learned company of Protestant exiles

---

2. Still useful is the overview of David Daiches, *The King James Version of the English Bible: An Account of the Development and Sources of the English Bible of 1611 with Special Reference to the Hebrew Tradition* (Chicago: University of Chicago Press, 1941), 75–138. See also G. Lloyd Jones, *The Discovery of Hebrew in Tudor England: A Third Language* (Manchester: Manchester University Press, 1983). The "sacred" dimension of much humanist scholarship is appropriately emphasized by Paul Oskar Kristeller, *Renaissance Thought: The Classic, Scholastic, and Humanist Strains* (New York: Harper Torchbooks, 1961).

who found refuge in Geneva during the reign of Mary Tudor.[3] This essay focuses on one segment of their version, the book of Exodus, if only—or especially—because that is what the woodcut at the center of the title page invites readers to do.

Prologue: William Tyndale's Revolutionary Initiative and Legacy

The course of the Reformation in Europe is usually reviewed by emphasizing the contributions of major reformers—most notably Luther, Zwingli, and Calvin. In England, however, there is no fully comparable "magisterial" figure. Instead, reform was a long, drawn-out, bitterly contentious, and all too often deadly civil drama that fluctuated in prevailing cause and policies during the reigns of the last four Tudor monarchs (Henry VIII [1509–1547], Edward VI [1547–1553], Mary I [1553–1558], Elizabeth I [1558–1603]). Furthermore, reform extended through and beyond the seventeenth-century reigns of their Stuart successors.[4] Most divisive was a question that remained at the center of the British drama: by whom and how should the authority of Scripture be exercised in the interests of sound Christian faith and practice?

---

3. *The Geneva Bible: A Facsimile of the 1560 Edition* (Madison: University of Wisconsin Press, 1969). In addition to Berry's "Introduction," 1–28, see the cogent overviews of Stanley Morison, *La Bible Anglaise de Genève, 1560 (The Geneva Bible)* (Gèneva-Berne: Editions Histoire et Typographie, 1972); Gerald Hammond, *The Making of the English Bible* (New York: Philosophical Library, 1983), 89–136; and, especially, Femke Molekamp, "Genevan Legacies: The Making of the English Geneva Bible," in *The Oxford Handbook of the Bible in Early Modern England, c. 1530–1700*, ed. Kevin Killeen, Helen Smith, and Rachel Willie (Oxford: Oxford University Press, 2015), 38–53 (with a focus on this edition as a carefully designed "study Bible").

4. For a detailed review of sixteenth-century developments, which can only be briefly sketched here, see David Daniell, *The Bible in English: Its History and Influence* (New Haven: Yale University Press, 2003), 113–388. For seventeenth-century developments, see especially Emma Major, "'That glory may dwell in our land': The Bible, Britannia, and the Glorious Revolution," in *The Oxford Handbook of the Bible in Early Modern England*, ed. Killeen et al., 427–48; and Kim Ian Parker, "'A king like other nations': Political Theory and the Hebrew Republic in the Early Modern Age," in *The Oxford Handbook of the Bible in Early Modern England*, ed. Killeen et al., 384–96.

There were several serious options debated already during the final quarter-century of King Henry's reign. Should authoritative exposition and application of scriptural witnesses remain—as had been the case since late antiquity—a monopoly of the established church, committed to upholding Latinate doctrinal tradition and maintaining the sacramental rites that assured the spiritual health of the faithful? Or, as Luther and other reformers were insisting, should laity as well as clergy have access to Scripture through accurate and literate translations, in order to facilitate a renewal of pristine Christian piety as attested in the earliest New Testament records? And, if a more "democratizing" hermeneutical agenda was implemented by means of an "authorized" English translation of Scripture, what kinds of interpretive guidance should published editions be permitted to include, or should they exclude, in order to establish and safeguard the text's true "meaning"?

Confronting the Key Issues

The vernacular Bible debate was initially engaged by King Henry in 1521 and, shortly thereafter, by William Tyndale (also known as William Hychins), a young, linguistically talented scholar and ostensibly virtuous cleric who had become an advocate of Luther's work as reformer. The king's first contribution was a Latin treatise defending the orthodox doctrine of seven sacraments.[5] This *Assertio* ("Defense") was written to debunk Luther's claim that Scripture only supported two sacraments as directly instituted by Christ. In 1528, the king published an English translation of Luther's personal response to this treatise, together with his own reply. He also added a preface in which he not only expanded his earlier rebuke but also charged that Luther had recently aided and abetted "two leude persons borne in our realme

---

5. Facsimile edition: *Assertio septum sacramentorum adversus Martin Luther* (Ridgewood, NJ: Gregg, 1966). The volume also includes the letter from Pope Leo X to the king, bestowing on him the honorific *Fidei Defensor*, "Defender of the Faith," as reward for his defense of Catholic orthodoxy. In the context of the king's separation from Rome, this title was withdrawn by papal decree, but it was restored to the king by act of Parliament in 1544 and continued to serve as a mandate for the crown's sometimes imperious role in ecclesial affairs.

for the translating of the Newe testament in to Englisshe . . . ."⁶ The oblique reference is to Tyndale and a younger associate, William Roy. And the scriptural text in view is Tyndale's translation of the Greek New Testament, whose printing in Cologne was thwarted in 1525 but successfully completed a year later in Worms, quite likely with Luther's help. Smuggled copies soon reached England, to the delight of some and the horror of others, among them Sir Thomas More, soon to become "Lord High Chancellor" of the realm (1529–1532).⁷ According to the king, who here and elsewhere seems to be echoing More, Tyndale's translation is erroneous, exhibiting "many corruptions of that holy text," and is further contaminated by "prefaces and other pestylent gloses in the margentes for the advancement and setting forthe of his [i.e., Luther's] abhomynable heresyes . . . ."

In the same year, Tyndale published abroad *The Obedience of a Christian Man* (Antwerp, 1528).⁸ Although clearly written in response to the royal proscription of his New Testament translation, Tyndale here addresses neither the king nor his other critics. He appeals instead to the English-speaking public, articulating an agenda for and the revolutionary purpose of his own and other vernacular translations of the Scriptures. Tyndale's case is succinctly sketched in the opening "epistle."⁹ In the body of the work, he develops this with a three-part argument. First, drawing upon Romans 13 but also incorporating comments on other key passages in both biblical Testaments (e.g., Deut 17:8-20), he affirms that "obedience" to legitimate degrees of authority—royal, judicial, and familial—is fundamental to God's created order. At the same time, these Scriptures abundantly attest that those endowed with such authority are held accountable. They are chosen by divine decree to exercise limited sovereignty, for the

---

6. Facsimile edition: Henry VIII, *Answere unto a Certaine Letter of Martyn Lther* [sic], English Experience 322 (Amsterdam: Theatrum Orbis Terranum, 1971), 8.

7. See David Scott Kastan, "'The noyse of the New Bible': Reform and Reaction in Henrician England," in *Religion and Culture in Renaissance England*, ed. Claire McEachern and Debora Shuger (Cambridge: Cambridge University Press, 1997), 46–68.

8. William Tyndale, *The Obedience of a Christian Man*, ed. David Daniell (1528; repr., London: Penguin Books, 2000).

9. Ibid., 1–25.

well-being of God's people, with wisdom and humility and not for their own personal gain or aggrandizement (e.g., Deut 1:9-18; 1 Pet 5:1-11). Second, when the Church of Rome appropriated for itself worldly power and wealth, it falsified its mandate to govern God's spiritual realm on Christ's behalf (e.g., John 17:6-21; 18:33-37). Its imperialistic policies and institutions were erected on the fractured foundation of Jerome's Latin "Vulgate" translation of the "*Hebraica veritas*" and the Greek New Testament. A primary mechanism for this falsification was implementation of the claim that scriptural witnesses are protean, replete with the potential to yield multiple types or layers of "meaning," some of which could only be discovered through "allegorical" and related forms of imaginative interpretation.[10] Third, the antidote to Rome's tyrannical, monopolistic, and idiosyncratic misuse of Scripture is recognizing that individual biblical texts have in each case a unitary, literary-contextual sense that can be established through sound, humanist philology. Moreover, this "plain sense" should be faithfully conveyed to lay readers as well as clerical readers through informed vernacular renderings. In the first and final analysis, then, Scripture itself, made accessible to the Christian public—which is blessed with God's spiritual empowerment to distinguish between truth and falsehood—is the only reliable arbiter of what its texts "say" and what they "mean."[11]

While Tyndale's three-part argument is much less forthcoming in addressing scriptural witnesses to civil disobedience, that possibility is implicit throughout, especially in his remarks about papal abuse of mundane power and the need of the English Church to rid itself of the idolatrous debris of Roman encroachment.[12] The toxic issues of aggressive reform and counter-reform would remain in the forefront of the British drama for more than a century.

---

10. Ibid., 156–80.

11. Ibid., 24; see also 191.

12. Thomas More's *A Dialogue Concerning Heresies* (1529) charged that, in this respect, Tyndale was far more "puffed vp with the poyson of pryde, malice, and enuye" than Luther (Thomas Lawler, Germain Marc'hadour, and Richard C. Marius, eds., *A Dialogue Concerning Heresies: Part 1, The Text*, vol. 6 of *The Complete Works of St. Thomas More* [New Haven: Yale University Press, 1981], 424–26). On Tyndale's "revolutionary" agenda and legacy, see Daniell, *The Bible in English*, 146–47, 157–59.

Tyndale's Old Testament Translations and Their Survival

The controversy between King Henry and Tyndale began as a "war of words" (including, to be sure, some episodes of book burning). It entered a new phase in the 1530s and soon turned lethal, when the king's preoccupation with negating Tyndale's influence became obsessive, though also more complicated by his own marital dilemma. His efforts to annul his marriage to Catherine of Aragon, followed by a secret marriage to Anne Boleyn in 1533, resulted in an irreparable break with Rome. These developments also alienated Thomas More, who refused to accept the legitimacy of the king's claim of "supremacy" that preempted papal authority. More was soon convicted for treason and executed on July 6, 1535. The most important roles in replacing him were acquired by two cautious advocates for reform, Thomas Cromwell and Thomas Cranmer, both of whom assisted the king in the annulment and remarriage maneuvers and then served as high officials in his administration. Cromwell held the position of vice-regent, "Lord Privy Seal," from 1536 until he was himself convicted for treason and executed on July 28, 1541. Cranmer became "Archbishop of Canterbury" (1534–1556); in this capacity he continued to mediate between Tyndale's ardent supporters and their opponents, working to establish an independent Anglican liturgy and polity under auspices of the crown. Later, in Mary Tudor's purge of Protestant leaders, he too was executed for treason and heresy.[13]

With the publication in 1530 of his translation of the Hebrew Torah, printed in Antwerp by Hans Luft, Tyndale took a major step toward completing an English version of the whole Christian Bible.[14] This "manual" edition (*octavo*) begins with a seven-page "epistle"

---

13. Diarmaid MacCulloch, *Thomas Cranmer: A Life* (New Haven: Yale University Press, 2017).

14. The translation (still in older English, but with "normalized" spelling, punctuation, and filling-out of abbreviations) is conveniently available in David Daniell, *Tyndale's Old Testament: Being the Pentateuch of 1530, Joshua to 2 Chronicles of 1537, and Jonah, Translated by William Tyndale* (New Haven: Yale University Press, 1992). In this essay, however, I have regularly cited Tyndale's original idiom, accessible online (identified by the abbreviation TEP=Tyndale's English Pentateuch): https://ia802706.us.archive.org/26/items/ThePentateuch/ Tyndale_William-The_Pentateuch-STC-2350-1724_01-p1to383.pdf.

and an eight-page "prologue showing the use of the scripture." In both of these, he insists that his earlier New Testament and now his English Pentateuch are intended primarily to set "the plain text and literal sense" coherently before the eyes of lay people.[15] The pursuit of Tyndale instigated by King Henry led to his capture near Antwerp in May 1535. During his incarceration in the castle of Vilvorde, near Brussels, Tyndale continued to translate the Old Testament, completing Joshua through Kings, as well as 1–2 Chronicles and Jonah, before he was condemned to death as a heretic in August 1536. Several weeks later, in early October of 1536, he was executed by strangulation, with his corpse then burned at the stake.

Miles Coverdale, an Augustinian friar and graduate of Cambridge University, had apparently become closely associated with Tyndale in Antwerp during the early 1530s. He may have helped another assistant, John Rogers, to secure drafts of the translations of later parts of the Old Testament that Tyndale had been able to finish before his execution. Soon thereafter, and with support from Cranmer, each of these disciples produced a "first" full version of the English Bible. Coverdale's Bible, published in 1535 (most likely in Antwerp) and reprinted two years later in London, used his own translation from Latin and German versions, but reflected some of Tyndale's controversial choices for rendering key New Testament terms.[16] Rogers's

---

15. Each of the last four pentateuchal books, which are printed with a clean "roman" type, has its own brief introduction. The translated text is presented in a single column, with occasional annotations in the margins. Exodus has forty-five such notes; most are explanatory of textual contents but some take critical or caustic aim at the papacy and its policies. E.g., the marginal comment at Exod 32:27 reads (TEP): "The popes bull sleeth moo than Aarons calfe, euen a hundred thousand for one heere of them." For the eleven woodcuts included in his Exodus (in the tradition of those found already in Lyra and "as they appeared in Luther's Pentateuch of 1524"), see James Strachan, *Early Bible Illustrations: A Short Study Based on Some Fifteenth and Early Sixteenth Century Printed Texts* (Cambridge: University Press, 1957), 76.

16. Because Coverdale's translation lacked foundation in the Hebrew and Greek texts, the 1535 and 1537 editions of his Bible are primarily significant as witnesses to an upturn in the acceptability of Scripture in English. The exquisite 1535 title-page woodcut by the younger Hans Holbein features a depiction of King Henry in the lower panel, distributing the text of "God's words" to English clergy and nobility; the 1537 reprinted edition is dedicated to him. See Berry,

Bible was published in Antwerp, also in 1537, with pseudonymic attribution to "Thomas Matthew" as the translator.[17] Three-quarters of this translation preserved Tyndale's work. For the remaining Old Testament books, Rogers borrowed from Coverdale's 1535 Bible. Archbishop Cranmer and vice-regent Cromwell had persuaded a hesitant King Henry, who seems to have remained unaware that these two English Bibles used Tyndale's anathematized translations, to approve their publication in England.[18] Then, in 1539, the king also gave his reluctant consent for the creation of another, more "official" English translation. This yielded Coverdale's revision of the Matthew Bible, printed as a large folio that earned the name Great Bible (Fig. 4.1).[19] Due to the inclusion of the archbishop's laudatory preface, the second and subsequent editions became widely known as Cranmer's Bible.

There is a double irony to be noted here. The efforts of Rogers and Coverdale, coordinated by Cranmer and Cromwell, preserved and distributed Tyndale's legacy, even under the aegis of royal license. Nevertheless, the earlier Coverdale and Rogers Bibles, and more so the Great Bible with its intimidating size and iconic appearance, are conspicuous attempts at circumscription and political "gentrification" of authoritative Scripture in the vernacular. The Great Bible

---

"Introduction," 2–3; and Daniell, *The Bible in English*, 176–89 (and, for the woodcut, figure 10).

17. Joseph W. Johnson, "Introduction to the Facsimile Edition," in *Matthew's Bible: A Facsimile of the 1537 Edition Combining the Translations of William Tyndale & Miles Coverdale*, ed. John Rogers (Peabody: Hendrickson, 2009), viii–x. Below the elaborately framed title-page woodcut is the claim that this version is "set forth with the kinges most gracyous lycence."

18. The king soon after regretted his permission. See Daniell, *The Bible in English*, 228–29; and Susan Wabuda, "'A day after doomsday': Cranmer and the Bible Translations of the 1530s," in *The Oxford Handbook of the Bible in Early Modern England*, ed. Killeen et al., 23–37.

19. Berry, "Introduction," 3–4. The printing of the first edition of 1539 is attributed to Richard Grafton and Edward Whitchurch, but the typesetting was most likely done abroad and, like the Matthews Bible, uses both "black letter" type and folio format. In addition to content headings at the tops of the pages and brief summaries at the beginnings of chapters, the first printing and later editions displayed decorative woodcuts and a minimal number of marginal cross references (see Fig. 4.1).

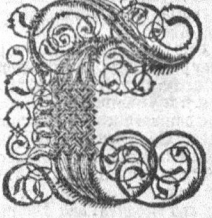

Figure 4.1. Leaf 22 obverse [beginning of Exodus], Great Bible, 1539. Photo Credit: Special Collections, William Smith Morton Library, Union Presbyterian Seminary.

was promulgated along with rules for restricted usage. Its extraordinary title-page woodcut—depicting in the upper panel a messianic King Henry downloading a copy of "God's Word [*Verbum Dei*]" with his right hand to the clerical establishment as an instrument of royal sovereignty and, with his left, another copy to empower similarly his civil officials—is best viewed as an unintended parody, not only of Holbein's frontpiece for the 1535 Coverdale Bible but, far more important, of what Tyndale sought to achieve by enabling the English public itself to read and study the scriptural traditions.[20]

King Henry died on January 28, 1547. In the final years of his reign he had encouraged parliamentary actions to hinder once again public access to any and all English translations of Scripture, but the program did not succeed. Moreover, popular interest in the now accessible narratives of the books of Samuel and Kings seems to have contributed to an energetic program for ecclesial reform that held sway during the brief, six-year reign of Edward VI, son of Henry and Lady Jane Seymour, whose family held Lutheran sympathies. Only nine at the time of his accession, Edward was celebrated by partisans as another "Josiah," the similarly youthful Judaean king credited with a thoroughgoing, iconoclastic reformation of the realm—a national cleansing that implemented a scriptural "Book of the Law" recovered from the Jerusalem Temple (2 Kgs 22:1–23:25).[21] The following reign of Mary I (1555–1558), a ferociously ardent Catholic, brought a brutal response. Not only were English Bibles confiscated and burned but Anglo-Protestant leaders such as John Rogers and Thomas Cranmer were executed; hundreds of others were also massacred. Some—the "Marian exiles"—sought refuge in Europe's major Lutheran enclaves. Among them were scholars who would produce, in remarkably short order, the English Geneva Bible of 1560 (Fig. 4.2).

---

20. See Daniell, *The Bible in English*, fig. 19; and Strachan, *Illustrations*, 78–80.

21. Daniell's discussion of this theme (*The Bible in English*, 229–35, 245) provides an important corrective to earlier views that failed to recognize its cogency as indicative of a shift toward a more militant Protestant position on iconoclastic reform.

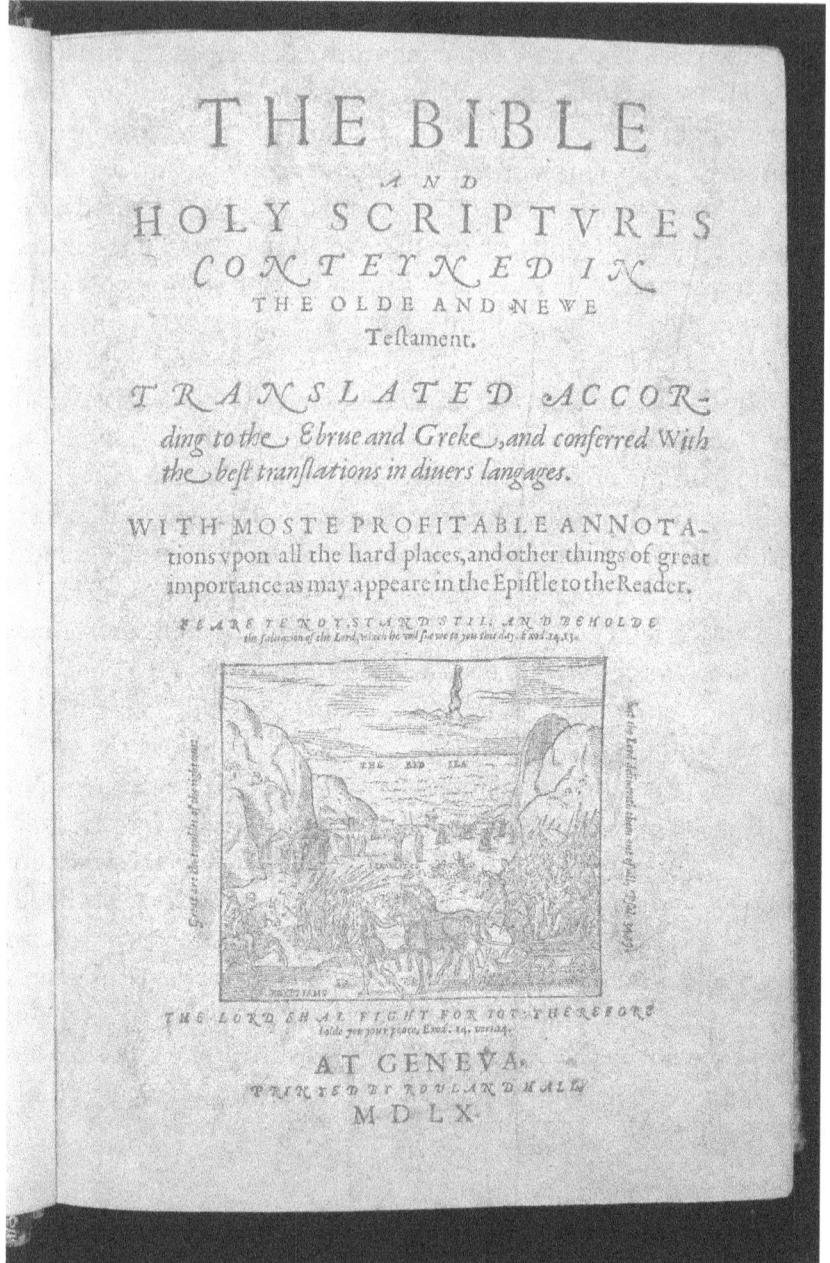

Figure 4.2. Title page, Geneva Bible, 1560. Photo Credit: Special Collections, Scheide Library, Princeton University.

The Legacy Renewed and Enriched

Unlike Richard Taverner's 1539 English Bible, which is generally considered an outlier,[22] the 1560 English Geneva Bible (EGB) belongs to the mainstream development of what is sometimes called the "Tyndale-King James tradition" of translation. Its linguistic profile marks the transition between Tyndale's often looser renderings and the more formal, elevated style adopted in the 1611 King James Version (KJV), which revised it. This assessment, however, is inadequate. It not only undervalues the contribution of the translation itself—with its close attention to Hebrew syntax, morphology, and semantics—but also overlooks what is conceptually distinctive and contextually most substantive and significant about EGB: its purposive design, the various supplementary contents it includes to facilitate expository study, and its coherently devised annotations. These complementary features were intended to renew William Tyndale's theo-political agenda for opening up the inspired treasures of Scripture before the broad English-speaking public, encouraging popular examination of them, shared comprehension, and faithful implementation.

Setting, Contributors, and Purpose

EGB is the timely creation of a competent team of highly motivated scholars. Their work was supported by a gathered community of exiles anticipating return to their homeland, when conditions allowed, and reengagement in the struggle for renewal of the English church. But EGB is also the product of a felicitous confluence of other circumstances that contributed immensely to its successful completion and reception.

The most important circumstance may well be the work's setting in the small yet strategically located and independent Swiss city-state of Geneva. During the middle decades of the sixteenth century, Geneva evinced a strong Protestant ethos—effectively cultivated by William Farel and John Calvin—which drew to it refugees from religious persecutions especially in nearby Italy and France, as well as others fleeing from Mary Tudor's bloody purge in England. Political independence also benefited the city's thriving printing industry

---

22. Daniell, *The Bible in English*, 219.

whose productivity in mid-century was exceeded in France only by printers in the considerably larger metropolis of Paris.[23] During this period in Geneva, revision and publication of vernacular Bibles, with Calvin's encouragement and sometimes his direct involvement, became the industry's mainstay. A related circumstance is Calvin's own productivity as theologian and biblical expositor during these mid-century decades, to which should be added his active sponsorship of humanist scholarship that found a home in his Genevan "Academy," where in 1555 Theodore de Beza began his tenure as Calvin's close associate and eventual successor.

Several features of EGB often identified as innovative, such as the use of verse numbers and roman type, had already been introduced a decade or so earlier in editions of Scripture published by French printers. Of greater import as a "first" is recognition that EGB was created through the collaborative effort of multiple scholars, resulting in a work that is coordinated in overall conception but not rigidly uniform in thematic contents. Within the version itself, the translators remain anonymous. However, some of them can be identified with confidence and their individual contributions inferred from what is otherwise known about them. Their leader was William Whittingham, who reached Geneva with a group of exiles in 1555, after a brief stay in Frankfurt; with him was John Knox, who became pastor of Geneva's English-speaking congregation.[24] With Calvin's support, Whittingham published an annotated translation of the Greek New Testament in 1557.[25] Using this work as a model, Whittingham most likely coordinated the whole EGB project and

---

23. See Francis M. Higman, *Piety and the People: Religious Printing in French, 1511–1551*, St. Andrews Studies in Reformation History (Aldershot, England: Scholar Press, 1996), 1–20; and Bettye Thomas Chambers, *Bibliography of French Bibles: Fifteenth- and Sixteenth-Century French-Language Editions of the Scriptures*, Travaux d'Humanisme et Renaissance, CXCII (Genève: Librairie Droz, 1983), xiii.

24. See Justine Walden, "Global Calvinism: The Maps in the English Geneva Bible," in *Shaping the Bible in the Reformation*, ed. Bruce Gordon and Matthew McLean (Leiden: Brill, 2012), 208–10.

25. Alfred W. Pollard, *Records of the English Bible: The Documents Relating to the Translation and Publication of the Bible in English, 1525–1611* (London: Henry Frowde; Oxford University Press, 1911), 24–26. Whittingham's English New

was specifically responsible himself for further revision of the New Testament translation. His counterparts, overseeing EGB's treatment of the Old Testament books, were probably Anthony Gilby and Thomas Sampson, scholars noted for their competence in Hebrew and Aramaic.[26]

Anonymity of those directly involved does not conceal differences of emphasis among them, apparent in both the annotations to various biblical books[27] and introductory statements about their principal goals. What they certainly shared, however, is a sense of the moment as a *providential* opportunity to affect a fundamental change in the piety and politics of the English church. This message is already prefigured in the title-page woodcut that depicts the Israelites departing from enslavement in Egypt but trapped between the Red Sea and the pursuing forces of Pharaoh. The three biblical quotations that frame this dramatic image, which reappears in the title page to the New Testament, attest its purpose as an exhortation to readers to see themselves—beleaguered during the Marian oppression—as experiencing anew the extreme peril and imminent deliverance of the "church" of ancient Israel: above, "Feare ye not, stand still, and beholde the saluacion of the Lord, which he will shewe to you this day. Exod.14,13"; below, "The Lord shal fight for you: Therefore holde your peace, Exod.14,14"; left side, "Great are the troubles of the righteous"; and, continued on the right, "but the Lord deliuereth them out of all, (Psal. 4:19)" (see Fig. 4.2). The message that the Red

---

Testament is, unfortunately, difficult to access. Daniell provides a good summary of its contents and character: *The Bible in English*, 278–90 and figs. 20, 22.

26. For identification of other members of the translation team and evidence that their assembly in Geneva was orchestrated, see Berry, "Introduction," 2–7; Morison, *La Bible Anglaise*, 74–76; and Daniell, *The Bible in English*, 277–78. Though they were not translators, important contributions to the project were made by Rouland Hall, the English printer who joined the exiles in Geneva, and John Bodley, an effective fundraiser. While Miles Coverdale's role in the project is unclear, his at least occasional presence in Geneva during this period is certainly noteworthy, if only as a figurehead for Tyndale's legacy.

27. E.g., in Gen 16:7[d], the "Angel of the Lord" who finds Hagar in the wilderness is identified as "Christ." But nothing comparable is suggested in annotations to Exodus passages where the surrogate or guiding "angel" theme is well attested (especially Exod 3:1; 14:19; 23:20-24; 33:2).

Sea encounter and other events narrated in the book of Exodus have direct, immediate theological relevance for EGB's readers is expressly articulated in "The Argument" that precedes the translation (Fig. 4.3) and once more at Exod 14:10, where the title-page woodcut appears again with accompanying comments (Fig. 4.4).[28]

Conspicuously different hermeneutical perspectives are underscored in EGB's two introductory "epistles," each dated April 10, 1560 (eighteen months after the coronation of Elizabeth Tudor). The first and longer epistle, which is addressed "To the Moste Uertvovs and Noble Qvene Elisabet" by "Your humble subiects of the English Churche at Geneua," defends the militant, iconoclastic aspect of Tyndale's reform agenda that was reasserted during the reign of Edward VI. Queen Elizabeth is urged to accept the role of reformer modeled by Zerubbabel, who inaugurated the postexilic restoration of the Jerusalem Temple (Ezra 4; 1 Esd 2). Inspired further by the examples of Josiah, Asa, and other reforming kings of Judah, she is encouraged to overcome with force any and all enemies, foreign and domestic, in order to rebuild "the Lords Temple, the house of

---

28. The comments alongside the woodcut at 14:10 make quite explicit the identification of the "Church of God" with the beleaguered Israelites, trapped between the Red Sea and the Egyptian forces. Striking here is the depiction itself and the marginal description of the physical setting: "for the Israelites had on ether side them, huge rockes & mountaines, before them the Sea, behinde them moste cruel enemies, so that there was no way left to escape to mans iudgement." This exaggerates the biblical account; its source is suggested by the marginal comment at 14:7 on the magnitude of Pharaoh's forces. The superscript "d" points readers to the subsequent marginal comment: "And toke six hundreth chosen charets, & [d] all the charets of Egypt / d Iosephus writeth that besides these charets there were 50000 horsemen, and 200000 fotemen." See Josephus, *Jewish Antiquities* 2.324, whose account continues: "Barring all routes by which they expected the Hebrews to attempt escape, they confined them between inaccessible cliffs and the sea; for it was the sea in which terminated a mountain whose rugged face was destitute of tracks and prohibitive for retreat. Accordingly, occupying the pass where the mountain abuts upon the sea, they blocked the passage of the Hebrews, pitching their camp at its mouth, to prevent their escape to the plain" (2.324–25; trans. H. St. J. Thackeray, *Josephus IV: Jewish Antiquities, Books I–IV*, LCL [London: William Heinemann, 1967], 306–309). Josephus is cited once more in EGB Exodus, in a note to the illustration of "The Tabernacle" at 26:15 (leaf 37): "Iosephus writeth that euerie boarde was an handful thicke" (see *Jewish Antiquities* 3.116–17).

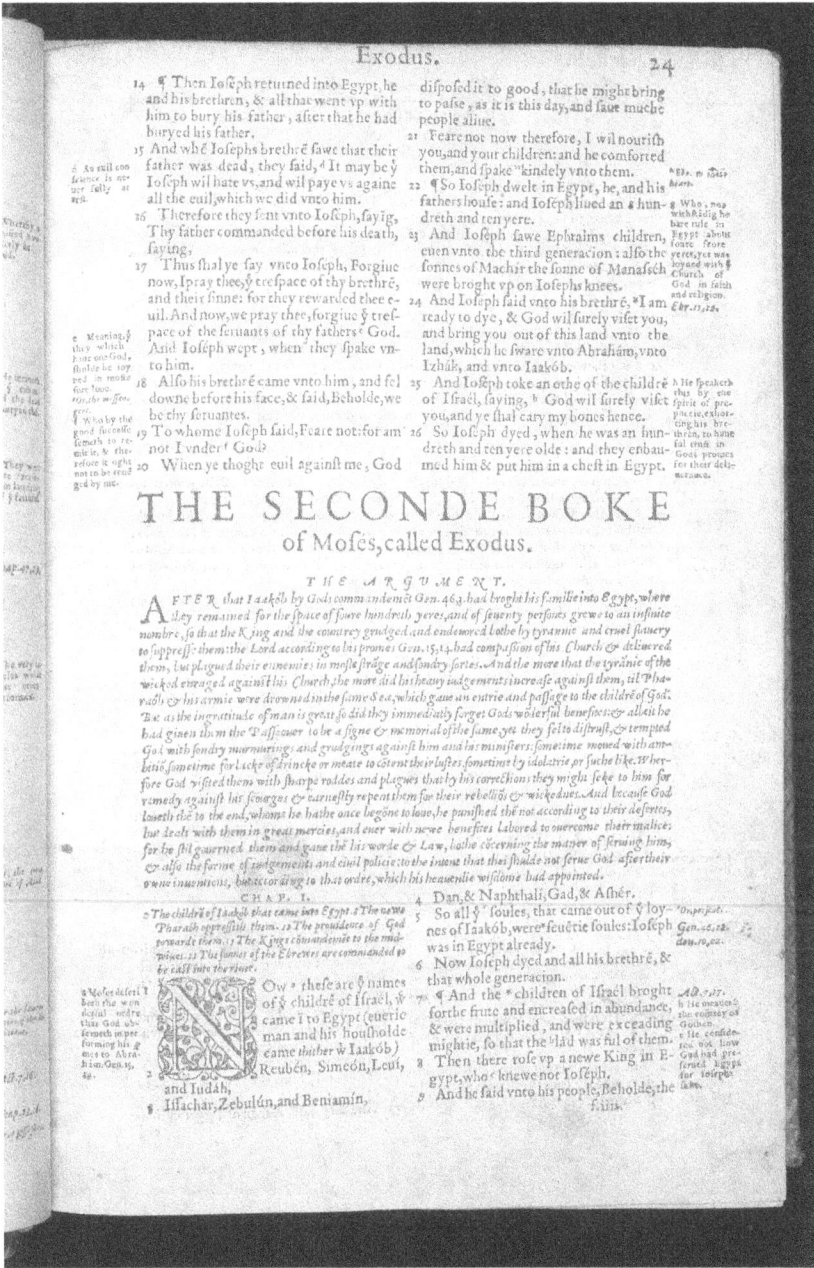

Figure 4.3. Leaf 24 obverse [beginning of Exodus], Geneva Bible, 1560. Photo Credit: Special Collections, Scheide Library, Princeton University.

Figure 4.4. Leaf 30 reverse [Exodus 14:10-26 with woodcut illustration of Red Sea Event], Geneva Bible, 1560. Photo Credit: Special Collections, Scheide Library, Princeton University.

God, the Church of Christ, whereof the Sonne of God is the head and perfection." Scripture, of course, now newly accessible in EGB for public study, provides the necessary mandate that acknowledges not royal "supremacy" over the church but Christ's, while also legitimating the queen's divine commission to serve him. The following general epistle, referenced already on the title page, makes a considerably more modest and informative appeal to readers. It sketches the purpose of the volume's supplementary resources and explains how the translation proper is augmented with marginal notes of several kinds to aid users to "atteine to the true and simple meaning" of the text.

Format and Supplements

Complementary features of overall design and coordinated contents enhance the effectiveness of EGB as a popular "study Bible," distinguishing it in size, affordability, and "para-textual" resources from its English predecessors. At the same time, EGB's novelty must be qualified by recognizing the work's great indebtedness to the series of French Bibles—which were consecutive revisions of Pierre Olivétan's 1535 translation—produced by Robert Estienne and other Genevan printers during the 1550s.

Most earlier English and French Bibles are folios, with each page (or leaf) of text displaying a header followed by two columns of translation that leave margins sufficiently wide to accommodate any notes (so both Rogers's Matthew Bible and Coverdale's Great Bible). The handsome folio edition published by Estienne in 1553 is the first of the whole Bible to employ numbered verses in the left margins of columns (Fig. 4.5).[29] This alignment has the significant effect of treating each biblical verse as a discrete textual-syntactical unit. Numbered verses are also a feature of Whittingham's 1557 New Testament, although like Tyndale's 1530 Pentateuch it is *octavo* in size, with a single column of text that allows for marginal notes. While this reduced format made the work convenient and less expensive, it

---

29. T. H. Darlow and H. F. Moule, *Polyglots and Languages Other Than English*, vol. 2 of *Historical Catalogue of the Printed Editions of Holy Scripture in the Library of the British and Foreign Bible Society* (London: The Bible House, 1911), 388 (#3719). Chambers (*Bibliography of French Bibles*, 195–196 [#172]) identifies the 1553 Estienne Bible as establishing the "base" for French editions until 1588.

Figure 4.5. Leaf 20 obverse [beginning of Exodus], Robert Estienne French Bible, 1553. Photo Credit: Special Collections, Scheide Library, Princeton University.

could not easily accommodate long texts, such as a complete Bible. EGB adopted a compromised *quarto* design. Each page of translated text is still able to display a header (with the name of the book in the center and a terse identification of its principal topic at the left margin and leaf number at the right) and parallel columns of text printed in roman type.

In comparison with Estienne's 1553 French Bible, the system for distinguishing various kinds of marginalia in EGB is elaborate. Asterisks in the text indicate marginal cross-references (as already in Roger's Matthew Bible and Coverdale's Great Bible); there are 180 of these in Exodus. Sigla resembling italicized and regular quotation marks distinguish respectively between marginal notes that give alternative renderings of the Hebrew (101 in Exodus) and those that render the "literal" Hebrew when the main translation has adopted a more intelligible English wording (49 in Exodus). Interpretive annotations, meant to clarify what the text says and means, are indicated by sequential roman letters elevated in the text, chapter by chapter; there are 451 of these in Exodus.

Supplements to the annotated translation proper include the "Arguments" (printed with italic type) introducing each biblical book, short content summaries at the beginnings of chapters (also using italics), two appended "tables" that index Hebrew "Propre Names" and "The Principal Things That Are Conteined in the Bible," two brief chronological lists, five maps, and twenty-six illustrative woodcuts with annotations. In addition to the title-page depiction of the Red Sea event, found also with Exod 14, ten of these woodcuts appear at appropriate places in Exod 25–30 to portray the tabernacle and related paraphernalia. The important, overall effect of these additional resources is to support the historical authenticity of the biblical narratives.[30] Much of this supplementary material, particularly the chapter summaries and woodcuts, is borrowed from or adapts what is included in Estienne's 1553 French Bible and its

---

30. Walden, "Global Calvinism," 187–215 (with particular attention to the map following leaf 77 reverse, which traces Israel's route from Goshen to Canaan on the basis of Num 33).

successors, especially so the 1560 *quarto* printed by Antoine Rebul, which is a close counterpart to EGB.[31]

EGB's Exodus Translation and Interpretive Marginalia

While Tyndale's agenda permeates EGB, he is nowhere mentioned in the work itself, nor do the translators suggest they are revising either Rogers's Matthew Bible or Coverdale's Great Bible, which preserved his legacy. Not only for the majority of books of the Latter Prophets and Writings (as well as the Apocrypha), which Tyndale had not translated, but for those he had finished—Exodus in particular—EGB's title-page claim to publish the Scriptures "translated according to the Ebrue and Greek, and conferred With the best translations in diuers langages" is quite credible. (The translators, of course, made liberal use of Tyndale's renderings when they found them cogent.) Moreover, with some confidence, the Hebrew edition they translated can be identified as the one printed in Sebastian Münster's *Hebraica biblia* (Basel, 1534), together with his annotated Latin translation (Fig 4.6).[32]

Münster's Hebrew text may be characterized as "Masoretic lite." It consists of the vocalized Hebrew, verse by verse, using terminal *sôp pāsûq* and, usually, medial *ʾatnaḥ* to indicate major clause syntax. But it does not represent *metheg, sillûq*, and detailed cantillation, or the traditional paragraph divisions (*pārāšîyôt*), or the larger apparatus that distinguishes the so-called Masoretic (M) *textus receptus* of the second edition of Daniel Bomberg's *Biblia Rabbinica* (Venice, 1524–1525). Of direct relevance, too, are Münster's Latin annotations that include frequent references to Targum Onqelos (T^O), the popular Jewish commentaries of Rashi and Abraham Ibn Ezra, and David Kimchi's Hebrew lexicon.[33]

---

31. Chambers, *Bibliography of French Bibles*, 268–70 (#263). EGB's woodcuts were apparently borrowed from those in the 1560 Rebul edition (Darlow and Moule, *Historical Catalogue* 2:390; Pollard, *Records*, 27).

32. Jones, *Discovery of Hebrew*, 46–48 (Fig. 6).

33. There is one marginal reference to "Kimchi" in EGB's Exodus, at 38:8d, on the polished metal "mirrors" contributed by serving women to make the bronze basin and stand for the tabernacle complex. The proximate source for

INTERPRETIVE RECEPTION OF THE BOOK OF EXODUS IN THE ENGLISH GENEVA BIBLE 111

Figure 4.6. Initial leaf of Exodus in S. Münster, *Hebraica biblia*, 1534. Photo Credit: Special Collections, William Smith Morton Library, Union Presbyterian Seminary.

Characteristics of the Translation

Several distinctive features of EGB's "literal" approach to translation, in comparison with Tyndale's freer style (which, to repeat, is not strictly governed by Hebrew versification), are illustrated already by its rendering of Exod 1:1-4:

TEP: "These are the names of the children of Israel, which came to Egypte with Iacob, every man with his housholde: Ruben, Simeon, Leui, Iuda, Isachar, Zabulon, Beniamin, Dan, Neptali, Gad and Aser."[34]

EGB: 1] "Now[a] these are the names of the children of Israél, who came in to Egypt (euerie man and his housholde came *thither* with Iaakób)
2] Reubén, Simeón, Leuí, and Iudáh,
3] Issachár, Zebulún, and Beniamín,
4] Dan, & Naphthalí, Gad, & Ashér."

Tyndale does not represent the initial conjunction of v. 1 and smooths the verse's syntax as indicated by the ʾatnaḥ; he renders vv. 2-4 as a simple list of the eleven sons of Jacob who migrated to Egypt with their father (to join Joseph, who was already there). EGB, on the other hand, renders the initial conjunction with temporal "Now," adding marginal note "a" with an explanation of its import as a link to the Genesis narratives: "Moses describeth the wonderful ordre that God obserueth in performing his promes to Abrahám, Gen.15,13." It identifies v. 1b as a parenthetical clause, and because "*thither*" has no literal equivalent in the Hebrew text, it is italicized. In vv. 2-4, EGB carefully renders the Hebrew conjunction, which—together with versification—is used to distinguish subgroups among Jacob's male offspring. Conspicuous here, too, is EGB's qualified practice of representing the literal spelling and accentuation of Hebrew personal names. The 1611 KJV adopts EGB's rendering of these verses,

---

this is probably Münster's annotation (*ad loc.*), which reflects Kimchi's *Sefer Ha-shorashim* (339–40, *marōt*); see also Rashi, *Exodus*, 212.

34. Roger's Matthew Bible and Coverdale's Great Bible are essentially TEP here, though note (see Fig. 4.1) that Coverdale's Great Bible lacks "Zebulun"!

dropping only the italicized "*thither*" in the parenthesis of v. 1b and the accents on the names in vv. 2-4.

Although the italicized "*thither*" does seem superfluous in 1:1, often elsewhere the device is a useful aid to English intelligibility. In 32:32, for example, the Hebrew text omits the apodosis of Moses' conditional oath. Tyndale and KJV simply gloss over the ellipsis:

> TEP: "Yet forgeue them their synne I pray thee: If not wype me out of thy boke which thou hast written."

> KJV: "Yet now, if thou wilt forgiue their sinne; and if not, blot me, I pray thee, out of thy Booke, which thou has written."

A likely sense of the omitted apodosis is supplied in italics by EGB:

> 32] "Therefore now if thou pardone their sinne, *thy mercie shal appeare*: but if thou wilt not, I pray thee, rase me out of thy boke, which thou hast written."[35]

Another interesting example of EGB supplementing the literal Hebrew in the interest of English intelligibility is found in 18:11b, the conclusion to Jethro's confession of the Lord's "greatness" among the gods. The text of M is a puzzlement: *kî baddābār ʾăšer zāddû ʿălêhem*. Tyndale renders this clause word for word, leaving the sense quite murky; KJV uses the italic device to augment the Hebrew, in order to support a contextual interpretation that understands *ʿălêhem* to refer to the Lord's elevation "above" other gods:

> TEP: "for because that they dealt prowdly with them."

> KJV: "for in the thing wherein they dealt proudly against them, *hee was* aboue them."

EGB's translation, with accompanying marginal note, facilitates the "measure for measure" interpretation already found in the tannaitic *Mekilta*, T°, and Rashi, which understands the "they" to be not the

---

35. Rashi (*Exodus*, 185) notes this is an ellipsis; he supplies an omitted apodosis: "Well and good" (*hărê ṭôb*).

other "gods" but the Egyptians and the "them" to be the oppressed Israelites: "for as they haue dealt proudely with them, *so are they* [e] *recompensed.* / e For they, that drowned the children of the Israelites, perished them selues by water."[36]

Also noteworthy is EGB's closer attention to Hebrew verbal morphology and syntax than is often exhibited in TEP and KJV.[37] A striking example is the disjunctive initial clause of 24:1, where M has *wĕʾel-mōšeh ʾāmar*. This inverted word order is rendered by TEP and KJV as equivalent to a *waw*-consecutive preterit construction (implying a continuation or renewal of the preceding address of God to Moses): "And he said to Moses." EGB, however, recognizes the inversion to express in this context a pluperfect sense: "Now he had [a] said vnto Moses." Marginal note "a" provides an explanation: "When he called him vp to the mountaine to giue him the lawes, beginning at the 20. chap. hitherto."[38] The literary import of this is to identify the rites of covenant-making narrated in 24:1-14 as the direct continuation of the initiation of the covenant in chapters 19–20; in effect, too, the "Covenant Code" of Exod 21–23 is bracketed as supplemental legislation, subordinate to the "moral law" of the Decalogue.

In cases where the sense of a Hebrew term is ambiguous, obscure, or otherwise deemed problematic, EGB typically adopts or cites in the margin interpretations that have the strong support of Jewish sources. For example, in 2:16 Reuel (so named in 2:18) is identified as "priest of Midian [M *kōhēn midyān*]," with the support of most ancient versions. But EGB adds a marginal alternative, "*Or, prince.*" This reflects T⁰ (*rabbāʾ*, which is informed by considerable debate in rabbinical texts about whether Reuel/Jethro, though a chief of his own people, had ever been or remained a legitimate *kōhēn*.[39] More interesting is the appropriate rendering of the *hapax* form *wĕʾanwēhû* in 15:2, which G (*kaì doxásō autón*) and V (*et glorificabo*

---

36. See Rashi, *Exodus*, 93; cf. Exod 1:22.

37. See, e.g., the marginal rendering of Qal infinitive absolute plus Qal perfect at 3:16 and the emphasis on distinguishing Qal and Hipʿil forms in notes at 4:20 and 10:14.

38. See Rashi, *Exodus*, 128.

39. Rashi, *Exodus*, 9.

eum) understand to mean "and I will glorify him" (and so still TEP). EGB, however, adopts the interpretation attested in T°, which understands the Hip'il imperfect form to be denominative of *nāweh* "dwelling, habitation," sometimes referring to the Jerusalem temple (Exod 15:13; Ps 79:7; Isa 33:20):[40]

> T°: "and I will build for him a sanctuary [*wĕʾebnê lēh maqdīšāʾ*]."
>
> EGB: "and I wil[b] prepare him a tabernacle. / b To worship him therein."
>
> KJV: "and I will prepare him a habitation."

In sum, EGB aims at literalness in its fidelity to the Hebrew text but not at the expense of English intelligibility.

Character and Purposes of the Interpretive Marginalia

In comparison with the density of marginal notes in Genesis, Psalms, the prophetic books, and most of the New Testament (Romans and Revelation in particular), EGB's annotations in Exodus are generally terse and spare in number. This disparity is no doubt representative of the theological weight traditionally ascribed to what Kendall Soulen has called "the standard canonical narrative," whose model was largely a creation of Justin Martyr and Irenaeus of Lyon in the Patristic Period. The plot of this overarching narrative focuses on the salvation history of humankind. It commences in Genesis with the creation and fall, and the "call" of Abraham that initiates "preparation for the Gospel"; Jesus the Christ, whose crucial advent is foreseen by the Old Testament prophets, is at once the "new Adam" and the unique, incarnate divine savior whose redemptive death and resurrection begin God's restoration of the created order to its pristine, pre-sinful condition. But this model is skewed by its incompleteness: it "... renders the center of the Hebrew Scriptures—the eternal covenant between the God of Israel and the Israel of God—ultimately indecisive for understanding how God works as Consummator and

---

40. Ibid., 75b; *Mekilta de-Rabbi Ishmael, Shirta* 3.46–49 (Lauterbach, 2/25–26).

as Redeemer to engage creation in lasting and universal ways."[41] In strong, corrective contrast to this model—*yet without negating it*—EGB's interpretation of Exodus recognizes it to be the hermeneutical keynote to a more comprehensive and coherent reading of the scriptural narrative in which the church is not only prefigured by but already participates in the covenantal, theopolitical history of ancient Israel. To use Calvin's apt metaphor, the drama of Israel's deliverance from servitude in Egypt and covenant-making at Sinai-Horeb reveals "as in a bright mirror, the incomparable power, as well as the boundless mercy, of God in raising up, and as it were engendering his Church."[42]

Together with the introductory "Argument" and the brief chapter summaries, EGB's marginal annotations to Exodus exemplify faithfully the exegetical agenda outlined in the opening "epistle" to readers. In order to guide students to discern "the true and simple meaning" of the biblical texts, the notes have three complementary aims: first, to provide data that facilitate basic "understanding," especially where the biblical text is difficult or obscure; second, to identify the "declaration of the text," which means its principal testimony or message; and third, to indicate appropriate "application," how the message should contribute to theological comprehension of "God's glories" and the "edification" of "his Church."

Most of the annotations in Exodus aim at basic "understanding," providing information about what the translated text "says." They treat such matters as:

- biblical place names and geography (e.g., 1:7[b] [Goshen], 3:1[a, b] [Sinai/Horeb], 10:19[g] [the Red Sea], 12:37[q] [the journey from Ramses to Succoth]);
- the identities of persons (e.g., 1:15[d] [Shiprah and Puah], 6:20[g] [Amram and Iochebed], 6:23[i] [Amminadab], 17:8[e] [Amalek]);

---

41. R. Kendall Soulen, *The God of Israel and Christian Theology* (Minneapolis: Fortress, 1996), 16.

42. John Calvin, *Commentaries on the Four Last Books of Moses Arranged in the Form of a Harmony*, trans. C. W. Bingham, vol. 1 (Grand Rapids: Eerdmans, 1950), xv. Cf. Tyndale, *Obedience*, 5.

- the Israelite-Jewish calendar and culture (e.g., 13:4ᶜ [Abib], 14:24ˡ [morning watch], 16:15ᶠ [manna], 16:36ᑫ [Ephah], 19:1ᵃ [Sivan], 30:13ʰ [value of the Sheqel]);
- unusual themes and cultic practices (e.g., 3:4ᵈ [the Lord's angelic surrogate], 13:13ᵍ,ʰ [first born], 14:8ᵉ [sense of "high hand"], 19:4ᵈ [the metaphor "eagles wings"], 28:4ᶜ [the priestly "Ephod"], 28:30ⁿ [the "Urim and Thumim"], 33:7ᶜ ["Ohel-moed"]).

The declarative annotations identify what the plain-sense renderings of biblical texts, interpreted contextually and theologically, "mean." For instance, annotation "d" to the description of Moses in 6:12 as "of vncircumcised lippes" comments on both the literal sense of the metaphor and its larger significance (in this case with reference to the "standard canonical narrative"): "Or, barbarous and rude in speache. & by this worde (vncircumcised) is signified the whole corruption of mans nature." The command in 23:19 that "*yet* shalt thou not seeth a kid in hisˡ mothers milke" elicits the comment (note "l"), "Meaning that no frutes shulde be taken before iust time: & thereby brideled all cruel & wanton appetites."

A prominent concern is "theodicy," that is, annotations that defend the sovereignty and providence of God in response to details of the complicated narrative interactions between God, Moses, and Pharaoh. Thus the setting adrift of infant Moses in the ark by his mother is to be interpreted not as an act of desperation but of confident faith: "Committing him to the providence of God, whome she colde not kepe from the rage of the tyrant" (2:3ᵇ). In 9:16, the Lord's hardening of Pharaoh's heart in order "to declare my ᵈ Name throughout all the world" is explained in note "d" to mean: "That is, that all the world may magnifie my power in ouer coming thee." Similarly, in 11:9 God informs Moses, "Pharaoh shal not heare you, ᵈ that my wonders may be multiplied in the land of Egypt. / d God hardeneth the heartes of the reprobat, that his glorie thereby might be the more set forthe, rom.9,17."

Already in these instances, and quite often elsewhere in EGB's Exodus, the "declarative" sense expressed in chapter summaries and marginal annotations is indicative of Calvin's proximate influence.⁴³ This is conspicuous in the treatment of the book's legislative corpora, where Calvin's views on the revelatory character and threefold uses of Mosaic law are simply presupposed.⁴⁴ The chapter summary to Exod 21 describes the laws that follow (identified as "The iudiciales" in the topical header) as "Temporal and ciuile ordinances, appointed by God, . . . : the obseruation whereof doeth not iustifie a man, but are giuen to bridel our corrupt nature, which else wolde breake out into all mischief and crueltie." The two "tables" of the Decalogue in 20:1-17 are identified using Calvin's enumeration, while the specific annotations on commandments of the "seconde table" in vv. 12-17 are declaratively interpreted on the basis of "synecdoche"— understanding the literal wording to imply a more inclusive sense.⁴⁵ Accordingly, the text and fuller sense of the homicide prohibition in v. 13 yields: "Thou shalt not ⁱ kil. / i But loue and preserue thy brothers life."

Only once, in the description of the ark at 25:17, does an annotation declare an explicitly Christological meaning for the "plain sense" renderings in text and margin: "Also thou shalt make a ᵍ Merciseat of pure gold / Or, couering: or, propitiatorie. / g There God appeared mercifully vnto them: and this was a figure of Christ." Note, too, by implication, God's redemptive presence on behalf of the ancient Israelite community and its individual members is the crux of the "ceremonial" laws that characterize the elaborate tabernacle-temple cultus, whose original function is now assumed and perfected through the priestly ministry of Christ (cf. 12:14ⁱ; 40:15ᵈ).

Not surprisingly, the theopolitical priorities of the Exodus annotator are also evident in annotations that aim at "application." Thus the hardships and anxieties experienced by the Israelites, in

---

43. For an overview of John Calvin's views on divine sovereignty and providence, see *Institutes of the Christian Religion*, vol. 1, ed. John T. McNeill, trans. Ford Lewis Battles, Library of Christian Classics 20 (Philadelphia: Westminster, 1960), 210–28.

44. *Institutes of the Christian Religion*, II.7.3–13 (ed. McNeill, vol. 1, 351–62); II.8.51 (ed. McNeill, vol. 1, 415–16).

45. *Institutes of the Christian Religion*, II.8.8–10 (ed. McNeill, vol. 1, 374–76); II.8.35–50 (ed. McNeill, vol. 1, 401–15).

Egypt and beyond—and, concomitantly, also by the church in its continuing struggle to achieve renewal—are lessons in trusting that God will always provide enough to sustain the life of his people. At 3:2, for instance, the applied meaning is analogically derived: "Then the Angel of the Lord appeared vnto him in a flame of fyre, out of the middes of a ᶜ bushe: / c This signifieth that the Church is not consumed by the fier of afflictions, because God is in the middes therof."[46]

Application includes a few annotations that are restrictive, cautionary, or moralizing. One such occurs at 3:22: "ᵖ For euerie woman shal aske of her neighbour, and of her that soiourneth in her house, iewels. / p This example may not be followed generally: thogh at Gods commandment thei did it iustly, receiuing some recompense of their labours" (cf. 15:20ᵏ). Another that seems to fit here is the annotation to 1:19 that gives a two-part judgment on the actions of the Hebrew midwives: "And the midwiues answered Pharaóh, Because the Ebrewe ᵍ women *are* not as the women of Egypt: for they are liulie, and are deliuiered yer the midwife come at them. / g Their disobedience herein was lawful, but their dissembling euil." Though scarcely "bitter" or polemical in tone, this annotation became infamous when, during the Hampton Court Conference of January 1604, King James I identified it as indicative of a dire threat posed by EGB to the authority of the British monarchy and the stability of the English national church.[47]

Some Consequences

David Daniell has argued persuasively that EGB—initially published in 1560 with numerous reprints and revised editions in various

---

46. See also 4:14ᵉ; 6:7ᵇ; 10:3ᵇ; 14:14ʰ; 16:4ᶜ, 16:18ⁿ; 17:7ᵈ.

47. Also so identified were 2 Chr 15:16 (where EGB has "And King Asa deposed Maacah *his* ⁱ mother from her regencie, because she had made an idole: / i Or grandmother: & herein he shewed that he lacked zeale for she oght to haue dyed bothe by the couenant, and by the Lawe of God: but he gaue place to foolish pitie, & wolde also seme after a sorte to satisfy the Lawe."); and Matt 2:12 ("And after they were warned of God in a dreame, that they shulde ⁱ not go againe to Herode, they returned into their countrey another way. / i Promes oght not to be kept, where Gods honour and preaching of his trueth is hindered; or els it oght not to be broken"). Cf. Daniell, *The Bible in English*, 431–36.

formats thereafter—"was the most significant book in English for the following hundred years."[48] Its reception was enthusiastic from the outset among the general public, especially those Protestants influenced by Calvin's theology who sought more vigorous, thorough reform of the English church and who came to be known as "Puritans." Similarly, an edition of EGB published in Edinburgh in 1579 was endorsed by Scotland's "Privy Council" for purchase and study by "every substantial householder," thus finding a favored reception among Presbyterians.[49] On the other hand, EGB was, at best, tolerated by Queen Elizabeth and the episcopacy of the Anglican church they sought to redefine after the trauma of Mary's reign. Their attempt to consolidate included production of an authorized English revised translation—the Bishops' Bible (1568)—which was intended to counter EGB's popularity and aggressive theopolitical agenda; it was a debacle.[50] The 1611 KJV and its revisions did eventually succeed in replacing, or at least outlasting, EGB, in part because the translators adopted (without specific acknowledgement) EGB's philologically astute English translation as a base while also implementing the stern mandate of King James to eschew any and all expository marginalia, as a safeguard against seditious or idiosyncratic interpretations.[51]

Finally, if KJV benefited in significant measure not only from Tyndale's foundational work but also from the advanced scholarship of EGB's translators, it is all the more important to recognize the fundamental difference in the ways these latter versions feature the translated scriptural texts. KJV was initially printed as a large folio. Its elaborate frontispiece engraving by Cornelis Bol displays, from top down, the Hebrew Tetragrammaton, a dove (representing divine inspiration), the seated figures of Peter and Paul with other apostles

---

48. Daniell, *The Bible in English*, 221.

49. See Maurice Betteridge, "The Bitter Notes: The Geneva Bible and Its Annotations," *The Sixteenth Century Journal* 14 (1983): 41–62; Molekamp, "Genevan Legacies," 51–52.

50. Hammond, *The Making of the English Bible*, 137–57; Daniell, *The Bible in English*, 338–47.

51. Pollard, *Records*, 54; Karen L. Edwards, "The King James Bible and Biblical Images of Desolation," in Killeen et al., eds., *The Oxford Handbook of the Bible in Early Modern England*, 71–82.

standing around them, and the façade of a foundation wall with the figures of Moses and Aaron in niches flanking a central title-box; at the four corners of the page are depictions of the evangelists.[52] This imagery projects solemn, divinely bestowed authority. The array of empowered biblical persons forms an intimidating barrier between the profane world without and the sacred realm within, where the translated text of Scripture—printed in ornamental black letter—is enshrined. While there are cross-references and occasional marginal notes to the translation itself, with alternative renderings of Hebrew and Greek terms, none offers guidance in exposition. Here the projected hermeneutical sense is one of an iconic, self-sufficient literary artifact—divine word rendered into elevated English text—whose legitimate curator is the established church.

As we have seen, the title-page woodcut of EGB invites readers to view their own current plight mirrored in the crisis of the Israelites, trapped by the forces of Pharaoh at the Red Sea, but with God's epic deliverance at hand. And throughout, EGB treats the translated scriptural texts not as an inviolable literary inner sanctum but as reliable witnesses to the history of God's creative and redemptive relationship with humankind, centered on the community of Israel and the messianic ministry of Jesus the Christ. Above all, the general "epistle" informs its readers of how the work of translation and the paratextual supplements and marginalia are designed to engage them in sound, meaningful exposition of these scriptural witnesses. In short, they are encouraged themselves to become competent exegetes in order to nurture their Christian faith and practice.

Tyndale's legacy as translator and reformer survived concerted efforts to silence it. So too has its coherently designed and implemented revision in EGB, which has shaped the mainstream of biblical scholarship and exegesis in the Reformed Tradition for almost five centuries.

---

52. Accessible online; also, e.g., Daniell, *The Bible in English*, fig. 27.

Bibliography

Berry, Lloyd E. "Introduction to the Facsimile Edition." Pages 1–28 of *The Geneva Bible: A Facsimile of the 1560 Edition*. Madison: University of Wisconsin Press, 1969. Repr., Peabody: Hendrickson, 2007.

Betteridge, Maurice. "The Bitter Notes: The Geneva Bible and Its Annotations." *The Sixteenth Century Journal* 14 (1983): 41–62.

Calvin, John. *Commentaries on the Four Last Books of Moses Arranged in the Form of a Harmony*. Translated by C. W. Bingham. Vol. 1. Grand Rapids: Eerdmans, 1950.

———. *Institutes of the Christian Religion*. Edited by John T. McNeill. Translated by Ford Lewis Battles. 2 vols. Library of Christian Classics 20–21. Philadelphia: Westminster, 1960.

Chambers, Bettye Thomas. *Bibliography of French Bibles: Fifteenth- and Sixteenth-Century French-Language Editions of the Scriptures*. Travaux d'Humanisme et Renaissance CXCII. Genèva: Librairie Droz, 1983.

Daiches, David. *The King James Version of the English Bible: An Account of the Development and Sources of the English Bible of 1611 with Special Reference to the Hebrew Tradition*. Chicago: University of Chicago Press, 1941.

Daniell, David. *The Bible in English: Its History and Influence*. New Haven: Yale University Press, 2003.

———. *Tyndale's Old Testament: Being the Pentateuch of 1530, Joshua to 2 Chronicles of 1537, and Jonah, Translated by William Tyndale*. New Haven: Yale University Press, 1992.

Darlow, T. H., and H. F. Moule. *Polyglots and Languages Other Than English*. Vol. 2 of *Historical Catalogue of the Printed Editions of Holy Scripture in the Library of the British and Foreign Bible Society*. London: The Bible House, 1911.

Edwards, Karen L. "The King James Bible and Biblical Images of Desolation." Pages 71–82 in *The Oxford Handbook of the Bible in Early Modern England, c. 1530–1700*, ed. Killeen, Smith, and Willie.

Ferrell, Lori Anne. "The Church of England and the English Bible, 1559–1640." Pages 261–71 in *The Oxford Handbook of the Bible in Early Modern England, c. 1530–1700*, ed. Killeen, Smith, and Willie.

Hammond, Gerald. *The Making of the English Bible*. New York: Philosophical Library, 1983.

Henry VIII. *Answere unto a Certaine Letter of Martyn Lther* [sic]. The English Experience 332. Amsterdam: Theatrum Orbis Terranum, 1971 [1528].

———. *Assertio septum sacramentorum adversus Martin Luther*. Ridgewood, NJ: Gregg, 1966 [1521].

Higman, Frances M. *Piety and the People: Religious Printing in French, 1511–1551*. St. Andrews Studies in Reformation History. Aldershot, England: Scholar Press, 1996.

———. "'Without Great Effort, and with Pleasure': Sixteenth-Century Geneva Bibles and Reading Practices." Pages 115–22 in *The Bible as Book: The Reformation*. Edited by Orlaith O'Sullivan. London: British Library, 2000.

Johnson, Joseph W. "Introduction to the Facsimile Edition." Pages viii–x in *Matthew's Bible: A Facsimile of the 1537 Edition Combining the Translations of William Tyndale & Miles Coverdale*. Edited by John Rogers. Peabody: Hendrickson, 2009.

Jones, G. Lloyd. *The Discovery of Hebrew in Tudor England: A Third Language*. Manchester: Manchester University Press, 1983.

Kastan, David Scott. "'The noyse of the New Bible': reform and reaction in Henrician England." Pages 46–68 in *Religion and Culture in Renaissance England*. Edited by Claire McEachern and Debora Shuger. Cambridge: Cambridge University Press, 1997.

Killeen, Kevin, Helen Smith, and Rachel Willie, editors. *The Oxford Handbook of the Bible in Early Modern England, c. 1530–1700*. Oxford: Oxford University Press, 2015.

Kimchi, Rabbi Davidis. *Sefer Ha-shorashim [Radicum liber; sive, Hebraeum bibliorum lexicon cum animadversionibus Eliae Levitae]*. Edited by Jo. H. R. Biesenthal and F. Lebrecht. Berlin: G. Bethge, 1847.

Kristeller, Paul Oskar. *Renaissance Thought: The Classic, Scholastic, and Humanist Strains*. New York: Harper Torchbooks, 1961.

Lauterbach, Jacob Z., trans. *Mekilta de-Rabbi Ishmael*. 3 vols. Philadelphia: Jewish Publication Society of America, 1976.

Lawler, Thomas. Germain Marc'hadour, and Richard C. Marius, eds. *A Dialogue Concerning Heresies: Part 1, The Text*. Vol. 6 of *The Complete Works of St. Thomas More*. New Haven: Yale University Press, 1981.

MacCulloch, Diarmaid. *Thomas Cranmer: A Life*. New Haven: Yale University Press, 2017.

Major, Emma. "'That glory may dwell in our land': The Bible, Britannia, and the Glorious Revolution" Pages 427–48 in *The Oxford Handbook of the Bible in Early Modern England, c. 1530–1700*, ed. Killeen, Smith, and Willie.

Molekamp, Femke. "Genevan Legacies: The Making of the English Geneva Bible." Pages 38–53 in *The Oxford Handbook of the Bible in Early Modern England, c. 1530–1700*, ed. Killeen, Smith, and Willie.

Morison, Stanley. *La Bible Anglaise de Genève, 1560 (The Geneva Bible)*. Gèneva-Berne: Editions Histoire et Typographie, 1972.

Münster, Sebastian. *Hebraica biblia*. Vol 1. Basileae: Ex officinis Michaelis Isingrinii & Henrici Petri, 1524.

Parker, Kim Ian. "'A king like other nations': Political Theory and the Hebrew Republic in the Early Modern Age." Pages 384–96 in *The Oxford Handbook of the Bible in Early Modern England, c. 1530–1700*, ed. Killeen, Smith, and Willie.

Pollard, Alfred W. *Records of the English Bible: The Documents Relating to the Translation and Publication of the Bible in English, 1525-1611*. London: Henry Frowde; Oxford University Press, 1911.

Rashi (Rabbi Shlomo Yitzchaki). *Exodus*. Vol. 2 of *Pentateuch with Targum Onkelos, Haphtaroth and Rashi's Commentary*. Translated by M. Rosenbaum and A. M. Sildermann. New York: Hebrew Publishing Company, n.d.

Soulen, R. Kendall. *The God of Israel and Christian Theology*. Minneapolis: Fortress, 1996.

Strachan, James. *Early Bible Illustrations: A Short Study Based on Some Fifteenth and Early Sixteenth Century Printed Texts*. Cambridge: University Press, 1957.

Tyndale, William. *The Obedience of a Christian Man*. Edited and with an Introduction and Notes by David Daniell. 1528. Repr., London: Penguin Books, 2000.

Wabuda, Susan. "'A day after doomsday': Cranmer and the Bible Translations of the 1530s." Pages 23–37 in *The Oxford Handbook of the Bible in Early Modern England, c. 1530–1700*, ed. Killeen, Smith, and Willie.

Walden, Justine. "Global Calvinism: The Maps in the English Geneva Bible." Pages 187–215 in *Shaping the Bible in the Reformation*. Edited by Bruce Gordon and Matthew McLean. Leiden: Brill, 2012.

5

Finoglio's *Joseph and Potiphar's Wife* at Harvard
Biblical Reception Meets Art Historical Methodology

Heidi J. Hornik and
Mikeal Joseph Parsons

It is with great pleasure that we contribute this study to honor our dear friend and colleague, Samuel E. Balentine, whose groundbreaking work on the Hebrew Bible helped to inspire this work.

Introduction

Joseph and Potiphar's Wife depicts a story of failed seduction of a morally justified servant who remains loyal to his faith and his master. Paolo Finoglio's oil on canvas painting from the mid-seventeenth century depicts the moment in the Genesis 39 narrative when Potiphar's wife dramatically grabs Joseph's garment to bring him into her bed (Fig. 5.1). The tenebrist lighting and stark contrast of colors enhances the drama and characterizes the Baroque style in which Paolo Finoglio (ca. 1590–1645) painted. Finoglio (also Finoglia), a Caravaggesque artist and a colleague of Artemisia Gentileschi

Figure 5.1. Paolo Finoglio, *Joseph and Potiphar's Wife*, ca. 1634. Oil on canvas. 232.7 x 193.7 cm. Harvard Art Museums/Fogg Museum, Cambridge, MA. Gift of Samuel H. Kress Foundation. Photo Credit: President and Fellows of Harvard College.

(1593–ca. 1656), rarely painted Hebrew Bible narratives. The relationship of biblical reception and art historical methodology in Paolo Finoglio's *Joseph and Potiphar's Wife* in the Harvard Art Museums will be utilized to create a visual exegesis. The biblical narrative, placement within the artist's *oeuvre*, comparison to contemporary depictions of the story, and the iconographical significance of the garment all contribute to this visual exegesis.[1]

Genesis 39—The Narrative of Joseph and Potiphar's Wife

Joseph's garment plays a pivotal role in Finoglio's painting and in the narrative about Joseph and Potiphar's wife in Genesis 39. Joseph has been taken down to Egypt and is a slave in the house of one of Pharaoh's officials named Potiphar (Gen 39:1). Potiphar, the captain of the guard, puts Joseph in charge of his entire household. Joseph is successful in that role and in everything he does because the Lord is with him (vv. 3-6). Despite the Lord blessing the household of Potiphar, trouble arises because the master's wife wants to seduce the handsome young Joseph. Joseph repeatedly refuses her advances and does not want to commit adultery or be disloyal to his master (vv. 7-10). One day he is in the house alone with her, and she calls to him to lie with her. As he tries to leave, she grabs his garment, but he escapes her grasp and flees the house. The wife then calls for her servants and falsely accuses Joseph of seducing her, using his garment as false evidence (vv. 11-15). Verses 12-18 repeatedly mention the garment. It is her "proof" of violation, and Potiphar believes her (vv. 16-20). This is not the first time that a garment has caused Joseph undue harm. Of course, Joseph's more famous story has to do with

---

1. Research for this article was supported by a 2019 Allbritton Grant for Faculty Research with study in Madrid and at the Prado. Our appreciation to Professor Mark Anderson (Baylor University) and Drs. Joseph Koerner and Jeffery Hamburger (Harvard University) for their support at various stages of this project for both Hornik and Parsons. The Harvard Art Museums curatorial and drawing departments enabled us to study the files and drawings as well as the painting on several occasions. Andrés Úbeda de los Cobos, Director of Conservation, Museo del Prado in Madrid, was also very generous with his time during Hornik's study of the Finoglio paintings in storage. Special thanks to Katie Burton for her careful and thorough assistance in the foundational research.

a robe and his brothers' jealousy of the garment (Gen 37:3-4). That story ends with Joseph trapped in a well (37:23-24), and this story concludes with him being imprisoned (39:20). Once again, the Lord is with Joseph, and he gains the trust of the keeper of the prison, who gives him authority over the other prisoners (39:21-23).

Paolo Finoglio, Painter of the Neapolitan Baroque

Paolo Finoglio's *oeuvre* provides vital context for understanding his interpretation of this biblical narrative. There are at least four paintings signed "*Neapolitanus*" by Paolo Domenico Finoglio.[2] They are the *Baptism of Valerian, Martyrdom of St. Januarius, St. Dominic*, and the *Triumph of Bacchus*.[3] Finoglio is believed to have been born around 1590 in the village of Orta di Atelia, just north of Naples. He began his training under Mannerist painter Ippolito Borghese (d. 1627).[4] Finoglio probably continued his study with Battistello Caracciolo (1578–1635), an artist who modeled himself strongly after one of the founders of the Italian Baroque style, Caravaggio (1571–1610).[5] Caravaggio's influence on Finoglio was exemplified through the ten lunettes Finoglio created early in his career. These works depict the *Founders of the Religious Orders* in the Sala Capitolare (1620–ca. 1626) in the Certosa of St. Martin, Naples.[6] Finoglio

---

2. Riccardo Lattuada, "Finoglia [Finoglio], Paolo Domenico," *Grove Art Online*, Oxford University Press, 2003.

3. Regarding the signature on the *Baptism of Valerian, Martyrdom of St. Januarius*, and *St. Dominic*, see Lattuada, "Finoglia [Finoglio], Paolo Domenico." Hornik was able to see the signature on the *Triumph of Bacchus* in the Museo del Prado, Madrid, with Andrés Úbeda de los Cobos, Director of Conservation, on 11 September 2019.

4. For the theories regarding Finoglio's trainings, see Pierluigi Leone de Castris, "Il giovane Finoglio," in *Paolo Finoglio e il Suo Tempo: Un Pittore Napoletano alle Corte degli Aquaviva*, ed. Silvia Cassani and Maria Sapi (Naples: Electa, 2000), 33–42.

5. De Castris, "Il giovane Finoglio," 33.

6. For illustrations of these works, see Silvia Cassani and Maria Sapi, eds., *Paolo Finoglio e il Suo Tempo: Un Pittore Napoletano alle Corte degli Aquaviva*, 87–91. For a more extensive study of the Certosa, see John Nicholas Napoli, "Fashioning the Certosa di San Martino: Ornament, Illusion, and Artistic Collaboration in Early-Modern Naples" (UMI diss., Princeton University, 2003).

also painted an altarpiece at this time, *Circumcision of Christ* (Fig. 5.2), which still remains on the left side wall of the Sala di Capitole in S. Martino.[7] When compared to two Caravaggio altarpieces for Neapolitan churches produced ca. 1606–1607, the *Flagellation* (San Domenico Maggiore) and the *Seven Works of the Misericordia* (Fig. 5.3), Pio Monte della Misericordia), the strong influence of tenebrism, dramatic gesture, centralized composition, and intense contrasting colors is apparent in the *Circumcision*. Finoglio likely would have studied Caravaggio's works and possibly even met the painter during his two brief stays in Naples between 1607 and 1610.[8] At the impressionable age of seventeen, Finoglio certainly would have heard about the notorious artist. In 1632, Finoglio returned to work for the Certosa of St. Martin and completed a cycle of the life of the saint for the chapel dedicated to him.[9]

Between 1629 and 1630, Finoglio painted a series of *Immaculate Conception* altarpieces in and around Naples that combine Caravaggesque effects of light with elongated figures of the late Mannerist style.[10] During this time, Finoglio was employed by wealthy private clients, acting as a copyist and art dealer in association with Tommaso della Vigna and Tiberio Mazzucco.

Naples was under Spanish rule since 1504, and its occupants enjoyed a life of pleasure and indulgence in various social and cultural rituals including the commissioning of art. Despite the eruption of Vesuvius in 1631 (which just missed the city), Naples was one of the richest art markets in Italy. Diego Velázquez (1599–1660), painter to King Philip IV (r. 1621–1665) of Spain, arrived in 1630 with

---

7. Cassani and Sapi, *Paolo Finoglio e il Suo Tempo*, 149.

8. See Silvia Cassani and Maria Sapio, eds., *Caravaggio: The Final Years* (Naples: Electa, 2005, published in conjunction with the exhibition shown at The National Gallery in London from 23 February–22 May 2005).

9. For the Life of St. Martin scenes, see Annachiara Alabiso, "Paolo Finoglio a San Martino," in *Paolo Finoglio e il Suo Tempo*, ed. Cassani and Sapi, 43–52, 150.

10. The Immaculate Conception altarpieces were painted for S. Lorenzo Maggiore, Naples; The Church of the Annunziata, Airola; and S. Francesco in Montesarchio (today in Lille, Musée des Beaux-Arts). See Lattuada, "Finoglia [Finoglio], Paolo Domenico." See also Cassani and Sapi, eds., *Paolo Finoglio e il Suo Tempo*, 154–56.

Figure 5.2. Paolo Finoglio, *Circumcision of Christ*, 1626. Oil on canvas. 255 x 170 cm. Sala Capitolare, Certosa di S. Martino, Naples. Photo Credit: Public Domain.

the entire Spanish retinue and probably visited Jusepe de Ribera's (1591–1652) studio.[11]

Several Baroque artists moved to Naples to take advantage of the wealth and prosperity of one of the two largest metropolitan centers (along with Paris), including Artemisia Gentileschi, Domenichino (1581–1641), Lanfranco (1582–1647), Poussin (1594–1665), Ribera (1591–1652), and Stanzione (1585–1656). Artemisia left Venice to avoid the plague in 1630, and her decision to go to Naples was motivated by the possibilities for patronage given the Spanish

---

11. Riccardo Lattuada, "Artemisia and Naples, Naples and Artemisia," in *Orazio and Artemisia Gentileschi, Father and Daughter Painters in Baroque Italy*, ed. Keith Christiansen and Judith Mann (New Haven: Yale University Press, 2001, published in conjunction with the exhibition shown at the Museo del Palazzo Venezia in Rome, the Metropolitan Museum of Art in New York, and the St. Louis Art Museum), 381.

Figure 5.3. Caravaggio, *Seven Works of the Misericordia*, 1606–1607. Oil on canvas. 390 x 260 cm. Church of Pio Monte della Misericordia, Naples. Photo Credit: Public Domain.

viceroy's desire to purchase paintings.[12] Her first signed and dated Naples work was the *Annunciation* in 1630.[13]

Each of these painters was requested by King Philip IV to decorate his Buen Retiro Palace in Madrid in the second wave of commissions. The first round was awarded to artists working in Rome by agents of Gaspar de Guzmán y Pimentel, count duke of Olivares.[14] The second round was larger and entrusted to Olivares's brother-in-law, the Spanish viceroy Manuel de Zúniga y Fonesca, count of Monterrey, and assigned in Naples between 1631 and 1637.[15] According to newly discovered documents, the seven painters listed above were working on these paintings from 1633 to 1642.[16] Stanzione, Artemisia Gentileschi, and Paolo Finoglio worked together on scenes from the life of St. John the Baptist.[17] Their five canvases were intended for the hermitage of San Juan, built by Count-Duke Olivares in 1634 in the park of the Buen Retiro in Madrid. The six scenes include Artemisia's *Birth of Saint John the Baptist* and Stanzione's *Annunciation to Zaccharias, Saint John the Baptist Taking Leave of His Parents, Saint. John the Baptist Preaching,* and *The Beheading of Saint John the Baptist.* Paolo Finoglio's *Saint John the Baptist in Prison* has been lost. The proportional division of the paintings (four to Stanzione and

---

12. Elizabeth Cropper, "Life on the Edge: Artemisia Gentileschi, Famous Woman Painter," in *Orazio and Artemisia Gentileschi*, ed. Christiansen and Mann, 269.

13. Lattuada, "Artemisia and Naples," 378–91. See Stefano Causa, "Gli Amici Nordici del Caravaggio a Napoli," *Prospettiva* 93/94 (Jan–April 1999): 142–57.

14. Lattuada, "Artemisia and Naples," 380.

15. Ibid.

16. Mercedes Simal López, "Nuevas noticias sobre las pinturas para el Real Palacio del Buen Retiro realizadas en Italia (1633–1642)," *Archivio Espanol* 84/335 (July–September 2011): 245–60. For an extensive study with bibliography, see Andrés Úbeda de los Cobos, ed., *Paintings for the Planet King: Philip IV and the Buen Retiro Palace* (Madrid: Museo Nacional del Prado; London: Paul Holberton, 2005; published in conjunction with the exhibition shown at the Museo Nacional del Prado in Madrid from 6 July–27 November 2005).

17. Mercedes Simal López, "Nuevas noticias," 252. See also Cropper, "Life on the Edge," 269.

one each to Artemisia and Finoglio) probably indicated the importance of each artist in the eyes of the patron at the time.[18]

Finoglio's pictures were beginning to receive the attention they deserved, evidenced by their inclusion in several important exhibitions on Artemisia.[19] Finoglio also collaborated again with Artemisia (who painted *Baptism of St. Celsus*), along with Lanfranco, Stanzione, and Agostino Beltrano, in the choir of the Pozzuli Cathedral, Naples, in the mid to late 1630s, but these works are in terrible condition and unable to be studied.[20] Finoglio and Artemisia had much in common. Through a comparison with Artemisia's *Esther Before Ahaseurus* (Fig. 5.4), it is possible to see that they shared an ability to create compositions with monumental figures and to paint drapery with texture, dynamic color, and dramatic lighting.[21]

Joseph and Potiphar's Wife should be dated ca. 1634 and placed during this period when Artemisia and Paolo were working on the same painting project for the Buen Retiro palace. They were exchanging stylistic ideas for life-size figures, brilliant fabrics, and intense compositional lighting to the point that their work could be confused. In fact, *Joseph and Potiphar's Wife* carried an attribution to Artemisia Gentileschi for nearly ten years, as will be explained subsequently. According to art historian Roberto Longhi, Artemisia's *Birth of Saint John the Baptist*, ca. 1633–1635, is an example of her ability to recreate an effective domestic interior using Caravaggio's tenebrist leanings as well as painting figures emerging out of darkened shadows.[22] These are some of the techniques that Paolo Finoglio learned from Artemisia and implemented in *Joseph and Potiphar's Wife*.[23]

---

18. Lattuada, "Artemisia and Naples," 382.

19. Francesca Baldassari, *Artemisia Gentileschi e il Suo Tempo* (Milan: Skira Editore, 2016, published in conjunction with the exhibition shown at the Palazzo Braschi in Rome from 30 Nov 2016–7 May 2017), 60, fig. 4.

20. Lattuada, "Artemisia and Naples," 383.

21. Ibid., 384.

22. Christiansen and Mann, eds., *Orazio and Artemisia Gentileschi*, 406.

23. These features also support our new dating of the painting, which will be discussed later.

Figure 5.4. Artemisia Gentileschi, *Esther before Ahaseurus*, ca. 1628–1630. Oil on canvas. 208.3 x 273.7 cm. Metropolitan Museum of Art, New York. Photo Credit: Public Domain.

The Triumph of Bacchus is evidence of Finoglio's continued participation in the decoration of the Buen Retiro Palace after moving to Conversano in 1635.[24] As stated above, this is one of the paintings that has the signature visible. It is part of the History of Rome cycle containing twenty-eight extant paintings, along with another six mentioned in Charles II's will, originally commissioned by Philip IV's representatives to painters in Rome and Naples in 1634.[25] *The Triumph of Bacchus*, painted after 1635, also exhibits Finoglio's

---

24. Úbeda de los Cobos, ed., *Paintings for the Planet King*, 176.

25. See "*The Triumph of Bacchus*," by Paolo Domenico Finoglia, Museo del Prado, https://www.museodelprado.es/en/the-collection/art-work/triunfo-de-baco/026cc3f1-964e-4dd8-8b0d-ddb6654025bc.

return to the style of Battistello Caracciolo, evident in the violent chiaroscuro and the exaggerated features of the figures.[26]

In a recent study in preparation for the 2005 exhibition at the Prado, *El Palacio del Rey Planeta: Felipe IV y el Buen Retiro*, scholars attributed the *Triumph of Bacchus* (Prado), a *Gladiator's Fight* (Patrimonio Nacional), and *Masinissa Mourning Over the Death of Sophonisba* (Prado) to Finoglio.[27] Although it is difficult to date the paintings, it is believed that they are after 1635 when the artist moved to Puglia and was in the court of Giangirolamo II Aquaviva d'Aragona, Conte di Conversano.[28] Finoglio worked on a cycle of the ten scenes from the *Gerusalemme Liberata* (today in the Museo Civico, Conversano) that was a pictorial representation of Torquato Tasso's poem decorating Aquaviva's castle in Conversano.[29] His final project was for the Church of Saints Cosmas and Damian that was founded in Conversano (Puglia) in 1635 by Aquaviva and his wife, Isabella Filomarino. The signed works depicting *St. Dominic*, the *Baptism of Valerian*, and the *Martyrdom of St. Januarius* were all located there and show the influence of Artemisia's painting.[30] This supports a dating of *Joseph and Potiphar's Wife* to ca. 1630–1635 when he was most directly influenced by Artemisia and before he left for Puglia.[31] Finoglio enjoyed the patronage of Il Aquaviva d'Aragona and Conte di Conversano in Puglia until his death in 1645.[32]

---

26. Úbeda de los Cobos, ed., *Paintings for the Planet King*, 204.

27. Ibid., 169–70, 177–82, 187–88, 204.

28. Giacomo Lanzilotta and Francesco Lofano, eds., *Paolo Finoglio e il Suo Seguito: Pittori a Conversano nei Decenni Centrali dei Seicento* (Galatina, Italy: Congedo, 2012, published in conjunction with the exhibition shown at the Pinacoteca Comunale in Conversano from 8 Sept–28 Oct 2012).

29. Alain Tapié and Alain Fleischer, eds., *Paolo Domenico Finoglio: La Jérusalem Délivrée* (Paris: Somogy, 2010, published in conjunction with the exhibition shown at the Palais des Beaux-Arts in Lille).

30. Cassani and Sapi, *Paolo Finoglio e il Suo Tempo*, 163–64.

31. Christiansen and Mann, *Orazio and Artemisia Gentileschi*, 411.

32. Lattuada, "Finoglia [Finoglio], Paolo Domenico."

Harvard's *Joseph and Potiphar's Wife*

Finoglio's *Joseph and Potiphar's Wife* is an oil on canvas that measures 91⅝ x 76¼ inches. It currently carries a date of ca. 1640, but we suggest a date of ca. 1634 as more accurate and indicative in the shared stylistic characteristics of Paolo Finoglio and Artemisia Gentileschi while working together in Naples between 1630 and 1635.[33] This picture was sold to the Kress Collection by Robert Bothers in 1950 and was a gift to the Fogg Art Museum in 1962.[34] The Samuel H. Kress Foundation created unprecedented programs between 1929 and 1961 dedicated to sharing the artistic legacy of Europe with the American people.[35] At the time when it was a gift to the Fogg, it was simply identified as "A Biblical Theme by a Roman Painter."[36] In 1968, Everett Fahy, Director of the Fogg, attributed the painting to Artemisia Gentileschi, and this was agreed upon by numerous Italian Baroque scholars.[37] Freedberg announced in his 1978 publication that the label for the painting had been changed, presumably by director Everett Fahy, to Paolo Finoglio.[38] Several scholars agree with

---

33. In addition to Artemisia's *Birth of Saint John the Baptist* discussed and illustrated below, please also see her *Lot and His Daughters*, from this period of stylistic exchange at the Toledo Museum of Art, http://emuseum.toledomuseum.org/objects/55087/lot-and-his-daughters?ctx=180a36ad-7ee0-442e-9a83-568c96d5457e&idx=0.

34. For a color illustration, see "Paolo Finoglia, Joseph and Potiphar's Wife," https://www.harvardartmuseums.org/art/228639.

35. For more on the Kress Foundation, see http://www.kressfoundation.org/collection/history/.

36. This is recorded in private correspondence between Miss Marie Schneider of Plainview, New York, who requests a photograph and updated attribution from Mrs. Phoebe Peebles, Archivist, Fogg Museum of Art. Curatorial files accessed on 1 March 2019 at the Harvard Art Museums. Thank you to Ms. Erica Lawson for facilitating our visit.

37. Ward Bissell, letter to Mr. Everett Fahy on 19 February 1969; Mina Gregori, *70 Pitture e Sculture del '600 e '700 Fiorentino* (Florence: Officine Grafiche Vallecchi, 1965), 9; Fern Rusk Shapley, *Paintings from the Samuel H. Kress Collection, Italian Schools XVI–XVIII Century* (London: Phaidon, 1966), 84–85, fig. 152.

38. Sydney J. Freedberg, "Lorenzo Lotto to Nicolas Poussin," *Apollo* 107/195 (May 1978): 389–97.

Freedberg, and the attribution, for the most part, remains today.[39] The large painting was conserved in 1990 with support from a two-year award from the Getty Grant Program and is permanently installed today in the Harvard Art Museums.[40]

Visual Exegesis and Formal Analysis

The scene depicts a story in Genesis 39 where Joseph tries to escape the advances of the wife of his master, Potiphar. The wife grabs onto the fabric of Joseph's cloak to prevent his retreat and tears part of it away. She later uses this torn cloth to falsely accuse him of inappropriate sexual advances towards her. *Joseph and Potiphar's Wife* was painted in the Baroque period, when many artists intended to separate themselves from the Renaissance through the use of intense colors and stronger contrasts in light. Though there was a stylistic change from the Renaissance, Christianity and biblical narratives remained popular themes and inspirations for Baroque artists. The Baroque style also frequently depicted a specific moment in time to give the painting additional drama. This painting in particular is successful because it reveals the narrative of the work through precise scene selection, subject, tenebrist light, facial expression, revealing

---

39. For an attribution to Finoglio, see Nicola Spinosa, *La Pittura Napolentana del '600* (Milan: Longanesi, 1984), pl. 35; Kristin A. Mortimer and William G. Klingelhofer, *Harvard University Art Museums: A Guide to the Collections* (Cambridge: Harvard University Art Museums; New York: Abbeville Press, 1986), 159; Edgar Peters Bowron, *European Paintings Before 1900 in the Fogg Art Museum: A Summary Catalogue including Paintings in the Busch-Reisinger Museum* (Cambridge: Harvard University Art Museums, 1990), 49, 107, 344; Roberto Contini and Gianni Papi, *Artemisia* (Rome: Leonardo-De Luca Editori, 1991), 70, 72; Ferdinando Bologna, *Battistello Caracciolo e il Primo Naturalismo a Napoli* (Naples: Electa, 1991), 291–92; Cassani and Sapi, *Paolo Finoglio e il Suo Tempo*, 104, 153–54; Christiansen and Mann, *Orazio and Artemisia Gentileschi*, 384, 386; Matthias Waschek et al., *Ideal [Dis-]Placements: Old Masters at the Pulitzer* (St. Louis: Pulitzer Arts Foundation, 2008), 11, 42; Baldassari, *Artemisia Gentileschi e il Suo Tempo*, 60. For a discussion in favor of Artemisia, see Mary D. Garrard, *Artemisia Gentileschi: The Image of the Female Hero in Italian Baroque Art* (Princeton: Princeton University Press, 1989), 80, 506; R. Ward Bissell, *Artemisia Gentileschi and the Authority of Art: Critical Reading and Catalogue Raisonné* (University Park: Pennsylvania State University Press, 1999), 121, 316–17.

40. *Director's Report (Harvard University Art Museums)*, No. 1990/1991 (1990–1991): 34.

body language, and a dark background that emphasizes the events of the foreground.

For a narrative image to be successful, the image must depict a scene that conveys its position as the consequence or result of a previous scene and the cause of the one that follows. This dual role is often achieved in a scene that is the climax of a story. Finoglio was constrained to one absolute moment in time, so every detail in the image becomes highly significant. Providing both the context for the image as well as developing the future implications, all within one scene, is undoubtedly difficult yet successfully achieved by Finoglio. It is made possible by an intentionally important moment in the narrative, which in this case is the climax.

The Cloth

There are two possible subjects of Finoglio's *Joseph and Potiphar's Wife*. The first is that the characters are the central element of the painting. In the case of written work, a story is often centered on one or more characters and their interactions with one another. However, to take this position is to assume that the narrative of the image must follow its source directly and fails to give the necessary attention to detail in the painting, which, as proven earlier, is critical in understanding the narrative of the image itself. The second option then, and the one that will be discussed here, is that the subject of the painting is the use of cloth throughout the composition. The cloth is not only the visual central point of the work but presents a physicality that provides multiple insights to Finoglio's narrative. For example, in every instance, the cloth is heavily folded, which contrasts strongly with the smoothness of the exposed skin of the figures.

According to Riccardo Lattuada, the confusion in the attribution of this panting first to Artemisia Gentileschi and now to Paolo Finoglio occurs precisely because of Finoglio's adept skill in describing textiles in minute detail.[41] He states, "This kind of mutual borrowing can be found in images of female figures, inspired by the stole models that enjoyed success in seventeenth-century Naples."[42] He further comments that the frontality of the figure in the protagonist's arrogant

---

41. Lattuada, "Artemisia and Naples," 384.

42. Ibid., 387.

expression, as well as in the execution of the rich and satiny material with its artfully arranged folds, is typical of Finoglio.[43]

The cloth makes up the sheets, the clothes, and the background of the image. It physically joins the two characters through their clutch of Joseph's cloak. Cloth also associates Potiphar's wife with temptation as the drapery cloth of her dress reveals her bare breast and thigh while merging seamlessly with the sheets on the bed. The cloth flows throughout the image, distinguishable only by the different colors Finoglio chooses for each garment. The cloth hangs and possesses a large number of folds throughout the image, making it appear to be heavy and present in some areas and seductively revealing in others. The cloth dominates the forms of the figures, which suggests the potential outcomes. The qualities of the cloth foreshadow Joseph's condemnation as it weighs on him literally and figuratively. The fact that Finoglio elects to make cloth the subject rather than the characters does not compromise the success of his narrative picture. This choice should be viewed as necessary since he is working within the confines of a specific moment. In fact, if Potiphar's wife and Joseph were the subjects of the painting, the painting would simply become a depiction of a scene within a multipart story and would fail to have the dramatic qualities and narrative focus that it displays now. By choosing the cloth as the subject of the painting, Finoglio creates a narrative that can be understood even without prior knowledge of the biblical account on which it was based.

Tenebrist Lighting, Beauty, and Figural Gesture

Another important element of Finoglio's painting is the lighting. The contrast of dark and light through the use of shadows was popular in the Baroque period and is used in this painting to convey meaning to the viewer. The use of tenebrism creates a dramatic spotlight effect on select parts of the painting. The brightest part of the image is the arm of Potiphar's wife, which is being used to grab Joseph's cloak. Coupled with the whiteness of the sheets and her dress, the light represents what could be, should Joseph succumb to her temptation. Her right breast and right thigh are seductively revealed in this intentionally bright part of the painting. In contrast, the shadow and

---

43. Ibid.

darkness represent where Joseph hopes to retreat, literally and figuratively out of sight and out of mind of Potiphar's wife. Perhaps the most definitive contrast in lighting is between his right foot and his left foot. Each foot is what is known as a "Greek foot," meaning the second toe is longer than the big toe. This was believed by the Greeks to be aesthetically pleasing and perhaps was related to the Golden Ratio.[44] The Greek foot is present in the *Venus de Milo* from the early second century BCE. It was copied by the Romans and throughout history as evidenced in such works as Michelangelo's *David* (1504) and Bartholdi and Eiffel's *Statue of Liberty* (1876). This feature contributes to Joseph's beauty and desirability. Although Joseph has not been one of his major publication interests, Samuel E. Balentine does comment on Joseph's wisdom as a chaste young male who refuses the advances of Potiphar's wife.[45]

The right foot is the only part of Joseph that is in the same vertical plane as Potiphar's wife. As a result, it is the most illuminated. A diagonal shadow connects Joseph's right foot to his left foot, which, by contrast, is the part of his body farthest away from the female figure and the closest to escaping. It is also placed in the darkest parts of the painting. While there is a clear struggle happening between Potiphar's wife and Joseph in the upper body of each figure, there is an equal struggle personally for Joseph in the lower half of his body as he battles the sexual desire she presents him with. The positioning of Joseph's right leg and its proximity to her naked thigh extending out over the cloth of the sheets intensifies the sexual tension between the two of them. Specifically, the nakedness of each figure's leg and the closeness of those limbs to each other works in conjunction with the surrounding cloth to create a diamond shape connecting several of the themes mentioned earlier. The curtains are pulled up, but they reveal only darkness, so the scene is refocused on the sheets and the figures every time the viewer's eye wanders into the background.

A third important element of the work is the facial expressions of the characters. By studying each character's expression, conclusions

---

44. For more on the Greek toe, see J. Park Harrison, "On the Relative Length of the First Three Toes on the Human Foot," *The Journal of the Archaeological Institute of Great Britain and Ireland* 13 (1884): 258–69.

45. Samuel E. Balentine, *Job*, SHBC (Macon, GA: Smyth & Helwys, 2006), 521.

can be drawn about the power dynamic between the two, their feelings about the current situation, as well as future consequences based on how the current struggle develops. Potiphar's wife's face appears seductive yet calm. It is not the expression she would have if she were truly struggling to seize Joseph's cloak. Rather, she understands the situation and power she possesses. Her lips are slightly separated as she may be surprised that Joseph resists her, since she has the ability to inflict consequences on Joseph if he does not act according to her wishes. Potiphar's wife's eyes give off the feeling of slight disappointment, yet she is not distressed by his resistance. This again confirms that she knows she has the upper hand in the situation.

Joseph's facial expression is also worthy of discussion. He does not appear to be struggling particularly hard to get the cloth back. Joseph seems to know there will be negative consequences regardless of his choice, thus his face reveals a kind of disappointment that he has found himself in such a situation. Joseph seems more focused on the larger problem that such a situation could occur so easily, and he is not focused on escaping the woman's grasp. The facial expressions give a feeling of resolve and the sense that this is a situation that occurred often between the wife of a powerful man and his slave or servant. Neither figure is particularly alarmed at what is happening, and we return to the instance at hand and what the potential resulting consequences may be. The subjects' facial expressions greatly help determine the narrative for Finoglio. If he focused solely on the present action and the faces represented only the struggle for the cloak, the image would be a scene from a story. But because there is such complexity and insight into the thoughts of these figures, a narrative can be constructed while the scene remains recognizable.

A final detail of the painting that also should be analyzed is the body language of the characters. Much like what is revealed in the faces, the body language presents the viewer with a narrative, not just a scene. Like the conclusion drawn from the expressions, there is little physical struggle between the characters. Presumably Potiphar's wife grabbed Joseph's cloak as he began his retreat, yet her grip on the cloak is loose since her fingers are not clenched. It is also important that Joseph turns around to grab the cloak with both hands. He is certainly much stronger than the woman, and it would be more effective for him to use the full weight of his body generated from the momentum of leaving to escape with his back to her. Instead, he makes an about face to pull the cloak. It is likely he is turning back around to further contemplate his choice or, perhaps, to glance at the beauty of the flesh revealed by the cloth of the sheet. The advances of a powerful man's wife would have been a strong temptation, especially given the potential punishment he may receive by resisting. Joseph places his weight on the left side of his body, which appears to be more of a passive position of resistance than if he had been depicted turned with his back towards her. It is as if he hopes she will be the one to make the conscious choice to drop his cloak rather than allowing the decision to be determined by him. This goes back to the power dynamic and Joseph's hope that Potiphar's wife will no longer desire him sexually, since then there may be no consequences for his resistance.

To assist in our dating, we consider Finoglio's *Christ and the Adulterous Woman* ca. 1634 (Fig. 5.5).[46] Although at 4x5 feet, the painting is not as monumental as *Joseph and Potiphar's Wife* (7.6x6.4 feet), it exhibits similar compositional characteristics such as the importance of the drapery in telling the story, the tenebrist light, and the implications that can be drawn between the central two figures resulting from color and body position. All of the figures, in both pictures, are positioned in the foreground with a black background to accentuate the activity before us. The characters behind Christ and the woman are not only in a black space with varying forms of headdress but also wear darker clothing, which is a strong contrast to the rose, white, and golden drapery chosen for the two primary figures of the narrative. These similar colors worn by the "good" protagonists, devoid of head covering, contrast with the figures left in the shadows who are judging the adulterous woman. In *Joseph and Potiphar's Wife*, Finoglio uses the contrasting colors of the white surrounding the wife and the darker tunic of Joseph to create opposition and tension between them. The central area behind them is black, and they are forced into a shared space constructed by the dark curtain of the canopy positioned above and to their sides. Although the drapery in

---

46. Brizia Minerva, "Paolo Finoglio, *Cristo e l'adultera*," in *Artemisia Gentileschi e il Suo Tempo*, 250; Lanzilotta and Lofano, *Paolo Finoglio e il Suo Seguito*, 68; Cassani and Sapi, *Paolo Finoglio e il Suo Tempo*, 99, 151.

Figure 5.5. Paolo Finoglio, *Christ and the Adulterous Woman*, ca. 1634. Oil on canvas. 120 x 149 cm. Museo Provinciale Sigismondo, Lecce. Photo Credit: Public Domain.

both *Joseph and Potiphar's Wife* and *Christ and the Adulterous Woman* functions as clothing, it is also the indicator of space in an otherwise flat composition. There is not a defined background, so the wrinkles and placement of cloth create dimensionality in both pictures.

In *Christ and the Adulterous Woman*, the tenebrist light illuminates the left portion of the face and clothing of both the woman and Christ. The position of their heads is identical, but Christ raises his right hand with open palm and leads our gaze towards the woman. The drapery hanging from Christ's right arm exaggerates this gesture, while the exposed neckline of the woman reveals her soft, white skin. The exposed skin of the neck and hands of the woman are closest to the hand of Christ. In *Joseph and Potiphar's Wife*, it is the legs that we notice through the tenebrist spotlighting effect. They are nearest to each other, creating a sexual tension between the protagonists rather than the calming, blessing gesture of Christ towards the adulterous woman. In a gesture of acceptance, the eyes and head of the woman are lowered towards her clasped hands as she receives Christ's blessing amid all the turmoil. In contrast, the two hands of Joseph and the left hand of the wife pull the cloth between them, causing both bodies to tighten, and emphasize the opposition between them. This struggle with the cloth forces the wife to steady her weight with her opposite hand, resulting in the revealing of her intensely lit right breast as her white undergarment falls off her shoulder. Her right thigh is also exposed as it bends outwards towards the viewer, casting a shadow on the bedsheet between her and the right leg of Joseph. This brings the viewer's eye back to Joseph's bare leg (and aesthetically pleasing Greek foot), and the circular momentum begins again for the viewer, only this time with heightened sensuality.

Popularity of the Subject and the Prominence of the Cloth

Depictions of Joseph and Potiphar's wife throughout the Renaissance and Baroque, both in Italy and north of the Alps, frequently rely on the placement of the cloth to tell the story. Although this occurs in painting, the most popular medium of exchanging ideas at this time was through the circulation of the reproductive print.[47] The subject appears in both the reproductive print collections of Marcantonio Raimondi (1480–1534), a Renaissance engraver (and assistant to Raphael) who made prints copying paintings by his contemporaries, and the *Illustrated Bartsch*, a nineteenth-century collection of prints utilized as sources for European Old Master painters from 1400–1850 compiled by Adam von Bartsch.[48] The *Illustrated Bartsch* includes the etching by Bartolomeo Passarotti (1529–1592) after the 1550 drawing by Taddeo Zuccaro (1529–1566).[49] Zuccaro's *Joseph and Potiphar's Wife* (Fig. 5.6) is a pen and brown ink with brown wash that is in the Metropolitan Museum of Art today.

Joseph and Potiphar's wife maintain varied stages of both being fully clothed as in the work of Raphael, as copied by Marcantonio Raimondi (Fig. 5.7), to both depicted completely nude (Fig. 5.8) by the German engraver Sebald Beham (1500–1550). There are also varying stages of aggression depicted in the gestures of both protagonists. They range from playful, almost conversational versions as seen in the 1610 oil on canvas by Ludovico Cigoli (1559–1613) to

---

47. A more extensive study of the subject of Joseph and Potiphar's wife as depicted in Renaissance and Baroque paintings, drawings and prints is in a forthcoming publication.

48. For more information on the *Illustrated Bartsch*, see https://www.artstor.org/collection/illustrated-bartsch/.

49. For the Passarotti etching, see Babette Bohn, "Passarotti and Reproductive Etching in Sixteenth-Century Italy," *Print Quarterly* 5/2 (June 1988): 117.

extremely volatile confrontations as in the Taddeo Zuccaro drawing (see Fig. 5.6).[50] The Zuccaro is one of the most aggressive in movement of the various types, and the wife wraps her arms around Joseph to rip the tunic off his back. In all of these versions, the drapery has a role in telling the story conveyed through its placement, length, thickness, shape, texture, and, in the case of paintings, how it is lit and its color.

There are a number of points that distinguish Finoglio's work as a multidimensional narrative rather than simply a single scene. The use of scene selection makes the work recognizable and opens up the potential for a narrative. This is shared with many of the other examples illustrated here. But the prominence of cloth provides an alternative subject that allows for a deeper exploration of the themes of the story present in this image as well as others. In the Finoglio, the dramatic light accentuates the diverse roles of, and interaction between, the two characters, while the facial expressions and body language provide the viewer with an entrée into the cultural commonality of such a scene at this time. It also offers insight into the thoughts and conflicts of each of the characters at the moment of this confrontation. Despite what may have been thought of as a constraint or limitation to creating a narrative with only the ability to capture one moment, Finoglio actually proves to be effective in conveying a narrative both to viewers who understand the story from Genesis and to those who are encountering the scene for the first time through this painting.

---

50. Cigoli's *Joseph and Potiphar's Wife*, located in the Galleria Borghese in Rome, can be viewed on the Web Gallery of Art at https://www.wga.hu/html_m/c/cigoli/joseph_p.html.

Figure 5.6. Taddeo Zuccaro, *Joseph and Potiphar's Wife*, ca. 1550. Pen and brown ink, brush and brown wash, heightened with white gouache over traces of black chalk, on blue paper. 13.2 x 11.2 cm. Metropolitan Museum of Art, New York. Bequest of John and Alice Steiner, 2003. Photo Credit: Public Domain.

Figure 5.7. Marcantonio Raimondi (after Raphael), *Joseph Fleeing from Potiphar's Wife*, ca. 1515–1525. Engraving. 20.7 x 124.1 cm. Metropolitan Museum of Art, New York, Harris Brisbane Dick Fund, 1941. Photo Credit: Public Domain.

Figure 5.8. Sebald Beham, *Joseph and Potiphar's Wife*, 1544. Engraving. 8.1 x 5.6 cm. National Gallery of Art, Washington, D.C., Rosenwald Collection. Photo Credit: NGA Images Open Access.

Bibliography

Baldassari, Francesca, ed. *Artemisia Gentileschi e il Suo Tempo.* Milan: Skira Editore, 2016. Published in conjunction with the exhibition shown at the Palazzo Braschi in Rome from 30 Nov 2016–7 May 2017.

Balentine, Samuel E. *Job.* SHBC. Macon, GA: Smyth & Helwys, 2006.

Bissell, R. Ward. *Artemisia Gentileschi and the Authority of Art: Critical Reading and Catalogue Raisonné.* University Park, PA: Pennsylvania State University Press, 1999.

Bohn, Babette. "Passarotti and Reproductive Etching in Sixteenth-Century Italy." *Print Quarterly* 5/2 (June 1988): 115–27.

Bologna, Ferdinando. *Battistello Caracciolo e il Primo Naturalismo a Napoli.* Naples: Electa, 1991.

Bowron, Edgar Peters. *European Paintings Before 1900 in the Fogg Art Museum: A Summary Catalogue including Paintings in the Busch-Reisinger Museum.* Cambridge, MA: Harvard University Art Museums, 1990.

Cassani, Silvia, and Maria Sapio, eds. *Caravaggio: The Final Years.* Naples: Electa, 2005. Published in conjunction with the exhibition shown at The National Gallery in London from 23 Feb–22 May 2005.

——, eds. *Paolo Finoglio e il Suo Tempo: Un Pittore Napoletano alle Corte degli Aquaviva.* Naples: Electa, 2000.

Causa, Stefano. "Gli Amici Nordici del Caravaggio a Napoli." *Prospettiva* 93/94 (Jan–April 1999): 142–57.

Christiansen, Keith, and Judith Mann, eds. *Orazio and Artemisia Gentileschi, Father and Daughter Painters in Baroque Italy.* New Haven: Yale University Press, 2001. Published in conjunction with the exhibition shown at the Museo del Palazzo Venezia in Rome, the Metropolitan Museum of Art in New York, and the St. Louis Art Museum.

Contini, Roberto, and Gianni Papi. *Artemisia*. Rome: Leonardo-De Luca Editori, 1991.

Director's Report (Harvard University Art Museums) (1990–1991): 34–37.

Freedberg, Sydney J. "Lorenzo Lotto to Nicolas Poussin." *Apollo* 107/195 (May 1978): 389–97.

Garrard, Mary D. *Artemisia Gentileschi: The Image of the Female Hero in Italian Baroque Art.* Princeton: Princeton University Press, 1989.

Gregori, Mina. *70 Pitture e Sculture del '600 e '700 Fiorentino.* Florence: Officine Grafiche Vallecchi, 1965.

Harrison, J. Park. "On the Relative Length of the First Three Toes on the Human Foot." *The Journal of the Archaeological Institute of Great Britain and Ireland* 13 (1884): 258–69.

Lanzilotta, Giacomo, and Francesco Lofano, eds. *Paolo Finoglio e il Suo Seguito: Pittori a Conversano nei Decenni Centrali dei Seicento.* Galatina: Congedo, 2012. Published in conjunction with the exhibition shown at the Pinacoteca Comunale in Conversano from 8 Sept–28 Oct 2012.

Lattuada, Riccardo. "Finoglia [Finoglio], Paolo Domenico." *Grove Art Online.* Oxford: Oxford University Press, 2003.

López, Mercedes Simal. "Nuevas noticias sobre las pinturas para el Real Palacio del Buen Retiro realizadas en Italia (1633–1642)." *Archivio Espanol* 84/335 (July–September 2011): 245–60.

Mortimer, Kristin A., and William G. Klingelhofer. *Harvard University Art Museums: A Guide to the Collections.* Cambridge: Harvard University Art Museums; New York: Abbeville Press, 1986.

Paolo Finoglia, *Joseph and Potiphar's Wife*, Harvard Art Museums, https://www.harvardartmuseums.org/art/228639.

Shapley, Fern Rusk. *Paintings from the Samuel H. Kress Collection, Italian Schools XVI–XVIII Century.* London: Phaidon, 1966.

Spinosa, Nicola. *La Pittura Napolentana del '600.* Milan: Longanesi, 1984.

Tapié, Alain, and Alain Fleischer, eds. *Paolo Domenico Finoglio: La Jérusalem Délivrée.* Paris: Somogy, 2010. Published in conjunction with the exhibition shown at the Palais des Beaux-Arts in Lille.

Úbeda de los Cobos, Andrés, ed., *Paintings for the Planet King: Philip IV and the Buen Retiro Palace.* Madrid: Museo Nacional del Prado; London: Paul Holberton, 2005. Published in conjunction with the exhibition shown at the Museo Nacional del Prado in Madrid from 6 July–27 Nov 2005.

Waschek, Matthias, Marjorie B. Cohn, Judith Mann, and Stephan Wolohojian. *Ideal [Dis-]Placements: Old Masters at the Pulitzer.* St. Louis: Pulitzer Arts Foundation, 2008.

Part II

Wisdom's Depths

Practicality in a World of Hubris[1]

Walter Brueggemann

It is a privilege to join in a vigorous salute to Sam Balentine, surely the most generative scholar in our field in his generation. I am glad to count Sam as a friend and mentor and to celebrate his penetrating honesty in dealing with the text.

In what follows I take up the elusive question of Job 28:12, "Where shall wisdom be found?"[2] My discussion of the question, however, requires a bit of gerrymandering, because the texts on which I focus here (and have focused more generally) do not match up with those that have preoccupied Sam. For that reason, I take up the question of Job 28:12, richly informed by Sam's work, to see how the question plays out in the books of Kings.

I.

Balentine's "Connections" on Job 28 conclude with open-ended questions and a final question mark, in a recognition that the text allows no simple resolution.[3] Along the way, Balentine enunciates two principles in response to Job's question from which I take my

---

1. I am greatly indebted to Davis Hankins, who helped me to complete this paper.

2. The translations in this essay are from the NRSV unless otherwise noted.

3. Samuel E. Balentine, *Job*, SHBC (Macon, GA: Smyth & Helwys, 2006), 429–35.

lead. First, quoting Paul Fiddes's insight, "the wisdom God possesses . . . is of a completely practical sort," Balentine concludes, "Both God and humans plot their course, focus their objectives, and use their capacities in practical—not theoretical—ways."[4] We will be on the lookout for *practical wisdom* in the books of Kings.

Second, Balentine notes with reference to the King of Tyre in Ezekiel 28 that "the king is corrupted by his acquisitions, and like them [the first couple] he is driven from God's presence (vv. 16–18). There is then a significant biblical tradition that affirms that hubris, specifically in terms of the acquisition and corruption of wisdom, is a form of rebellion against God that leads to alienation and judgment."[5] Balentine comments on this sorry scenario: "If the objective is selfish, if humans seek wisdom in order to subvert God's creational design or to supplant God as Creator, then they can expect to be thwarted and judged."[6] Then, in the next sentence, in a return to an accent on the practical, Balentine ends with a wonderment: "But what if humans seek only after that which God has offered? What if their quest is only for the 'righteousness and justice' that God promises to those who are 'upright' and 'blameless' (Prov 2:7; cf. 2:9)?"[7] Balentine leaves that an open question with at least the possibility that, to those who do "righteousness and justice," the matter is different than to those who act corruptly in hubris. In what follows, I will appeal to Balentine's principles of *hubris and practicality* in an approach to the books of Kings, in order to see if the books of Kings consist in an epistemological struggle between those who use "wisdom" for quite different ends, a struggle that, according to the theological perspective of the books of Kings, is definitional for the character and future of Israel. And we may say, a struggle that is definitional today for the viability and future of the human community as it lives amid the fragility of God's creation. Here then is my question: What if the books of Kings constitute a response to the question of Job 28:12, "Where shall wisdom be found?"

---

4. Ibid., 431.

5. Ibid., 432.

6. Ibid.

7. Ibid.

II.

Given that the books of Kings present a theological exposition of the dynastic line of David in Jerusalem, our first candidate as possessor of wisdom is the long line of kings who presided over the Jerusalem establishment. These kings are surrounded by an entourage of scribes and sages, and they have access to all the best learning and whatever there was of the generation of new knowledge (cf. Prov 25:1). As with every major concentration of power, these kings want to claim that they know most and best. At the outset of this royal narrative, moreover, is Solomon who in his great success is presented as a champion of wisdom. This is evident in his passion for collecting wisdom (1 Kgs 4:29-34): "People came from all the nations to hear the wisdom of Solomon; they came from all the kings of the earth who had heard of his wisdom" (v. 34). The narrative of 1 Kgs 3:16-28, moreover, ends with a formula of amazement: "All Israel heard of the judgment that the king had rendered; and they stood in awe of the king, because they perceived that the wisdom of God was in him, to execute justice" (v. 28).[8] In a summary statement, Solomon's wealth is linked to his wisdom:

> Thus King Solomon excelled all the kings of the earth in riches and in wisdom. The whole earth sought the presence of Solomon to hear his wisdom, which God had put into his mind. Every one of them brought a present, objects of silver and gold, garments, weaponry, spices, horses, and mules, so much year by year. (1 Kgs 10:23-25)

It has been usual, in pious interpretation, to take this trajectory of Solomon's wisdom at face value. I have proposed, however, that the Solomonic narrative in Kings is to be read ironically, thus casting the king's "golden" reputation in doubt and suggesting rather that this narrator-interpreter intended not to celebrate Solomon but to expose him in his self-deception and hubris.[9] We may notice specifically four matters in the narrative of Solomon's wisdom that invite ironic

---

8. Cf. 1 Kgs 5:12; 10:4-8; 11:41.

9. Walter Brueggemann, *Solomon: Israel's Ironic Icon of Human Achievement* (Columbia: University of South Carolina Press, 2005).

awareness. First, the grandiose temple of Solomon was premised on the assumption that Solomon could capture YHWH's presence in the temple to perpetuity as an assured patron of his regime (1 Kgs 8:23-53). Already in the narrative of dedication, however, we are otherwise on notice. In 1 Kgs 8:9 it is observed that the ark of presence is empty. In 1 Kgs 8:27 it is recognized that even this splendid house cannot box in the glory of God. Guaranteed temple presence is a royal illusion.

Second, Solomon's splendid capitol and grandiose temple depended on tax revenue for which the king devised an elaborate tax-collecting apparatus (1 Kgs 4:7-19). The enterprise was so lucrative that two of the king's sons-in-law (Ben-abinadab and Ahimaaz) presided over tax districts (1 Kgs 4:11, 15). The king's capacity to maintain such an exploitative system that provided surplus wealth for the economic elite at the expense of subsistence peasants, however, is given the lie in the narrative of 1 Kgs 12:1-19.[10] Solomon's son, Rehoboam, is even more foolish than his father. The assumption that such wealth "happily" funded the royal city was false.[11]

Third, Solomon's propensity for the collection of horses, chariots, gold, proverbs, and wives seemed limitless (1 Kgs 10:14-25). There was no impediment to his limitless accumulation; yet the ominous conclusion of 1 Kgs 11 reports that Solomon's aggressive collection of wives and concubines did him in:

> Among his wives were seven hundred princesses and three hundred concubines; and his wives turned away his heart. For when Solomon was old, his wives turned away his heart after other gods; and his heart was not true to the LORD his God, as was the heart of his father David. (vv. 3-4)

But, of course, these many women were not any exception to his regime of acquisition. They were a part of the fabric and exhibit

---

10. Roland Boer, *The Sacred Economy of Ancient Israel* (Louisville: Westminster John Knox, 2015) has fully characterized the system of extraction over which one such as Solomon presided. On pp. 202–203 he nicely identifies the ruling class in that economy as "non-producing" who maintain their extravagant life by economic extraction.

11. Cf. 1 Kgs 10:8 on the "happy ones."

of his accumulation that had long since transcended the old-fashioned limits of the Torah. The narrator can see that the collection of wives is a Torah violation: "King Solomon loved many foreign women . . . concerning which the LORD had said to the Israelites, 'You shall not enter into marriage with them, neither shall they with you; for they will surely incline your heart to follow their gods'" (1 Kgs 11:1-2). Thus Torah looms over the splendor of Solomon in his acquisitiveness. In like manner his accumulation and the propulsion of entitlement violated Torah and could not stand (cf. Deut 17:14-20). It turns out that Solomon's wisdom was in fact a long-running, sustained act of foolishness.

Thus in the remembered teaching of Jesus in the Gospel of Luke (in one of only two mentions of Solomon by Jesus) we are offered a discerning measurement of Solomon: "Consider the lilies, how they grow: they neither toil nor spin; yet I tell you, even Solomon in all his glory was not clothed like one of these" (Luke 12:27). In the foregoing parable in Luke 12:13-21, the great accumulator who is so eagerly successful is, in the end, termed a fool who brings destruction on himself (v. 20). Because of the subsequent mention of Solomon, it is not much of a stretch to conclude that the fool in the parable is none other than Solomon, whose wisdom turns out to be lethally foolish.

Fourth, the king's capacity for self-sufficiency and autonomy is vigorously and pervasively challenged in the narrative of Kings. In what I have termed "the Deuteronomic proviso," the narrative forcefully reiterates the conditionality of the Torah:[12]

> *If* you will walk in my ways, keeping my statutes and my commandments as your father David walked, then I will lengthen your life. (1 Kgs 3:14)
>
> *If* you will walk in my statutes, obey my ordinances, and keep all my commandments by walking in them, then I will establish my promise with you, which I made to your father David. (1 Kgs 6:12)

---

12. Brueggemann, *Solomon*, 139–59.

And then more fully:

> *If* you walk before me, as David your father walked, with integrity of heart and uprightness, doing according to all that I have commanded you, and keeping my statutes and my ordinances, then I will establish your royal throne over Israel forever, as I promised your father David. . . . *If* you turn aside from following me, you or your children, and do not keep my commandments and my statutes that I have set before you, but go and serve other gods and worship them, then I will cut Israel off from the land that I have given them. (1 Kgs 9:4-7)

The reiterated "if" of Torah collides with the self-sufficiency of royal wisdom and the assurance that royal wisdom guaranteed limitless acquisition and security; such wisdom is an illusion that will, perforce, end in disaster.

The long line of kings that follow Solomon in Jerusalem in the books of Kings are variously successful and variously committed to Solomon's practice of avarice and acquisitiveness. Given the recurring strictures of the prophets against the regime and its elite support, there is no good reason to assume that the royal house would have, in any effective way, departed from the vision of autonomy, self-sufficiency, and acquisitiveness that we see grounded in royal ideology and its companion, hubris. That ideology of hubris evidently eliminated the old "if" of Torah conditionality. Thus the long run of the dynasty is *a history of hubris* that could claim godly legitimacy. Such practice is, in the eyes of these narrators, a consummate act of foolishness.

The single unmistakable exception to this long run of hubris is King Josiah (2 Kgs 22–23).[13] As King Josiah is narrated, we are told, "When the king heard the words of the book of the law, he tore his clothes" (2 Kgs 22:11). This is not the response of a hubristic king who thinks he needs to answer to no transcendent authority. Rather this king (a quite exceptional king in his dynasty!) is responsive to the teaching of the scroll:

---

13. Josiah's grandfather, Hezekiah, is a near exception as well, except that the narrative of the reign of Hezekiah ends with some accommodating compromise (2 Kgs 18–20).

> Go, inquire of the LORD for me, for the people, and for all Judah, concerning the words of this book that has been found; for great is the wrath of the LORD that is kindled against us, because our ancestors did not obey the words of this book, to do according to all that is written concerning us. (2 Kgs 22:13)

Because of his responsiveness, Josiah is regarded by the prophet Huldah as peculiarly favored by YHWH:

> Because your heart was penitent, and you humbled yourself before the LORD, when you heard how I spoke against this place, and against its inhabitants, that they should become a desolation and a curse, and because you have torn your clothes and wept before me, I also have heard you, says the LORD. Therefore, I will gather you to your ancestors, and you shall be gathered to your grave in peace; your eyes shall not see all the disaster that I will bring on this place. (2 Kgs 22:19-20)

The subsequent report that the king was killed in battle does not detract from this quite peculiar prophetic approbation of the king (2 Kgs 23:28-30). Josiah apparently did not participate in the recurring hubristic practices of acquisitiveness and self-sufficiency so characteristic of his royal family.

This testimony in the royal narrative is seconded, remarkably, by the prophet Jeremiah who contrasts Josiah with his son, Jehoiakim, who promptly returned to the "normalcy" of acquisitive exploitation. In Jer 22:13-19 Jehoiakim is condemned by the prophet for his grandiose self-exhibit that is made possible by the exploitation of his workers.[14] By contrast "your father" (Josiah) did exactly the opposite:

> Woe to him who builds his house by unrighteousness,
> and his upper rooms by injustice;
> who makes his neighbors work for nothing,
> and does not give them their wages;

---

14. The contrast between Josiah and Jehoiakim is further explicated by the report that while Josiah "tore his clothes" in an act of penitence (2 Kgs 22:11), Jehoiakim tore the scroll when it was read to him in an act of defiance (Jer 36:23). The use of the same term suggests an intentional contrast in the two reports.

> who says, "I will build myself a spacious house
> with large upper rooms,"
> and who cuts out windows for it,
> paneling it with cedar,
> and painting it with vermillion.
> Are you a king because you compete in cedar? . . .
> But your eyes and heart are only on your dishonest gain,
> for shedding innocent blood,
> and for practicing oppression and violence. (Jer 22:13-15, 17)

Surely such foolishness will come to a bad end:

> Therefore thus says the LORD concerning King Jehoiakim son of Josiah of Judah:
> They shall not lament for him, saying,
> "Alas, my brother!" or "Alas, sister!"
> They shall not lament for him, saying,
> "Alas, lord!" or "Alas, his majesty!"
> With the burial of a donkey he shall be buried—
> dragged off and thrown out beyond the gates of Jerusalem. (Jer 22:18-19)

By contrast "your father" (Josiah) did exactly the opposite:

> Did not your father eat and drink
> and do justice and righteousness?
> Then it was well with him.
> He judged the cause of the poor and needy;
> then it was well.
> Is not this to know me? says the LORD. (Jer 22:15-16)

By his care for the "poor and needy," Josiah did exactly "justice and righteousness," the very marks that Balentine singles out as ordinary conduct of the "upright and blameless." An inference that may be drawn is that Josiah, unlike the rest of his dynasty, was indeed a carrier of wisdom.

Balentine wonders, "What if their quest is only for the 'righteousness and justice' that God promises to those who are 'upright and blameless?'"[15] Nowhere is it said that Josiah is "wise" or possesses wisdom. It is affirmed, however, that his practice toward the poor and needy was "to know me," that is, to know YHWH. Without the word "wisdom," this verdict concerning Josiah could intend to assign wisdom to him that begins in "the fear of the Lord."

This remarkable king, however, is a glaring exception to the royal history of hubris. Thus we may indeed conclude, in response to Job's question, that wisdom is not to be found in royal environs, much as the royal placeholders could pretend. But the kings are surely remembered as those in Israel who boast of wisdom, might, and wealth, although they neglected that in which YHWH delights ("steadfast love, justice, and righteousness") (Jer 9:23-24 [MT 9:22-23]). We must look elsewhere to see where wisdom might be found in the books of Kings.

III.

When we seek alternative candidates as carriers of wisdom in the books of Kings, we inescapably turn to Elijah and Elisha, the central characters in the prophetic narratives of 1 Kgs 17–2 Kgs 9.[16] This extended narrative decisively interrupts the royal narrative and attests to a very different social reality that features the practice of a very different epistemology. In this prophetic narrative, the kings of Israel appear hardly at all, being portrayed as impotent and irrelevant to the ongoing life of society.[17] Thus,

- In 2 Kgs 4:1-7 Elisha enacts resistance to the debt economy over which the king surely presides, and he performs an alternative act of well-being that emancipates the desperate widow from

---

15. Balentine, *Job*, 432.

16. Here I will limit my attention to four Elisha narratives that I have studied most closely, but the same general case can readily be made for all the narratives of the two prophets.

17. Walter Brueggemann and Davis Hankins, "The Affirmation of Prophetic Power and Deconstruction of Royal Authority in the Elisha Narratives," *CBQ* 76 (2014): 58–76.

her menacing creditors. The king does not appear but surely stands behind the creditor.[18]

• In 2 Kgs 5:1-27 Elisha sees to the healing of the Syrian leprous general and insists that the healing requires no co-pay. The (unnamed) king of Israel, by contrast, is incapable of making any effective response to the reality of leprosy: "Am I God, to give death or life, that this man sends word to me to cure a man of his leprosy?" (v. 7).

• In 2 Kgs 6:8-23 Elisha manages to end the military hostility between Syria and Israel, so that "the Arameans no longer came raiding into the land of Israel" (v. 23). The (unnamed) king of Israel, by contrast, has no clue about peacemaking and only wants to escalate hostility by a counter-act of violence. He does not know "the things that make for peace" (Luke 19:42).

• In 2 Kgs 6:24–7:20 the (unnamed) king of Israel is helpless in the face of famine. He recognizes his own incapacity and voices a dismissive appeal to deliverance by God: "No! Let the LORD help you. How can I help you? From the threshing floor or from the wine press?" (6:27).

It seems clear enough that the narrative quite intentionally portrays the absent or unnamed kings of Israel as an irrelevance to the practical needs of society. These narratives function, with reference to the kings, as a deliberate deconstruction and exposé of royal power and imply that real power for life can only be found elsewhere.[19] And of course the "elsewhere" of real social transformation is located in the person of Elisha, who owes nothing to royal claims.

Thus in turn we are able to watch as Elisha commits, one after another, restorative acts that are beyond royal administration:

---

18. For an exposition of the extraction system over which the king presided in such societies see Douglas E. Oakman, *Jesus and the Peasants* (Eugene, OR: Wipf & Stock, 2008), and idem., *Jesus, Debt, and the Lord's Prayer: First Century Debt and Jesus' Intentions* (Eugene, OR: Wipf & Stock, 2014). While Oakman focuses on the later system of Rome, the general pattern of exploitation recurs.

19. In my earlier exposition of these narratives, *Testimony to Otherwise: The Witness of Elijah and Elisha* (St. Louis: Chalice, 2001), I have used the term "otherwise" instead of "elsewhere." The point is the same.

- In 2 Kgs 4:1-7 Elisha inexplicably causes the needy widow to receive extravagant amounts of olive oil so that she can return to a viable life. His performance in this episode is without comment or explanation. We are not told that he did anything identifiable, but the oil was ample.
- In 2 Kgs 5:1-27 Elisha's enactment of the healing is simple, dispatching the mighty general to the modest Jordan River: "Go, wash in the Jordan seven times, and your flesh shall be restored and you shall be clean" (v. 10). The remainder of the narrative affirms that Elisha is a master of leprosy so that he is able to reassign it to the predatory Gehazi (v. 27).
- In 2 Kgs 6:8-23 we see that Elisha is a powerful man of prayer: "Then Elisha prayed: 'O LORD, please open his eyes that he may see.' . . . Elisha prayed to the LORD, and said, 'Strike this people, please, with blindness.' . . . Elisha said, 'O LORD, open the eyes of these men so that they may see'" (vv. 17, 18, 20). These events are without comment. But the decisive act of Elisha that evokes the end of hostility is a more mundane, practical act: "Set food and water before them so that they may eat and drink; and let them go to their master" (v. 22). Elisha, in response to the (unnamed) king of Israel, refuses the usual practice of "seeing like a state" to which the king is committed.[20]
- In 2 Kgs 6:24–7:20 the social crisis is that food is scarce and therefore too expensive for poor people to purchase. The means whereby food becomes plentiful enough at low prices so that poor people have access is the improbable "sound" (*qôl*) that frightens the Syrians and causes them to abandon their food supply. Elisha's role in this odd episode consists only in his refusal to give in to the royal economy of scarcity, and his anticipation of abundance soon to come: "Tomorrow about this time a measure of choice meal shall be sold for a shekel, and two measures of barley for a shekel, at the gate of Samaria" (7:1). He delivers a severe reprimand, moreover, to the royal official who doubts his anticipation: "You shall see it with your own eyes, but you shall not eat from it" (7:2). Elisha does not even reappear in the denouement of this narrative. The narrative simply

---

20. James C. Scott, *Seeing Like a State: How Certain Schemes to Improve the Human Condition Have Failed* (New Haven: Yale University Press, 1998).

reiterates Elisha's earlier anticipation and reprimand and shows how his anticipation worked itself out in actual practice. The end result is that the cynical royal officer could not engage the alternative reasoning of Elisha, reasoning that falls outside the capacity of royal rationality. The sum of these narratives surely left Israel, in its many retellings, filled with amazement that such gifts of life happened outside the royal regime.

IV.

Since our theme is wisdom, we may ask what kind of skill set Elisha exhibits. To be sure, there is something odd and inscrutable about Elisha's restorative actions; it is plausible, however, to think his actions are odd only when we "see like a state," and imagine that the world operates according to the rationality of the royals. But this prophetic narrative begins at a different place and remains insistently outside the rationality of the royal state. In an appeal to James C. Scott, I have proposed that Elisha refuses the technical competence of such a state, a competence here shown to be ineffective, and offers a very different reality.[21] To be sure, that alternative reason is firmly grounded in and authorized by appeal to "the word of the LORD." In its actual performance, however, we may notice that this alternative reason that has transformative capacity arises "from below," not from throne or temple. I have found Scott's characterization of *mētis* to be helpful in reading the Elisha narratives afresh: "*Mētis* is better understood as the kind of knowledge that can be acquired only by long practice at similar but rarely identical tasks, which require constant adaptation to changing circumstance."[22] This knowledge, unlike the technical mastery of the urban elites who surround the king, is "local," "partisan knowledge as opposed to generic knowledge," "plastic, local, and divergent":[23]

---

21. Walter Brueggemann, "Totalized *Techne* vs. Neighborly *Metis*," *Tenacious Solidarity: Biblical Provocations on Race, Religion, Climate, and the Economy*, ed. Davis Hankins (Minneapolis: Fortress, 2018), 3–28.

22. Scott, *Seeing Like a State*, 177.

23. Ibid., 318, 332.

It is in fact the idiosyncrasies of *mētis*, its contextualness, and its fragmentation that make it so permeable, so open to new ideas. *Mētis* has no doctrine or centralized training. . . . The big mistake of the rationalist . . . is to assume that "tradition," or what is called "practical knowledge," is rigid, fixed, and unchanging—in fact it is "preeminently fluid."[24]

Scott shows how "seeing like a state" seeks to erode and nullify the force of practical competence, that is, folk knowledge of how to manage the inscrutable aspects of lived reality. Thus it is my judgment that Elisha's art of transformation is *mētis*—local, partisan folk knowledge that defies the rationality of the throne, a rationality that seeks to overcome such folk capacity by the assertion of technique in a passion for scale, speed, and efficiency. Thus consider the following:

- In 2 Kgs 4:1-7 it is the mobilization of the neighborhood that is featured in the collection of oil; all the resources of the neighborhood are recruited for the rescue of the widow.
- In 2 Kgs 5:1-27 it is the appeal to "river healing" that transforms the general, even while it annoys him.
- In 2 Kgs 6:8-23 Elisha has the conviction that food generously given can counter hostility and break the cycle of alienation. There is nothing magical about this act except the magic of material generosity.
- In 2 Kgs 6:24–7:20 it is Elisha's conviction that royal scarcity could not prevail because the food-giving capacity of God's world would outlast royal parsimony in a resolve of abundance. This conviction about abundance is well voiced in the sketch of Della and Athey Keith offered by Wendell Berry: "They had about them a sort of intimation of abundance, as though, like magicians, they might suddenly fill the room with potatoes, onions turnips, summer squashes, and ears of corn drawn from their pockets. Their place had about it that quality of bottomless fecundity, its richness both in evidence and in reserve."[25] Elisha does a like "magic" of abundance.

---

24. Ibid., 332.

25. Wendell Berry, *Jayber Crow: A Novel* (Washington, D.C.: Counterpoint, 2000), 181.

None of this is to deny or resist the transcendent power of God attested in these acts of transformation. But when that transcendent power of transformation is specifically enacted and embodied amid state technique, it is carried through folk drama "from below" that works outside the agency of the state. My impression is that in our usual reading of these narratives, there is such accent on the transcendent "word of the Lord" that we fail to notice the practicality and effectiveness of ordinary folk practice.

Balentine will not be certain that God gives wisdom even to those who seek "only that which God has offered."[26] We can note, however, that Elisha is indeed occupied with the "righteousness and justice" that enhance the well-being of the community. But second, and more important for Balentine, is the fact that Elisha's work is eminently practical, concerned with daily life as it was lived by his vulnerable contemporaries: quoting Fiddes's argument that "the wisdom God possesses . . . is of a completely practical sort," Balentine concludes, "Both God and humans plot their course, focus their objectives, and use their capacities in practical—not theoretical—ways."[27] Thus,

- In 2 Kgs 4:1-7 Elisha saves the widow and her son from starvation by an abundance of oil.
- In 2 Kgs 5:1-27 Elisha engages in the bodily healing of the desperate Syrian general after the best "science" of the general's own regime could do nothing.
- In 2 Kgs 6:8-23 Elisha finds a practical way to interrupt a bloody conflict between perennial enemies.
- In 2 Kgs 6:24–7:20 Elisha's anticipation of abundance counters the regime of scarcity grounded in hubris.

What an inventory of practicality: oil, healing, end of war, and food!

The technique of absent or unnamed kings could do nothing in a practical way. The alternative that matters is God-given *mētis*. I suggest, at least provisionally, that we may answer Job's question: wisdom is to be found outside the precincts of power among those

---

26. Balentine, *Job*, 432.

27. Ibid., 431.

who live in hope and share the quotidian gifts of creation that are all around. It turns out that the prophetic narratives in the books of Kings are not only an *interruption* of the royal time line. They are an assertive *subversion* of royal claims that intends to bear witness to another way of being in the world that does not "see like a state," that does not reduce lived reality to rational control, and that does not rely too much on pedigreed time lines but finds resources for transformation amid the unadministered agents of social reality. It is no wonder that Elijah, an antecedent to Elisha, is termed by King Ahab "my enemy" (1 Kgs 21:20). These characters are the enemy of the state because they enact and exhibit the power for life that is well beyond the aegis of the regime. While the force of *technique* aims to displace the power of *mētis*, transformative power from below continues nonetheless to reappear. The Elisha narrative attests the staying power of such capacity in the face of the hubristic regime of technique.

V.

If this narrative *interruption and subversion* of the royal narrative is indeed an alternative in ancient Israel representing an alternative epistemology (how we know what we know), this alternative is an invitation for our own scholarly work. It may draw some of our energy away from our preoccupation with the "history that has been written by winners" with excessive focus on the claims of the royal state. It invites greater attention to the claims of peasant folk that operate with a very different rationality. This alternative, of course, is exactly what is happening in our discipline as our energy turns away from "historical criticism" that is reflective of imperial rationality to "social scientific" methods. Yet even our "social scientific" methods do not characteristically allow for *the inscrutable and transcendent* that operate in, with, and under the neighborhood.

It may be that the books of Kings are designed to exhibit *a history of hubris* that is countered by *a narrative of practicality* that leaves no *monuments* but only *memories* that last as long as monuments but are not susceptible to royal reason.[28] One can observe the long-term

---

28. Such durable, empowering memory figures large in the work of Wendell Berry. See John Leax, "Memory and Hope in the World of Port William,"

bias in our discipline that has most often dismissed the Elijah-Elisha narratives as "legend," which means they are not a reliable witness to "real" historical reality. In a knowing reflection on Gunkel's genres, Jay Wilcoxen offers a contrast between these two modes of attestation:

> Sagas as a literary type can be distinguished from historical writing as a literary type by five polarities: 1) They differ in mode of transmission: saga by oral tradition, history by writing. 2) They differ in subject matter: saga deals with things in the private worlds of men, particularly family relations; history deals with public and particularly political events. 3) They differ in the resources on which they depend: saga draws on tradition and imagination; history on witnesses and records. 4) They differ in part, at least, in the probability of the action they relate: saga tends to be credulous, incorporating the miraculous and the improbable; history, to be credible, confining itself to the possible and the probable. Finally, 5) they differ in their ends or purposes: saga is poetic in tone, aiming to entertain and inspire; history is prosaic, aiming to inform.[29]

This inventory fairly reflects the assumptions of much of critical scholarship. But on the fourth point, the terms "credulous," "miraculous," and "improbable" reflect the modernist tilt of scholarship that tends to "see like a state." On the fifth point, the tasks of "entertaining and inspiring" fall far short of the gravitas of the subversive alternative suggested here. It is exactly this dismissive judgment about the "legends" that needs to be reconsidered, reflecting the extent to which critical scholarship has aligned itself with modernist assumptions of privilege, objectivity, and domination. Such a perspective has caused scholarship to dismiss the most important claims of the prophetic tradition.

Beyond the small scope of our scholarship, the issue of *technique and mētis* is of immense importance for our contemporary political economy. With the seemingly limitless growth of technological

---

Wendell Berry: Life and Work, ed. Jason Peters (Lexington: University Press of Kentucky, 2007), 66–75.

29. Jay A. Wilcoxen, "Narrative," *Old Testament Form Criticism*, ed. John H. Hayes (San Antonio: Trinity University Press, 1974), 60.

empires and the limitless accumulative capacity of the powerful wealthy, our common life becomes increasingly defined by scale, speed, and efficiency. What is being lost in that collusion of knowledge and power is the legitimacy of *the local and the neighborly* that depend on face-to-face interaction at a pace other than the rush to commoditization. With the domination of technique, already operative with Solomon, our democratic institutions are less and less effective, and our imperious top-down decision-making causes human reality to be reframed as commodity. As Jacque Ellul has made clear, in the midst of dominating technique, politics is an illusion as policy is covertly made by moneyed people and business executives without regard for the common good.[30] The prophetic narrative attends to the common good that is systemically disregarded by the Davidic royals.

The resistance of this subversive alternative of the local and the "partisan" (as distinct from the "universal") is urgent in the face of the power or technique. Thus the dramatic conflict between *the history of hubris* and *the narrative of practicality* that we have found in the books of Kings is immediately contemporary in our political economy. The practical performance of neighborly "righteousness and justice" is urgent if our humanness is to be preserved.

This struggle accents, yet again, the wonderment of Job: "Where shall wisdom be found?" (28:12). We are in our society seduced into thinking that wisdom is to be found in the dominant rule of technological knowledge that easily colludes with elitist entitlement power. The tradition of subversion, however, knows that such knowledge and power is an imperial form of wisdom; we might suspect, even now, that wisdom will not be found in that combination but in *the narratives of practicality* that have to do with transformative bodily responses to *poverty* (as in 1 Kgs 4:1-7), *sickness* (as in 1 Kgs 5:1-27), *violence* (as in 1 Kgs 6:8-23), and *hunger* (as in 1 Kgs 6:24–7:20). Among the most important voices in this alternative narrative of practicality is Wendell Berry, who relentlessly insists on the disciplines of frugality, restraint, and diversity enacted locally

---

30. Jacque Ellul, *The Political Illusion*, ed. Konrad Kellen (Eugene, OR: Wipf & Stock, 2015).

in the neighborhood.³¹ As with Elijah and Elisha, Berry sounds old-fashioned and irrelevant in a technological postindustrial economy. But like those ancient prophetic narratives, the wisdom Berry articulates and performs is not so readily dismissed as we are tempted to do. Thus the contest of the books of Kings continues to insist that attention must be paid to the ways of neighborly humanness about which the history of hubris does not know.

VI.

I finish with two peeks into the New Testament. In Matt 11:25-30, in a note peculiar to the Gospel of Matthew, Jesus affirms that "these things" concerning the coming kingdom of heaven are not available to "the wise and intelligent" but to "infants," the little people who have no claim to power, control, pedigree, or worldly wisdom. The saying is enough to make one suspect that Jesus locates "wisdom" not with those who possess the forms of power but with his simple followers who are enjoined to be like him, "gentle and humble in heart" (v. 29). To ask "where shall wisdom be found?" is to wonder "who gets it?" "The scholars and the wise, who could explain much but missed the revelation in their midst (11:25a) did not get it. Those who did get it are 'babies,' the unpretentious 'little ones' who made no claims but could be given the gift of revelation, which comes from God alone (11:25b-27)."³² The contrast between *the wise* and *the infants* in this odd affirmation is an echo, I submit, of the struggle in the books of Kings between *the history of hubris* and *the narratives of practicality*. The "infants" who follow him were to be about the practical work of God's future.

In 1 Cor 1:25 Paul asserts that "God's foolishness is wiser than human wisdom." God's foolishness confounds the wise of the world in the same way that the prophets confounded the kings of Israel.

---

31. These virtues turn up everywhere in the corpus of Wendell Berry. In *The Art of Loading Brush: New Agrarian Writings* (Berkeley: Counterpoint, 2017), 8–9, he offers a "characterization of agrarianism." In *The World-Ending Fire: The Essential Wendell Berry* (Berkeley: Counterpoint, 2017), 232, he avers, "We must achieve the character and acquire the skills to live much poorer than we do." On p. 263, he judges, "The *duty* of the older generation is to be embarrassingly old-fashioned."

32. M. Eugene Boring, "The Gospel of Matthew," *NIB* 8:275.

Then Paul identifies those who follow that summons to foolishness. They are not wise by human standards; they are not powerful or of noble birth (v. 26). But they are charged nonetheless with transformative work. These two texts, I submit, follow from the struggle in the books of Kings, and in turn they aid our reading of the books of Kings.

This reading of the books of Kings, moreover, brings us back to the wisdom tradition itself in probing the question of Job 28:12. It seems clear enough from the foregoing that wisdom is indeed located "below," whereas the claim of wisdom "from above" is illusionary. This way of reading, then, brings us close to the articulations of the books of Job and Ecclesiastes. In the book of Job, in the end, the wisdom of the friends (who know from above) is rejected by YHWH, and Job is commended for speaking "what is right," that is, speaking wisdom (42:7-8). Job is not unlike Elisha, an outsider to social reputation and social influence (Job 30).[33] It is, moreover, exactly his displacement as a social outsider, requiring him to learn "from below," that brings him to the wisdom that YHWH commends.

In like fashion in the book of Ecclesiastes, the royal figure of "Solomon" is presented as all-knowing. But the "royal fiction" of Eccl 1:12–2:26 shows that such royal claims are without substance and are fraudulent. The real wisdom attested in the book of Ecclesiastes is of a quotidian variety that rejects the pretense of royal transcendence and draws close to the lived reality of food, drink, and work. This is not unlike Elisha who is preoccupied with food, health, peace, and economic viability. "Instead Qohelet evokes a loose set of concrete activities that make possible affective experiences and social relations . . . . Qohelet's moral agent thus emerges at a site of shared alienation that harbors the potential to constitute social solidarities, affective experiences, and political creations beyond the normative."[34] Thus it is possible to see the struggle between the wisdom of *hubris* and the wisdom of *practicality* in the books of Kings as having strong parallels in the *hubris* of Job's friends and the *hubris* of royal Solomon, and

---

33. Cf. Davis Hankins, "Wisdom as an Immanent Event in Job 28, Not a Transcendent Ideal," *VT* 63 (2013): 210–35.

34. Davis Hankins, "The Internal Infinite: Deleuze, Subjectivity, and Moral Agency in Ecclesiastes," *JSOT* 40 (2015): 57–58.

the *practicality* of Job and the *practicality* of the honest critical voice of Qohelet. This close parallel suggests that the connections between the "sapiential" and the "historical" in Israel's literature are close and compelling. All of these traditions struggle with the question of Job 28:12. In Job 28 after the dismissal of human wisdom (vv. 1-19), the verses that follow conclude otherwise. In vv. 23-27 wisdom belongs to God. Then in verse 28, wisdom is assigned to "humankind" of a certain ilk, those who fear YHWH and avoid evil: that is wisdom! No great imagination is required to see the same practical wisdom performed by Elisha who lives "from below," who generates futures not available to the kings who know "from above." The unnamed kings are as impotent and helpless as are Job's friends and "royal Solomon."

Thus we have clues beyond the questions with which Balentine ends his discussion. The aphorisms of Job 28:28 and Eccl 12:13 know where wisdom is to be found. In the books of Kings, we have narrated practical wisdom in the figure of Elisha. It is no stretch to conclude that wisdom is not among those who imagine knowledge as power; it is rather situated among those who are "weak, low, and despised in the world" who eventually bring to naught the wisdom of the world.[35] Wisdom is placed among the displaced.

Bibliography

Balentine, Samuel E. *Job*. SHBC. Macon, GA: Smyth & Helwys, 2006.

Berry, Wendell. *The Art of Loading Brush: New Agrarian Writings*. Berkeley: Counterpoint, 2017.

———. *Jayber Crow: A Novel*. Washington, D.C.: Counterpoint, 2000.

———. *The World-Ending Fire: The Essential Wendell Berry*. Berkeley: Counterpoint, 2017.

Boer, Roland. *The Sacred Economy of Ancient Israel*. Louisville: Westminster John Knox, 2015.

---

35. Cf. 1 Cor 1:28.

Boring, M. Eugene. "The Gospel of Matthew." *NIB* 8:87–506.

Brueggemann, Walter. *Solomon: Israel's Ironic Icon of Human Achievement.* Columbia: University of South Carolina Press, 2005.

———. *Tenacious Solidarity: Biblical Provocations on Race, Religion, Climate, and the Economy.* Edited by Davis Hankins. Minneapolis: Fortress, 2018.

———. *Testimony to Otherwise: The Witness of Elijah and Elisha.* St. Louis: Chalice, 2001.

———, and Davis Hankins. "The Affirmation of Prophetic Power and Deconstruction of Royal Authority in the Elisha Narratives." *CBQ* 76 (2014): 58–76.

Ellul, Jacque. *The Political Illusion.* Edited by Konrad Kellen. Eugene, OR: Wipf & Stock, 2015.

Hankins, Davis. "The Internal Infinite: Deleuze, Subjectivity, and Moral Agency in Ecclesiastes." *JSOT* 40 (2015): 43–59.

———. "Wisdom as an Immanent Event in Job 28, Not a Transcendent Ideal." *VT* 63 (2013): 210–35.

Leax, John. "Memory and Hope in the World of Port William." Pages 66–75 in *Wendell Berry: Life and Work.* Edited by Jason Peters. Lexington: University Press of Kentucky, 2007.

Oakman, Douglas E. *Jesus and the Peasants.* Eugene: Wipf & Stock, 2008.

———. *Jesus, Debt, and the Lord's Prayer: First Century Debt and Jesus' Intentions.* Eugene: Wipf & Stock, 2014.

Scott, James C. *Seeing Like a State: How Certain Schemes to Improve the Human Condition Have Failed.* New Haven: Yale University Press, 1998.

Wilcoxen, Jay A. "Narrative." Pages 57–98 in *Old Testament Form Criticism.* Edited by John H. Hayes. San Antonio: Trinity University Press, 1974.

"God Set Infinity into Their Minds"
Qohelet's Quest to Comprehend the Incomprehensible

Heather Woodworth Brannon

> *I should like to thank my mentor, Samuel E. Balentine, for encouraging me to pursue this particular project under his guidance as a student at Union Presbyterian Seminary in 2017. Without his thoughtful insight and steadfast support, I may have never discovered the immense gratification of thinking about thinking.*

Samuel E. Balentine begins his quest to examine biblical wisdom literature with the Joban question, "Where shall wisdom be found?" (Job 28:12).[1] This perennial question has plagued thinkers across generations. In the pursuit of wisdom, those who look to biblical texts quickly find themselves grappling with the boundary between divine Wisdom (with a capital *W*) and human wisdom (with a small *w*). For Balentine, both Job and Qohelet speak of the latter, in that wisdom "remains open to divine revelation without being

---

1. Samuel E. Balentine, *Wisdom Literature*, CBS (Nashville: Abingdon, 2018), 6.

closed to autonomous thinking and discovery."[2] Job and Qohelet's dissonant voices within the wisdom tradition exemplify the human desire to seek knowledge by pressing upon the boundaries set by the divine rather than subordinating to the limitations of knowledge. Expanding our view beyond the sacred scrolls, the nature of wisdom in other disciplines (e.g., cognitive science) and religious traditions (e.g., Buddhism) continues to challenge and illuminate what is found in the Bible.

The contemporary thinker considering the Joban question stands at a crossroads with numerous routes from which to choose. Each possibility invites thinkers to explore the complex relationship between the divine and human, revelation and reason, and piety and autonomy. The hope is that all paths lead to the ultimate source of hidden wisdom. The reality, however, is that humans may never reach this final destination. Out of discouragement, the search for wisdom may be abandoned because cognitive limitations hinder any potential progress. The act of surrendering acknowledges that there is nothing new to be discovered under the sun and that wisdom is as pointless as chasing the wind. Those who cease their search are resigned to "eat, drink, and take pleasure in all their toil" because the source of wisdom is inaccessible.[3]

Balentine's close readings of Job and Qohelet present a profoundly different approach to the search for wisdom, however. He suggests that the intellectual journey itself is not a means to an end but, as these texts reveal, a divine invitation to explore and test human boundaries. According to Balentine, "the quest for wisdom was a process of thinking about thinking that resisted closure, for knowledge was itself always a moving target, a journey more than a destination."[4] Such a search for wisdom enables humans to discover the unknown and discern the limits of human cognition. From this perspective, the boundaries of knowledge are meant to be pressed upon and transcended, not enforced and obeyed.

With this essay, I wish to express my deep appreciation for Balentine's imaginative approach to the interpretation of wisdom literature,

---

2. Balentine, *Wisdom Literature*, 161.

3. Eccl 2:24-26; 3:12-13, 22; 5:18-20 [MT 5:17-19]; 8:15; 9:7-9; 11:7-10.

4. Balentine, *Wisdom Literature*, 22.

especially his proposal that the hiddenness of wisdom is indeed God's invitation to search for the unknown. As a tribute to the influence of his approach, this essay will explore Qohelet's engagement with the Joban question by examining Qohelet's quest to comprehend the incomprehensible. Qohelet embodies Balentine's proposal in that it is the journey itself that shapes Qohelet's thinking and that enables him to imagine the infinite within the finite.[5]

Within the book of Ecclesiastes, Qohelet's persistent pursuit to understand the logical underpinnings of reality leads him to chase the unattainable. God holds the definitive answers that Qohelet seeks with his heart, yet Qohelet refuses to address God directly. His use of the designation "the God" emphasizes his perception of God as hidden behind an impenetrable veil of secrecy (*hāʾĕlōhîm*, thirty-two times with the definite article). This distance between Qohelet and "the God" manifests itself in his observation that God has set *hāʿōlām* ("infinity") into the human *lēb* ("heart" or "mind") (3:11). Qohelet believes that *hāʿōlām* has the potential to disclose what God has done from the beginning to the end but that this potential is deceptive because humans cannot comprehend God's plans, no matter how hard they may try. Nonetheless, Qohelet unyieldingly "[desired] to follow knowledge like a sinking star, beyond the utmost bound of human thought."[6] Without God's direct involvement in the process, though, Qohelet cannot gravitate any further toward divine knowledge. Why then did Qohelet continue this endless intellectual pursuit in spite of the obvious outcome?

This essay engages this critical question by examining the trajectory between divine intention and human cognition. Central to this task is a reconsideration of what it means for God to "set *hāʿōlām*" into Qohelet's *lēb* in 3:11b—an idiom that is notoriously difficult to translate and understand. In an effort to gain clarity, many commentators place the exegetical emphasis on determining the most accurate meaning of *hāʿōlām* in 3:11b, without considering its impact on

---

5. In this essay, I refer to Qohelet as "he" or "him," with the recognition that Qohelet's explicit gender is not revealed. Qohelet's gender and gender inequality within Ecclesiastes will be discussed further toward the end of this essay.

6. Alfred Lord Tennyson, "Ulysses," in *Tennyson: Poems* (London: Everyman's Library, 2004), 88–90.

Qohelet. The inscrutable nature of *hāʿōlām* renders the exact purpose of its presence in the *lēb* difficult to articulate. The temptation for many readers is to assume that *hāʿōlām* is an epistemological barrier that hinders human cognition. Thus, the question of why Qohelet subsequently ignores this epistemological obstacle is often overlooked. I suggest that *hāʿōlām* is a catalyst for cognition rather than an obstacle to knowledge. God's intentional placement of *hāʿōlām* into Qohelet's *lēb* enables him continually to reengage his mind in the process of thinking about thinking in order to understand his own human limitations and to discover more than he thought was possible.

In the remainder of this essay, I demonstrate this transformation of Qohelet's cognition by (1) defining the functions of *lēb* and *hāʿōlām*; (2) evaluating how Qohelet uses his mind; (3) demonstrating Qohelet's increased sense of perception; (4) determining the impact of Qohelet's increased perception on his thought process; and (5) summarizing my findings in light of the Joban question.

The Function of *lēb* and *hāʿōlām* in Ecclesiastes

The idiom in 3:11 (*hāʿōlām nātan bĕlibbām*, "[God] set infinity into their minds") occurs once in Ecclesiastes and is found nowhere else in the Hebrew Bible. Determining the function of this idiom requires close attention to its terminology. In this section, I analyze three concepts within the idiom: (1) the function of *lēb*; (2) the impact of God "setting" something in the *lēb*; and (3) the function of *hāʿōlām* within the *lēb*.[7]

The term *lēb* is not unique to Ecclesiastes; it occurs approximately 602 times throughout the Hebrew Bible. The *lēb* was understood to accommodate a variety of functions, including emotions (e.g., joy in Exod 4:14; pain in 1 Sam 1:8), intellectual functions (e.g., remembrance in Deut 4:9; perception in 1 Sam 4:20), will and deliberation (e.g., Isa 10:7; Jer 22:17), and as an instrument of wisdom (e.g., Prov

---

7. Both *lēb* and *hāʿōlām* are complicated terms in the Hebrew Bible in general and Ecclesiastes in particular. It is not my purpose here to explain every occurrence of these terms. Rather, I will provide a brief semantic analysis of the terminology in order to contextualize the idiom in 3:11 properly. For a comprehensive analysis of *lēb* in the Hebrew Bible, see Michael Carasik, *Theologies of the Mind in Biblical Israel* (New York: Peter Lang, 2006).

2:10; Eccl 1:16).⁸ The word *lēb* occurs forty-two times in the book of Ecclesiastes. Qohelet deliberately directs his own *lēb* both to think ("mind") and to feel ("heart").⁹ When Qohelet's *lēb* serves as the seat of intellect and functions cognitively, I render the term as "mind" (see, e.g., Eccl 2:3, "I searched with my mind how to cheer my body with wine—my mind still guiding me with wisdom"). When *lēb* is used in connection with pleasure and functions emotively, I render the term as "heart" (e.g., Eccl 2:10, "I kept my heart from no pleasure, for my heart found pleasure in all my toil"). The immediate context helps readers determine whether *lēb* functions cognitively or emotively and should be translated as "mind" or "heart."

There are a few occasions when the *lēb* functions as a receptacle to hold what God sets into it, yet it is not simply a storage unit for idle thoughts and feelings. In the Hebrew Bible, there are nine occurrences of God setting something into the *lēb* that occur with the verb *nātan* ("to set"): wisdom (1 Kgs 10:24; 2 Chr 9:23), the law (Ezra 7:27; Jer 31:33), a vision (Neh 2:12), the ability to assemble genealogy (Neh 7:5), gladness (Ps 4:7 [MT 4:8]), the fear of God (Jer 32:40), and *hāʿōlām* (Eccl 3:11b).¹⁰ God's deliberate act of setting something into the mind or heart is a way for God to influence human behavior, which demonstrates that *lēb* is receptive to internal stimuli.

Understanding the function of *lēb* in 3:11b requires a reexamination of the frequently disputed object, *hāʿōlām*. Much like

---

8. F. Stolz, "*lēb*, heart," *Theological Lexicon of the Old Testament*, trans. M. E. Biddle, ed. Ernst Jenni and Claus Westermann, vol. 2 (Peabody: Hendrickson, 1997), 638–42.

9. I do not intend to argue that cognition and emotion are fully distinct from one another. As cognitive scientists have shown, the two often overlap. Biblical Hebrew captures the overlap between cognition and emotion with the use of a single term (*lēb*) for these and other faculties. See, e.g., Antonio Damasio, *Looking for Spinoza: Joy, Sorrow, and the Feeling Brain* (Orlando: Harcourt, 2003), 147–50, 184–220.

10. There are two other instances of God as the subject of *nātan* in connection to *lēb*: God who gives a trembling heart (Deut 28:65) and God who "has not given (you) a mind to understand" (Deut 29:4 [MT 29:3]). These instances are not included in my discussion because they do not demonstrate God setting something into the *lēb*.

lēb, *hāʿōlām* is difficult to define because of its ambiguous nature. Furthermore, there are 440 occurrences of the word in the Hebrew Bible, making it a challenge to define the term adequately. There are approximately ten broad understandings of *ʿōlām* in the Hebrew Bible outside of Ecclesiastes that are relevant to this study: "definiteness" (Gen 3:22), "as long as one lives" (Ex 21:6), "into the indefinite future" (Deut 23:4), "forever" (1 Kgs 2:33), "forever and ever" (1 Chr 16:36), "everlasting" (Isa 26:4), "for a long time" (Isa 42:14), "long" (Isa 63:19), "long ago" (Jer 2:20), and "ancient" (Jer 5:15).[11] One common factor among these occurrences of *ʿōlām* is a reference to time, whether past, present, or the indefinite future.

The seven occurrences of *ʿōlām* in Ecclesiastes (1:4, 10; 2:16; 3:11b, 14; 9:6; 12:5) occur in contexts that denote temporality and do not refer to the philosophical sense of eternity.[12] Five of these occur with the preposition *lĕ* ("to/for," 1:4, 10; 2:16; 3:14; 9:6). In 1:4, *lĕʿōlām* is connected to the verb "to stand" (*ʿāmād*) and denotes duration and stability ("the earth remains forever"). Ecclesiastes 3:14 emphasizes the stability of God's works, which cannot be changed by human beings ("whatever God does endures forever"). Combined with the negative particle (*ʾên*) and an emphasis on death, *lĕʿōlām* indicates "no enduring [remembrance]" in 2:16 and "never again" in 9:6. The occurrence in 1:10 appears in the plural (*lĕʿōlāmîm*) with a singular verb (*hāyâ*) to denote the remotest time in the past ("ages before us"). The remaining two instances of *ʿōlām* occur in 12:5 and 3:11b without the preposition *lĕ*. In 12:5, the expression "eternal home" connotes one's grave.[13]

---

11. See, e.g., Ludwig Koehler, Walter Baumgartner, and Johann J. Stamm, *Hebrew and Aramaic Lexicon of the Old Testament (HALOT)*, trans. and ed. Mervyn E. J. Richardson, vol. 1 (Leiden: Brill, 1994–1999), 798–99.

12. For a detailed account of *ʿōlām* in Ecclesiastes, see A. Schoors, *The Preacher Sought to Find Pleasing Words: A Study of the Language of Qohelet, Part II Vocabulary* (Leuven: Peeters, 2004), 221–25.

13. In Ecclesiastes, God gives (*nātan*) more than just *hāʿōlām*. Although Qohelet does not communicate directly with God, God (not Qohelet) continues to initiate points of contact with human beings through giving. God initiates the act of giving ten out of seventeen times (59%). According to Qohelet, God gives human beings a preoccupation (1:13; 3:10); wisdom, knowledge, and joy (2:26 [2x]); the work of gathering and heaping (2:26); a few days of life (5:17; 8:15);

The context of temporality is crucial for rendering *hā'ōlām* (with the definite article) in 3:11b.[14] Preceding this idiom, Qohelet describes antithetical pairs of activities within time (3:1-8). Following the idiom, Qohelet claims that the impact of *hā'ōlām* on humans is that "they cannot find out the work which (the) God has done from the beginning to the end" (3:11c). In this context of perception, trying to find (*māṣā'*) something does not imply a physical task. The act of searching refers to human cogitation, the quest to discover and understand the events in time that are under God's control. For the first time in the book, Qohelet claims that God's plans cannot be discovered (3:11c), which he seeks to affirm through an ongoing investigation. I suggest then that the observation in 3:11c—the unknowability of God's plans—serves as Qohelet's initial hypothesis, which drives his inquiry for the remaining nine chapters of the book.[15]

Many commentators view Qohelet's observation in 3:11c as a declarative statement, thus interpreting *hā'ōlām* as an epistemological barrier and translating *hā'ōlām* as "ignorance."[16] Such a view posits

---

wealth, possessions, and honor (5:18; 6:2); and the life-breath (12:7). Each of these contributions is either something that may help one survive (e.g., wealth) or something that separates humans from the deity (e.g., preoccupation).

14. For a discussion on time in Ecclesiastes, see Mette Bundvad, *Time in the Book of Ecclesiastes* (Oxford: Oxford University Press, 2015), especially 99–114.

15. The particle of relation (*'ăšer*) may lead to a number of translations, thus altering the meaning of 3:11. For example, if *'ăšer* is translated "so that," then *hā'ōlām* may be considered a barrier to knowledge. My translation, "yet," emphasizes the irony of *hā'ōlām* in the human mind. *hā'ōlām* is the potential to think beyond what one believes is possible, even though one cannot know everything. The choice of translation, however, does not stand in contrast to my proposal that 3:11c is Qohelet's initial hypothesis and that infinity is a cognitive stimulus.

16. The ambiguous meaning of *hā'ōlām* has led to a variety of translations, including a rejection of the word as it could be written defectively with the definite direct object marker. This apparent error, however, could be intentional on the part of the author to create ambiguity. There are possible connections to Proto-Semitic and Ugaritic, *ġlm* ("to be dark/darkness"). Thus, some scholars translate the noun as "secret" or "darkness/ignorance." On the other hand, the Ugaritic verb *'lm* ("to be known") and the noun "eternity," the Arabic noun *'lm* ("knowledge"), and MHeb verb *'ālam* ("to be concealed/hidden") further complicate how one may translate this word using comparative Semitics (see *HALOT*,

that God, the oppressor, actively hinders human cognition and the human capacity to engage the temporal order.[17] Yet the immediate context of 3:11b and semantic understanding of *ʿôlām* both indicate that *hāʿōlām* has some connection to time. In this context, *hāʿōlām* is best translated as "infinity," or that which transcends time. Infinity is an unlimited, indefinite duration of time that only God can fully comprehend.[18] Infinity undoubtedly impacts Qohelet's ability to think.[19] When God set infinity into the human *lēb*, God intended for humans to think and imagine beyond what they thought was possible.

How Qohelet Uses His Mind

In this section, I establish how Qohelet uses his mind throughout Ecclesiastes, thus creating a framework in which to detect changes in his thought process both before and after God sets infinity in his mind. I do not intend to offer a psychoanalysis of Qohelet, but rather literary observations regarding the structure of the book. Two key idioms—"I set my mind" and "I said in/with my mind"—demonstrate Qohelet's ability to acquire knowledge without assistance from God. By both analyzing and tracing the occurrences

---

798–99; 834–35; Gregorio del Olmo Lete and Joaquín Sanmartín, *A Dictionary of the Ugaritic Language in the Alphabetic Tradition*, Third Revised Edition, trans. and ed. Wilfred G. E. Watson [Leiden: Brill, 2015], 154–55; 316). In Hebrew, *hāʿōlām* may be amended to the word *ʿāmal* ("toil"), which is a motif throughout the book. Other translations include "border," "barrier," "world," "universe," "the work of God," and "duration" (Schoors, *Preacher*, 223–25). The goal of this paper is not to determine the exact rendering of this word but to examine what impact *hāʿōlām* has on Qohelet's thought process.

17. Bundvad, *Time*, 101–14. C. L. Seow emphasizes the irony of the situation, which is the ability of humans to know what God has done in the moment, yet they "bypass the moment in order to grasp the totality of existence," which is not possible. See *Ecclesiastes*, AB 18C (New York: Doubleday, 1997), 163, 173.

18. Davis Hankins also chose to translate *hāʿōlām* as "infinity" in 3:11b. He offers an interesting perspective of infinity in "The Internal Infinite: Deleuze, Subjectivity, and Moral Agency in Ecclesiastes," *JSOT* 40/1 (2015): 43–59.

19. Given the cognitive functioning here, the term *lēb* in 3:11b is best rendered "mind."

of these key idioms throughout the book, it is then possible to explicate Qohelet's increased perception and comprehension after infinity.

The first idiom, "I set my mind," occurs five times in Ecclesiastes (1:13, 17; 8:9, 16; 9:1). In all occurrences, Qohelet is the subject of the verb "to set" (*nātan*). The act of setting his mind to do something indicates a desire to acquire knowledge, which goes beyond mere observation (akin to seeing with the eyes, *rā'â*). Qohelet's intentional engagement in the cognitive process allows him to set a goal (1:13, 17), analyze what he has observed (8:9), and state a conclusion by processing gathered data (8:16; 9:1). At no point does Qohelet involve God, whether by requesting guidance or demanding answers. As an autonomous thinker, Qohelet believes that his mind is the optimal tool for the intellectual task.

The second idiom, "I said in/with my mind," occurs six times in Ecclesiastes (1:16; 2:1, 15 [2x]; 3:17, 18). In each occurrence, Qohelet is the subject of the verb "to speak" (*dābar* in 1:16; 2:15b; *'āmar* in 2:1, 15a; 3:17, 18). The idiom includes the pronoun "I" (*'ănî*, except 2:15b) in various combinations with the prepositions "in" (*bĕ*) and "with" (*'im*).[20] These two verbs—"to speak" and "to think"—denote critical thought, careful reflection, and reasoning. The six times Qohelet speaks in or with his mind enable him to establish his authority (1:16), start his experiment (2:1), engage in reflection (2:15a), make a bold claim (2:15b), state God's intentions (3:17), and justify God's intentions (3:18).[21] When Qohelet speaks

---

20. For an overview of this idiom in the Hebrew Bible, see Carasik, *Theologies*, 115–18, 120–24.

21. Thomas Krüger believes that 3:17 (along with 2:26; 7:26; 8:5, 12-13) is a secondary gloss and should not be attributed to the original author because it is a corollary to Qohelet's own thought. Likewise, Samuel L. Adams notes that the close repetition of identical phrasing in 3:17-18 is not indicative of Qohelet's careful rhetorical style. I consider 3:17, however, to be an integral part of Qohelet's thought process. Similar repetition of this idiom occurs in 2:15 (2x; note *'āmar* in 2:15a and *dābar* in 2:15b), which has not been deemed a secondary gloss. Given this pattern, I suggest that the repetition in 3:17-18 is characteristic of Qohelet's rhetorical style and is a reflection of his ongoing cogitation. See Thomas Krüger, *Qohelet: A Commentary*, ed. K. Baltzer, trans. O. C. Dean (Minneapolis: Fortress, 2004), 15; Samuel L. Adams, *Wisdom in Transition: Act and Consequence in Second Temple Instructions*, JSJSup 125 (Leiden: Brill, 2008), 142.

in or with his mind, Qohelet treats his mind like a conversation partner. Once again, Qohelet does not involve God in his intellectual inquiry, relying primarily on his mind to analyze information in order to gain understanding. His internal thought process is meant to be shared with, not concealed from, readers, which may or may not include God.[22] Qohelet's mind, therefore, plays a prominent role in acquiring knowledge and internally processing what he has learned.[23]

Thus far, I have established that Qohelet's mind (*lēb*) is integral to his thought process by showing that the use of his mind is for careful reflection and the acquisition of knowledge. His inquiry does not depend on God or conversations with others to learn something new. Qohelet both sets and speaks with his mind continually throughout the book. He periodically reengages his mind in order to set goals, critically examine his observations, and state conclusions. Qohelet's cognitive reengagement is exhibited by closely following the occurrences of these two *lēb* idioms throughout the book, especially the order in which they occur. The linear progression of these idioms will create a framework in which to understand his overall thought process.

Detecting Qohelet's Increased Sense of Perception

Examining the overall occurrences of the two *lēb* idioms in the entire book highlights a substantial gap in which they do not occur between 3:19 and 8:8. One must wonder what Qohelet's mind is doing during this period, especially given the frequent occurrences of the two *lēb* idioms before infinity in 3:11b.

---

22. Nowhere in Ecclesiastes does God speak to God's own heart. In the Hebrew Bible, this divine reflective utterance occurs only one time (Gen 8:21).

23. Michael V. Fox has written extensively on Qohelet's epistemology, especially the importance of Qohelet's *lēb*. See "Qohelet's Epistemology" in *HUCA* 58 (1987): 137–55; *Qohelet and His Contradictions* (Sheffield: Sheffield Academic, 1989), 79–120; *A Time to Tear Down and a Time to Build Up: A Rereading of Ecclesiastes* (Grand Rapids: Eerdmans, 1999), 71–96.

1:13	I set my mind
1:16	I said with my mind
1:17	I set my mind
2:1	I said with my mind
2:15a	I said with my mind
2:15b	I said with my mind
3:11b	Infinity set into their minds
3:11c	Qohelet's initial hypothesis
3:17	I said with my mind
3:18	I said with my mind
3:19–8:8	**No occurrences of *lēb* idioms**
8:9	All this I observed, setting my mind
8:16	When I set my mind
9:1	All this I set to my mind, examining it all

A closer reading of the text indicates that occurrences of the verb of perception, "to see" (*rāʾâ*), frequently increase after 3:11 during this interim period.[24] Among the forty-seven occurrences of the verb in the book, Qohelet reports seeing or attempting to see something firsthand twenty-five times (*rāʾîtî*). Before infinity, Qohelet sees something only five times: deeds under the sun (1:14), wisdom (2:12), how wisdom excels folly (2:13), the need for *carpe diem* (2:24), and the business that God gave humans (3:10).

After God sets infinity into Qohelet's mind, there is a considerable increase in his sense of perception. He reports seeing something twenty additional times, including injustice in the world (3:16; 7:15); the unknowability of fate (3:22; 9:11); oppression (4:1; 5:13 [MT 5:12]); the origins of envy (4:4); perpetual dissatisfaction (4:7; 6:1); the limits of wisdom (4:15); *carpe diem* (5:18 [MT 5:17]); lack of wisdom in humans (7:27); human ignorance (7:29); human-inflicted injustice (8:9); unjust behavior of the wicked (8:10); business on earth (8:16); all the work of God, which is beyond comprehension (8:17); the value of wisdom (9:13); evil (10:5); and the unpredictability of the social order (10:7). Qohelet's perception of the world

---

24. Other perception verbs (e.g., to feel, hear, etc.) do not appear to play a major role in Ecclesiastes. One area that merits further consideration is the emotive function of *lēb* in connection with verbs of perception.

shifts from conventional observations (1:1–3:10) to ethical atrocities, including horrific injustices and imposed human limitations that can hardly be avoided (3:16–12:14).

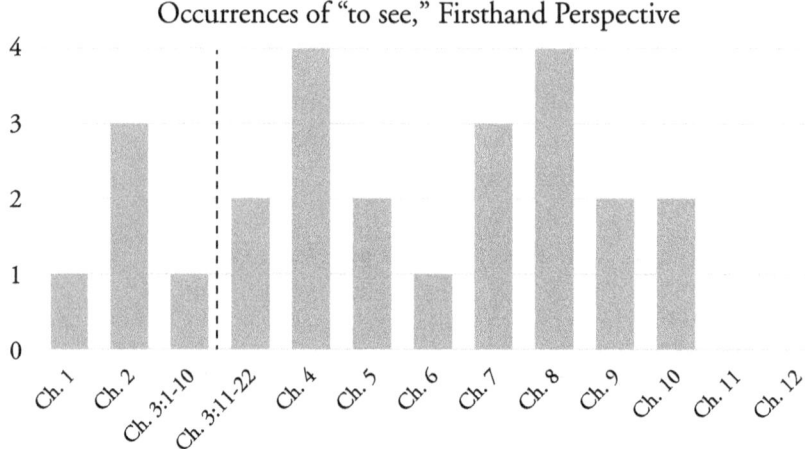

This comparison indicates a significant increase of roughly 400 percent in Qohelet's ability to perceive. His primary method of data collection is through personal observations. For Qohelet, seeing is knowing; an increase in his perception enables him to learn and reason without relying on proverbial wisdom or divine revelation.

I suggest that the presence of infinity in Qohelet's mind directly causes his increased perception through an epistemological shift from seeing to knowing in 3:9-15. Before infinity, Qohelet saw that God has preoccupied humans in order to halt their potential inquiry (3:10). In 3:11, God invites Qohelet (and humans) to imagine the infinite within the finite. Qohelet hypothesizes that, in spite of infinity, humans will never discover God's plans (3:11c). Qohelet's ongoing inquiry indicates his desire to test this hypothesis. Infinity, then, stimulates Qohelet's investigation for the purpose of testing his hypothesis and reporting what he has learned.

Qohelet offers several inferences immediately after infinity that reflect his initial hypothesis in 3:11c. Qohelet is able to know and confirm four realizations: (1) it is good for humans to experience pleasure (3:12); (2) they should eat, drink, and take pleasure in their inevitable toil (3:13); (3) God is not confined by time, and humans cannot alter God's plans, so humans should stand in awe before God

(3:14); and (4) no events—past, present, or future—are exceptional (3:15). These preliminary inferences guide Qohelet's ongoing investigation. His increased perception enables him to collect valuable data and push the boundaries of his cognition.

3:10	I have seen (*rā'îtî*) the business that God has given to humans to be occupied with.	
3:11a	God has made everything suitable for its time;	"to see"
3:11b	God set infinity (*hā'ōlām*) into their minds	
3:11c	yet they cannot find out the work which God has done from the beginning to the end.	
Epistemological shift		
3:12	I know (*yāda'tî*) that there is nothing good for them, except to rejoice, and to do well as long as they live.	
3:13	[I know] all people should eat, drink, and take pleasure in all their toil. This is a gift from God.	"to know"
3:14	I know (*yāda'tî*) that whatever God does, God endures forever; nothing can be added to it and nothing can be taken from it; and God has made it so that they may stand in awe before God.	
3:15	[I know] that which is already has been, and that which is to be already is. God seeks what has been pursued.	

The Impact of Increased Perception on Qohelet's Thought Process

With infinity as the catalyst for Qohelet's curiosity, he is able to make diverse observations and form substantive conclusions that were previously not possible. Qohelet's period of increased perception is marked by the use of the verb "to know" (*yāda'*). Within the entire book, Qohelet claims to know something firsthand four times despite the thirty-six occurrences of the verb. Before infinity in 3:11b, Qohelet knows something once: both the wise and fools have the same fate (2:14). After 3:11, Qohelet knows something three times: humans should do well in life, take pleasure in their toil, and fear God (8:12). These conclusions, however, are a limited representation of the impact of Qohelet's increased perception on his thought process. Qohelet's reluctance to declare what he knows—as indicated through the lack of first-person occurrences of *yāda*ʿ—exemplifies his recognition that there is more to be learned, thus he must continue thinking about thinking.

The occurrences of the two key idioms in which the term *lēb* appears—"I set my mind" and "I said in/with my mind"—best illustrate how Qohelet's increased perception affects his ability to form substantial conclusions. Qohelet's initial hypothesis is that humans cannot find out the work that God has done from the beginning to the end (3:11c). This proposition guides his inquiry through reflection (3:16-22), observation (4:1–8:15), and a report of his findings (8:16–9:1). Directly after the epistemological shift from seeing to knowing (3:10-15), Qohelet sees injustice and speaks to his mind twice (3:16-18). This reengagement with his mind leads to the conclusion that humans cannot alter their fate (3:19-22). But Qohelet is not satisfied with his findings. For several chapters, Qohelet actively observes the world around him in order to collect additional data (4:1–8:15). He neither speaks with nor sets his mind again until he has gathered sufficient data.

This sets the stage for Qohelet's final report concerning his quest to discover the unknown. The overwhelming quantity of observations that he collected requires reengagement with his mind in order to process the data (3:19–8:8). Qohelet's first attempt to set his mind results in further observation about injustice (8:9-15).[25] His next

---

25. A rare idiom in Ecclesiastes, "I turned my mind," occurs only once in 7:25 and indicates a reengagement of Qohelet's mind before 8:9. Qohelet also reemphasizes his initial hypothesis in 7:14. I did not include these examples because they are not directly related to my suggested framework. They do, however, continue to support my proposal that Qohelet's initial hypothesis (3:11c) drives his inquiry through a period of increased perception, resulting in a considerable delay of reengagement with his mind.

attempt to set his mind results in a profound affirmation of his initial hypothesis (3:11c; 8:16): (1) no one can find out all that is happening under the sun (8:17a); (2) humans will never learn this information, no matter how persistently they seek it (8:17b); and (3) even those who claim to know everything cannot find this out (8:17c).

The reaffirmation of Qohelet's initial hypothesis might suggest that he should discontinue his quest to discover God's work because he has proved that his initial hypothesis is, indeed, accurate. Yet Qohelet paradoxically continues his inquiry by setting his mind one last time to examine his collective observations and share what he has learned (9:1-12). Qohelet reports that (1) God controls the fate of all humans, righteous and wicked; the same fate comes to everyone (9:1-3); (2) the living are better off than the dead because they can have hope (9:4-6); and (3) all people should enjoy life to the fullest (9:7-12). Qohelet can now attest that humans cannot find out God's plans or engage in the temporal order for personal gain or preservation. He confidently confirms his initial hypothesis with no need to reengage his mind for the remainder of the book.

3:11b	Infinity set into their minds
3:11c	**Qohelet's initial hypothesis: humans cannot find out what the God has done from the beginning to the end**
3:17	I said with my mind
3:18	I said with my mind
3:19–8:8	Period of increased perception (data collection)
8:9	Reengagement of Qohelet's mind: all this I observed, setting my mind
8:16	**Confirmation of his initial hypothesis: when I set my mind**
9:1	Additional inquiry: all this I set to my mind, examining it all

Qohelet's realization that he cannot know God's work might have stopped other thinkers from continuing the quest to discover what is hidden. Yet for Qohelet, his diverse observations allow him to think even more deeply about what it means to be alive. He observes that life is filled with unfortunate challenges; therefore, humans should savor every moment of their lives before their ultimate demise (9:7-9). He also discovers that thought, knowledge, and wisdom are a vital part of being human (9:10). Although Qohelet cannot comprehend the entirety of God's work, he recognizes the wondrous opportunity to expand the limits of his own understanding through continued observation and reflection. Qohelet's intellectual journey emphasizes the importance of the human mind in helping to understand lived experiences.

It should not be overlooked that Qohelet's consistent reliance on his mind throughout the entire book is an indication of his overwhelming sense of divine abandonment.[26] At no point does the deity appear, intervene, or speak to Qohelet. In light of this experience, Qohelet then perceives God to be unreliable and disengaged from creation in an unjust world. He deems it unnecessary to ask God questions, request assistance, or even lament in the midst of his deep despair. Therefore, Qohelet resorts to skepticism, which is an intensification of his sense of divine abandonment.[27]

Yet Qohelet's primary goal is to detect God at work in the world, that is, to perceive God's presence, not God's hiddenness. Although Qohelet is unable to experience God's presence in a satisfying way, this does not mean that God is disconnected from humans. God's setting of infinity into Qohelet's mind is both an indicator of God's presence and a way of redirecting Qohelet back toward God. Infinity drives Qohelet's desire to experience the presence of God, thus enabling him to think deeply about complex issues, to appreciate moments of pleasure, and to imagine life closer to Eden. Qohelet's pursuit of wisdom is the continuous redirecting of himself toward God. Thus God is both present and hidden in this book, by actively initiating Qohelet's intellectual pursuit yet providing ample space for Qohelet to be an autonomous thinker.

Qohelet demonstrates the importance of thinking about thinking by unceasingly reengaging his mind, without the conscious realization that God stimulates his open-ended intellectual journey. God's setting of infinity into Qohelet's mind significantly increases his sense of perception and helps him imagine the infinite within the finite.

---

26. For an impressive exegetical treatment of the notion of God's hiddenness in the Hebrew Bible, see Samuel E. Balentine, *The Hidden God: The Hiding of the Face of God in the Old Testament* (Oxford: Oxford University Press, 1983).

27. Balentine, *The Hidden God*, 167–70.

Without infinity as the catalyst for his curiosity, Qohelet would never have reaped the abundant benefits of the journey itself. Infinity enables him to make rich observations about the world, which, in turn, enable him authoritatively to report a more complex understanding of his cognitive limits. Although Qohelet appears to pursue this quest independently, at the heart of his investigation was not his brilliant mind but the God who indirectly initiated his persistent pursuit to learn.[28] Qohelet's intellectual quest demonstrates a trajectory between divine intention and human cognition, which is a reminder to Qohelet's readers that the act of thinking about thinking is a gift from God.

One final question deserves consideration: Is the process of thinking about thinking available to everyone? In Qohelet's world, the privilege of seeking wisdom was reserved for the sages, likely composed only of men. According to Qohelet, finding a wise woman is nearly impossible: "One [wise] man (*ʾādām*) among a thousand I found, but a [wise] woman (*ʾiššâ*) among all these I have not found" (7:28). Scholars have not reached a consensus on the role of women in this book. For some readers, this verse is seen as among many statements sprinkled throughout the book that severely limit women's contributions to the wisdom enterprise.[29] Katharine J. Dell, however, proposes translating *ʾādām* as "human being" (not "man," *ʾîš*) and *ʾiššâ* as Woman Wisdom in 7:28, thus rendering the elusive search for wisdom a universal quest for all humans.[30]

---

28. Qohelet does not include the definite article in 3:10 when referring to God (*ʾĕlōhîm*), which is the subject of the verb *nātan* in 3:11, yet he includes the definite article (*hāʾĕlōhîm*) immediately after infinity is set into the mind. It seems that Qohelet's perception of God as a distant deity is not consistent within this pericope.

29. For further reading, see Jennifer L. Koosed, "Ecclesiastes," in *Women's Bible Commentary*, ed. Carol A. Newsom, Sharon H. Ringe, and Jacqueline E. Lapsley (Louisville: Westminster John Knox, 2012), 243–46 and idem, *(Per)mutations of Qohelet: Reading the Body in the Book* (New York: T&T Clark, 2006).

30. Katharine J. Dell offers a brief discussion on various feminist readings of 7:23-29 in *Interpreting Ecclesiastes: Readers Old and New* (Winona Lake: Eisenbrauns, 2013), 84–94. For additional feminist scholarship on Ecclesiastes, see Russell L. Meek and David J. H. Beldman, *A Classified Bibliography on Ecclesiastes* (New York: T&T Clark, 2019), 123–24.

Following Dell, I propose that thinking about thinking is available to everyone since God places infinity into the minds of all humans, regardless of gender, race, sexuality, ability, or other factors. The author's use of the expression *bĕnê hā'ādām* ("humans") in 3:10 and its reference in 3:11b (placing infinity into their [i.e., human beings'] minds) reflect a broader scope.[31] For Qohelet, God is impartial to the divisions that humans construct within society. A close reading of this text suggests that—even in Qohelet's androcentric context—infinity is innate in every human being and cannot be suppressed. God intends for all intellectually curious humans to cogitate and to wonder.

Returning to the Joban Question

In returning to the Joban question, "where shall wisdom be found?" (Job 28:12), Qohelet does not offer a satisfying answer that directs humans to hidden wisdom.[32] Yet it is precisely the desire to see what is hidden and to discover the unknown that expands the cognitive limits of human beings. Or, as Balentine astutely notes, "where knowledge is elusive, imagination is empowering."[33] For Balentine, both Job and Qohelet allow wonder to stimulate their curiosities and provoke challenging questions because "there is more to be learned about the meaning of life than subordination to its limitations."[34] Those who have read Balentine's scholarship—and especially the privileged thinkers who have studied and worked with him—can attest that he exemplifies this model of pressing upon the outermost limits of intellectual inquiry. Balentine's robust imagination, courage to engage in challenging interdisciplinary work, and willingness to grapple with notoriously difficult texts is of great inspiration to this writer. As his student and faithful friend, I cannot imagine a more

---

31. In 3:10 and 3:11b, the presence of the definite article in *hā'ādām* denotes a universal meaning, referring to the whole of humankind, not specifically men. 7:28 lacks the definite article (i.e., *'ādām*); therefore, the meaning is not clear, especially in contrast to *'iŝŝâ*. For further discussion, see Schoors, *Preacher*, 44–49.

32. For a fascinating discussion on the Joban question, see Samuel E. Balentine, *Job*, SHBC (Macon, GA: Smyth & Helwys, 2006), especially 418–29.

33. Balentine, *Wisdom*, 157.

34. Ibid., 158.

exceptional embodiment than him of what it means to embrace God's gift of infinity in the mind.

Bibliography

Adams, Samuel L. *Wisdom in Transition: Act and Consequence in Second Temple Instructions.* JSJSup 125. Leiden: Brill, 2008.

Balentine, Samuel E. *The Hidden God: The Hiding of the Face of God in the Old Testament.* Oxford: Oxford University Press, 1983.

———. *Job.* SHBC. Macon, GA: Smyth & Helwys, 2006.

———. *Wisdom Literature.* CBS. Nashville: Abingdon, 2018.

Bundvad, Mette. *Time in the Book of Ecclesiastes.* Oxford: Oxford University Press, 2015.

Damasio, Antonio. *Looking for Spinoza: Joy, Sorrow, and the Feeling Brain.* Orlando: Harcourt, 2003.

Del Olmo Lete, Gregorio, and Joaquín Sanmartín. *A Dictionary of the Ugaritic Language in the Alphabetic Tradition.* Third Revised Edition. Translated and Edited by Wilfred G. E. Watson. Leiden: Brill, 2015.

Dell, Katharine J. *Interpreting Ecclesiastes: Readers Old and New.* Winona Lake: Eisenbrauns, 2013.

Fox, Michael V. "The Innerstructure of Qohelet's Thought." Pages 225–38 in *Qohelet in the Context of Wisdom.* Edited by A. Schoors. Leuven: Leuven University Press, 1998.

———. *Qohelet and His Contradictions.* Sheffield: Sheffield Academic, 1989.

———. *A Time to Tear Down and a Time to Build Up: A Rereading of Ecclesiastes.* Grand Rapids: Eerdmans, 1999.

Hankins, Davis. "The Internal Infinite: Deleuze, Subjectivity, and Moral Agency in Ecclesiastes." *JSOT* 40/1 (2015): 41–59.

Isaksson, Bo. *Studies in the Language of Qohelet: With Special Emphasis on the Verbal System.* Stockholm: Almqvist & Wiksell International, 1987.

Jenni, Ernst, and Claude Westermann. *Theological Lexicon of the Old Testament, Volume 2*. Translated by Mark E. Biddle. Peabody: Hendrickson, 1997.

Koehler, Ludwig, and Walter Baumgartner. *The Hebrew and Aramaic Lexicon of the Old Testament, Volume II*. Leiden: E.J. Brill, 1995.

Koosed, Jennifer L. "Ecclesiastes." Pages 243–46 in *Women's Bible Commentary*. Edited by Carol A. Newsom, Sharon H. Ringe, and Jacqueline E. Lapsley. Louisville: Westminster John Knox, 2012.

———. *(Per)mutations of Qohelet: Reading the Body in the Book*. New York: T&T Clark, 2006.

Krüger, Thomas. *Qohelet: A Commentary*. Hermeneia. Minneapolis: Augsburg Fortress Press, 2004.

Meek, Russell L., and David J. H. Beldman. *A Classified Bibliography on Ecclesiastes*. New York: T&T Clark, 2019.

Schoors, Antoon. *The Preacher Sought to Find Pleasing Words: A Study of the Language of Qohelet, Part II Vocabulary*. Leuven: Peeters, 2004.

Seow, C. L. *Ecclesiastes*. AB 18C. New York: Doubleday, 1997.

Strong, James. *The New Strong's Expanded Exhaustive Concordance of the Bible*. Nashville: Thomas Nelson, 2001.

Tennyson, Alfred Lord. "Ulysses." Pages 88–90 in *Tennyson: Poems*. London: Everyman's Library, 2004.

Wisdom through Symbolic Objects
The Second Temple Intellectual Context of Symbolic Bodies in and beyond Proverbs 1–9[1]

Phillip Michael Lasater

> *I warmly dedicate this paper to Samuel E. Balentine. While teaching me many things and introducing me to an interdisciplinary vision of biblical studies, he helped me sense the myriad ways in which "biblical interpretation matters." The emphatic statement that "biblical interpretation matters" was the focus of the first lecture I ever heard him deliver, and it remains in my mind still today.*

How might the language usage in biblical texts supply a window into the way that scribes interpreted the material world?[2] That is

---

1. Collegial input was important in this study's development. I am sincerely thankful to Françoise Mirguet (Arizona State University), and the Alttestamentliches Forschungsseminar (Universität Zürich), for their thoughtful feedback on earlier versions of this paper. Whatever shortcomings remain are my own.

2. Samuel E. Balentine notes that the scribes behind the book of Proverbs sought to understand life's purpose as well as "the nature of the world." See his *Wisdom*

the question of this essay, which takes Proverbs 1–9 as a point of departure. In these instructional texts, the seemingly nonphysiological use of physiological terms can give us glimpses into scribal views of physical objects or materiality. Terms that include body parts are about something other than body parts. How should we make sense of it when a noun like *lēb*, "heart," does not plainly indicate a "heart"? What accounts for the gap between a corporeal term on the one hand and its plain referent on the other? For the scribes responsible for Prov 1–9, it seems that words are not the only things that "mean"; material objects also "mean," and their meanings can influence the use of words written by scribes, and encountered by readers, in and beyond these texts. Indeed, Prov 1–9 can be understood prospectively as part of what Second Temple Jewish wisdom was becoming, with Philo and other, later writings contributing to a shared worldview.[3] Historically, the capacity of objects to mean is what lay behind allegory and its secondary, literary manifestation in the use of written words. In Second Temple period compositions, the meanings of worldly objects seem to have generated equivocal meanings of words in texts that speak of those objects, a point that applies within and beyond the book of Proverbs in so-called post-biblical Jewish literature.

As the academic designation indicates, wisdom literature or instructional literature has a lot to say about "wisdom" (*ḥokmâ*) or, more broadly, "instruction" as something that can be acquired, taught, and practiced (e.g., *tôrâ*, *mûsār*, *daʿat*). Furthermore, at least in Prov 1–9, not all "instruction" is equal. Pointing out this fact alone says nothing new, as a brief glance at the past century of Proverbs scholarship illustrates. Many times, scholars have questioned what to

---

Literature, CBS (Nashville: Abingdon, 2018), 11.

3. On reading prospectively, see Hindy Najman, "Jewish Wisdom in the Hellenistic Period: Towards the Study of a Semantic Constellation," in *Is There a Text in This Cave? Studies in the Textuality of the Dead Sea Scrolls in Honour of George J. Brooke*, ed. Ariel Feldman, Maria Cioată, and Charlotte Hempel, STDJ 119 (Leiden: Brill, 2017), 466 and 472, where Najman concludes that "there is sufficient correlation between the Greek and Hebrew constellations of terms to warrant the claim that these contemporaries inhabited a shared worldview." See also Hindy Najman, "Ethical Reading: The Transformation of the Text and the Self," *JTS* 68/2 (2017): 525.

make of the way that Prov 1–9 juxtaposes parental teaching on the one hand with divine, personified wisdom on the other. This issue has spawned much redaction-critical work, and this work presupposes some kind of difference between varieties of instruction in these chapters—varieties that some scholars have sought to explain in terms of a linear development from "non-theological" to "theological" wisdom, whereas others have doubted whether such a linear shift in fact occurred.[4] Amid the diverging conclusions about redaction, what seems agreed upon is that Prov 1–9 does indeed present more than one sort or level of instruction and of knowledge. Disagreement emerges through the question of how these levels relate to each other, with human bodies sharing in the same allegedly "non-theological" and "theological" foci. Is their relation just a coincidental byproduct of literary transmission? Or might these levels capture something important in a Second Temple period intellectual project?

Since literary-historical conclusions influence this discussion, I should acknowledge that I find Prov 1–9 to be a largely unified late-Persian or Hellenistic period composition, whose pairing of parental teaching with divine, personified wisdom does not warrant diachronic reconstruction.[5] Literary growth is neither the only nor the most promising way to explain this distinction in this text. An

---

4. For the idea of a shift from non-theological to theological wisdom, see William McKane, who posits a time "before and after [wisdom's] subjection to Yahwistic piety" (*Proverbs: A New Approach*, 2nd ed. [London: SCM, 1977], 263). By contrast, for the argument that an already theological wisdom increased its theological emphasis, see H. H. Schmid, *Wesen und Geschichte der Weisheit* (Berlin: Verlag Alfred Töpelmann, 1966), 144–45. Cf. Gerhard von Rad, *Weisheit in Israel*, 4th ed. (Neukirchen-Vluyn: Neukirchener Verlagsgesellschaft, 2013 [orig. 1970]), 73 n. 12. Finally, Katharine Dell argues that "there was an ongoing tension between the human-sided wisdom and the God-given dimension," which may have characterized wisdom "from earliest times" (see her *'Get Wisdom, Get Insight': An Introduction to Israel's Wisdom Literature* [Macon, GA: Smyth & Helwys, 2000], 30).

5. For a date in the Hellenistic period, see Konrad Schmid, *Literaturgeschichte des Alten Testaments: Eine Einführung* (Darmstadt: Wissenschaftliche Buchgesellschaft, 2008), 180–83; and Michael Fox, *Proverbs 1–9: A New Translation with Introduction and Commentary*, AB 18A (New York: Doubleday, 2000), 6. Samuel L. Adams is open to a date in either the Persian or the Hellenistic period (*Wisdom in Transition: Act and Consequence in Second Temple Instructions*, JSJSup 125 [Leiden: Brill, 2008]).

alternative for understanding the relationship between parental and divine wisdom is to focus on how acquiring instruction depends on tutoring key human faculties like the *lēb*, "heart" (but also *nepeš*, "soul, life"), which the scribes behind Prov 1–9 understood as, in theory, open to different levels of knowledge.[6] While the *nepeš* does receive attention in Prov 1–9, the primary anthropological term is the *lēb*, through which pupils receive wisdom. In this vein, a major issue needing clarification is why words for body parts have meanings in Prov 1–9 that can hardly be called physiological—a point that raises questions about what the word *lēb* referenced as well as about how the referenced object itself was understood. Michael Fox and Christopher Ansberry have observed a number of commonalities (≠ borrowing) between Greek literature and Prov 1–9, and this paper joins arguments along these lines.[7] In this case, the argument has to do with allegorical or symbolic understandings of physical objects, one being the *lēb*. Using Prov 1–9 as a starting point, the argument I want to make is that the use of physiological terms suggests that at least some biblical scribes had an allegorical or symbolic view of the physical world, which is more directly attested, as well as contested, in the history of reception. This use of words might give glimpses into biblical writers' ontology. The main biblical texts for consideration are Prov 4 and Prov 2. A careful look at the terminology in these texts raises questions of ancient and early-modern intellectual history that can enhance our understanding of Prov 1–9, those who produced it, and how they compare to later interpreters of Jewish Scriptures.

---

6. For more on this hierarchy of knowledge, see Phillip Michael Lasater, *Facets of Fear: The Fear of God in Exilic and Post-exilic Contexts*, FAT II 104 (Tübingen: Mohr Siebeck, 2019), 177–217.

7. Michael Fox, "Ethics and Wisdom in the Book of Proverbs," *HS* 48 (2007): 75–88; idem, "The Epistemology of the Book of Proverbs," *JBL* 126 (2007): 669–84; Christopher B. Ansberry, "What Does Jerusalem Have to Do with Athens? The Moral Vision of the Book of Proverbs and Aristotle's *Nicomachean Ethics*," *HS* 51 (2010): 157–73.

Distinguishable yet Intertwined Levels of Instruction in Proverbs 1–9

In Prov 4, the opening lecture clearly emphasizes the teacher's own instruction for the student, with the teacher's former experience under his mentor paralleling the current relationship:

Proverbs 4:1–5		
1.	Hear, O sons, <u>the father's instruction</u>; listen attentively to know understanding.	שמע בנים מוסר אב והקשיבו לדעת בינה
2.	For <u>I have given</u> you good teaching; do not forsake <u>my instruction</u>.	כי לקח טוב נתתי לכם תורתי אל־תעזבו
3.	For I was a son to my father, the tender and prized one of my mother,	כי־בן הייתי לאבי רך ויחיד לפני אמי
4.	<u>He taught me</u> and said to me, "May your *lēb* take hold of <u>my words</u>. Keep <u>my commandments</u> and live."	וירני ויאמר לי יתמך־דברי לבך שמר מצותי וחיה
5.	Acquire wisdom, acquire understanding; do not forget nor turn aside from <u>the words of my mouth</u>.	קנה חכמה קנה בינה אל־ תשכח ואל־תט מאמרי־פי

Proverbs 4:1-5 is about intergenerational instruction between teachers and students. The initial sentence identifies "the father's instruction" as a way of knowing, a way of gaining understanding that the current teacher had received from his "father" or teacher (v. 1, *lāda ʿat bînâ*; note the retrospective v. 3). In vv. 2 and 4, this parental instruction consists of "good teaching" and "my *tôrâ*," as well as "my words" and "my commandments." In addition to these first-person suffixes, v. 5 locates the instructive words' origin in the mentor's own "mouth" (*ʾimrê-pî*). This is a human wisdom. The text envisions a process of habituation where, through a quasi-parental model, mentors help pupils train their affective and cognitive faculties

to resist certain inclinations and to pursue others. Such training of human faculties—in this case, the *lēb*—enables the acquisition and practice of the teacher's wisdom. In v. 4, colon A introduces the *lēb* as the subject of a jussive, making the heart the focus of third-person assessment. That is, the heart is subject to oughts: "May your *lēb* take hold of my words." It should act in one way rather than another. While training is required, the heart apparently has a natural openness toward instruction. It is the *lēb* that can and should "grasp" (*tāmak*) these normative "words," as though they were objects (note 3:18, *tāmak* + wisdom as "the tree of life").[8] This activity of the *lēb* in "grasping" instruction is what enables the pupil to honor colon B's imperative of keeping the teacher's commandments for the sake of life or flourishing: "Keep my commandments and live" (4:4). The next verse sums up the issue as a matter of acquiring wisdom, which is an imperative to be obeyed: "Acquire wisdom, acquire insight." This imperatival call to acquire wisdom presupposes the malleability of the *lēb*, which must be responsive by "taking hold" of the instructor's words and by the pupil's ongoing attunement to them (vv. 4-5). As noted earlier, the end of v. 5 states that this avenue toward wisdom rests on the mentor's authority: "the words of my mouth." Proverbs 4 thus emphasizes parental wisdom and the ethical role of the *lēb* in acquiring it.

Proverbs 2:1-6 is another text that comments on the *lēb*, which is again related to the acquisition of wisdom. In this case, it is a divine wisdom from YHWH. This wisdom is not interchangeable with the human wisdom mentioned in Prov 4.[9] But denying their interchangeability does not mean that they are unrelated or assignable to different literary histories; there is fluidity between the interpersonal wisdom of Prov 4 and the theologically endowed wisdom of Prov 2. The one should lead to the other, as illustrated in the compound, conditional statement of 2:1-6:

---

8. See the comments about this text in Jacqueline Vayntrub, "Like Father, Like Son: Theorizing Transmission in Biblical Literature," *HeBAI* 7 (2018): 500–26, here 516–17.

9. In several respects, Prov 2–3 build on the speech by personified Wisdom in 1:20-33 and anticipate her speech in Prov 8, where it becomes even more explicit that this personified Wisdom originates from YHWH (8:22-24; cf. earlier 2:6; 3:19-20).

Proverbs 2:1-6		
1.	My son, if you take <u>my words</u> and store up <u>my commandments</u> with[in] you,	בני אם־תקח אמרי ומצותי תצפן אתך
2.	making your ear (*ʾōzen*) attentive to wisdom and guiding your *lēb* to insight (*tĕbûnâ*)	להקשיב לחכמה אזנך תטה לבך לתבונה
3.	if you call for understanding and call out for *tĕbûnâ*,	כי אם לבינה תקרא לתבונה תתן קולך
4.	if you seek it like silver and search it out like treasures,	אם־תבקשנה ככסף וכמטמונים תחפשנה
5.	then you will understand the fear of YHWH and find divine knowledge,	אז תבין יראת יהוה ודעת אלהים תמצא
6.	for YHWH gives wisdom; <u>from his mouth</u> come knowledge and *tĕbûnâ*.	כי יהוה יתן חכמה מפיו דעת ותבונה

The divine instruction here anticipates other passages in Prov 1–9, which emphasize the possibility of substantial unity between transcendent rationality and this-worldly rationality.[10] *Ḥokmâ* is the unifying element, and the *lēb* is the anthropological equipment for acquiring it. Even though the father speaks in 2:1-6, in contrast to the previous text, he stresses a different and indeed higher level of knowing whose content does not seem restricted to the written lectures of Prov 1–9. This higher level is *daʿat ʾĕlōhîm*, "divine knowledge" (2:5). Both parental wisdom and divine wisdom are in view here, but with the former seeming to operate as a venue for "finding" the latter. The conditional clauses (*ʾim*, "if") in vv. 1-4 about parental

---

10. See the discussion in Carol A. Newsom, "Evil in the Hebrew Bible: The Case of the Wisdom Literature," in *Evil: A History*, Oxford Philosophical Concepts, ed. Andrew P. Chignell (Oxford: Oxford University Press, 2019), 60–81, where she observes how in Proverbs the created order, and its rationality, is "the same rationality that the wise understand and enact" (67). She also discusses helpfully these issues in Job and Ecclesiastes. For a reception-historical treatment of how such concerns relate to Ecclesiastes, see Phillip Michael Lasater, "Not So Vain After All: Hannah Arendt's Reception of Ecclesiastes," *JBRec* 6/2 (2019): 163–96.

wisdom lead up to vv. 5-6 about divine wisdom and the envisioned outcome (*ʾoz*, "then") of "finding" *daʿat ʾĕlōhîm*, which is apparently the same as the *daʿat* and *tĕbûnâ* that come not from the instructor's "mouth" but rather from YHWH's "mouth" (v. 6, *mippîw*, for divine instruction; cf. 4:5, *ʾimrê-pî*, for the teacher's instruction). Identical terms are used here for conceptually distinct levels of instruction (cf. vv. 1-2 and vv. 5-6). The noun *tĕbûnâ* serves as an example (vv. 2, 3, 6, 11): in 2:1-2, after the teacher introduces "my words," which impart a human *tĕbûnâ*, he tells the student to "raise your voice" in supplication for a *tĕbûnâ* that may or may not be human (2:3). This ambiguity in 2:3 is heightened by the fact that, by 2:6, a divine *tĕbûnâ* certainly is in view, coming from YHWH's own "mouth." Lower and higher levels appear complementary. Moreover, fostering a particular condition for the *lēb* is indispensable for attaining each level of knowledge, which implies that the scribes behind Prov 1–9 regarded ethics as being, in some sense, preparatory for epistemology. For them, knowledge requires that certain normative conditions are already in place, with the *lēb* being inextricable from knowledge and normative conditions alike.

In Prov 2, such normative conditions involve securing a particular inclination for the parallel nouns *lēb* and *ʾōzen*, each of which can denote a body part but neither of which is chiefly physiological here or in other, similar texts (see note 52 on 4Q252).[11] As is well known, the word *lēb* suggests a governing locus of thought, feeling, and agency, with *ʾōzen* resembling this usage at times (e.g., 4Q416 2 iii 18; see also the usage of *ʾōzen* in note 52). In multiple sources, both words have to do with a human capacity for and receptivity to authoritative instruction as well as revelation, and their usage in this way can overlap. Like the *ʾōzen*, the *lēb* may "hear," implying that straightforward sensory experience is not always the concern. In a context that is also about wisdom, 1 Kgs 3:9 mentions Solomon's

---

11. The combination of *lēb* + *nāṭâ* is unusual in Prov 1–9, applying not to a person but to abstractions like wisdom, discernment, etc. The closest parallel is the late Ps 119, where talk of the heart's "inclinations" applies to divine *tôrâ* (see also Ps 141:4; note the "ear's" inclination in Ps 49:5). For further discussion, see Bernd Schipper, *Hermeneutik der Tora: Studien zur Traditionsgeschichte von Prov 2 und zur Komposition von Prov 1–9*, BZAW 432 (Berlin: de Gruyter, 2012), 88–90.

desire for a *lēb šōmēaʿ*, "hearing *lēb*." On its own, the incongruent sensory combination of "hearing" + *lēb* illustrates the inadequacy of a plain or literal meaning for either term: Solomon asks for normative conditions to be satisfied so that understanding may come. Here in Proverbs 2, the scribes' connection between ethics and epistemology is clear when the father in 2:7-9 outlines the import of virtuous practice and then points to a result of "understanding" (v. 9, *bîn*), since this wisdom from YHWH will "enter into your *lēb*" (v. 10). In these texts, it seems safe to say that, even though these terms can and do denote body parts, these terms for body parts are best interpreted as both *including* and being *about* something other than literal body parts. The question is, "Why?" Why did it make sense to use words for corporeal items in this way? To answer this question, we need to consider the relationship between the word *lēb*, the object to which it refers, and the location of meaning.

This non-literal usage of terms for body parts may hint that, according to the scribes behind the book of Proverbs, language does not circumscribe meaning. Both words and objects can "mean." This distinction becomes clearer if we contextualize influential, modern approaches to meaning and their indebtedness to early-modern theoretical changes. These changes involved how people read biblical texts and the physical world. Against this background, we can better apprehend a symbolic or allegorical conception of objects, as well as this conception's intellectual adherents, whose so-called post-biblical ideas may have grounding within the instructional literature of Prov 1–9.[12]

The next section contrasts ideas from Second Temple wisdom with some modern notions that consider objects by themselves as "dead matter" devoid of meaning, so that individuals provide or

---

12. To say that allegory is post-biblical is to suggest that it post-dates "the Bible," which, as a number of studies have stressed, is an anachronism in studies of ancient Judaism insofar as "the Bible" was not clearly defined until well after interpreters, including canonized scribes such as Paul (e.g., Gal 4:24), had already been reading Scripture allegorically. For a thoughtful treatment of canonization and the nature of textual authority, see Hindy Najman, "The Vitality of Scripture Within and Beyond the 'Canon,'" *JSJ* 43 (2012): 497–518. See also Timothy H. Lim, *The Formation of the Jewish Canon* (New Haven: Yale University Press, 2013), 52–53.

project their own meaning, through intention or otherwise. Such contrasts help identify ways that modern biblical scholarship's institutional and intellectual history refracts scholarly views of what many ancient readers thought about themselves and their texts. If we engage in modern, philological research with insufficient self-criticism, there may be "cracks in our presumption" of bracketing our hermeneutical biases.[13]

Reforming Words and Things

The repercussions of early-modern changes remain present for today's scholars of ancient literature, so we should be clear about some easily overlooked differences where researchers may presume common definitions between modernity and antiquity that are quite divergent (e.g., words, texts, materiality, and meaning).

In the sixteenth century, the Protestant Reformation's disputes altered not only the institutions of Western Christianity but also people's conceptions of Scripture and its wording. Separating Scripture from what Michael C. Legaspi calls a "divine economy of meaning" oriented toward the world,[14] the Bible's meaning came to be sought wholly in its written words, which may or may not clearly communicate their authors' intent. The humanist motto *ad fontes* came to work in conjunction with the Protestant motto *sola scriptura*. For many Reformers and Enlightenment figures, the de-institutionalized Bible became first and foremost a freestanding text, whose purportedly original and thus preferable version was the oft-sought means for Reformers to mend doctrinal divisions—provided, of

---

13. For this phrase, see David A. Lambert, "Refreshing Philology: James, Barr, Supersessionism, and the State of Biblical Words," *BibInt* 24 (2016): 342. Lambert later asks, "Could there be a new or updated philology that points to the historicity or contingency—that is to say, the intrinsic instability and ideological basis—of our 'word meanings'?" (353). A fitting place to begin is to think about a strict association between "words" and "meanings."

14. Michael C. Legaspi, *The Death of Scripture and the Rise of Biblical Studies*, Oxford Studies in Historical Theology (Oxford: Oxford University Press, 2010), 3. He goes on to write that "Instead of looking *through* the Bible in order to understand *the truth about the world*, eighteenth-century scholars looked directly at the text, endeavoring to find new, ever more satisfactory frames of cultural and historical reference by which to understand *the meaning of the text*" (26).

course, that confessionally opposed Reformers could unite around one reading.[15] Indeed, words came to monopolize meaning.[16] However unintentionally, this change proved congenial to Europe's transforming political and intellectual landscape where individuals tried to make sense of biblical texts, as well as the natural world, in new ways.

An influential, modern conception of meaning in language is that meaning arises via a word's designation of a thing, whether the thing in question is concrete or abstract. The idea is that meaning emerges through words' representation of objects. More exactly, the idea is that words' meanings are attached *through an individual's mental images* to external things, which, strictly speaking, are without meaning on their own. One could call this view a mediational or designative theory, according to which our words impart meaning to objects in the world. Historically, this way of thinking has coincided with early-modern individualist theories of knowledge that are rooted in the work of Descartes.[17] Descartes held that knowledge arises only when inner states of mind accurately represent a reality outside of the mind. These inner states of mind are the medium of knowledge. Knowledge arises not by someone's directly grasping objects or ideas but rather through an individual's subjective states, so long as these states accurately represent that which resides in the world or "outside"

---

15. Ibid., 18–26.

16. Notably, when discussing the text-critical collaboration between the Protestant Louis Cappel (1585–1658) and the Catholic Jean Morin (1591–1659), Legaspi suggests that, for Cappel, philology had replaced the priesthood (ibid., 21; see also 23).

17. Charles Taylor, "Overcoming Modern Epistemology," in *Faithful Reading: New Essays in Theology and Philosophy in Honour of Fergus Kerr, OP*, ed. S. Oliver et al. (London: Bloomsbury, 2013), 46. Descartes' basic approach to issues of the mind and language has survived even among schools of thought that reject the philosophical anthropology and substance dualism on which Descartes' arguments depended (e.g., Humean empiricism; contemporary physicalists; etc.). See further idem, *The Language Animal: The Full Shape of the Linguistic Capacity* (Cambridge: Harvard University Press, 2016), 13–14. See also the discussion in Dennis Patterson, "Review of M. R. Bennett and P. M. S. Hacker's *Philosophical Foundations of Neuroscience*," *Notre Dame Philosophical Reviews: An Electronic Journal*, 10 September 2003, https://ndpr.nd.edu/news/philosophical-foundations-of-neuroscience/.

the mind, so to speak. This theory depends heavily on an inside-outside component, with the former (i.e., "inside") being the domain of knowledge and meaning. The individual is viewed independently from the world and remains always at a distance from it, so that what is known is never the world itself but rather an individual's subjective representations of whatever presumably lies "outside."[18]

Reminiscent of Descartes, Nick Riemer in his book *Introducing Semantics* discusses what he calls "the semiotic triangle": thought/psychology, symbol, and referent. He exemplifies how a designative theory of language usually depends on an intellectual descendent of Cartesian thinking. At the end of the discussion, Riemer argues the following:

> This leads to the important point that we do not have any access to the world as it actually, objectively is. The only referents we can know are ones which are perceived by our senses or imagined in our minds: ones for which, in other words, we have **mental representations**. . . . The world of referents, that is, must be considered not as a world of real external entities, but as a world of representations which are *projected* by the mind. Another way of putting this would be to say that the world of referents is *within* the domain of psychology. As humans with minds, we have no access to *the* world, with a definite cast of fixed, pre-established referents. (original emphasis)[19]

---

18. Given this emphasis on an individual's interior life as the theoretical starting and concluding point, it is not surprising that these early-modern notions of knowledge and language have fostered types of skepticism that side firmly with one pole of Descartes' dualism (e.g., solipsism, where only the individual self is knowable and real) and physicalism (e.g., only matter is real). On the resultant skepticism from these early-modern theories, see Taylor, "Modern Epistemology," 43. For a contrast between ancient Israelite and modern European attitudes toward the heart and notions of subjectivity, see Silvia Schroer and Thomas Staubli, *Die Körpersymbolik der Bibel* (Darmstadt: Wissenschaftliche Buchgesellschaft, 1998). Schroer and Staubli suggest that modern European attitudes separate "the heart" from striving, rationality, and thought, aligning it instead with accepted, rejected, or misunderstood gestures, as well as with freedom (56).

19. Nick Riemer, *Introducing Semantics* (Cambridge: Cambridge University Press, 2010), 14–15.

Riemer's comments illustrate how modern, designative theories of meaning have a strongly subjectivizing and atomizing thrust. They abstract the individual, the mind, and language from broader background conditions, focusing on the seemingly isolated phenomena of signs, referents, and an individual's "mental representations," which manufacture or project linguistic meaning. Meaning here is separated from objects, being associated instead only with words, which in turn have their place in an individual's psychology. As we will see, this dissociation of meaning from objects, and the turn toward individual subjects, correlates with the early-modern emphasis on authorial intent as the determinative factor of textual meaning, where words' meanings are required to align with an author's subjective states or psychology (i.e., "intention"). Without individuals to project meaning onto a psychologically constructed "world of referents," objects on their own have no meaning.[20] This outlook is a companion to the idea that natural objects can only be understood through quantitative, not qualitative, description.[21] Objects as such have neither an intrinsic purpose (i.e., *telos*) nor a symbolic capacity of pointing to something beyond themselves. So in this scenario, only words "mean"; objects do no such thing. As hinted in the introduction, this theory of language, like others, is a window into an ontology—one that has been important for Western modernity.[22]

Scholars from a range of disciplines have traced this dissociation of meaning from physical objects to the early-modern period in Europe, particularly to the Reformation era and its ramifications during the Enlightenment, where what we know as biblical studies surfaced as a discipline.[23] This conception of materiality arose

---

20. Riemer, *Introducing Semantics*, 15.

21. Thomas Nagel, *The Last Word* (Oxford: Oxford University Press, 2001), 21, points out that "the ordinary methods of science are basically Cartesian." See also Taylor, *The Language Animal*, 14.

22. Taylor, "Modern Epistemology," 44.

23. Peter Harrison, *The Bible, Protestantism, and the Rise of Natural Science* (Cambridge: Cambridge University Press, 2001 [orig. 1998]), 64–120; Brad S. Gregory, *The Unintended Reformation: How a Religious Revolution Secularized Society* (Cambridge: Harvard University Press, 2012), 112–23, esp. 113 on *sola*

partially out of a pragmatic, methodological concern for examining nature with a strict focus on efficient causality, and partially out of a widespread trend of anti-Aristotelianism at the time. In neither case was this notion of objects an empirical discovery.[24] Nonetheless, the result in the early-modern period was that matter or physical reality was redefined as an exclusively quantitative, not qualitative, concept to be understood mathematically, mechanistically, causally. The longstanding idea that natural things have meanings and, relatedly, intrinsic purposes was dismissed, fostering the instrumental mentality that "[t]he purposes things serve are extrinsic to them," that things are not to be understood "in terms of supposedly normative patterns at work in them," patterns that offer instruction and moral standards.[25] Among earlier advocates, to deny, for example, the Aristotelian theory that things have normative, essence-based *teloi* was a way of defending divine sovereignty; to suggest otherwise was believed to limit divine volition and to overestimate the reliability of human knowledge.[26] Theological motivations, then, lay behind this non-teleological and non-symbolic redefining of natural things. The historian of science Peter Harrison has shown how, in key ways, this redefinition of physical reality was rooted in hermeneutical shifts

---

scriptura and *sola ratio* as rival answers to the challenges of the Reformation era; see also Charles Taylor, *A Secular Age* (Cambridge: Harvard University Press, 2007), 97–99.

24. See Leszek Kołakowski, *Metaphysical Horror*, rev. ed. (Chicago: University of Chicago Press, 2001 [orig. 1988]), who notes that the driving, utility-oriented idea was that "the idea of experience should be applied restrictively, to concepts that are, or might be, useful in dealing with objects, and therefore somehow 'better' or 'genuine'" (20). For more on the turn against Aristotle during this period, see Thomas Nagel, *Mind and Cosmos: Why the Materialist Neo-Darwinian Conception of Nature Is Almost Certainly False* (Oxford: Oxford University Press, 2012), 32; and Edward Feser, *Scholastic Metaphysics: A Contemporary Introduction* (Heusenstamm: Editiones Scholasticae, 2014), 12–18. And classically, but with specific emphasis on moral theory, see Alasdair MacIntyre, *After Virtue: A Study in Moral Theory*, 3rd ed. (Notre Dame: University of Notre Dame Press, 2007 [orig. 1981]).

25. Taylor, *A Secular Age*, 97–98.

26. Peter Harrison, *The Territories of Science and Religion* (Chicago: University of Chicago Press, 2015), 80–81. See also Gregory, *The Unintended Reformation*, 38; Taylor, *A Secular Age*, 97.

especially among early Protestant Reformers.[27] To summarize Harrison's argument briefly, the Protestant, hermeneutical shift toward literalism in reading the book of Scripture fostered a literalism in reading the book of nature.

How these two "books" were read had long been intertwined. Well before the medieval articulation of "nature" as an organizational category for physical reality, the interpretation of authoritative texts and various objects had interlocked not only within, but also prior to, Christian literature.[28] The physical world was conceived in qualitative and symbolic terms, eventually paralleling textual interpretation in how the world was to be "read."[29] Nor does a symbolic outlook along these lines seem to come only from Greek influence (e.g., 4Q252 5, frag. 6; note the "tropological" view of animals in Prov 6:6; Job 12:7; etc.).[30] While the plain or literal meaning of texts

---

27. Harrison, *Territories*, 79–81; idem, *Natural Science*, 64–120.

28. See Philo's *Allegorical Commentary* and the *Physiologus*. On Philo's *Allegorical Commentary*, see Louis H. Feldman, James L. Kugel, and Lawrence H. Schiffman, eds., *Outside the Bible: Ancient Jewish Writings Related to Scripture* (Philadelphia: The Jewish Publication Society, 2013), 902–903. The *Physiologus*, which may have been composed by a disciple of Origen in the second century CE, was a systematized, highly influential account of natural things' meanings that in various, and competing, ways had been discussed well before the second century CE. See Harrison, *Natural Science*, 11–33, 39–44.

29. Harrison, *Natural Science*, 44–63, 65.

30. On the instructive dimension of the physical world in ancient Jewish contexts, see Tova Forti, *Animal Imagery in the Book of Proverbs* (Leiden: Brill, 2008), who states that, for scribes, the physical world was admired and assessed because of the "wisdom" it contained and the "unconscious intelligence of beasts, who share a mysterious and at times esoteric knowledge inaccessible to human beings" (1–2; see also 101–29). Even though Forti does not mention allegory, there is deep concord between what she describes and allegorical conceptions of the world from antiquity. The *word* "allegory" first appears in Greek writings. The earliest known attestation of derivatives from the stem ἀλληγορ are in fragmentary rhetorical writings by the Epicurean Philodemus (ca. 110–40 BCE), as discussed by Hans-Josef Klauck, *Allegorie und Allegorese in synoptischen Gleichnistexten*, 2nd ed.(Neutestamentliche Abhandlungen 13; Münster: Aschendorff, 1978), 39–41. On early Greek usages of allegory, see Glenn W. Most, "The poetics of early Greek philosophy," in *The Cambridge Companion to Early Greek Philosophy*, ed. A. A. Long (Cambridge: Cambridge University Press, 1999), 339–41.

and objects was acknowledged in antiquity, it was often one layer of meaning among others on a vertical scale. In Christian circles such as the Alexandrians, literal meaning was the least important. Even for the Antiochene school of interpretation, which emphasized a text's plain meaning, plain meanings were neither the only nor the highest ones.[31] Although some early Christians adhered to a hermeneutic of reading Scripture only literally, such readings of Scripture, according to Manlio Simonetti, may be considered radical in their day.[32] More commonly, the hermeneutical coexistence of literal, moral, and allegorical meanings of texts entailed that texts were somewhat equivocal.

Attempting to eliminate anything other than a literal or plain meaning in written words was an early-modern novelty fueled by the Reformation era's theological disputes. For example, Reformers tended to downgrade concrete, ritual practices and to dismiss or destroy physical icons, which were specific ways of denying meaning to semantically charged objects and, in the process, aligning meaning with words alone—namely, written, scriptural words. The gradual redefinition of physical, including religious, objects was related to a transformed way of reading biblical texts.[33] Fueling the hermeneutical transformation was, on the one hand, a widely shared fascination with origins (i.e., *ad fontes*; e.g., authorial intent or *Ur*-meaning; *Urtext*, etc.), and, on the other hand, Reformers' elevation of the Bible *as text* to unprecedented levels of authority separable from ecclesial institutions. The principle of Scripture alone as having the final say in doctrinal disputes required reducing its ambiguity as much as possible, which bolstered the appeal of literal, and supposedly

---

31. In the fourth century, Antiochene interpreters like Diodore of Tarsus (died ca. 390 CE) and Theodoret of Cyrus (died ca. 460 CE) spoke of higher meanings (*theōria*) that surpassed the plain meaning (*lexis*) of texts but argued that the former should be methodologically constrained by the former. See Michael Graves, *The Inspiration and Interpretation of Scripture: What the Early Church Can Teach Us* (Grand Rapids: Eerdmans, 2014), 15.

32. Manlio Simonetti, *Biblical Interpretation in the Early Church: An Historical Introduction to Patristic Exegesis* (New York: T&T Clark, 2001), 13.

33. Harrison, *Natural Science*, 115.

author-intended, readings.³⁴ There was a felt need for textual meaning to be single and determinate, not multilayered and equivocal.³⁵ A reduction of textual meaning to the literal coalesced with and intensified a denial of objects as symbolic, as natural bearers of meaning: literalism in one area helped promote literalism in the other. The early Protestants' rejection of allegorical interpretation was a logical outgrowth of reforming objects and words alike. Indeed, substantial change resulted from gainsaying that the cosmos was a locus of signs, where objects point beyond themselves to various truths. When that was opposed, texts no longer needed to account for various truths, but only for one, namely, a writer's personal intent.³⁶ The claim that biblical texts are univocal lay at the heart of this literalist turn.

Keeping in mind these intellectual transitions is indispensable for seeing how, during the same period, allegory came to be viewed not as "an approach to the world" that may be reflected in texts³⁷ but rather as a literary or linguistic device as such, and a disreputable one at that.³⁸ Writing in the seventeenth century about the inter-

---

34. For a fuller discussion of this issue, see Gregory, *The Unintended Reformation*, 74–128. On these heightened expectations for the Bible, which was then contrasted with tradition, see the comments in Diarmaid MacCulloch, *Reformation: Europe's House Divided, 1490–1700* (London: Penguin Books, 2003), 101.

35. Harrison, *Natural Science*, 111, 113.

36. On allegory and the multiplicity of truths to be addressed, see Mark Elliot, "Allegory and Allegorical Interpretation," in *Oxford Encyclopedia of Biblical Interpretation*, ed. Steven L. McKenzie (Oxford: Oxford University Press, 2013), 17–27, who notes that, for ancient readers, "allegory does not serve to get across one truth but to map relationships of invisible *truths*" (19; original emphasis). See also Simonetti, *Biblical Interpretation*, 11–12.

37. Harrison, *Natural Science*, 91.

38. On allegory's early-modern disrepute, with the further issue of allegory's relationship to typology, see Hindy Najman, "Cain and Abel as Character Traits: A Study in the Allegorical Typology of Philo of Alexandria," in *Past Renewals: Interpretive Authority, Renewed Revelation and the Quest for Perfection in Jewish Antiquity*, JSJSup 53 (Leiden: Brill, 2010), 207–18, where Najman notes how "Since the reformation, scholars have denigrated allegorical interpretation (e.g., in the writings of Philo of Alexandria and Origen), because it appeared far removed from the literal sense of Scripture," as well as how "anti-allegorical polemics ... still find their way into current scholarship" (208). Similarly, see Simonetti, *Biblical Interpretation*, 6–12.

pretation of Genesis and anticipating later emphasis on projection (cf. Riemer's quote above), the Swiss theologian Jean Le Clerc remarked that allegory warrants "Indignation" in view of "this Libertine way of Interpreting the Scripture, which wholly depends upon the Fancy of the Interpreter."[39] According to Le Clerc, allegory consists of "[committing] Violence upon [Moses'] words."[40] It was "violence" because written words in their plain sense are determinate for Le Clerc. Discernible behind his comments about allegory is the revised understanding of matter from the previous century: meaning was being reconfigured not as a feature of the world but as the work or product of individuals, so that words came to monopolize meaning, and meaning in turn was to be sought chiefly in the psychology, the intent, of individual writers, whether Moses or otherwise. If the world is not a depository of signs and *teloi* where natural objects point to various truths, then, so the reasoning goes, plain descriptive language is the one plausible form of meaning in biblical texts' presentation of the world.

By contrast, in pre-Reformation or non-Protestant settings where a symbolic view of the world was in play, a common assumption was that texts needed to be read in more than one way in order to do justice to the referenced objects, which were themselves polysemous. One should note that such a view of objects as polysemous would likely affect how authors used words in texts, since the use of a word may presuppose an object's symbolic dimensions (which may be happening with *lēb* in Prov 1–9). As evidenced by arguments from antiquity that the same text should be read plainly and allegorically alike, allegory was not mainly an attempt to salvage otherwise nonsensical texts; rather, it was an attempt to understand a symbolic cosmos through articulating the plural meanings of what a text references, whether the referenced items were natural, constructed, or abstract (Philo in *Leg.* 2.89; later, Augustine in *Doctr. chr.* 3.10.14).[41]

---

39. Jean Le Clerc, *Twelve Dissertations out of Monsieur Le Clerc's Genesis*, trans. Mr. Brown (London: R. Baldwin, 1696), 144. See also Harrison, *Natural Science*, 91, 109.

40. Le Clerc, *Twelve Dissertations*, 143.

41. Adam Kamesar, "Biblical Interpretation in Philo," in *The Cambridge Companion to Philo*, ed. A. Kamesar (Cambridge: Cambridge University Press,

For that reason, allegory was not limited to "obviously" symbolic texts but was applied to narratives, laws, and so on.[42] Even though the meanings of things, especially hostile creatures, could be regarded as imperfectly grasped or hidden, their meanings were nonetheless presupposed as real by virtue of something's having been created.[43] Accordingly, biblical texts were thought to be equivocal not because of the texts' words *per se* or because of an author's carelessness but rather because of the symbolic nature of the referenced objects. Allegory was less about linguistics, more about ontology. So even if an author did not consciously intend to allegorize, reading a text allegorically could remain plausible due to the symbolic dimensions of referenced items such as light, sun,[44] water, animals,[45] places, ritual objects, certain body parts, and so on. This sort of outlook seems to have been more widespread in the Second Temple period than scholars acknowledge. The linguistically documented use of allegory in the New Testament does not mark a radical break but rather stands within a broader interpretive tradition (Gal 4:24, *allēgoreō*, "to allegorize"). I turn now to some noticeably diverse examples from

---

2009), argues that Philo basically shared the same attitude toward allegory that Augustine later made more explicit (80). Elliot, "Allegory and Allegorical Interpretation," makes a similar observation when he writes, "Allegory then should not be seen as having been simply a 'last resort' for puzzling texts."

42. Klauck, *Allegorie und Allegorese*, writes "Es sei daran erinnert, daß in der Väterzeit und im Mittelalter die allegorische Exegese keineswegs ausschließlich auf Gleichnisse angewandt wurde. Bevorzugte Objekte der Allegorese waren z.B. atl Geschichts- und Gesetzestexte, die man nur so theologisch und homiletisch glaubte auswerten zu können. Das ändert sich erst in der Neuzeit" (5).

43. On animals, see the remarks in Forti, *Animal Imagery*, 2; and also Harrison, *Natural Science*, 13–15.

44. On Egyptian solar imagery during the ninth through eighth centuries BCE, see Othmar Keel and Christoph Uehlinger, *Gods, Goddesses, and Images of God in Ancient Israel* (Minneapolis: Fortress, 1998), 278–81; and with relevance to the temple, note the seal of "Ashna" (272, 275; cf. the imagery in Isa 6:1-5). For the same set of reapplied images in later biblical texts, see William P. Brown, *Seeing the Psalms: A Theology of Metaphor* (Louisville: Westminster John Knox, 2002), 81–103.

45. Forti, *Animal Imagery*, treats various ways in which animals contained important instruction, including for the operation of human society (101–35).

the late Second Temple period, which include Josephus, Philo, and Qumran, after which I will return to Prov 1–9.

Symbolic Conceptions of Natural and Constructed Objects in the Second Temple Period

Not known as a representative of allegory, Josephus wrote in the *Antiquities* about the tabernacle's entrance being struck by rays of sunlight, which he appears to interpret symbolically in view of the Hebrew Bible's "light theology" (*Ant.* 3.6.3; cf. the eastward orientation of the Jerusalem temple, facing the sunrise). In a number of Hebrew Bible texts, there is a resemblance between light and the sun on the one hand and *kābôd* or sanctuary presence on the other (cf. *kĕbôd-ʾēl* and *šemeš* in Ps 19:2–7).[46] In biblical passages like Ps 19, sunlight (*x*), whose literal sense is acknowledged by mentioning "heat" (*ḥammâ*, Ps 19:7), nonetheless means or signifies something beyond itself (*y*). Its meaning was multilayered: to say that *x* is or means *y* is not to abandon the former but to elaborate on it. Given their resemblances, "a sun is . . . YHWH god" in Psalm 84 (v. 12, *kî šemeš . . . yhwh ʾĕlōhîm*; see also Ps 104:1; Isa 60:19; etc.). Likewise, Josephus seems interested not in sunlight as a physical phenomenon but rather in that toward which sunlight points. Turning to constructed, ritual objects, Josephus then speaks about what various, physical aspects of the tabernacle itself mean:

> However, this proportion of the measures of the tabernacle proved to be an imitation of the system of the world; for that third part thereof which was within the four pillars, to which the priests were not admitted, is, as it were, a heaven peculiar to God. But the space of the twenty cubits is, as it were, sea and land, on which men live, and so this part is peculiar to the priests only. (*Ant.* 3.6.4)

---

46. Similar reflections on the symbolic dimensions of light are widely attested beyond ancient Israel and Judah, as Thomas Staubli has emphasized ("'Let there be light!' Concepts of Light in Ancient Near Eastern Iconography and in the Bible," [forthcoming]). See also Benjamin D. Sommer, "Nature, Revelation, and Grace in Psalm 19: Towards a Theological Reading of Scripture," *HTR* 108 (2015): 387–88; and Brown, *Seeing the Psalms*, 84.

In this neighboring passage, Josephus identifies not sunlight but rather a ritual item (*x*) as pointing toward transcendent meanings (*y*). As he words it, the tabernacle is "an imitation of the system of the world," including "a heaven peculiar to God."

Philo of Alexandria is a more obvious case. Language for Philo is capable of a right fit with "being" in the thick, Platonic sense of "being," so literal description cannot spell the end of inquiry.[47] In his *Allegorical Interpretation*, for instance, he writes of rain and springs of water as pointing to "the superabundance of [God's] wealth and [God's] own goodness" (*Alleg. Interp.* 1.3.34). He was no doubt capable of describing rain and springs literally in terms of, say, liquid that fosters plant growth, but, more importantly for him, they signify truths beyond themselves. Similarly, in the Genesis story of creation, the placement of humans into a world of potentially threatening animals has to do with unruly passions that need to be tamed: what needed to be "ruled" was the soul's own movements that steer people either toward or away from goodness (*Creation* XXVI).[48] The wild animals lead Philo to reflect on sources of instability in ethically maintaining the human soul, not within the material, natural world.[49]

Directly pertinent to our original question about physiological terms in Prov 1–9, Philo writes allegorically about the human heart in multiple texts. The noun *kardia*, "heart," is documented thirty-nine times in his corpus,[50] where he moves seamlessly between literal, ethical, and symbolic usages of the word. While one might

---

47. Kamesar, "Biblical Interpretation in Philo," 70–71. See also Harrison, *Natural Science*, 29–30, 43.

48. Later Christian interpreters read the text similarly, such as Augustine in *Confessions* 13.21 and Jerome in *CCSL* 75.11f. On the passions' threat to Torah practice, see further Feldman, Kugel, and Schiffman, eds., *Outside the Bible*, 882–83; Harrison, *Natural Science*, 47–50.

49. For a reception-historical treatment of how wild creatures in the book of Job have been read ethically, theologically, and politically, see Samuel E. Balentine, *Have You Considered My Servant Job?: Understanding the Biblical Archetype of Patience* (Columbia: University of South Carolina Press, 2015), 177–201.

50. See Peder Borgen, Kåre Fuglseth, and Roald Skarsten, *The Philo Index: A Complete Greek Word Index to the Writings of Philo of Alexandria* (Leiden: Brill, 2000), 186.

quibble with the following table's divisions, Philo's own emphases with *kardia* can be grouped into at least four classes (mostly excluding scriptural quotations). As the table demonstrates, physiological or literal emphases, while present, are the least frequent:

Emphasis	Literary source
The soul and/or virtues	*Leg.* 1:68; *Sac.* 136; *Post.* 85, 137; *Mut.* 123, 237-38; *Somn.* 1:30-32, 33; *Somn.* 2:180; *Spec.* 1:213-15, 218, 304; *Spec.* 4:137; *Virt.* 183; *Praem.* 80
Creation theology	*Opif.* 117-18; *Leg.* 1:12; *Leg.* 2:6; *Det.* 90; *Somn.* 1:30-32, 33
Misc. resemblances	*Mos.* 1:188-89; *Spec.* 1:6; *QG* 2:3
Physiological	*Leg.* 1:59; *Prov* 2:17

Philo is clearly aware of the heart's literal, physiological importance (e.g., *Leg.* 1:59; *Prov* 2:17). But its relation to other body parts leads him to reflect on the heart's material place in the body's sevenfold division, which resembles not only the soul's sevenfold division but also the sevenfold, logical structuring of the Bible's opening creation story. Thus, bodily observations are related to ethical, exegetical, and creation-theological concerns.[51] The heart's crucial role for the soul and virtue formation is why a material, corporeal heart is unfit for sacrifice on the altar: since the soul undergoes not only virtuous but also vicious movements, the heart's "opposite qualities" would profane the holy altar (here *Sac.* 136; see also *Spec.* 1:213-15, 218). Ethics and creation theology translate directly into material considerations for what it would mean to offer a bodily organ on an altar.

This seamlessness between symbolic, ethical, and literal talk of the heart is possible because there is no such thing as "mere" matter for Philo. Material objects need to be interpreted in various ways. Insofar as matter originates from the creator, it is a venue for and points, even if obliquely, toward divinity. According to Philo's earlier

---

51. On Philo's approach to Gen 1 as a non-chronological account of creation, see Roberto Radice, "Philo's Theology and Theory of Creation," in *The Cambridge Companion to Philo*, ed. A. Kamesar (Cambridge: Cambridge University Press, 2009), 133.

work, where he shows more reservations toward Stoicism, natural objects' receptivity toward mind is a case in point:

> How, then, is it natural that the human intellect, being as scanty as it is, and enclosed in no very ample space, in some membrane, or in the *kardia* (truly very narrow bounds), should be able to embrace the vastness of the heaven and of the world, great as it is, if there were not in it some portion of a divine and happy soul, which cannot be separated from it? For nothing which belongs to the divinity can be cut off from it so as to be separated, but it is only extended. (*Det.* 90)

Although Philo rejects some Stoic arguments that matter contains divine *physis* or "nature," matter for Philo is not anything mere; it belongs to the transcendent source of materiality even if that source's nature is shrouded.[52] The creator is indirectly perceptible to the world, comparable to YHWH in Prov 1–9, where one can "find the knowledge of God" through a divinely granted wisdom that both characterizes creation and enters virtuous human hearts (Prov 2:1-10, here v. 5). As Philo puts it in *Somn.* 1:32-34, what is "incomprehensible" (*akatalēptos*) is indirectly channeled by matter, itself being receptive to "a fragment of divinity" (*apospasma theion*).

---

52. In this regard, Philo resembles his predecessor Aristobulus. On Philo's negative theology, see Maren R. Niehoff, *Philo of Alexandria: An Intellectual Biography* (New Haven: Yale University Press, 2018), 210–16; on Aristobulus's relevance, see Radice, "Philo's Theology," 135–36. Philo and his contemporaries' views of "matter" are not interchangeable with the early-modern, non-teleological conceptions of "matter" that encouraged theories where any higher-level phenomena (e.g., mind or the illusion thereof) are determined by lower-level physical laws. On the context of this outlook's historical origins, see Nagel, *Mind and Cosmos*, 35–36; Gregory, *The Unintended Reformation*, 56–64; and Feser, *Scholastic Metaphysics*, 12–18. Specifically on Philo's attitude toward the body, see Françoise Mirguet's discussion of Philo's positive language about the material body "welcoming" the soul as a host country welcomes an exile—thus portraying not only the material body but also diaspora as positives. Mirguet's paper is relevant for considering the symbolic capacity of bodies. Philo's writings are good for showing how ancient contrasts between "body" and "soul" do not map directly onto early-modern contrasts between "body" and "soul," since the notions of matter and the soul had both undergone transformation. For more on Philo in a broader Second Temple context, see Françoise Mirguet, "Introductory Reflections on Embodiment in Hellenistic Judaism," *JSP* 21 (2011): 18.

These issues in Philo's conception of matter seem informed by his attitude toward *logos*, which he equates to some extent with *sophia*—a divinely grounded, connective medium between the immaterial creator and the material world.[53] Hence, like a garment, the divine *logos* has "put on" (*endyō*) "earth and water and air and fire, as well as the things coming from them" (*Fug* 110). The heart is one such material item. In substantial respects, Philo's creation theology and stance toward materiality seem to be in concord with the intellectual project summed up in Prov 1–9 during the Second Temple period. This is not an argument for borrowing or influence between sets of texts. It is an argument for intellectual overlap or hermeneutical common ground between Second Temple wisdom as exemplified within and beyond texts like Prov 1–9 and Philo (both of which can be compared with hermeneutical family resemblances at Qumran; e.g., 4Q252).[54]

What I have called a semantically charged notion of constructed and natural objects can inform studies of the allegorical tendency of the scribes behind Prov 1–9. These tendencies are hardly limited to the oft-studied figures of personified Wisdom on the one hand and

---

53. Radice, "Philo's Theology," 138, 145.

54. Lasater, *Facets of Fear*, 199–202. According to George Brooke, 4Q252 is a commentary on Genesis that could be a copy of an earlier manuscript tradition. See his discussion in Feldman, Kugel, and Schiffman (ed.), *Outside the Bible*, 211. Indeed, 4Q252 displays a symbolic view of objects, such as Judah's "staff," which indicates "the covenant of kingship." Symbolic conceptions of body parts are also at Qumran, such as the clause *gālâ ōzen*, "to uncover the ear"—an epistemological expression for receiving revelation. This use of physiological language seems grounded within the Hebrew Bible itself, as argued by Samuel I. Thomas, "Hearing the Vision: גלה אזן in Qumran Sectarian Texts," *HeBAI* 5 (2016): 59–74. Thomas puts it well when he writes that the issue "was *at least* hearing, even if it was not only hearing" (65). Hence, despite being a non-conformist group, the *Yaḥad* was not isolated in its symbolic hermeneutics. See Jean-Baptiste Humbert, "Qumran," in *The Oxford Encyclopedia of the Bible and Archaeology*, ed. Daniel M. Master (Oxford: Oxford University Press, 2013), 203. On the wider dispersement of the group beyond the site at Qumran, see John J. Collins, *Beyond the Qumran Community: The Sectarian Movement of the Dead Sea Scrolls* (Grand Rapids: Eerdmans, 2010), 65–69.

the strange woman (≈ personified Folly) on the other.⁵⁵ Concrete terminology for the body was semantically charged, with physiological words like *lēb* being used to signify higher or transcendent human capacities, including these scribes' goal of acquiring, even participating in, divinely grounded wisdom (note also *nepeš* [8:36]; cf. *ōzen*, which only "inclines" toward human instructors).⁵⁶ Indeed, the educational aim in Prov 2 is to foster proper "inclinations" for the *lēb*, which only under the right circumstances can receive divine wisdom (2:6, 10).⁵⁷

A neglected question about this usage of bodily terms is, "Why?" When using the word *lēb*, the scribes behind Prov 1–9 were informed by broader, shared conceptions of the referenced object, which, in addition to being the seat of rationality and feeling, had a long history of pointing to human standing before deities—even where neither the word *lēb* itself nor philological equivalents appear. Not only the word but also the object stood for something. Heart amulets provide some clues in this direction, since they occasionally, but notably not always, are inscribed with "heart" wording. With Egyptian imagery, language, and divine names, the heart amulets discovered in the Levant are centuries older than Prov 1–9, but, in the imagery's

---

55. For discussions of these personifications, see Fox, *Proverbs 1–9*, 134–41; Konrad Schmid, "Schöpfung im Alten Testament," in idem, ed. *Schöpfung* (Tübingen: Mohr Siebeck, 2012), 105–106; Katharine Dell, *'Get Wisdom, Get Insight'*, 19–21.

56. The occurrences of *lēb/lēbāb* are in 2:2, 10; 3:1, 3, 5; 4:4, 23; 5:12; 6:14, 18, 21, 32; 7:3, 7, 10, 25; 8:5; 9:4, 16. The occurrences of *nepeš* are in 1:18, 19; 2:10; 3:22; 6:16, 26, 30, 32; 7:23; 8:36. On this participatory project, see Lasater, Facets of Fear, 204, 213. The occurrences of *ōzen* are in 2:2; 4:20; 5:1, 13. The one occurrence of *rûaḥ* is in 1:23. Focusing on imagery in the Psalms, Florian Lippke has recently argued that creation theology informs the body terminology in the Psalms, where notions of "relatedness" ("Bezogenheit") and "interweaving" ("Verwobenheit") undergird a correspondence between human and divine bodies. See Florian Lippke, "Gottebenbildlichkeit in anthropomorphischer Dimension: Belege aus dem Psalmenbuch," in *Ich will dir danken unter den Völkern: Studien zur israelitischen und altorientalischen Gebetsliteratur. Festschrift für Bernd Janowski zum 70. Geburtstag*, ed. Alexandra Grund, Annette Krüger, and Florian Lippke (Gütersloh: Gütersloher Verlagshaus, 2013), 108–109.

57. Schipper, *Hermeneutik der Tora*, 88–90.

application, this cultural interchange between Egypt and the Levant suggests a degree of common ground in how people understood this object's meanings.[58] A few amulets identify Amun-Re as the true refuge of the "heart," displaying the long tradition of the heart as signifying human standing before deities.[59] Other heart amulets can be placed in the late Neo-Babylonian period.[60] Furthermore, these amulets may suggest a wider, presupposed understanding or "social imaginary" for the heart's semantics, since amulets were common, tangible possessions that forged "a direct relationship between their wearer and a deity."[61]

For whatever reason, the most common attestation of such heart imagery in the Levant is not iconographic but textual, though the textual attestations of the Hebrew word *lēb* seem to assume the referenced object's symbolic layers, which were theologically oriented. Within Prov 1–9 and its discourse on levels of wisdom that are graspable by a *lēb* rightly inclined, the quest for divinely grounded wisdom is compatible with what we see elsewhere in the semantics of heart imagery. As the parental instructor in Prov 2–3 introduces

---

58. See the description in Christian Herrmann and Thomas Staubli, *1001 Amulett: Altägyptischer Zauber, monotheisierte Talismane, säkulare Magie* (Stuttgart: Katholisches Bibelwerk, 2010), 133.

59. One was found at Beth-Shemesh (eighteenth dynasty, 1479–1292 BCE), http://www.bible-orient-museum.ch/bodo/details.php?bomid=16468. One was found in the Samarian highlands at Tell el-Farah (eighteenth dynasty, 1479–1292 BCE), http://www.bible-orient-museum.ch/bodo/details.php?bomid=17933.

60. One was found at Ashkelon (664–525 BCE), http://www.bible-orient-museum.ch/bodo/details.php?bomid=19904. Another was found at Tel Akko (664–525 BCE), http://www.bible-orient-museum.ch/bodo/details.php?bomid=19556.

61. For a discussion of some of these Egyptian or "Egyptianizing" amulets, see Angelika Berlejung, "Divine Presence for Everybody," in *Divine Presence and Absence in Exilic and Post-Exilic Judaism*, ed. Nathan MacDonald and Izaak J. De Hulster, FAT II 61 (Tübingen: Mohr Siebeck, 2013), 72. The phrase "social imaginary" is from Taylor's *Secular Age*, 171–76. Although he discusses developments in the modern period, his comments about concrete practice are pertinent here: "The relation between practices and the background understanding behind them is therefore not one-sided. If the understanding makes the practice possible, it is also true that it is the practice which largely carries the understanding" (173).

a higher, divine wisdom that enters the *lēb* and gives life (2:10; 3:16-20), he also introduces this text block's creation theology: "YHWH in wisdom founded the earth; he established the heavens in *tĕbûnâ*" (3:19; note the insufficiency of an exclusively human viewpoint in 3:5-8, where *yāda'* in v. 6 ≈ *da'at 'ĕlōhîm* in 2:5).[62] In some Second Temple period Jewish writings, creation theology plays a significant role in encouraging allegory based on sets of resemblances, and in Prov 1–9 we may have a case where the roots of so-called "post-biblical" tradition are active within biblical texts themselves.[63]

In Gerhard von Rad's book *Weisheit in Israel*, he argues, correctly to my mind, that a core claim of the creation theology in Prov 1–9 is that physical reality itself has a meaning. That seems to be his point when he writes that the figure of personified Wisdom amounts to "den von Gott der Schöpfung eingesenkten »Sinn«," as well as creation's embedded yet discoverable secret ("[das] Schöpfungsgeheimnis") (see esp. 3:19; 8:22-36).[64] Von Rad's treatment of Proverbs reinforces the supra-linguistic reach of meaning that we have summarily observed in Second Temple period literature. He suggests that, according to Prov 1–9, the physical world is suffused with "[einen] von Gott eingesenkten Sinn," implying a background understanding where tangible, as well as bodily, items signify higher capacities and realities. The kind

---

62. The lecture in Prov 3 expands on, and connects linguistically with, themes from Prov 2 about divine wisdom and the limits of human understanding, which, in the logic of Prov 1–9, is something that should be transcended. I have addressed the relationship between these chapters in my dissertation.

63. On creation theology as the framework for "Gottebenbildlichkeit" in the Psalms, see the discussion in Lippke, "Gottebenbildlichkeit in anthropomorphischer Dimension," 108–109; Harrison, *Natural Science*, 14–15. See Michael Fishbane, *Biblical Interpretation in Ancient Israel* (repr., Oxford: Clarendon, 1989), 2. See further the detailed summary of this phenomenon of a growing tradition in Louis C. Jonker, "Introduction," *HeBAI* 2 (2013): 275–76. For the link between exegesis and reception, see Hermann Spieckermann, "From Biblical Exegesis to Reception History," *HeBAI* 1 (2012): 327–50.

64. In English, these phrases could be rendered as "the divinely grounded meaning of creation" and "the secret of creation." See further Gerhard von Rad, *Weisheit in Israel*, 4th ed. (Neukirchen-Vluyn: Neukirchener Verlagsgesellschaft, 2013 [orig. 1970]), 157, 181–82. See also the comments of Roland Murphy, "Wisdom and Creation," *JBL* 104 (1985): 9–10.

of world depicted is one where divine wisdom is "poured out" or "woven" into the created, material order.⁶⁵

For these scribes, matter is not something "mere." What has not received enough notice is the major divergence in conceptions of matter or physical reality as such between Prov 1–9 and the modern, literalist turn outlined earlier, and how this same divergence coincides with early-modern efforts to overcome allegory.⁶⁶ With contemporary interest in "materialist" theories of religion, it should be stressed that contemporary scholars may be applying an internally different understanding of matter from what ancient scribes would recognize.⁶⁷ Stated minimally regarding Proverbs, these scribes' conception of created order coupled with scribal culture's bookishness contain the elements for an allegorical or symbolic approach to the world—an approach that later interpreters sought to systematize and that even later Protestant interpreters sought to overturn. These contested elements seem inchoate but nonetheless present in the thinking of Prov 1–9.

By attending to the intellectual climate of the Hellenistic and early Roman periods, I have tried to contextualize Prov 1–9 within the intellectual framework of later Second Temple Jewish wisdom. Contrasting this framework with the early-modern literalist turn invites philologists to reflect on the straightforwardness of, and rationale for, privileging plain or literal meanings. Ancient Jewish scribes' symbolic or semantically charged conception of the physical, created world may help explain the repeated, symbolic use of physiological terms like *lēb*. As an entity with a range of endowed meanings,

---

65. In Prov 8:23, one may interpret the verb *nskty* either as MT's Nif. pf. 1st person singular of I *nsk* ("to pour out"), i.e., *nissaktî*; or alternatively as Nif. pf. 1st person singular of II *skk* ("to weave, form"), i.e., *nĕsakkōtî*. The latter would maintain the speech's gestational imagery for the relationship between wisdom and YHWH (cf. II *skk* in Ps 139:13, where, like Prov 8:22ff., one also finds *qnh*).

66. For discussion of this effort in the nineteenth century, see Klauck, *Allegorie und Allegorese*, 4–12, who discusses what he calls "[den] antiallegorische[n] Ansatz."

67. For discussion of these approaches, see Julian Droogan, *Religion, Material Culture and Archaeology* (London: Bloomsbury, 2013), who notes that a sharp polarization of "spiritual" against "material" is "deeply entrenched in the thinking processes of modernity" (3).

including intellectual and affective capacities, as well as one's position before YHWH, the *lēb* was understood to situate pupils on a vertical spectrum of escalating and eventually divine wisdom that, in these scribes' reasoning, is attainable through combining virtuous practice with diligent study: an epistemology anchored in ethics. In Prov 1–9, it is through a symbolic object that one receives this wisdom.

Bibliography

Adams, Samuel L. *Wisdom in Transition: Act and Consequence in Second Temple Instructions*. JSJSup 125. Leiden: Brill, 2008.

Ansberry, Christopher B. "What Does Jerusalem Have to Do with Athens? The Moral Vision of the Book of Proverbs and Aristotle's *Nicomachean Ethics*." *HS* 51 (2010): 157–73.

Balentine, Samuel E. *Have You Considered My Servant Job?: Understanding the Biblical Archetype of Patience*. Studies on Personalities of the Old Testament. Columbia: University of South Carolina Press, 2015.

———. *Wisdom Literature*. CBS. Nashville: Abingdon, 2018.

Berlejung, Angelika. "Divine Presence for Everybody." Pages 67–93 in *Divine Presence and Absence in Exilic and Post-Exilic Judaism*. Edited by Nathan MacDonald and Izaak J. De Hulster. FAT II 61. Tübingen: Mohr Siebeck, 2013.

Borgen, Peder, Kåre Fuglseth, and Roald Skarsten. *The Philo Index: A Complete Greek Word Index to the Writings of Philo of Alexandria*. Leiden: Brill, 2000.

Brown, William P. *Seeing the Psalms: A Theology of Metaphor*. Louisville: WJK, 2002.

Collins, John J. *Beyond the Qumran Community: The Sectarian Movement of the Dead Sea Scrolls*. Grand Rapids: Eerdmans, 2010.

Dell, Katharine. *'Get Wisdom, Get Insight': An Introduction to Israel's Wisdom Literature*. Macon, GA: Smyth & Helwys, 2000.

Droogan, Julian. *Religion, Material Culture and Archaeology*. London: Bloomsbury, 2013.

Elliot, Mark. "Allegory and Allegorical Interpretation." Pages 17–27 in *Oxford Encyclopedia of Biblical Interpretation*. Edited by Steven L. McKenzie. Oxford: Oxford University Press, 2013.

Feldman, Louis H., James L. Kugel, and Lawrence H. Schiffman, eds. *Outside the Bible: Ancient Jewish Writings Related to Scripture*. Philadelphia: The Jewish Publication Society, 2013.

Feser, Edward. *Scholastic Metaphysics: A Contemporary Introduction*. Heusenstamm: Editiones Scholasticae, 2014.

Fishbane, Michael. *Biblical Interpretation in Ancient Israel*. Repr., Oxford: Clarendon, 1989.

Forti, Tova. *Animal Imagery in the Book of Proverbs*. Leiden: Brill, 2008.

Fox, Michael. "The Epistemology of the Book of Proverbs." *JBL* 126 (2007): 669–84.

———. "Ethics and Wisdom in the Book of Proverbs." *HS* 48 (2007): 75–88.

———. *Proverbs 1–9: A New Translation with Introduction and Commentary*. AB 18A. New York: Doubleday, 2000.

Graves, Michael. *The Inspiration and Interpretation of Scripture: What the Early Church Can Teach Us*. Grand Rapids: Eerdmans, 2014.

Gregory, Brad S. *The Unintended Reformation: How a Religious Revolution Secularized Society*. Cambridge: Harvard University Press, 2012.

Harrison, Peter. *The Bible, Protestantism, and the Rise of Natural Science*. 2nd ed. Cambridge: Cambridge University Press, 2001.

———. *The Territories of Science and Religion*. Chicago: University of Chicago Press, 2015.

Herrmann, Christian, and Thomas Staubli. *1001 Amulett: Altägyptischer Zauber, monotheisierte Talismane, säkulare Magie*. Stuttgart: Katholisches Bibelwerk, 2010.

Humbert, Jean-Baptiste. "Qumran." Pages 203–12 in *The Oxford Encyclopedia of the Bible and Archaeology*. Edited by Daniel M. Master. Oxford: Oxford University Press, 2013.

Jonker, Louis C. "Introduction." *HeBAI* 2 (2013): 275–86.

Kamesar, Adam. "Biblical Interpretation in Philo." Pages 65–91 in *The Cambridge Companion to Philo*. Edited by Adam Kamesar. Cambridge: Cambridge University Press, 2009.

Keel, Othmar, and Christoph Uehlinger. *Gods, Goddesses, and Images of God in Ancient Israel*. Minneapolis: Fortress, 1998.

Klauck, Hans-Josef. *Allegorie und Allegorese in synoptischen Gleichnistexten*, 2nd ed. Neutestamentliche Abhandlungen 13. Münster: Aschendorff, 1978.

Kołakowski, Leszek. *Metaphysical Horror*. Rev. ed. Chicago: University of Chicago Press, 2001.

Lambert, David A. "Refreshing Philology: James, Barr, Supersessionism, and the State of Biblical Words." *BibInt* 24 (2016): 332–56.

Lasater, Phillip Michael. *Facets of Fear: The Fear of God in Exilic and Post-exilic Contexts*. FAT II 104. Tübingen: Mohr Siebeck, 2019.

———. "Not So Vain After All: Hannah Arendt's Reception of Ecclesiastes." *JBRec* 6/2 (2019): 163–96.

Le Clerc, Jean. *Twelve Dissertations out of Monsieur Le Clerc's Genesis*. Translated by Mr. Brown. London: R. Baldwin, 1696.

Legaspi, Michael C. *The Death of Scripture and the Rise of Biblical Studies*. Oxford Studies in Historical Theology. Oxford: Oxford University Press, 2010.

Lim, Timothy H. *The Formation of the Jewish Canon*. New Haven: Yale University Press, 2013.

Lippke, Florian. "Gottebenbildlichkeit in anthropomorphischer Dimension: Belege aus dem Psalmenbuch." Pages 93–120 in *Ich will dir danken unter den Völkern: Studien zur israelitischen und altorientalischen Gebetsliteratur. Festschrift für Bernd Janowski zoom 70. Geburtstag*. Edited by Alexandra Grund, Annette Krüger, and Florian Lippke. Gütersloh: Gütersloher Verlagshaus, 2013.

MacCulloch, Diarmaid. *Reformation: Europe's House Divided, 1490–1700.* London: Penguin Books, 2003.

MacIntyre, Alasdair. *After Virtue: A Study in Moral Theory.* 3rd. ed. Notre Dame: University of Notre Dame Press, 2007.

McKane, William. *Proverbs: A New Approach.* 2nd ed. London: SCM, 1977.

Mirguet, Françoise. "Introductory Reflections on Embodiment in Hellenistic Judaism." *JSP* 21 (2011): 5–19.

Most, Glenn W. "The poetics of early Greek philosophy." Pages 332–62 in *The Cambridge Companion to Early Greek Philosophy.* Edited by A. A. Long. Cambridge: Cambridge University Press, 1999.

Murphy, Roland. "Wisdom and Creation." *JBL* 104 (1985): 3–11.

Nagel, Thomas. *The Last Word.* Oxford: Oxford University Press, 2001.

———. *Mind and Cosmos: Why the Materialist Neo-Darwinian Conception of Nature Is Almost Certainly False.* Oxford: Oxford University Press, 2012.

Najman, Hindy. "Cain and Abel as Character Traits: A Study in the Allegorical Typology of Philo of Alexandria." Pages 207–18 in *Past Renewals: Interpretive Authority, Renewed Revelation and the Quest for Perfection in Jewish Antiquity.* JSOJSup 53. Leiden: Brill, 2010.

———. "Ethical Reading: The Transformation of the Text and the Self." *JTS* 68/2 (2017): 507–29.

———. "Jewish Wisdom in the Hellenistic Period: Towards the Study of a Semantic Constellation." Pages 459–72 in *Is There a Text in This Cave?: Studies in the Textuality of the Dead Sea Scrolls in Honour of George J. Brooke.* Edited by Ariel Feldman, Maria Cioată, and Charlotte Hempel. STDJ 119. Leiden: Brill, 2017.

———. "The Vitality of Scripture Within and Beyond the 'Canon.'" *JSJ* 43 (2012): 497–518.

Newsom, Carol A. "Evil in the Hebrew Bible: The Case of the Wisdom Literature." Pages 60–81 in *Evil: A History*. Edited by Andrew P. Chignell. Oxford Philosophical Concepts. Oxford: Oxford University Press, 2019.

Niehoff, Maren R. *Philo of Alexandria: An Intellectual Biography*. New Haven: Yale University Press, 2018.

Patterson, Dennis. "Review of M. R. Bennett and P. M. S. Hacker's *Philosophical Foundations of Neuroscience*." *Notre Dame Philosophical Reviews: An Electronic Journal*. 10 September 2003. https://ndpr.nd.edu/news/philosophical-foundations-of-neuroscience/.

Rad, Gerhard von. *Weisheit in Israel*. 4th ed. Neukirchen-Vluyn: Neukirchener Verlagsgesellschaft, 2013.

Radice, Roberto. "Philo's Theology and Theory of Creation." Pages 124–45 in *The Cambridge Companion to Philo*. Edited by A. Kamesar. Cambridge: Cambridge University Press, 2009.

Riemer, Nick. *Introducing Semantics*. Cambridge: Cambridge University Press, 2010.

Schipper, Bernd. *Hermeneutik der Tora: Studien zur Traditionsgeschichte von Prov 2 und zur Komposition von Prov 1–9*. BZAW 432. Berlin: de Gruyter, 2012.

Schmid, Hans Heinrich. *Wesen und Geschichte der Weisheit*. Berlin: Verlag Alfred Töpelmann, 1966.

Schmid, Konrad. *Literaturgeschichte des Alten Testaments: Eine Einführung*. Darmstadt: Wissenschaftliche Buchgesellschaft, 2008.

———. "Schöpfung im Alten Testament." Pages 71–120 in *Schöpfung*. Edited by Konrad Schmid. Tübingen: Mohr Siebeck, 2012.

Schroer, Silvia and Thomas Staubli. *Die Körpersymbolik der Bibel*. Darmstadt: Wissenschaftliche Buchgesellschaft, 1998.

Simonetti, Manlio. *Biblical Interpretation in the Early Church: An Historical Introduction to Patristic Exegesis*. New York: T&T Clark, 2001.

Sommer, Benjamin D. "Nature, Revelation, and Grace in Psalm 19: Towards a Theological Reading of Scripture." *HTR* 108 (2015): 376–401.

Spieckermann, Hermann. "From Biblical Exegesis to Reception History." *Hebrew Bible and Ancient Israel* 1 (2012): 327–50.

Staubli, Thomas. "'Let there be light!' Concepts of Light in Ancient Near Eastern Iconography and in the Bible" (forthcoming).

Taylor, Charles. *The Language Animal: The Full Shape of the Linguistic Capacity*. Cambridge: Harvard University Press, 2016.

———. "Overcoming Modern Epistemology." Pages 43–60 in *Faithful Reading: New Essays in Theology and Philosophy in Honour of Fergus Kerr, OP*. Edited by S. Oliver et al. London: Bloomsbury, 2013.

———. *A Secular Age*. Cambridge: Harvard University Press, 2007.

Thomas, Samuel I. "Hearing the Vision: גלה אזן in Qumran Sectarian Texts." *HeBAI* 5 (2016): 59–74.

Vayntrub, Jacqueline. "Like Father, Like Son: Theorizing Transmission in Biblical Literature." *HeBAI* 7 (2018): 500–26.

Ethics and Character Formation in Biblical Wisdom Texts

John Barton

It is a great pleasure and privilege to dedicate this paper to Samuel Balentine, whom I have known for forty years and whose contribution to biblical studies has been so significant.

In this paper, I want to present, and recommend, the ideas in two recent studies of the ethics of wisdom. One is by Anne W. Stewart: *Poetic Ethics in Proverbs: Wisdom Literature and the Shaping of the Moral Self*.[1] The other work is by one of the editors of this volume: Patricia Vesely's *Friendship and Virtue Ethics in the Book of Job*.[2] I think these studies constitute an important contribution to the study of ethics in wisdom, a somewhat neglected topic. Stewart and Vesely

---

1. Anne W. Stewart, *Poetic Ethics in Proverbs: Wisdom Literature and the Shaping of the Moral Self* (Cambridge: Cambridge University Press, 2016).

2. Patricia Vesely, *Friendship and Virtue Ethics in the Book of Job* (Cambridge: Cambridge University Press, 2019).

show that there is indeed a virtue ethic in the Hebrew Bible, illustrating it from various wisdom texts. They have moved the discussion of biblical ethics on to a very considerable extent.

But to explain my interest in these books, I need to go back to an article on virtue ethics that I published some twenty years ago in *Studies in Christian Ethics*.[3] Virtue ethics has become a central concern of writers on ethics in many traditions, both religious and nonreligious, and my concern in my article was to ask whether there is anything approximating it in the Bible. The article is "Virtue in the Bible" and was reprinted in my collected essays *Understanding Old Testament Ethics: Approaches and Explanations*.[4] At the beginning I set out four features commonly found in an ethic of virtue.

First, virtue ethics tends to be concerned less with a set of decisions about difficult cases and more with commitment to a particular lifestyle. The virtue ethicist is concerned with the fixed and stable moral dispositions from which ethical decisions flow. Ethics is more centrally about the general tenor of a person's day-to-day life than about deciding on hard cases.

Second, virtue ethics stresses the centrality of moral formation and the development of a moral character over time. This is one of the things I want particularly to focus on in this paper.

Third, moral rules that do exist are more a distillation from many good decisions made by virtuous people than hard-and-fast rulings that have to be obeyed. Aristotle, the fount of virtue ethics, stresses the accumulation of experience by a wise person rather than an external set of rules that are simply binding. Rules of thumb are by no means excluded, but the life of virtue is a matter of extended experience rather than of obedience to external norms.

And fourth, to live a life of virtue one needs a moral vision, the ability to "read" the successive situations one finds oneself in and to live consistently and in an examined way.

In my article I dealt with all four of these features, and I argued that on the whole the Bible does not contain much that is conducive

---

3. John Barton, "Virtue in the Bible," *Studies in Christian Ethics* 12/1 (1999): 12–22.

4. John Barton, *Understanding Old Testament Ethics: Approaches and Explanations* (Louisville: Westminster John Knox, 2003).

to a virtue ethic. In so far as it does, the best place to look is probably in narrative texts—where we see characters struggling to live well in difficult circumstances—rather than in law or wisdom. And I was sceptical in particular of finding virtue thinking in the wisdom literature, above all because it seemed to me to lack the second feature just described: the idea of moral formation and progress in the virtuous life. I wrote,

> . . . there are no Laodicean moralists in the wisdom literature. Everyone is either good or bad, wise or foolish. Living the good life appears to be an absolute, with no gradations or variations. Proverbs operates in some ways with a similar pattern of thought to that in Deuteronomy, where Moses lays before the people of Israel as a whole a choice between good and evil, the way of life and the way of death (e.g. Deut. 30:15), a tradition that continues throughout the Old Testament and re-emerges in the New Testament and other early Christian literature: one may think of the "two ways" teaching in *The Epistle of Barnabas* and the *Didache*. Ethical choice is a once-for-all affair which sets one's feet either on the way to life or on the way to death: there are no half-measures. This does not seem to me very like what a virtue ethic is asserting about human character, despite superficial resemblances. And I think the same could be said, for example, of Paul. The Pauline epistles abound in the language of virtues and vices, but the subtlety which sees everyone as a mix of the two, or as living a life in which virtue is *cultivated* and vice therefore [progressively] rooted out seems largely lacking. People belong in one of two camps. Nevertheless in Paul there are of course more nuanced ideas, such as the way the indwelling Spirit shapes the believer, which may well be able to contribute to a virtue ethic. The Old Testament wisdom literature, however, seems to me to inhabit a cruder world of thought, where character is indeed all important but is seen as fixed and unchanging, almost at times as predetermined.[5]

And again:

> . . . taken at face value, Proverbs eschews most ideas of moral progress. Hebrew culture differs from Greek on precisely this issue: the

---

5. Barton, "Virtue in the Bible," 14.

Hebrew Bible does not operate with any idea that one can grow in virtue, but sees virtue as something one either has or lacks. It is true that if you give instruction to a wise man he will become wiser still (Prov. 9:9), but there is no point in giving instruction to a fool, because he will persist in his folly just as much as before.[6]

I went on to suggest that the Bible speaks not about moral progress but about conversion, not about formation of character but about radical change. Ethical action in the Bible is most commonly not part of a long sequence of wise decisions but is part of absolute obedience to external norms. So, I argued, virtue ethics is not native to the Bible. A virtue ethicist might *use* biblical material—a point I shall return to—but the Bible does not encapsulate a virtue ethic. It is not about the gradual formation of character.

Now Anne Stewart's book is a head-on attack on arguments such as these. She describes my presentation of the ethics of Proverbs, which draws on a widespread way of thinking about the wisdom literature, as "the simplicity thesis": that is, the theory that everything in Proverbs, particularly, is drawn in black and white and is, to use my own word, "crude." She writes,

> A tacit assumption of much wisdom scholarship is the presumed naïveté, simplicity, or rigidity of the worldview represented by Proverbs, particularly by the sentences of Prov 10–29. While this is certainly not a universal presumption, its pervasiveness is obscured by the implicit ways in which such notions inform certain conclusions about the nature of wisdom, the development of the literary tradition, and the differences among the wisdom books . . . [Thus R. B. Y. Scott] implies that the book contains a kind of wisdom that is characterized by a "mechanical oversimplification" that is divorced from reality, caught instead in the "lofty clouds of theorizing." And Scott is certainly not alone in this presumption. Walther Zimmerli spoke of wisdom's "naïve optimism and the unhistorical approach to life as necessary emanations from this basic rationalistic attitude."[7]

---

6. Ibid., 15.

7. Stewart, *Poetic Ethics*, 73.

It is this idea that leads to the common belief that Job and Qoheleth represent a "crisis" in the wisdom tradition, as they question such naïve assumptions about the simple contrast between the righteous and the wicked, wise people and fools, and press for more nuance—or even deny the basic wisdom scheme altogether.

All this, Stewart argues, is an error. Far from being crude and simplistic, Proverbs concerns itself with education and training in virtue. Central to this is the idea of *mûsār*, traditionally rendered "discipline":

> Within Proverbs, the formation of the student's capacity for . . . complex forms of moral reasoning is tied to the concept of *mûsār* . . . . *Mûsār* is at the heart of the book's purpose, as stated from its opening words: to know wisdom and *mûsār* (1:2), to acquire the *mûsār* of sagacity (1:3). . . . As Michael V. Fox explains, *mûsār* is more than practical teaching but is "a moral insight or a quality of moral character." . . . it is . . . a conceptual category in the book that refers to the task of formation. It is not simply the lesson itself or the action of correction, although the term refers at times to both of these, but it is more broadly the nature of the education that the sages advance. In this sense, it is a multifaceted concept that extends to various modes of intellectual, emotional, and moral development.
>
> Behind the concept of *mûsār* is a sophisticated moral psychology that presumes the complexity of the human person. Accordingly, *mûsār* is a task not only of verbal or physical correction, but of training the student's intellect, emotion, and perception such that his faculties are equipped for navigating the world. Thus the effect of *mûsār* is not described simply as intellectual assent to certain principles, but rather it is a process of acquiring right perception, the proper perspective to see and experience the world.[8]

Stewart goes on to discuss *mûsār* as having four aspects: rebuke, motivation, desire, and imagination.

Rebuke or reproof can be found in the poem in Prov 1:20-33, where wisdom is portrayed as warning the young of the dangers of ignoring her commands. The person addressed is singled out for contrast with the crowd of wrongdoers, as one who is amenable to

---

8. Ibid., 78.

correction, and as potentially one who "listens to me" and who "will dwell securely and be at ease from dread of trouble" (v. 33). Proverbs presents a picture of what Stewart calls "educated moral selfhood": "moral equipment is innate, but exists in potential only."[9] Its development depends on a willingness to accept instruction and to adapt to moral demands. It is true that "fools" cannot receive instruction; but, against the "simplicity thesis," those who are simple but not foolish can learn from good teachers and can advance in virtue and understanding.

Motivation is also crucial to the programme of education in Proverbs, and the motivations for good conduct are nearly all future-orientated, promises of the benefits that will accrue from good behaviour. But, against what I argued in my book *Ethics and the Old Testament*,[10] Stewart maintains that this is not based on a crude model in which good conduct almost automatically leads to blessing and bad conduct to disaster: Proverbs is not so simplistic. Rather, the book treats the self-interested assumption that doing good will lead to reward as a factor in motivating the actor to genuinely good behaviour. Good conduct can lead to wealth, honour, protection, and life.[11] But these are more like side effects of living well than direct incentives to action: ". . . character, consequence, motive, and context are complexly intertwined."[12] There is no strict "act-consequence" system at play: there is an awareness that, while one can expect a reward for right living, in the end all is in the hands of God, and it is his blessing that makes one truly rich (Prov 10:22). Wisdom, furthermore, is desirable for its own sake, even apart from any material or other benefits it may bring.

Desire, indeed, is a major theme in Proverbs and is not reducible to a simple wish for good things. It is an "internal source of motivation."[13] It must be purified so that it is directed to the right

---

9. Ibid., 98.

10. John Barton, *Ethics and the Old Testament* (London: SCM, 1998; 2nd ed., 2002).

11. Stewart, *Poetic Ethics*, 105.

12. Ibid., 119.

13. Ibid., 137.

ends—surely an idea akin to character formation, if anything in Proverbs is. The feminine personification of wisdom is meant to show the young man for whom Proverbs is intended how to desire wisdom rather than the "strange woman," a spiritualization of desire that seems to me to have some resemblances to Plato. "Proverbs indicates that the nature of the search for wisdom is itself elusive and prolonged, for it both offers and resists full satiation, leaving the student desiring more . . . . wisdom's elusiveness is not indicative of a frustration or complaint, but it functions to impel the continued search for wisdom."[14] This shows that Proverbs is concerned with a progressive growth in understanding, which at once destroys the simplicity thesis.

Imagination is also central to Proverbs and equally incompatible with the simplicity thesis, which presupposes a severe lack of imagination in Israel's sages. Imagination can be seen especially in the wide range of metaphors that occur in the book. "Moral reasoning . . . is fundamentally imaginative in the sense that it is not strictly governed by the literal application of absolute moral laws but proceeds by metaphorical understanding of morality and social interaction."[15] The extensive use of metaphor shows clearly that Proverbs is designed to appeal to the imagination, not merely to the conscience, and that it expects the reader to think deeply about his moral commitments, not simply obey an external norm. The book has a complex texture that is unknown to proponents of the simplicity thesis.

There is much more in Stewart's stimulating book, but I hope this gives an idea of its general themes. My own sense is that she has succeeded in demolishing the simplicity thesis that I along with others have defended and has shown how much more subtle and nuanced Proverbs is than we ever thought. Wisdom was for a long time the Cinderella of Old Testament study, its marginalization partly justified by the argument that it is dogmatic and unimaginative. In fact, it has as much complexity as the thought of the biblical historians, psalmists, or lawgivers, if it is read with care and attention. I would continue to defend the idea that there are dogmatic assertions in some wisdom texts—think of the egregious Psalm 37:25,

---

14. Ibid., 144.

15. Ibid., 181.

"I have been young, and now am old, yet I have not seen the righteous forsaken, or his children begging bread." But Stewart has shown that this is not the norm in wisdom, and particularly not in Proverbs, where the idea of instruction, *mûsār*, has a complexity and density that recalls the Hellenistic idea of *paideia*, a complete education in moral responsiveness. So, basically, I surrender! With hindsight, I am actually quite surprised that I defended the thesis I did. I think I wanted to stress that there were indeed ideas in the Hebrew Bible not conducive to a virtue ethic, but I leaned too far and did not do justice to wisdom in particular. I hope Stewart will be read by everyone interested not only in the wisdom tradition but in biblical ethics for the light it throws on this complex and subtle moral tradition.

I now turn to Patricia Vesely's work, *Friendship and Virtue Ethics in the Book of Job*. Here we have a further study of virtue ethics in the wisdom literature. It taps into current concerns with virtue and character ethics in biblical studies but is the first work as far as I know to apply these concerns to the book of Job. Likewise, it is the first to examine the theme of friendship in the book. Vesely treats the subject of virtue ethics by a careful examination of Aristotle and of the ethical tradition deriving from him, via Alasdair MacIntyre and, a bit more surprisingly, the Old Testament scholar Bruce Birch, whom however she shows to have contributed significantly to the tradition as it affects biblical ethics.[16] There are many quotations from Aristotle, showing close parallels with biblical ways of thinking that would have astonished those who, fifty years and more ago, argued for a "Hebrew/Greek thought contrast." More recently, scholarship has been more hospitable to seeing parallels between the Hebrew Bible and Aristotle, but this is the first book known to me that works over the similarities (and differences) in some detail. It is thus a considerable contribution to the literature on biblical ethics yet should also be read by classicists and philosophers.

Following the lead of Samuel E. Balentine, Vesely argues that the theme of friendship is central to the book of Job.[17] The "comforters"

---

16. See Bruce Birch, *Let Justice Roll Down: The Old Testament, Ethics, and Christian Life* (Louisville: Westminster John Knox, 1991).

17. Vesely, *Friendship and Virtue Ethics*, 1, quoting Samuel E. Balentine, *Job*, SHBC (Macon, GA: Smyth & Helwys, 2006), 445.

are criticised because of their failure in showing true friendship towards Job, which for the Hebrew Bible as for Aristotle is a moral failing. She shows that friendship is a test of character, which is a central theme in virtue ethics, as we have seen. A false friend is a great evil, much reflected on in the work of Ben Sira—see, for example, Sirach 6:8-13.[18] Friendship makes clear moral demands, as in Job 6:28-29, where Job insists that his friends should face him and recognize his sufferings, rather than harassing him. That is what virtue requires: it is not laid down anywhere in biblical law—how could it be?—but it is recognized throughout the wisdom literature and in much narrative, too. It is present in the prose frame of Job, where in the epilogue Job's new friends (and some of his old ones) welcome and celebrate him after his reversal of fortune.

Reflecting on Job 29–31, Vesely writes,

> In the society that Job depicts [in these chapters], proper relationships are of the utmost importance. Throughout his declaration of innocence, Job demonstrates that he has upheld his responsibilities to others and to God. He has cultivated the proper dispositions, perceptions, and intentions that generate compassionate, honest, generous, and just behavior. While the [Aristotelian] disposition of goodwill may provide the underlying foundation for his proper treatment toward others, he has sought after deeper and more intimate relationships with those whom he encounters. As Aristotle notes, without goodwill, friendship is impossible.[19]

A virtue ethic here helps to explain the whole texture and flavour of the book of Job in a way that other ethical models would fail to do. Thus Vesely, like Stewart, shows convincingly that the ideas of moral formation and the development of character, crucial to relationships of friendship, are central to Job and hence to the wisdom literature of which Job is such a significant part. Awareness of Aristotelian ethics opens up the understanding of Israelite literature and helps to reveal there, too, an ethic of virtue and character.

If I can scavenge any remains from my own earlier argument, with the help of Stewart's and Vesely's theses, I would mention two things.

---

18. Discussed in Vesely, *Friendship and Virtue Ethics*, 69.

19. Ibid., 220.

First, there is the idea that even texts that are not inherently concerned with moral formation can be used for that purpose. Famously or notoriously, stories in the so-called historical books have traditionally functioned in both Judaism and Christianity as moral *exempla*, even though they may not have been designed for that purpose, while laws prohibiting very specific actions have been broadened to have the whole of life in their purview. Many Christians down the ages have examined their consciences by using the Decalogue as a template for moral conduct in general, even though its original purport seems to have been much more restricted. Wisdom texts can certainly also function in that way whether or not they were designed for forming moral character. Even a text that says fools cannot be reformed can serve, in practice, to reform fools—rather as prophetic texts that say the end is coming and cannot now be avoided can be used to preach repentance, and thus to falsify themselves. From a text that argues that certain people are irreformable, a programme of reform can in fact be extracted, given the right hermeneutic.[20]

Second, there is no doubt that later wisdom at least does overtly thematize moral training. Such training, which is an essential idea in virtue ethics, is a major theme in the thought of Ben Sira, who is explicit about the way studying wisdom improves the moral character, and it follows a progressive path with identifiable stages:

> Wisdom teaches[21] her children
> and gives help to those who seek her.
> Whoever loves her loves life,
>   and those who seek her from early morning are filled with joy.
> Whoever holds her fast inherits glory,
>   and the Lord blesses the place she enters.
> Those who serve her minister to the Holy One;
>   the Lord loves those who love her.
> Those who obey her will judge the nations,

---

20. Stewart argues the stronger case, that Proverbs is not only designed to train the moral character but is generally *about* such training: that is its actual message. I must say she has convinced me that this is so. Even if it were not, however, Proverbs can still stand as a great tool in informing the human conscience and in producing good moral character.

21. I follow the Hebrew text here; the Greek has "exalts."

and all who listen to her will live secure.
If they remain faithful, they will inherit her;
    Their descendants will also obtain her.
For at first she will walk with them on tortuous paths;
    she will bring fear and dread upon them,
and will torment them by her discipline
    until she trusts them,
and she will test them with her ordinances.
Then she will come straight back to them again and gladden them,
    and will reveal her secrets to them.
If they go astray she will forsake them,
    and hand them over to their ruin. (Sir 4:11-19)

The idea of moral progress also starts to make more of an appearance in other works from the Second Temple period, for example, the Wisdom of Solomon:

If riches are a desirable possession in life,
what is richer than wisdom, the active cause of all things?
And if understanding is effective,
who more than she who is fashioner of what exists?
And if anyone loves righteousness,
her labours are virtues;
for she teaches self-control and prudence,
justice and courage;
nothing in life is more profitable for mortals than these.
(Wis 8:5-7)

There is sometimes also an emphasis on ascetic practices that will purify one's character. Thus in *Psalms of Solomon* 3 we read, "The righteous constantly searches his house to remove his unintentional sin" (a possible allusion to seeking out leaven before Passover?).[22] Compare Job 1:5:

And when the feast days had run their course, Job would send and sanctify them, and he would rise early in the morning and offer burnt-offerings according to the number of them all; for Job said,

---

22. Robert B. Wright, "Psalms of Solomon," *OTP* 2:654–55.

"It may be that my children have sinned, and cursed God in their hearts."

The term *formation* is quite appropriate here. Very striking in this connection is Job 31, which presents us with what I think is the only example of "self-examination" in the Old Testament, as Job thinks back over his conduct and acquits himself of one possible sin after another. This may, as is often thought, rest on Egyptian "negative confessions," but it moves into a world of personal spirituality that seems more sophisticated. Here (compare also Tobit 4) there is a concern for inner intentions that belongs to a self-consciously spiritual discipline, which is notably more gentle with enemies than, for example, the Psalms: gloating over their downfall is expressly forbidden.[23] The *Testaments of the Twelve Patriarchs* (not wisdom literature, but with many affinities to wisdom in the teaching placed in the mouth of each patriarch) evince similar ideals: the *Testament of Simeon* 4:4-5 commends Joseph for his forgiving spirit, part of his general integrity. By this time, the idea of improving oneself by deliberate ascetic and intentional exercises was established in Israel— it was not a peculiarity of the teaching of Jesus or of New Testament writers. There is, one may say, an art of living well: that is the ideal in Ben Sira particularly, and it is close to what we now mean by a virtue ethic.

It may be that there are analogies in Israelite thought to various much older Egyptian ideas about moral development. The importance of leading an orderly life is stressed from Ptah-hotep onwards

---

23. See further Vesely, *Friendship and Virtue Ethics*, 132–34, 163. She writes, for example,

> Job makes several attempts to rebut his friends' accusations against his "heart" and "eyes" and to profess his innocence with regard to the purity of his inner life. In 31:7, Job assures his hearers that his eyes have not led his heart astray . . . , and in 31:1, he asserts that he has covenanted with his eyes not to look improperly on a maiden. . . . As Job declares in 27:6, his heart has never reproached him . . . ; he is pure from the inside out. Both Job and his friends make claims that support one of virtue ethics' most basic tenets: morally culpable actions are fueled by flaws of character. One's inner attitudes, intentions, and perceptions are the source of wickedness and righteousness. (134)

and is still there in Amen-em-opet. The ideal of Egyptian wisdom is the quiet or silent man, someone who keeps his thoughts to himself and does not make a scene. He follows an inner path.

It should also be noted that a number of sources are concerned with good *thought* as well as good action. In Job 31, as we have seen, there is an interest in what goes on in the "heart"—that is, the mind—and this is also true of Psalms 15 and 101. In the Second Temple period the condemnation of idolatry is linked with an attack not only on the practical immorality but also on the intellectual corruption supposed to mark out idolaters, an idea that found its way down into the writings of Paul (see Rom 1:21-23), perhaps through Wisdom of Solomon 12:23–13:9. Having the right attitude towards God and other people is a frequent concern in the Psalms. Psalm 119, the lengthy acrostic about obedience to the Torah, is certainly concerned with training one's actions and one's thoughts alike:

> I treasure your word in my heart,
> > So that I may not sin against you.
> I will meditate on your precepts,
> > And fix my eyes on your ways,
> Give me understanding, that I may keep your law,
> > And observe it with my whole heart.
> Before I was humbled I went astray,
> > But now I keep your word.
> It is good for me that I was humbled,
> > So that I might learn your statutes. (Ps 119:11, 15, 34, 67, 71)

So the formation of moral character certainly occurs in biblical texts, not least in those we count as part of the wisdom tradition. Both Stewart and Vesely recognize this development, which is obvious in texts from the Second Temple period. As the above authors argue, an interest in character is already to be found in Proverbs, including what may be the earliest sections of that book, and in Job's presentation of friendship and his self-examination in chapter 31. The wisdom of these texts is not at all simplistic but anticipates later developments that are found in the Hellenistic age. Whether or not we refer to this as virtue ethics, it is certainly interested in moral training, and hence in the formation of character.

Bibliography

Balentine, Samuel E. *Job*. SHBC. Macon, GA: Smyth & Helwys, 2006.

Barton, John. *Ethics and the Old Testament*. London: SCM, 1998. 2nd ed., 2002.

———. *Understanding Old Testament Ethics: Approaches and Explanations*. Louisville: Westminster John Knox, 2003.

———. "Virtue in the Bible." *Studies in Christian Ethics* 12/1 (1999): 12–22.

Birch, Bruce. *Let Justice Roll Down: The Old Testament, Ethics, and Christian Life*. Louisville: Westminster John Knox, 1991.

Stewart, Anne W. *Poetic Ethics in Proverbs: Wisdom Literature and the Shaping of the Moral Self*. Cambridge: Cambridge University Press, 2016.

Vesely, Patricia. *Friendship and Virtue Ethics in the Book of Job*. Cambridge: Cambridge University Press, 2019.

Wright, Robert B. "Psalms of Solomon." *OTP* 2:639–70.

Job and the "Comforting" Chaos
William P. Brown

It is my delight to present this essay to Sam Balentine, from whose works over the years I have learned and benefited greatly.

It is customary among scholars today to highlight Job as a book that revels in polyphony, ambiguity, irony, and, for some, even parody.[1] At the very least, Job is a masterpiece of literary complexity replete with conflicting viewpoints lacking tidy resolution.[2] Indeed, Job's character is itself a study of literary, if not psychological, complexity. Drawing from H. L. Ginsberg's famous epithets, many identify "Job the Impatient" in the poetry (cf. 21:4b) over and against "Job the Patient" in the prose.[3] But this single binary by no means exhausts the

---

1. See references below. For parody, see Katharine J. Dell, *Job: Where Shall Wisdom Be Found? An Introduction and Study Guide*, T&T Clark Study Guides for the Old Testament 14 (London: Bloomsbury T&T Clark, 2017), 33–50; Bruce Zuckerman, *Job the Silent: A Study in Historical Counterpoint* (Oxford: Oxford University Press, 1991), esp. 93–136. For a parodic reading of Job's response to God, see Edward L. Greenstein, "The Problem of Evil in the Book of Job," in *Mishneh Todah: Studies in Deuteronomy and Its Cultural Environment in Honor of Jeffrey H. Tigay*, ed. Nili Sacher Fox, David A Glatt-Gilad, and Michael J. Williams (Winona Lake, IN: Eisenbrauns, 2009), esp. 359.

2. This is explored by Carol A. Newsom, who utilizes the dialogical approach of Mikhail Bakhtin to read Job as a "polyphonic" text (*The Book of Job: A Contest of Moral Imaginations* [Oxford: Oxford University Press, 2003], esp. 18–31).

3. According to Ginsberg, these contrasting descriptions point to distinct compositional layers in the book ("Job the Patient and Job the Impatient," in *Congress*

irreducible complexity of the protagonist's character, which exhibits a veritable array of polarities. There is Job the fearful[4] as well as Job the fearless,[5] Job the restrained[6] along with Job the unbridled,[7] Job both despairingly hopeless[8] and audaciously hopeful.[9] Job likens himself to a "windblown leaf" on the one hand (13:25) and a sea "dragon" on the other (7:12; cf. 6:21), all tenuously held together within a single, evolving character.[10]

Such complexity of character is brought to bear in Job's encounter with YHWH in chapters 38–42. Particularly pertinent is Job's final response, which is rife with interpretive possibilities. Carol Newsom, for example, offers five different translations of 42:6, which together do not exhaust "the various nuances that might be heard in the ambiguity of the Hebrew."[11] One could easily add more.[12] In any case, how one interprets Job's final response, what David Clines calls "one

---

Volume: Rome, 1968, IOSOT, VTSup 17 [Leiden: Brill, 1969], 88–111).

4. E.g., 3:24-25; 6:4; 23:15-16; 31:23.

5. E.g., 12:2-3; 13:3, 15b, 18-19; 23:4, 6-7; 31:37; cf. 9:34-35.

6. E.g., 6:24; 40:4; cf. 13:19.

7. E.g., 7:11; 10:1-2; 23:4.

8. E.g., 9:2-20; 13:15a; 14:7-10, 18-19; 19:13-16.

9. E.g., 16:18-19; 19:25; 23:6-7.

10. Note also Job's contradictory discourse in the third cycle of dialogues, particularly in light of 24:18-25 and 27:13-23, both of which stress the certainty of punishment for the wicked and the powerful (contra 21:2-26).

11. Carol A. Newsom, "The Book of Job," in *The New Interpreter's Bible* (Nashville: Abingdon, 1996), 4:628–29. See also William Morrow, "Consolation, Rejection, and Repentance in Job 42:6," *JBL* 105 (1986): 211–25. Others have reviewed a similar range of translational possibilities before arriving at a primary meaning: e.g., Samuel E. Balentine, *Job*, SHBC (Macon, GA: Smyth & Helwys, 2006), 693–95; Ellen J. van Wolde, "Job 42,1–6: The Reversal of Job," in *The Book of Job*, ed. Willem A. M. Beuken, BETL 114 (Leuven: Leuven University Press, 1994), 223–50; David J. A. Clines, *Job 38–42*, WBC 18B (Nashville: Thomas Nelson, 2011), 1204–24.

12. Including the most recent (and quite distinctive) translation offered by Terje Stordalen in "The Canonical Taming of Job (Job 42.1–6)," *Perspectives on Israelite Wisdom: Proceedings of the Oxford Old Testament Seminar*, ed. John Jarick (London: Bloomsbury T&T Clark, 2016), 187–207.

of the biggest surprises of the book,"[13] has much to do with how one interprets YHWH's answer, not to mention the book as a whole. In this essay, I attempt to diminish ever so slightly the semantic ambiguity of Job's response with what I consider to be the most obvious nuance of a highly contested verb (*nḥm*), but in so doing deepen ever so greatly the ambiguity of YHWH's answer. The (re)interpretation of YHWH's answer in light of Job's response and its significance for Job's character, it turns out, is the biggest surprise of all.

Job's Final Response

To take up Job's final response to YHWH is to dive into a cascade of exegetical cruxes, as the history of biblical commentary testifies all too well.[14] Job's final response in 42:1-6 features two statements introduced as conclusions in 42:3aβb and 42:6, signaled by *lākēn* and *ʿal-kēn* ("therefore") respectively. The former reads: "Therefore, I declared what I did not understand, things too wonderful (*niplāʾôt*) for me, which I did not know." Restating YHWH's opening address in 38:2, Job admits that he has spoken out of ignorance, specifically ignorance of YHWH's *niplāʾôt*, or "wonders." While the plural term frequently denotes divine works of victory on behalf of Israel (e.g., Josh 3:5; Mic 7:15; Pss 98:1; 106:22), it can also reference God's works in creation (Ps 136:4; Prov 30:18; cf. Ps 119:18), as it does particularly in Job (5:9; 37:5; 37:14). It seems appropriate that YHWH's answer to Job, featuring everything from the macrocosmic to the monstrous, from lions to Leviathan, would elicit a sense of fearful awe on the part of Job (and the reader).

Job's final words, however, take a different, if not surprising, turn. In the face of a multitude of possibilities, I offer my own translation:

> I heard you by the hearing of the ear,
> > but now my eye has seen you.

---

13. Clines, *Job 38–42*, 1222.

14. A thorough review of the scholarship up to 2011 is found in Clines's translation notes for 42:2-6 in *Job 38–42*, 2104–11.

> Therefore, I relent[15]
> and am comforted over dust and ashes. (42:6)

Before discussing the details, it is important to note at the outset that Job's concluding words respond to what his "eye has seen," namely God. But what Job has seen of God, as the divine speeches make abundantly clear, is inextricably tied to what Job has heard from God. And what Job has heard from God has everything to do with a poetically rich rendering of creation, presented in the divine speeches as a "self-revelation of creation," to borrow from Gerhard von Rad's definition of biblical wisdom.[16] While Job initially beholds "the whirlwind," complete with the definite article for theophanic emphasis (*hasseʿārâ;* 38:1; 40:6),[17] it is YHWH's voice, rather than YHWH's form or physique, that takes center stage, the verbal replacing the visual. For four chapters, no less, divine discourse rather than theophanic imagery mediates Job's encounter with the Deity. This striking asymmetry between YHWH's appearance, indicated by only one repeated word, and YHWH's lengthy discourse, coupled with Job's pronouncement that he has "seen" God in 42:6, has led some to posit an earlier account of divine theophany that focused more, if not exclusively, on physical appearance.[18] In any case, the

---

15. The meaning of the first verb (*mʾs*) is disputed. Space does not allow for a full discussion of its semantic possibilities. Briefly, I take the first line of Job's intention to formally withdraw his case against God. Throughout the book of Job, the verb *mʾs* is typically deployed to convey rejection or refusal. This is particularly clear whenever the verb takes an object (5:17; 8:20; 9:21; 10:3; 19:18; 30:1; 31:13), but it also applies in cases where the verb stands alone, as in 34:33 and 36:5, whose objects can easily be inferred from the context. Most decisive, however, is the last instance in which Job employs the verb prior to 42:6. In his self-oath, Job seeks divine judgment on whether he ever dismissed a formal grievance from his slaves: "If I have dismissed the case (*ʾemʾas mišpaṭ*) of my male slave or female slave when they submitted a complaint against me" (31:13). Such legal language applies equally well to 42:6.

16. Gerhard von Rad, *Wisdom in Israel*, trans. James D. Martin (Nashville: Abingdon, 1972), 144–76.

17. Brian R. Doak, *Consider Leviathan: Narratives of Nature and Self in Job* (Minneapolis: Fortress, 2014), 184–85.

18. So, e.g., Naphtali H. Tur-Sinai, *The Book of Job: A New Commentary* (Jerusalem: Kiryath Sepher, 1957), 512.

present text features not so much a theophany as a divine "logophany," for lack of a better term. YHWH speaks out of the tempest, yes, but a *verbal* tempest is what rages for the next four chapters.

It is thus through the power of poetic discourse that Job is enabled to "see" God, specifically something of God *vis-à-vis* creation. Or put more pointedly by Ellen van Wolde, Job testifies that he "has seen YHWH('s view)";[19] Job has seen creation from God's perspective. Job finds that all creation reflects something of God's wisdom and might.[20] While recognizing that this does not solve or alleviate the ambiguity of Job's words in 42:6, it does, I submit, provide a clear framework for its interpretive implications, as we shall see.

Having withdrawn his legal challenge against God,[21] Job pronounces the existential result of finding resolution in YHWH's answer, namely "comfort." Regardless of how the verb *nḥm* is translated in context, it fundamentally denotes a change of heart or mind and can exhibit a wide range of meaning from "regret" to "comfort." As in the case of the first verb (*mʾs*), the range of ancient versions admits to an uncertainty of meaning. But much like the first verb, the meaning that *nḥm* assumes elsewhere in the book contributes something significant to its nuance here. Indeed, consistency is its hallmark: the verb occurs six other times in the book of Job and always with the sense of "comfort," an undeniably prominent theme throughout the book.[22] One would think, then, that the default meaning of the verb in 42:6 is "comforted" or "comfort oneself," a meaning that, however, is not reflected in any standard English

---

19. Van Wolde, "The Reversal of Job," 248, cf. 234.

20. Often noted is theophanic imagery particularly in the figures of Leviathan and the warhorse. See, e.g., Newsom, *Book of Job*, 243, 251, 261; idem, "The Book of Job," 611; Norman C. Habel, *The Book of Job: A Commentary*, OTL (Philadelphia: Westminster, 1985), 547; Barry R. Huff, "Dipped in Filth and Clothed in Glory: Job's Transformation of Priestly Terms, Themes, Texts, and Theologies" (PhD diss., Union Presbyterian Seminary, 2017), 237.

21. Widely recognized is the pervasiveness of legal language in Job's discourse (e.g., 9:2-35; 10:2, 6-7, 17; 13:6-12, 17-28; 14:3; 16:8, 19-21; 19:5, 7, 25; 23:6).

22. Job 2:11; 7:13; 16:2; 21:34; 29:25; 42:11 (cf. the nominal form in 15:11).

translation except the CEB.²³ While its Niphal form is unique in Job, the meaning of "comfort" is well attested elsewhere in this stem and frequently in conjunction with the preposition *'al*.²⁴

Regarding the specific nuance of "comfort" in 42:6, there are at least two distinct possibilities: "Therefore, I relent and am comforted *on* dust and ashes." Here the preposition *'al* is simply locative in meaning (cf. Job 2:8, 12). Another possibility is to take the preposition to designate *for what* a person is consoled: "Therefore, I relent and am comforted *over/for* dust and ashes."²⁵ A clear example of this use occurs five verses later in the Epilogue: "And they comforted him *for* all the calamity (*'al kol-hārā'â*) that YHWH had brought against him" (42:11aβ; see also 2 Sam 13:39; Jer 31:15; Ezek 14:22). In both examples (42:6b, 11aβ), the object of the preposition *'al* indicates the reason that calls for comfort. In Job 42:11aβ, the reason is divinely wrought "calamity." In v. 6, it is "dust and ashes" (*'āpār wā'ēper*), whose significance remains a matter of debate.

David Lambert, for example, argues that the expression "dust and ashes" serves as a metonym for mourning: Job's concluding words mark his repudiation of and disengagement from mourning.²⁶

---

23. The translation of "comfort" has been rigorously argued by Thomas Krüger, "Did Job Repent?" in *Das Buch Hiob und seine Interpretationen*, ed. Thomas Krüger et al. (Zürich: Theologischer Verlag, 2007), 223–29. See also Clines, *Job 38–42*, 1208–209; Leo G. Perdue, *Wisdom and Creation: The Theology of Wisdom Literature* (Nashville: Abingdon, 1994), 180–81, 364 n.121.

24. For examples of *nḥm* denoting "comfort" in the Niphal, see Gen 24:67; 38:12; 2 Sam 13:39; Jer 31:15; Ezek 14:22; 31:16; cf. Gen 37:35 (Hithpael). Other possible meanings of *nḥm* in the Niphal include "change one's mind," "reconsider," or "regret" (Exod 13:17; 32:12, 14, 1 Sam 15:11, 29; Joel 2:13; Amos 7:3; Ezek 32:31 [contra NRSV]). Moreover, in nearly every case in which the phrase *nāḥam 'al* in the Niphal denotes a change of mind or reconsideration, the subject (most typically God) is in the position of changing the outcome of (potential) events that precipitated, or would precipitate, the concern in the first place (e.g., Exod 32:12, 14; 1 Chr 21:15; Joel 2:13; Amos 7:3; Jon 3:10; 4:2). Job is no such subject, and "dust and ashes" is no event. Greenstein argues for "take pity" in Job 42:6 and cites 2 Sam 13:39 for support, but this citation refers to David being comforted over Absalom's death.

25. Again, see 2 Sam 13:39; Jer 31:15; Ezek 14:22.

26. David Lambert, "The Book of Job in Ritual Perspective," *JBL* 134 (2015): 567. See also Clines, *Job 38–42*, 1220–22. Stordalen takes a similar tact but

Job, in other words, declares himself comforted over having had to mourn, say, the loss of his children (see Rabbinic Targum of Job). But another, more likely possibility is that Job is comforted for *being* "dust and ashes," in response to his earlier complaint in 30:19: "[God] has cast me into the mire (*ḥōmer*),[27] and I have become like dust and ashes (*wā'tmaššēl ke'āpār wā'ēper*)." Lambert's position, which is similar to Clines's,[28] does not fully take into account Job's own words in 30:19, which is key to understanding 42:6b. Here, the verbal pairing points to Job's own sense of mortal insignificance before God (cf. Gen 18:27), a particularly vivid way of re-describing his insignificance in 40:4.

For my argument, it is not necessary to narrow down the semantic possibilities of *nāḥam* in 42:6b to a single meaning. All these options could work, with varying degrees of success, and perhaps even better when considered together. Yes, Job does sit on his ash heap (2:8), and, yes, Job likens himself to "dust and ashes" (30:19), and, yes, Job no longer mourns or presses his case against YHWH from here on out. There may be no need to settle on an exclusive meaning for 42:6b. Moreover, to limit the meaning of *nāḥam* to a singular nuance (i.e., "comfort") is philologically reductive. (It is poetry after all.) Instead, I simply argue that the meaning of "comfort" *cannot be excluded* from the broader context of personal change to which Job testifies in his final words. Indeed, it is impossible to exclude it, given the consistent semantic weight the verb carries throughout the book. At the very least, "comfort" is semantically significant in Job's final response.[29] What remains wide open, however, is this question: What is it about YHWH's answer that prompts Job to find comfort? Put

---

arrives at the opposite conclusion with "Job . . . insisting on *completing* his rites of mourning" before God's display of power ("The Canonical Taming of Job," 196).

27. In Job 4:19, the term designates "clay" in parallel with "dust," both designating the mortal human body (cf. 10:9). In 13:12, *ḥōmer* is set in parallel with "ashes" to highlight the ineffectuality of the friends' discourse. Elsewhere, the term frequently designates potter's clay (Isa 45:9; 29:16; 41:25; Jer 18:4, 6), a metaphor for human creation (Isa 64:7).

28. Clines, *Job 38–42*, 1208–11, esp. 1211.

29. Cf. Van Wolde's concluding translation: "Therefore I . . . comfort myself/ repent of dust and ashes" ("Reversal of Job," 250).

more precisely, what can be gleaned from the content and function of divine discourse that brings about Job's comfort?

By declaring himself "comforted," Job acknowledges that God has succeeded in providing what his friends have failed to do, thus continuing a trajectory within the book that began in 2:11 and ends at 42:11. Outside of Job, the theme of "comfort" can signal the transition from mourning to joy (e.g., Jer 31:13; Isa 66:13-14). More broadly, it can indicate a change in one's condition and status, including legal status, as from neglect to favor (Ruth 2:10-13; Ps 86:17), from punishment to redemption (e.g., Isa 12:1; 40:1; 49:13), from loss of a loved one to gaining a new relationship (e.g., Gen 24:67; cf. 37:35), from distress unto death to new life and restoration (e.g., Ps 71:20-21). In all cases, "comfort" involves nothing less than transformation. Most well known are the opening words of Deutero-Isaiah (40:1), wherein "comfort" is correlated with Israel's change in status from punished to redeemed. Such redemption, moreover, is marked by dramatic transformation in a follow-up passage in which God's "comfort" converts Zion's wasteland into a veritable Eden (Isa 51:3).

If the community's comfort of Job helps to reverse the "calamity" with which YHWH afflicted Job (42:11), what then does YHWH's answer offer by way of "comfort" that mitigates, or even reverses, Job's own sense of mortal insignificance, of being "dust and ashes"? It is a counterintuitive question for many interpreters, for what "comfort" is there in an answer that refuses to explain why Job has been targeted for torment?[30] What "comfort" is there in a verbal theophany that seems to hammer home Job's own insignificance? Job's confession of comfort, surprising as it is, necessitates a rereading of YHWH's answer to find perhaps an even greater surprise than his response. Indeed, the introductory ʿal-kēn ("therefore") invites a retrospective look at YHWH's answer even as Job's reference to comfort may also anticipate what he will receive in the Epilogue (42:10-12). Upon his ash heap, before God and the sublime sweep of the cosmos, Job has not only been grasped by a sense of fearful wonder (42:3; cf. 40:4-5); he has also found solace concerning his state of desolation.

---

30. Note the irony of the friends' *explanatory* answers providing no comfort for Job.

The Contours of Awe

Job's response to YHWH's speeches, in short, reflects a seemingly intractable tension: awe on the one hand and comfort on the other. How does one reconcile the two? I suggest starting experientially rather than theologically. With a plethora of visually arresting images and metaphors marshalled by the poet, from singing stars and bursting Sea to birthing mountain goats and monstrous Leviathan, the poet provides in accumulative fashion a vivid panoramic experience of primordial awe. Regardless of the myriad theological point(s) made throughout the divine discourse, one thing seems clear: the YHWH speeches are meant to elicit most fundamentally an experience of fearful awe, as Job himself testifies in 42:3. Perhaps then it might be helpful to know something about the nature of awe for understanding what is going on in the divine speeches and in Job's response.

For that I turn to a foundational psychological study of awe, which locates this cognitively charged emotion "in the upper reaches of pleasure and on the boundary of fear."[31] Dacher Keltner and Jonathan Haidt identify two religious examples, one similar to that of Job's encounter with YHWH. In the dramatic climax of the *Bhagavad Gita*, the hero Arjuna asks the god Krishna, the Lord of the universe, to see the cosmos. In gracious response, Krishna grants him a "cosmic eye" that allows him to see both Krishna and the universe. Arjuna is filled with wonder, and his verbal response indicates that he is in a state of awe: "Things never seen before have I seen, and ecstatic is my joy; yet fear-and-trembling perturb my mind" (II.45). Or put more succinctly in a more recent translation, "Having seen what no mortal has seen, I am joyful, yet I quiver with dread."[32] Joy and fear, ecstasy and terror: such are the polarities of awe. Keltner and Haidt ask the question, how can awe be both "profoundly positive and terrifyingly negative" at the same time?[33] The same could be asked of Job.

---

31. Dacher Keltner and Jonathan Haidt, "Approaching Awe, a Moral, Spiritual, and Aesthetic Emotion," *Cognition and Emotion* 17/2 (2003): 297.

32. Stephen Mitchell, trans., *Bhagavad Gita: A New Translation* (New York: Three Rivers Press, 2000), 141.

33. Keltner and Haidt, "Approaching Awe," 303.

To answer this question from a research-oriented perspective, Keltner and Haidt identify "two central themes of the awe family," namely "vastness" and "accommodation."[34] The former designates anything "that is experienced being much larger than the self," hence its affinity with overwhelming power. The second central theme of awe, "accommodation," refers to the "process of adjusting mental structures that cannot assimilate a new experience."[35] This includes the experience of disorientation and confusion. Awe, thus, "involves the *need* for accommodation," which may or may not be successful.[36] Job's penultimate words in 42:2-3 testify to YHWH's overwhelming power (v. 2) as well as to Job's challenge of assimilating what YHWH has revealed to him. Moreover, the central themes of awe (vastness and accommodation) provide a helpful, stereoscopic lens through which to reread YHWH's revelation to Job.

Vastness

YHWH reveals a creation that consists of domains and dimensions extending far beyond Job's own purview, from the "pathway to where light dwells" (38:19) to the "gates of deep darkness" (v. 17) and "recesses of the deep" (v. 16), as well as the "storehouses" of snow and hail (v. 22) and the "expanse of the earth" (v. 18). There also lies the "waste and desolate land," a no-man's land where channels of rainwater irrigate the desert (vv. 25-27). Such domains testify, in Job's own words, to the "outskirts of [YHWH's] ways" (26:14), now brought front and center to his attention. YHWH has turned Job's world not so much "inside out" as outside in. But regardless of direction, YHWH shows Job the vastness of creation, a world so vast that it both swallows him up and scales him down. While the world according to YHWH provides Job no answer, no response to his protest of pain, it does by necessity draw Job outside of himself as he becomes lost in vast cosmic landscapes limned in poetry.

Creation's vastness points invariably to the One who exercises sovereign power over all creation, a God who "can do all things" and whose purposes "cannot be thwarted," as Job's own words testify

---

34. Ibid., 304.

35. Ibid.

36. Ibid.

(42:2). Earlier when YHWH invites him to respond, Job responds with self-professed silence and deference, complete with appropriate hand gesture, acknowledging YHWH's superior might (40:4-5). Job's silence, his refusal to respond, in turn, signals his state of awe. Immediately thereafter, YHWH challenges Job to do what only YHWH can do, namely, act with divine power, a challenge that drips with sarcasm (40:9-14). Job is thereby put in his place; he is no equal to YHWH. Job's perception of his lowly status vis-à-vis God corresponds to what Keltner and Haidt describe as "primordial awe," that is, "the emotional reaction of a subordinate to a powerful leader."[37] The power differential between Job and YHWH, of course, could not be greater.

Accommodation

Vastness and power cover much of the thematic substance of YHWH's answer to Job. But what of Job's reaction? His terse but telling response in 42:3 admits to abject ignorance, betraying a measure of disorientation or bewilderment. The world that YHWH reveals to Job both extends Job's understanding and at the same time upturns it. Job discovers a wildly dissonant cosmos that turns out to be a "comforting" chaos. How so?

The animals are key. The whirlwind speeches showcase various wild creatures, both near and far (38:39–39:30; 40:15–41:26). Each one is given its poetic due in YHWH's cosmic collage of life. The first animal, the lion, as with nearly every creature, is introduced with a challenge cast as a question: "Can you hunt prey for the lion, or fill the appetite of the young lions?" (38:39). Such a question effectively turns Job's world on its head. Contrary to what Job might have expected, YHWH does not challenge Job to kill the lion, as if to have him actually "gird up his loins" and exercise his physical prowess in the face of predatory danger. Rather, YHWH challenges Job to imagine himself *providing for* the lion (38:39; cf. Ps 104:21).

Also key for Job is the onager, or wild ass, a quintessentially free creature as admiringly described by YHWH in 39:5-8. The onager effectively reverses Job's cultural map: it scorns the "commotion" (*hămôn*) of the city while flourishing in the wilderness. Job, on the

---

37. Ibid., 306–307.

other hand, views the wilderness as the domain of chaos. Through divine poetry, Job is invited to see the world as the onager sees it, in direct contradistinction to his own. Moreover, the onager proves itself to be far different from what Job had surmised about this creature. For Job, the onager was a convenient metaphor to target outcasts eking out their survival on the margins: "Like onagers in the desert they go out to their toil, scavenging for food" (24:4b). From Job's perspective, the onager metaphorically maps the poor as pitiable scavengers subsisting in the wilderness. Harsher are Job's words six chapters later, which denigrate the poor as a "braying" "senseless brood" (30:7-8). But from YHWH's perspective, the onager is far from pathetic. The wilderness is this creature's natural element; the salt lands are its "dwelling places" (39:6). In YHWH's world, monstrous and marginal creatures are free to secure their livelihoods, which they pursue fiercely and with poetically infused dignity. They are subjects unto themselves, even as many of them are abhorrent in Job's sight.

Finally, Job complains that he has become "a brother of jackals and a companion of ostriches" (30:29), paired animals emblematic of mourning and urban desolation.[38] The statement is sarcastically ironic: Job has found "companionship," as it were, in a community whose members signify in his eyes only human tragedy, a companionship that he bitterly laments. Nevertheless, YHWH reveals that Job is in fact in good company with such animals of the wild, even the ostrich, who, although bereft of wisdom, stands fearlessly against "the horse and its rider" (39:18). Ostriches and jackals are nothing to complain about, YHWH claims, but all to wonder about.

Perhaps most dissonant and disconcerting for Job is YHWH's validation of chaos in creation. The movement of YHWH's revelatory answer, in fact, proceeds from creation to chaos, rather than the reverse, as is typical of ancient creation accounts.[39] The monstrous figure of Leviathan marks the culmination of creation in Job (cf. Ps 74:14; Isa 27:1). In YHWH's world, this monster of the deep not only thrives in the abyss but is elevated (!) to unrivaled royal status (41:26; cf. 40:11-12). It is Leviathan, not Job, much less humanity,

---

38. Cf. Isa 13:22; 34:13; Jer 9:10; 10:22; 49:33; 51:37; Mic 1:8.

39. Newsom, "The Book of Job," 597.

who bears royal status. Yes, chaos is "overturned" *in Job's eyes*, not by divine conquest but instead by divine approbation.

Such a radical revisioning of chaos entails a comparable revision of divine character. Often debated is the nature and extent of divine warrior characterization in YHWH's answer.[40] Warrior imagery is undoubtedly present in YHWH's answer, but it does not run destructively rampant as one finds in Job's own discourse (see 9:4-10; 12:13-25; 13:18-19; 26:7-14). In YHWH's discourse, warrior imagery is found, for instance, in the repeated challenge to Job to "gird up" his "loins," treating Job as a combatant (38:3; 40:7 [*geber*]). References are also made to meteorological "battle and war" (38:23), divinely summoned floods and lightning bolts (vv. 34-35), and YHWH's capability of killing Behemoth with the sword (40:19).[41] In 40:9-14, YHWH (sarcastically) challenges Job to take up the divine warrior role himself in order to vanquish the wicked (v. 14).[42]

Elsewhere, however, the warrior script gets rewritten in significant ways, such as in the description of the Sea (38:8-11). The passage eschews the rhetoric of conquest by featuring in its place the language of nurture and care. The Sea is likened to an infant, "born from the womb" (v. 8) and wrapped in a "swaddling band" (v. 9). The containment of the Sea's "proud waves" is established by divine pronouncement, not by violence (v. 11). No *Chaoskampf* rages here.[43] Indeed, nowhere in YHWH's description of creation's heights and depths is cosmic conflict presupposed: the "recesses of the deep" are not trampled (v. 16), darkness is given equal play to light (v. 19), and feminine agency parallels masculine agency with

---

40. For discussion and bibliography, see Doak, *Consider Leviathan*, 184–89.

41. The translation of this verse is debated and emendations are offered (e.g., Newsom, *Book of Job*, 250). Nevertheless, I take the text (MT) as it stands.

42. While YHWH offers Job the chance to play God for a day, it remains unclear whether YHWH actually does what YHWH challenges Job to do.

43. Contra Jon D. Levenson's flat reading of Job 38:8-11 (*Creation and the Persistence of Evil: The Jewish Drama of Divine Omnipotence* [San Francisco: Harper & Row, 1988], 15–16). See Rebecca S. Watson, *Chaos Uncreated: A Reassessment of the Theme of "Chaos" in the Hebrew Bible*, BZAW 341 (Berlin: de Gruyter, 2005), 278; Newsom, *Book of Job*, 244; Doak, *Consider Leviathan*, 192–93.

regards to precipitation (vv. 28-29). As for rain in the desert, divine action is cast not so much in terms of violent storm activity as in terms of channel construction (v. 25).[44] Most significantly, when the collage of animals is presented for Job's consideration, provision and freedom, rather than subjugation and conquest, are highlighted (e.g., 38:39-41; 39:6). Human mastery over these animals is consistently countered, while divine mastery is simply assumed but never exercised outright. The possibility of divine intervention always looms, but it seems scarcely needed in such a vibrant and vital world. Telling is the description of the warhorse, in which warrior imagery gallops at full stride (39:19-25). Leviathan, a monstrous warrior in its own right, proves invincible whenever challenged, elevated to unrivaled royal status (41:26).[45] Overall, warrior imagery in YHWH's answer is more theriomorphic than theomorphic. All in all, YHWH's reconstruction of creation and of divine character is not just an exercise in cognitive dissonance but an experience of cognitive implosion. Such is Job's challenge of "accommodation." Such is the phenomenology of awe.

Job Decentered

The two central themes of "vastness" and "accommodation" point to a dynamic that underlies the entirety of Job's experience of YHWH and creation: Job is thoroughly "decentered." He discovers throughout this wild and vast creation that he is not centrally or hierarchically related to any of it. He is forced to "accommodate" and, in turn, radically revise his worldview. Neurologist Patrick McNamara describes the phenomenon of decentering as a "temporarily decoupling of the Self from its control over executive cognitive functions" on the one hand, and "a search for some more effective controlling

---

44. An ancient Near Eastern parallel can be found in the role of the Igigi, a lower class of gods who were assigned such menial labor and consequently rebelled (*Atrahasis* I OBV i-iv).

45. Much debate has revolved around 41:4, which can be interpreted either as YHWH's boasting over Leviathan or YHWH's silencing of Leviathan's boasting. I favor the former (see the discussion in Newsom, *Book of Job*, 251).

agency over cognitive resources and mechanisms" on the other.[46] In other words, the self loses control or suffers a dramatic "reduction in agency,"[47] and searches for another pathway that leads to re-integration. In so doing, the self enters into a liminal state that is resolved either positively or negatively. One result is that the self is "enriched, transformed, and transfigured."[48] Such a pathway toward re-integration can also promote the self's "healing capacities,"[49] including comfort. On the negative side, "the decentering process can . . . lead to dangerous, disintegrative psychic states including fanaticism and psychotic and delusional states."[50] On the positive side, the process can involve "a flood of images and affects that resolves into a process of attempts at meaning and then finally insight and gratitude/joy."[51] And perhaps one could also add "comfort."

Job's Comfort

We can now reread the most disputed verse in the entire book with new understanding: "Therefore, I relent and am comforted over dust and ashes" (42:6). How could Job find "comfort" in the face of YHWH's decentering revelation? More broadly, how can such an experience be both "profoundly positive and terrifyingly negative"? Perhaps the answer is that Job's encounter with God, poetically mediated, is fundamentally meant to elicit an experience of awe—an experience of "decentering" that in the end turns out to be profoundly positive, "comforting" even, as much as it is overwhelming.

Where, then, in the divine discourse is Job able to find comfort amid his awe and sense of insignificance before God and creation? One could suggest that the very fact that YHWH communicated

---

46. Patrick McNamara, *The Neuroscience of Religious Experience* (Cambridge: Cambridge University, 2009), 5.

47. Ibid., 143.

48. Ibid., 5.

49. Ibid., 6.

50. Ibid.

51. Ibid., 143. McNamara goes on to describe how decentering is mediated chemically in the brain, including a reduction in serotonin, which inhibits executive control over matters of cognitive control or "prefrontal-temporal cortical function" (143), as well as heightens limbic activity (144).

with Job provides a comforting resolution. But nothing about God's fierce presence in the whirlwind is meant to be comforting. To the contrary, it is terrifying, given that the whirlwind imagery recalls the episode in the Prologue regarding the death of Job's children caused by a "great wind" (1:19). Moreover, the manner in which YHWH communicated, a rebuke of the highest, most brutal order, is by no means comforting either. So the reader is compelled to look for something *within* YHWH's answer that would have elucidated comfort for Job.

Behold Behemoth! Twice YHWH implores Job to direct his attention to Behemoth (*hinnēh*), as in the first line in 40:15 (cf. 16a): "*Voila* Behemoth, which I made with you (*ʾăšer-ʿāśîtî ʿimmāk*)!"[52] While the force of the preposition *ʿim* remains open to interpretation, the question persists: why would YHWH mention Job at all in connection with the "first/chief (*rēʾšît*) of God's works" (v. 19)? Perhaps the preposition is simply temporal in nuance, meaning "along with" or "at the same time of." But when read in the light of Job's bitter lament about being fraternally connected *with* "jackals" and "ostriches" (30:29), there is clearly more behind this simple preposition: Behemoth and Job share a connection, something in common. For all the alien otherness of creation, could it be that Job has found his place in the company of these wild creatures that he once held in derision or had considered fearfully repulsive? Regardless of the implications, this simple preposition cited in the only positive reference to Job in YHWH's answer invites reflection on what Job possibly shares with these creatures of the wild, beginning with Behemoth: alien identity, resistance to control, fearlessness, and, to state the obvious, lack of guilt. In God's creation, Job not only discovers himself sharing common creature-hood *with* the wild; he also sees something of himself in each of these creatures, all sharing in the irrepressible exercise of life. Using the language of Keltner and Haidt, Job has successfully "accommodated" YHWH's revelation of creation by discovering a connection with God's wild "kin-dom," the source of his self-professed comfort. What Job needed from the beginning, which his friends had failed to provide, was a sense of connection

---

52. OG omits the verb and reads, "Look at the wild beasts with you."

amid his suffering. Instead of finding it in his so-called friends, Job discovers it in a monster—the biggest surprise of all!

Job's confessed comfort, thus, adds another interpretive layer that only deepens the ambiguity of YHWH's harsh answer by highlighting its affirmative and transformative impact on Job. To take it one step further, the Joban poet invites the reader to imagine what Job's own poetic portrait might look like within YHWH's cosmic collage of creatures. In some ways, the Epilogue fulfills that function, as it features Job, "full of days," subverting patriarchal convention by sharing his inheritance with his daughters (42:15-17). However, that is only half the story, the story of Job placed back in his prosaic world, as he was in the beginning. But what about Job in the wild, in God's vast creation? What might Job's *poetic* portrait, partly descriptive, partly aspirational, be in relation to the other twelve poetic portraits of wildlife? In other words, what would YHWH say about Job *poetically?* Perhaps something such as this:

> Behold my servant Job!
>   A blameless and upright man is he.
> Among humans no one is so fierce as he;
>   among his peers he has no equal.
> Do you think you can chain his mouth shut?
>   Will he make supplications to you?
> Argue with him and think of the dispute,
>   you will not do it again!
> I will not keep silent concerning his mouth,
>   the words of his lips, the boldness of his speech.
> Although he may labor in vain without wisdom, he has no fear.
>   Indeed, he laughs at his friends and denounces their teachings.
> He scorns the tyranny of tradition;
>   he denounces the accusations of his detractors.
> Even if the dialogue is turbulent, he is not frightened;
>   he remains confident amid a torrent of backlash.
> He goes forth and does not repent.
>   Who has let this wild ass of a man go free?

In his detailed study of "nature narratives" in the book of Job, Brian Doak concludes that nature "teaches humans how to be human."[53] As profiled in YHWH's answer, nature bursts with the chaotic, messy, unrestrained exercise of life. Through this vivid self-revelation of creation, YHWH indirectly affirms the fearless, unrestrained, irrepressible side of Job the disputant by aligning him with the wild, fearless, irrepressible side of creation. YHWH's awe-filled answer, in the end, is indeed an invitation for Job to "gird up his loins" and be the fearless creature he was meant to be.

Bibliography

Balentine, Samuel E. *Job*. SHBC. Macon, GA: Smyth & Helwys, 2006.

Clines, David J A. *Job 38–42*. WBC 18B; Nashville: Thomas Nelson, 2011.

Dell, Katharine J. *Job: Where Shall Wisdom Be Found? An Introduction and Study Guide*. T&T Clark Study Guides for the Old Testament 14. London: Bloomsbury T&T Clark, 2017.

Doak, Brian R. *Consider Leviathan: Narratives of Nature and Self in Job*. Minneapolis: Fortress, 2014.

Ginsberg, H. L. "Job the Patient and Job the Impatient." Pages 88–111 in *Congress Volume: Rome, 1968*. IOSOT. VTSup 17. Leiden: Brill, 1969.

Greenstein, Edward L. "The Problem of Evil in the Book of Job." Pages 333–62 in *Mishneh Todah: Studies in Deuteronomy and Its Cultural Environment in Honor of Jeffrey H. Tigay*. Edited by Nili Sacher Fox, David A Glatt-Gilad, and Michael J. Williams. Winona Lake, IN: Eisenbrauns, 2009.

Habel, Norman C. *The Book of Job: A Commentary*. OTL. Philadelphia: Westminster, 1985.

Huff, Barry R. "Dipped in Filth and Clothed in Glory: Job's Transformation of Priestly Terms, Themes, Texts, and Theologies." PhD diss., Union Presbyterian Seminary, 2017.

---

53. Doak, *Consider Leviathan*, 229.

Keltner, Dacher, and Jonathan Haidt. "Approaching Awe, a Moral, Spiritual, and Aesthetic Emotion," *Cognition and Emotion* 17/2 (2003): 297–314.

Krüger, Thomas. "Did Job Repent?" Pages 217–29 in *Das Buch Hiob und seine Interpretationen*. Edited by Thomas Krüger et al. Zürich: Theologischer Verlag, 2007.

Mitchell, Stephen, trans. *Bhagavad Gita: A New Translation*. New York: Three Rivers Press, 2000.

Lambert, David. "The Book of Job in Ritual Perspective." *JBL* 134 (2015): 557–75.

Levenson, Jon D. *Creation and the Persistence of Evil: The Jewish Drama of Divine Omnipotence*. San Francisco: Harper & Row, 1988.

Morrow, William. "Consolation, Rejection, and Repentance in Job 42:6." *JBL* 105 (1986): 211–25.

Newsom, Carol A. "The Book of Job." Pages 317–638 in vol. 4 of *The New Interpreter's Bible*. Nashville: Abingdon, 1996.

———. *The Book of Job: A Contest of Moral Imaginations*. Oxford: Oxford University Press, 2003.

Perdue, Leo G. *Wisdom and Creation: The Theology of Wisdom Literature*. Nashville, TN: Abingdon, 1994.

Rad, Gerhard von. *Wisdom in Israel*. Translated by James D. Martin. Nashville: Abingdon, 1972.

Stordalen, Terje. "The Canonical Taming of Job (Job 42.1–6)." Pages 187–207 in *Perspectives on Israelite Wisdom: Proceedings of the Oxford Old Testament Seminar*. Edited by John Jarick. London: Bloomsbury T&T Clark, 2016.

McNamara, Patrick. *The Neuroscience of Religious Experience*. Cambridge: Cambridge University, 2009.

Tur-Sinai, Naphtali. H. *The Book of Job: A New Commentary*. Jerusalem: Kiryath Sepher, 1957.

Van Wolde, Ellen J. "Job 42,1-6: The Reversal of Job." Pages 223–50 in *The Book of Job*. Edited by Willem A. M. Beuken. BETL 114. Leuven: Leuven University Press, 1994.

Watson, Rebecca S. *Chaos Uncreated: A Reassessment of the Theme of "Chaos" in the Hebrew Bible*. BZAW 341. Berlin: de Gruyter, 2005.

Zuckerman, Bruce. *Job the Silent: A Study in Historical Counterpoint*. Oxford: Oxford University Press, 1991.

When Eternal Questions "Dance" within the Human Imagination
The Making of the Ballet Job: *A Masque for Dancing*[1]

Patricia Vesely

> *It is with deep appreciation that I dedicate this essay to Samuel E. Balentine, who first introduced me to* Job: A Masque for Dancing *many years ago and who taught me that the "dance" of biblical interpretation is an undertaking that is performed on multiple and varied stages in human life. Sam has been and will continue to be an inspiration for my exegesis of the Bible, of art, and of the questions that drive humanity's search for God.*

---

1. I am grateful to Emma Darbyshire of the Fitzwilliam Museum in Cambridge and Jack Glover Gunn of the V&A Museum in London for their kind and gracious help in obtaining manuscripts and photographs related to the ballet *A Masque for Dancing*.

In English artist William Blake's final illustration in his series of plates on the book of Job, Job and his family are shown standing in front of a large tree, joyfully playing musical instruments, while a feminine figure, symbolizing the arts, watches contentedly in the foreground. The sun is rising in the east, marking the beginning of a new day. In the biblical story, no reference is made to Job or his family taking up musical instruments in celebration of his restoration, yet this is an unmistakable focus of Blake's depiction of Job's renewal (Fig. 11.1).

Blake's decision to surround the restored Job with music and song indeed has historical roots. In the fourteenth and fifteenth centuries, Job was celebrated as the patron saint of music. Several illuminated manuscripts and altar panels dating from this period depict Job holding musical instruments.[2] The earliest connections between Job and music may be found in the first century BCE to first century CE text the Testament of Job, where Job is described playing the lyre for his maidservants (14:1-5) and bequeathing musical instruments to his daughters upon his restoration (52:4-7).[3] Yet the insertion of instruments by Blake in his final illustration of the Joban plates is not simply a nod of recognition toward Job's depiction as a musician.[4] According to Blake, humanity finds its way to God through artistic expression; art is thus essential to the human quest for spiritual renewal. Blake understood the "imagination" as the locus in which God is revealed to the individual and through which spiritual regeneration takes place.[5]

---

2. Samuel E. Balentine, *Have You Considered My Servant Job?: Understanding the Biblical Archetype of Patience*, Studies on Personalities of the Old Testament (Columbia: University of South Carolina Press, 2015), 41–43; Kathi Meyer, "St. Job as a Patron of Music," *The Art Bulletin* 36/1 (Mar 1954): 29–30.

3. R. P. Spittler, "Testament of Job: A New Translation and Introduction," *OTP* 1:844, 867.

4. By the nineteenth century, the time in which Blake was creating his portraits, this characterization for Job was no longer common. Balentine, *Have You Considered*, 41–43; Meyer, "St. Job as Patron of Music," 30.

5. J. G. Davies, *The Theology of William Blake* (Oxford: Clarendon, 1948), 64–70; Morris Eaves, *William Blake's Theory of Art* (Princeton: Princeton University Press, 1982), 67, 69; Kathleen Raine, *The Human Face of God: William Blake and the Book of Job* (New York: Thames and Hudson, 1982), 13–15; Christopher Rowland, *Blake and the Bible* (New Haven: Yale University Press, 2010), 9–10.

WHEN ETERNAL QUESTIONS "DANCE" WITHIN THE HUMAN IMAGINATION 269

Figure 11.1. William Blake, "So the Lord Blessed the Latter End of Job More than the Beginning," Plate XXI of William Blake, *Illustrations of the Book of Job*, 1823–1825. Engraving. 40.6 x 27.3 cm. Yale Center for British Art, New Haven, CT. Gift of J. T. Johnston Coe in memory of Henry E. Coe, Yale BA 1878; Henry E. Coe Jr., Yale BA 1917; and Henry E. Coe III, Yale BA 1946. Photo Credit: Public Domain.

The centrality of art in Blake's understanding of spiritual restoration further is underscored by contrasting Blake's last plate with the first in his series of Joban illustrations. In Plate 1, Job, his wife, and his children sit in front of the same large tree shown in the last plate. Hanging above them on the branches of the tree, unused, are the very instruments that are put to song in the last portrait. The sun is setting, indicating the beginning of Job's "night," or descent into darkness. The unused instruments suggest an untapped potential: there is more to life than Job initially perceives. In this opening illustration, Job is surrounded by flocks of sheep, tents, and doting children—he is clearly a prosperous man—but his "music" is silent. In Blake's drawings, Job's journey from spiritual slumber to spiritual awakening most poignantly is symbolized by the presence or absence of music and song, representative of artistic expression as a whole (Fig. 11.2).

Blake's portraits were first published in 1826, a few months before his death. Upon the one-hundredth anniversary of his death, author and Blake expert Sir Geoffrey Keynes sought to honor Blake with the creation of a ballet based on his "Illustrations to the Book of Job." According to Keynes, Blake's drawings "were asking for the chance to be put into motion . . . . they seemed to want to move from the page and on to the stage."[6] Telling the Joban story through a wide variety of artistic mediums—painting, music, and dance—was deemed appropriate by Keynes given Blake's own estimation of art as essential to the human journey towards spiritual fulfillment. Blake believed that his own artwork served to push humanity further along that journey toward a greater recognition of the God that is grasped through the imagination. The Joban ballet, for Keynes, would be another such effort.

For Blake, art must be an expression of the "the whole identity of the person" (Eaves, *William Blake's Theory of Art*, 67). Eaves explains, "Since the imagination is that identity, art is indeed the expression of imagination" (ibid.). Blake and other Romantic artists like Wordsworth and Shelley viewed art as restorative and, in some ways, salvific. Art is what restores integrity and wholeness to personal identity in "a culture flying to pieces under the specialized pressures of industrialization" (ibid., 67, 69–70).

6. Frank W. D. Ries, "Sir Geoffrey Keynes and the Ballet *Job*," *Dance Research: The Journal for the Society for Dance Research* 2/1 (Spring 1984): 19.

Figure 11.2. William Blake, "Thus Job Did Continually," Plate I of William Blake, *Illustrations of the Book of Job*, 1823–1825. Engraving. 40.6 x 27.3 cm. Yale Center for British Art, New Haven, CT. Gift of J. T. Johnston Coe in memory of Henry E. Coe, Yale BA 1878; Henry E. Coe Jr., Yale BA 1917; and Henry E. Coe III, Yale BA 1946. Photo Credit: Public Domain.

As with most works of art on a large scale, Keynes recognized that his ballet would need to be a collaborative effort. Keynes enlisted the following individuals: his sister-in-law and expert wood engraver, Gwendolen Raverat, for the set designs and costumes; Ralph Vaughan Williams, renowned composer and Raverat's cousin, for the musical score; and Ninette de Valois, professional dancer and founder of The Royal Ballet, for the choreography. Each of these participants found themselves deeply invested in the Joban story and sought to mold the production based on their own interpretations of the tale. Like the biblical story itself, the finished product came to life through dialogue and the contribution of multiple perspectives that were not always harmonious with each other.

In the remainder of this essay, I analyze the making of the Joban ballet with specific emphasis on Keynes's, Raverat's, and Vaughan Williams's input, which is known through a series of existing letters and early drafts of the ballet.[7] I focus on three particular issues that created dissonance among these collaborators: the question of Job's guilt, God's role in Job's suffering, and the nature of Job's restoration. Although marked by disagreement in its genesis, the finished product achieved Blake's aim of the revival of the human spirit through art, and *A Masque for Dancing* paved the way for the creation of The Royal Ballet of London, one of the most widely acclaimed ballet companies in the world.

The biblical text introduces Job as a man who is "blameless," "upright," "fearing God," and "turning from evil" (1:1, 8; 2:3; cf. 1:22; 2:10). Job's exemplary character appears indisputable in the opening narrative, yet not all readers of the text agree with the narrator's declaration of Job's innocence. John Calvin, for example, believed that Job is guilty of pride and self-righteousness; Elihu's reproof and God's storm theophany prompts his repentance and

---

7. That the script for the ballet went through a series of revisions is attested by the multiple drafts that were written by the various collaborators. At least seven different drafts exist in the Fitzwilliam Museum in Cambridge, England. The changes among the versions are telling with respect to the issues that led to disagreement and debate among the collaborators. The relevant material may be found in the album Geoffrey Keynes, "Blake's Job: A masque for dancing." All manuscripts were acquired with permission from the Fitzwilliam Museum, Cambridge, England.

subsequent restoration.[8] Others, such as Samuel E. Balentine, argue that the biblical author establishes Job's innocence so as to remove Job from any responsibility for his suffering and so that the focus of the tale rests on the question of what role, if any, God plays in innocent human suffering.[9] The collaborators of the Joban ballet wrestled with the question of Job's guilt as well. Since Blake's portraits served as the inspiration for the ballet, a brief explanation of Blake's evaluation of Job's moral standing is needed before examining the collaborators' vision for their leading figure.

Blake's opening illustration offers clues as to his assessment of Job's initial state. As noted, Job, his wife, and their children sit in front of a large tree upon whose branches hang numerous musical instruments. An open Bible lies on Job's and his wife's laps, and sheep and their sheepdog are sleeping peacefully in the foreground. The sun is setting in the west, and a crescent moon rises, signaling the onset of night.

Blake's drawings are full of symbolism: the instruments that lie unused, the setting sun, and even the sleeping sheep and sheepdog are all indications that Job himself is not fully "awake" but lies in a state of spiritual slumber. Something is missing in Job's life; he has not yet come into the full realization of life as God intended.

The texts that Blake includes in the margins around his drawings further clarify these symbolic images. Blake titles this plate "Thus did Job continually," a reference to Job's act of sacrificing during his children's feast days in order to compensate for any sins they might have committed (Job 1:4-5). In the lower corners is Job 1:1, "There was a Man in the Land of Uz whose Name was Job. & that Man was perfect and upright & one that feared God & eschewed Evil. & there was born unto him Seven Sons & Three Daughters." In the center of the lower margin Blake has added two texts from the New Testament: "The Letter Killeth, The Spirit giveth Life" (2 Cor 3:6), and "It is Spiritually Discerned" (1 Cor 2:14).

---

8. John Calvin, *Sermons from Job*, trans. Leroy Nixon (Grand Rapids: Eerdmans, 1952), 220–22, 276–84.

9. Samuel E. Balentine, *Job*, SHBC (Macon, GA: Smyth & Helyws, 2008), 27–28, 30–33. Cf. Patricia Vesely, *Friendship and Virtue Ethics in the Book of Job* (Cambridge: Cambridge University Press, 2019), 233–36.

The two texts from Corinthians are instructive for understanding Blake's conception of religion and the character of Job. For Blake, reality is spiritual. Humans are born into a "natural state" whereby they are caught up in the physical and material world, yet this is only a shadow of the true reality that lies beyond what is perceived through the senses. In order to access this deeper realm, one must be awakened in the spirit. Blake describes this journey as a movement from the "materialist self" to the "spiritual self."[10] This process of awakening occurs through God's revelation to humankind through the imagination.[11]

Blake believed the Joban story portrays the journey that every human must undertake from entrapment in the material world to liberation and spiritual awakening.[12] The first portrait in his illustrations offers clues that Job is, in part, responsible for his troubles. The texts Blake includes from Corinthians suggest that Job is caught up in material things. His repeated sacrificing, or "ritualistic morality," reveals a spiritual naiveté. Blake's final portrait depicting Job's restoration (replete with rising sun, instruments in use, and wakened animals) confirms these notions: occupying the same space as the texts from Corinthians in Plate 1 are the words "In burnt Offerings for Sin thou hast had no Pleasure" (Heb 10:6).[13]

---

10. Davies, *Theology of William Blake*, 40–47, 60–65.

11. Ibid., 64–70; Balentine, *Job*, 50; Eaves, *William Blake's Theory of Art*, 69; Raine, *Human Face of God*, 13–14; Rowland, *Blake and the Bible*, 9–10, 14.

12. Davies, *Theology of William Blake*, 41; Raine, *Human Face of God*, 13, 17, 20–24; Rowland, *Blake and the Bible*, 34–35, 45–48, 71.

13. Blake's depiction of Job in the opening scenes reflects his negative assessment of religion in nineteenth-century England. He criticized the church for having become stale and legalistic and critiqued thinkers such as Bacon, Locke, and Newton for their emphasis on reason and empiricism and their consequent disavowal of the imagination (Davies, *Theology of William Blake*, 14–15; Eaves, *William Blake's Theory of Art*, 67; Raine, *Human Face of God*, 11–13, 40–41; Rowland, *Blake and the Bible*, 11, 22–23). A religion that loses its connection with the spiritual realm becomes solely focused on morality, Blake surmised:

> The Spectre is the Reasoning Power in Man; & when separated
> From Imagination, and closing itself as in steel, in a Ratio
> Of the things of Memory. It thence frames Laws & Moralities

In Blake's eyes, Job begins his journey like every human—ignorant and falsely dependent on the material world. The question of moral guilt, however, was not central to Blake's understanding of the quest for spiritual wholeness.[14] Plate 1 reflects Job's "lethargic state": Job has not yet tapped into the far reaches of his imagination, which would enable his eyes to be opened to the Divine. Job thus is responsible for the sufferings that such blindness causes, but he is not guilty of any moral infraction. Job is, simply put, "asleep" to the true nature of God and the true nature of his own self.

Keynes, the initiator of the Joban ballet and a Blake expert, was careful to follow Blake's interpretations as closely as possible. In his scripts for the ballet, Keynes thus focuses on Blake's emphasis on the *internal* struggle depicted in the Joban plates. For him, the images of Job's wealth in Blake's opening illustration symbolize Job's reliance on material things, but Job's financial status in any literal sense is irrelevant to the tale.[15] Following Blake, Keynes attributes a kind of "materialism" to Job at the onset of the story that is indicative of his mistaken perception that the natural world is a reliable source of truth and knowledge that results in an ineffectual piety. As with Blake, the question of Job's moral guilt is not central to Keynes's interpretation of Job's suffering and renewal.[16]

To destroy Imagination! the Divine Body, by Martyrdoms & Wars. (*Jerusalem*, 74.10–13)

(All quotations of Blake are taken from David V. Erdman, ed., *The Complete Poetry and Prose of William Blake*, Newly Revised Edition [New York, Anchor Books, 1988]).

14. Raine, *Human Face of God*, 39, 84; Rowland, *Blake and the Bible*, 2–3, 11. Raine explains, "Throughout his prophetic writings Blake's call is never to repentance but to awakening: enlightenment, not repentance, was for him the way to know God" (*Human Face of God*, 39).

15. Allison Sanders McFarland, "A Deconstruction of William Blake's Vision: Vaughan Williams and *Job*," *International Journal of Musicology* 3 (1994): 345. Cf. Raine, *Human Face of God*, 215–16; Rowland, *Blake and the Bible*, 14–17.

16. "[W]hat precisely constitutes 'materialism' must be defined with caution. Blake does indeed decry materialism, by which he means anything not inherently spiritual. . . . His dismissal of Newton and Locke, among others, is scathing, and reveals that Blake believed analytical thought is a form of materialism" (McFarland, "Vaughan Williams and *Job*," 345. Cf. ibid., 346–47).

Early on in the project, Keynes enlisted his sister-in-law, Gwendolen Raverat, to help with the creation of the ballet. Raverat, a skillfully trained artist and wood engraver, brilliantly designed the sets to reflect the dual realms in which the Joban story alternates. One of Blake's portraits was to be displayed as the backdrop of each scene. The stage itself was divided into two halves: the back half, which was raised, represented the heavenly realm, and the lowered front half represented the earthly realm. A drop sheet could be lowered between the two halves if the focus fell on the earthly realm, while the front half could be darkened and the drop sheet raised if the focus lay on the heavenly realm.[17]

Raverat's involvement in the ballet extended well beyond the set designs, however. She became one of the principal writers of the script, and she and Keynes worked together on several drafts before Vaughan Williams and de Valois joined the project. Unlike Blake and Keynes, Raverat did not read Job as a story depicting humanity's quest for spiritual enlightenment; rather, she interpreted the tale as that of one man's guilt, repentance, and restoration.

Raverat begins her version of the ballet as follows:

> Act 1 *Earth*. (The front part of the stage only is seen).
> Sunset. The scene represents hilly country, where many flocks are feeding. Job and his whole family are seated under a tree in the middle of the stage. They are rich and prosperous shepherds, and a complacent materialism reigns all about them.[18]

After a dance performed by Job's children and a time of feasting in which Job participates,[19] Satan enters the stage behind them and beseeches God to appear. The drop sheet rises, revealing the character of God seated on the heavenly throne. Raverat then narrates, "Satan addresses Jehovah and accuses Job of the sin of materialism, pointing

---

17. Geoffrey Keynes, "Blake's Job: A masque for dancing," (album) p. 4, f1. Manuscripts acquired with permission from The Fitzwilliam Museum, Cambridge, England.

18. McFarland, "Vaughan Williams and *Job*," 362–63.

19. In the biblical text, only Job's children partake in the feasts (Job 1:4-5).

at Job as he sits in voluptuous contentment in the front part of the stage."[20]

By using phrases such as "complacent materialism," "the sin of materialism," and "voluptuous contentment," and by including Job in the feasting that takes place among his children, Raverat tips the moral scales in the direction of Job's guilt. According to Allison McFarland, Raverat's interpretation of Job's materialism was in keeping with her cultural setting in early twentieth-century England. Raverat, the granddaughter of Charles Darwin, grew up in Cambridge academic circles known for quasi-socialist sympathies.[21] Raverat's biographical memoir, *Period Piece: A Cambridge Childhood*, displays a perspective that is critical of the British upper class.[22] McFarland explains, "The first synopsis of the Job ballet, with Raverat as apparently the sole author, paints Job's sin in very bold strokes, and the sin is in action, not only in thought. In this version there is no doubt that Job has sinned because of his accumulation of wealth and possessions: the typescript at times lapses into language reminiscent of a socialist tract."[23] For Raverat, Job represents the elites of society whose interests in material comforts result in diminished conditions for the lower classes. In her interpretation, Job's moral failings are clear: he is guilty of the vices of greed and self-indulgence.

One cannot be certain whether audiences would have connected the images of Job's wealth with a spiritual blindness and ignorance, as Blake and Keynes imagined, or a greed and self-interestedness associated with the upper echelons of society, as Raverat intended. At least one participant rejected both of these interpretations, however, and sought to shape the story around a different model of the hero Job.

The composer of the musical score, Ralph Vaughan Williams, joined the project after Keynes and Raverat had drafted several versions of the script. Once he committed to the project it was clear that, like Raverat, he wished to be involved in shaping the story as

---

20. Keynes, "Blake's Job," p. 4, f2.

21. McFarland, "Vaughan Williams and Job," 346.

22. Gwendolyn Raverat, *Period Piece: A Cambridge Childhood* (London: Faber and Faber, 1952), 75–80, 102–104; McFarland, "Vaughan Williams and *Job*," 346.

23. McFarland, "Vaughan Williams and *Job*," 345–46.

well as providing his artistic talents. Vaughan Williams drafted his own version of the script, which he regularly shared with the others in the ongoing creation of the ballet. His notes include set, costume, and even choreographic instructions.[24] At one point Keynes expressed in frustration with Vaughan Williams, "He wished to introduce features having no connexion whatever with the designs, whereas it was my intention that the entire conception should be unadulterated Blake."[25]

Vaughan Williams's own rendition of the opening scene of the ballet is revealing. He begins with the following picture: "Job and his family sit in quiet contentment surrounded by flocks and herds."[26] A dance of Job's sons and daughters then takes place, which Vaughan Williams describes with intricate detail, naming who should dance and where they should be situated on the stage. After Satan's entrance and appeal to heaven, Vaughan Williams provides a description of God and Satan's interaction:

> God arises in His majesty and beckons to Satan. Satan steps forward at God's command. A light falls on Job. God regards him with affection and says to Satan 'Hast thou considered my servant Job?' Satan says 'Put forth Thy hand now and touch all that he hath and he will curse Thee to Thy face. God says, 'All that he hath is in thy power.' Satan departs.[27]

In his scripts, Vaughan Williams changes Keynes's and Raverat's language so as to exonerate Job from any possible sin or vice. The "complacent materialism" of Raverat has become a "quiet contentment," suggesting that Job is grateful for his blessings but is not, by any means, luxuriating in them inappropriately. Vaughan Williams deletes the reference to "Job's sin" by Raverat and includes the detail that God looks upon Job with affection, which further solidifies his portrayal of Job as an innocent human being.

---

24. Keynes, "Blake's Job," p. 9, f1.

25. McFarland, "Vaughan Williams and *Job*," 349; Ries, "Sir Geoffrey Keynes," 23.

26. McFarland, "Vaughan Williams and *Job*," 364.

27. Keynes, "Blake's Job," p. 9, f1; cf. Job 1:8-12.

At the outset of the Joban ballet, then, these three collaborators sought to introduce audiences to different versions of the character of Job. This leading role may have been a morally decent man who lacked spiritual insight; he may have been among the self-interested elite whose reliance on wealth rendered him guilty of pride and complacency; or he may have been an entirely innocent human being, someone who found favor in God's eyes and was blessed with many comforts as a result.

Not surprisingly, these diverse depictions of Job corresponded to different understandings of the character of God among the collaborators. A second point of controversy that arose in the making of the ballet was the issue of how to portray God on stage and what role this figure was to play in Job's sufferings.

Blake's own understanding of God is complex. His strong emphasis on divine immanence has led to the critique that his art blurs the distinction between Creator and creation.[28] Blake speaks of God as the fullness of the imagination that can be found within each human being. The imagination is "the Divine Body in Every Man," he writes, and creation is "the Divine Vision, And the sports of Wisdom in the Human Imagination, Which is the Divine Body of the Lord Jesus, blessed for ever."[29]

The intimate link between humanity and the ultimate reality that is Blake's God can be seen in the nearly identical depictions of God and Job in his drawings. In Plate 5, for example, two similar figures are situated in the central portions of the top and bottom halves of the drawing. Their beards are the same, their dress is the same, and both have the same despondent expression, heads tilted at exactly the same angle. One of the only visible differences is that the head of God, who is seated at the top, is tilted to the right, while that of Job, who occupies the bottom half, is tilted to the left (Fig. 11.3). For

---

28. Davies, *Theology of William Blake*, 55, 59–68.

29. Annotations to Berkeley's *Siris*, 219; *Milton*, 3.3–4. "I know of no other Christianity and of no other Gospel than the liberty both of body & mind to exercise the Divine Arts of Imagination, Imagination, the real & eternal World of which this Vegetable Universe is but a faint shadow, & in which we shall live in our Eternal or Imaginative Bodies when these Vegetable Mortal Bodies are no more" (*Jerusalem*, 77). See also Rowland, *Blake and the Bible*, 27–28, 45–48, 60–61.

Figure 11.3. William Blake, "Then Went Satan Forth from the Presence of the Lord," Plate V of William Blake, *Illustrations of the Book of Job*, 1823–1825. Engraving. 40.6 x 27.3 cm. Yale Center for British Art, New Haven, CT. Gift of J. T. Johnston Coe in memory of Henry E. Coe, Yale BA 1878; Henry E. Coe Jr., Yale BA 1917; and Henry E. Coe III, Yale BA 1946. Photo Credit: Public Domain.

Blake, the right side symbolizes the spiritual life, while the left side symbolizes the material world.[30] The similarities between the two figures, coupled with the change in direction of their heads, indicate that Job has not yet reached full identification with the Divine but that the potential to do so awaits.

In his effort to honor Blake's retelling of the Joban tale, Keynes names God "Job's Spiritual Self" in his scripts. Keynes was able to convince the others to keep this title, in part, because of the difficulties in trying to portray God as a character on stage.[31] In Keynes's narration, after God assents to Satan's request to inflict Job, God ("Job's Spiritual Self") steps down from the throne, and Satan triumphantly takes his place. This dramatic scene, for Keynes, signifies the reign of "Job's Materialist Self" over his life at this point. At the close of the story as Job beholds deeper spiritual realities, "Job's Spiritual Self" (God) returns to the throne.[32]

By locating Job's struggle internally as a reflection of the human journey from ignorance to spiritual enlightenment, the moral dilemma posed by God's involvement in allowing (or causing) innocent humans to suffer is removed for Keynes and Blake. If humans must all progress along this path in order to realize their true natures, then it is in their best interest to rid themselves of any dependence on material things. The instigator of Job's sufferings is not an independent and transcendent deity, for Keynes or Blake, but Job's own spiritual blindness.[33]

Raverat agreed to name God "Job's Spiritual Self" in the final rendition of the script, yet the focus of the Joban story, for her,

---

30. McFarland, "Vaughan Williams and *Job*," 343.

31. Keynes, "Blake's Job," p. 15, f2–3; Ries, "Sir Geoffrey Keynes," 23.

32. Ries, "Sir Geoffrey Keynes," 32–33; McFarland, "Vaughan Williams and *Job*," 364. For more on Satan as humanity's "Materialist Self," see Davies, *Theology of William Blake*, 62; Raine, *Human Face of God*, 195–200. Raine explains, "Satan, as the Selfhood or empirical ego, is not one of the eternal contraries of Good and Evil; nor is the victory of Imagination, who casts out the ego, the conquest of 'evil' by 'good'. Rather we see the triumph of 'the human existence itself' over a world of illusion, or 'error', as Blake says" (*Human Face of God*, 235).

33. See, e.g., Rowland, *Blake and the Bible*, 16–17, 46–47, 71.

remained Job's journey from guilt to repentance and restoration. Both God, whom Raverat names "Jehovah," and Satan have a hand in Job's troubles, but Job plays a role, too. For Raverat, Job's suffering serves as a punishment whereby he learns of his moral faults.

In Blake's drawings, Elihu is portrayed as a prophetic figure who reveals spiritual truths to Job.[34] In Raverat's version, Elihu plays a pivotal role in Job's restoration as well, but not because he functions as an enlightened sage. Raverat describes Elihu's appearance with words that continue to underscore the moralistic focus of her interpretation: "Elihu enters and rebukes Job for his materialism. 'Ye are old and I am very young.' A dance of youth and beauty. Job understands how he has sinned and has a true vision of the Deity."[35] The drop sheet, which had been lowered during Elihu's dance, is raised, and God, once again, appears seated on the heavenly throne.

For Raverat, Elihu succeeds in "opening Job's eyes" to his pride and self-interest. While Job's "punishments" (the loss of his possessions, children, and health) may seem excessive to audiences, Raverat's reading, at least, provides a logical explanation for Job's losses. A simple cause-and-effect principle is evident: Job's sins result in punitive measures that are aimed at initiating his repentance and restoration. Such an interpretation offers audiences a strong moral and social message: pride, greed, and excessive reliance on material possessions may lead to one's downfall.

Vaughan Williams, in keeping with his understanding of Job as a truly innocent human being, did not accept Keynes's or Raverat's interpretations of Job's sufferings. In his scripts, God is named, simply, "God."[36] His interpretation of the story raises a troubling scenario for audiences: Job is an innocent human being, God is the supreme Deity who has power to interfere with mortal lives, and Satan may show up at any time to initiate harm and destruction. Not only does Vaughan Williams remove the language of "sin" in his scripts, rendering the causes of Job's suffering (including God's role in it) uncertain; he also adds details that emphasize the tragic nature of Job's losses. After the death of Job's children, he inserts a funeral

---

34. Raine, *Human Face of God*, 205–12; Rowland, *Blake and the Bible*, 48.

35. Keynes, "Blake's Job," p. 4, f4–5.

36. McFarland, "Vaughan Williams and *Job*," 364–66.

cortege who process across the back of the stage as the messengers arrive to tell Job the sad news—a striking visual reminder to audiences of the gravity of such a loss.[37] In a letter to Raverat addressing the messengers' scene, he stresses, "It must be a dance at Job and not at the audience and it must be terrifying and not comic."[38]

The musician's own experiences may have caused him to resonate with the tragic elements of Job's story. Vaughan Williams served in the ambulance corps during World War I and was haunted by his experiences with the war for the remainder of his life.[39] Between 1916 and 1917, his unit was stationed in northern France where it was his responsibility to fetch the wounded from the trenches each night so that they could be brought to a safe place for treatment.[40] Vaughan Williams witnessed the terrifying nature of reality that is not always logical, and it seems he was adamant that Job's story reflect this aspect of life.

As the collaborators disagreed with respect to the nature of Job's character, they likewise did not see eye to eye over the question of what role God played, if any, in Job's trials. A third point of contention among them was the issue of how and to what degree Job's trials were resolved. What constituted Job's restoration? Or, on a more practical level, how would the ballet end?

Blake's final illustration depicts the completion of Job's spiritual journey. Job's "spiritual self" is awakened, and he now sees through the eyes of the imagination, represented by his engagement with the arts. In Blake's final portrait, Job is not simply restored to his initial state of well-being that existed prior to his struggles; he is transformed into a higher state.[41] Rather than sitting, he stands; instead of holding a book, he holds a harp; and his one hand that is not resting on the instrument is raised towards the heavens, indicating

---

37. Ibid., 367. This detail, in fact, was added in Keynes's final version of the ballet (Ursula Vaughan Williams, *RVW: A Biography of Ralph Vaughan Williams* [Oxford: Oxford University Press, 1964], 284).

38. Ries, "Sir Geoffrey Keynes," 23.

39. Vaughan Williams, *RVW*, 120–22, 132; McFarland, "Vaughan Williams and Job," 362.

40. Vaughan Williams, *RVW*, 120–22.

41. Rowland, *Blake and the Bible*, 14.

his deep connection to and understanding of spiritual matters. The sun is rising in the east, signaling the dawning of a new era for Job.

Keynes's version of the ballet reflects Job's new transformation. As Satan initiated the removal of "Job's Spiritual Self" from the heavenly throne, so Elihu enables its return by revealing to Job his true identity. After Elihu's "dance of youth and beauty," the drop sheet rises, revealing "Job's Spiritual Self" restored to the throne.[42] In Keynes's draft, Satan makes a second attempt to persuade Job's Godhead to afflict Job. Yet this time, Satan is "repelled and driven down by the Sons of the Morning," marking his last appearance on stage.[43] Keynes concludes the ballet with two parallel dances of rejoicing, one in heaven, performed by the angelic host, and one on earth, performed by Job and his household, who worship God with musical instruments, as depicted in Blake's painting (see Fig. 11.1). The curtain closes on the "new" Job who sits "in the sunrise of restored prosperity, surrounded by his family, upon whom he bestows a blessing."[44]

Raverat follows this basic sequence in her scenario, yet she departs from Keynes's assumptions that Job's troubles fully are resolved at the close of the story. In her earlier scripts, after the parallel dances of rejoicing in heaven and earth, the drop sheet falls, hiding the back half of the stage. Job and his family then engage in a "pastoral dance," during which "Satan comes in softly to spy and dances among them."[45] Although Satan has been banished from the heavenly throne, in Raverat's interpretation, he is not altogether banished from the earthly realm. In a later version of her script, the final scene unfolds with the pastoral dance occurring without the entrance of Satan. Job's children then depart, and Job is left alone with his wife. At this point, Raverat's instructions, in question form, read, "enter Satan to spy again?"[46]

---

42. McFarland, "Vaughan Williams and *Job*," 364. For Blake's depiction of Elihu as a prophetic sage, see Raine, *Human Face of God*, 203–18.

43. McFarland, "Vaughan Williams and *Job*," 364; see also Plate 16 of Blake's "Illustrations to the Book of Job."

44. Ibid.

45. Ries, "Sir Geoffrey Keynes," 31.

46. Keynes, "Blake's Job," p. 4, f5.

Raverat's inclusion of Satan in the final scene, whether as a participant in the last dance or as a voyeur from the sides, reveals her discomfort with the idea that Job has passed beyond any temptation toward moral laxity. If, as I suggest, Raverat interpreted the Joban story through the particular lens of class contentions during the early part of the twentieth century in England, then it would stand to reason that her warnings against greed and self-indulgence not be left on stage. Raverat's retelling of the Joban story is one that beckons audiences to continue the moral struggle against pride and complacency as they return to their daily lives. Raverat's scenario did not make it into the final production, however, as Keynes insisted on Satan's removal from both heaven and earth.[47]

Vaughan Williams, like Raverat, viewed Job's restoration with a certain ambiguity; his depiction of the final scene is perhaps the darkest of the three. The participants of the earthly dance of rejoicing are not identified as Job's children by Vaughan Williams; rather, the dancers are simply "young men and women."[48] His description of this dance, moreover, contains instructions not present in the others' versions. As he details the dance of "worship and musical instruments" that takes place, he adds the pointed note, "*But Job must not play an instrument himself.*"[49] For Vaughan Williams, the musician among the group, to deny Job this very mode of expression is striking, especially in light of the central role that music plays in Blake's understanding of human renewal and restoration.

The reasoning behind Vaughan Williams's emphasis on Job's exclusion from the musical chorus is open to interpretation, but it may be that Vaughan Williams did not believe a complete restoration for Job was possible after the losses that he experienced. Further details in his scenario accentuate the less celebratory tone of his ending. Vaughan Williams's staging of the final scene depicts a more contemplative Job than that of his collaborators. Keynes's last scene simply shows Job seated and "surrounded by his family upon whom

---

47. McFarland, "Vaughan Williams and Job," 359.

48. Ibid., 367.

49. Ibid. (emphasis added).

he bestows a blessing."[50] Vaughan Williams begins his final scene with Job, now "old and humbled," seated alone with his wife. Friends then come and offer him gifts, after which "Job stands and gazes on the distant cornfield."[51] Then, gradually, his three daughters enter and sit at his feet, and Job blesses them, still standing. These added details contribute to an image of a "restored Job" who may be both grateful for his new family and friends yet also pensive, not forgetting what has been lost. Perhaps Vaughan Williams's own experiences in the war impressed upon him the harsh reality that the loss of life is not so easily replaceable and that suffering leaves a mark on a person that does not always fully mend.[52]

Vaughan Williams was not always able to convince the others to incorporate his choreography, especially if it was deemed too much of a departure from Blake, but he did find ways to tell his story through the musical score. In his composition, each character has their own thematic line: the music of God and the Sons of Morning is melodic, legato, and full of "expansive melodies," for example, while Satan's music is marked by dissonance, descending chromatic scales, and repetitive figures.[53] Job's music is a combination of the two, sometimes mimicking God's more clearly and sometimes Satan's, depending on what is happening in the story. That Satan's banishment was not understood as final by Vaughan Williams can be heard in his scoring of this part of the tale. Rather than articulate Satan's exit from heaven with triumphant or resolute chords, the music is surprisingly calm. As McFarland writes, "The music of Satan's fall also has none of the drama of the Blake illustration. It is so curiously devoid of the intensity and emotion seen in the print. . . . Without

---

50. Ibid., 364.

51. Ibid., 366.

52. Vaughan Williams lost several of his closest friends to the war, including fellow composer George Butterworth. In a letter written to his friend Gustav Holst, he expressed his mounting grief: "I sometimes dread coming back to normal life with so many gaps—especially of course George Butterworth—he has left most of his MS to me—and now I hear that Ellis is killed—out of those 7 who joined up together in August, 1914, only 3 are left" (Vaughan Williams, *RVW*, 122).

53. McFarland, "Vaughan Williams and *Job*," 353–54.

seeing a staged production, the listener could never guess that this stately music represents Satan being driven out of Heaven."[54]

Even more telling, perhaps, is Vaughan Williams's musical narration of the final scenes. One might expect the motifs associated with God and the spiritual beings to dominate the music associated with Job's restoration, perhaps even rising to new heights; but, instead, one hears the dissonant chords associated with Satan lurking alongside the music of God.[55] Rather than ending on the musical key associated with the Deity and heavenly beings (G Major, or the tonic), Vaughan Williams ends on the minor third (B-flat), the interval associated with Satan.[56] Vaughan Williams's music thus depicts Job's restoration as not fully settled, suggesting to his listeners that the threat of evil is an inescapable and persistent element of human life.

One wonders if audiences would have picked up on these musical cues. It is likely that audiences would have interpreted *A Masque for Dancing* in ways that resonated with their own expectations and experiences. Perhaps some would see and hear a call to delve further into their imaginations, seeking new ways to commune with God through artistic expression. Some may have come away from the ballet having heard a moral tale issuing a warning against greed and complacency. Yet others may have left with a sobering awareness of life's "tragic notes," heard through the dissonant chords that mark the music's end.

While multiple, sometimes competing perspectives contributed to the final production of the ballet, it yet achieved, as Blake would have hoped, a kind of "new birth" for British culture. *A Masque for Dancing* was the first ballet to contain an all-English creative team: writer, composer, set designer, and choreographer. Keynes remarked in an interview in 1978, "I think it fair to call *Job* the first English ballet of the twentieth century; some histories of ballet state that *Job*

---

54. Ibid., 360.

55. Ibid., 361.

56. Ibid., 359. "[T]he arrival at B-flat at the end of the masque does not fulfill a purely musical purpose; rather it exists solely to delineate Satan's interval of the minor third. Vaughan Williams is symbolizing the persistence of evil even when all is seemingly resolved" (ibid.).

saved the English ballet."⁵⁷ *A Masque for Dancing* made its first public appearance with the Vic-Wells Ballet, the organization that later became The Royal Ballet, and the production set de Valois on the path to become one of the most well-known choreographers in the history of ballet.⁵⁸ *A Masque for Dancing* thus marked the beginning of a cultural phenomenon that has grown into one of the premiere ballet organizations in the world, one that continues to elevate the human spirit to new heights through the mediums of dance and music (Figs. 11.4 and 11.5).

As Balentine writes with respect to the multiplicity of ways the Joban story is "reread" throughout art and culture, "The question is not whether the first or the third reading is correct. It is whether and to what extent rereadings enlarge our understanding and our

---

57. Ries, "Sir Geoffrey Keynes," 30. Initially, Keynes took the ballet to Sergei Diaghilev, founder of the Ballets Russes, but Diaghilev rejected it as being "too English" (ibid., 19, 20). Keynes's response to this critique was "Well, it was. Quite true" (ibid., 20). Lydia Lopoktova, a professional ballet dancer who was married to Keynes's brother, John Maynard Keynes, replied upon seeing the performance, "Job was truly a thing for theatre, which I used to doubt. . . . My chief pleasure was that it differed from the Russian Ballet tradition—the most important merit of Job" (ibid., 25). *A Masque for Dancing* premiered at the Cambridge Theater in London in July 1931. Three weeks later it was taken to Oxford, then it returned to London where it was performed at the Old Vic Theatre. The ballet continued to run in London throughout the next several decades, with additional performances in Copenhagen and New York. It was last performed in 1972.

58. "Dame Ninette" is recognized internationally for her role in establishing English classical ballet as an art form distinct from the then-dominant Russian and French traditions. Apart from *Don Quixote*, which de Valois worked on later in her career, *Job* was her largest production. The ballet's large cast, theatrical designs, and dramatic narrative established de Valois as an artist capable of bringing together ballet and theater. Art critic Richard Capell wrote upon seeing a performance in 1934, "This is a masterpiece. Ballets containing even one little idea have been rare in the last sixteen years. Many have had no idea at all. The idea of *Job* is grand, and it is carried out with daring and nobility. Indeed a unique work—a ballet that attains to the sublime!" (Kathrine Sorley Walker, *Ninette de Valois: Idealist Without Illusions* [London: Dance Books, 1987], 115). De Valois was appointed a Dame of the Order of the British Empire in 1951 and was awarded the Order of Merit by Queen Elizabeth II in 1992, among many other honors, for her lasting influence on British culture (ibid., 295–96, 310–11).

Figure 11.4. J.W. Debenham, *Job: A Masque for Dancing*, 1931. Photograph. The Old Vic/Cambridge Theatre London. Victoria and Albert Museum, London. Photo Credit: J.W. Debenham/ Victoria and Albert Museum, London.

appropriation of ancient texts in new, perhaps surprising ways."[59] The collaboration involved in the making of the Joban ballet, which led the artists to wrestle with such fundamental issues as God's role in human behavior and the causes of human suffering, reflects each of their own stories and the struggle each generation faces concerning questions that do not allow for simple answers. The conversation and its resulting dramatic enactment of the story of Job in the ballet *A Masque for Dancing* is a vivid demonstration of how such questions of "eternity" find a home in the deepest places of our imagination.[60]

---

59. *Have You Considered*, 11.

60. Cf. Eccl. 3:11. See also Heather Woodworth Brannon's piece, "'God Set Infinity into Their Minds': Qohelet's Quest to Comprehend the Incomprehensible," in this volume.

Figure 11.5. William Blake, "When the Morning Stars Sang Together and All the Sons of God Shouted for Joy," Plate XIV of William Blake, *Illustrations of the Book of Job*, 1823–1825. Engraving. 40.6 x 27.3 cm. Yale Center for British Art, New Haven, CT. Gift of J. T. Johnston Coe in memory of Henry E. Coe, Yale BA 1878; Henry E. Coe Jr., Yale BA 1917; and Henry E. Coe III, Yale BA 1946. Photo Credit: Public Domain.

Bibliography

Balentine, Samuel E. *Job*. SHBC. Macon, GA: Smyth & Helwys, 2006.

———. *Have You Considered My Servant Job?: Understanding the Biblical Archetype of Patience*. Columbia: University of South Carolina Press, 2015.

Calvin, John. *Sermons from Job*. Translated by Leroy Nixon. Grand Rapids: Eerdmans, 1952.

Davies, J. G. *The Theology of William Blake*. Oxford: Clarendon, 1948.

Eaves, Morris. *William Blake's Theory of Art*. Princeton: Princeton University Press, 1982.

Eerdman, David V., ed. *The Complete Poetry and Prose of William Blake*, Newly Revised Edition. New York: Anchor Books, 1988.

Keynes, Geoffrey, "Blake's Job: A masque for dancing" (album: 1930–1981). Manuscripts acquired with permission from The Fitzwilliam Museum, Cambridge, England.

McFarland, Allison Sanders. "A Deconstruction of William Blake's Vision: Vaughan Williams and *Job*." *International Journal of Musicology* 3 (1994): 339–71.

Meyer, Kathi. "St. Job as a Patron of Music." *The Art Bulletin* 36/1 (March 1954): 21–31.

Raine, Kathleen. *The Human Face of God: William Blake and the Book of Job*. New York: Thames and Hudson, 1982.

Raverat, Gwendolyn. *Period Piece: A Cambridge Childhood*. London: Faber and Faber, 1952.

Ries, Frank W. D. "Sir Geoffrey Keynes and the Ballet *Job*." *Dance Research: The Journal for the Society of Dance Research* 2/1 (Spring 1984): 19–34.

Rowland, Christopher. *Blake and the Bible*. New Haven: Yale University Press, 2010.

Spittler, R. P. "Testament of Job: A New Translation and Introduction." *OTP* 1:829–68.

Vaughan Williams, Ursula. *RVW: A Biography of Ralph Vaughan Williams.* Oxford: Oxford University Press, 1964.

Vesely, Patricia. *Friendship and Virtue Ethics in the Book of Job.* Cambridge: Cambridge University Press, 2019.

Walker, Kathrine Sorley. *Ninette de Valois: Idealist Without Illusions.* London: Dance Books, 1987.

Part III

Torah in Wisdom and Wisdom as Torah

Woman Wisdom and Her Afterlife

Katharine J. Dell

It is a great pleasure and an honour to dedicate this essay to Sam, whom I have come to know through circles of the modern "wise" in the academy and with whom I worked on the editorial board of the Oxford Encyclopedia of the Bible and Theology. *I am a great admirer of his work and truly value his friendship.*

I want to begin with Veronese's *Allegory of Wisdom and Strength*, a famous Renaissance painting from Venice, dated 1565. In what seems like an unholy mixture of Hebrew and Roman imagery, we find Wisdom, personified as a Woman, contrasted with Strength, represented by the Roman god Hercules (the Roman equivalent of the Greek Heracles). This is not a contrast made in the biblical material on Wisdom; in fact, "strength" (*gĕbûrâ*) is one of Wisdom's qualities in Prov 8:14: "I have good advice and sound wisdom; I have insight, I have strength."[1] Ultimately, though, Wisdom's appeal to knowledge conquers strength any day: "Wise warriors are mightier than strong ones, and those who have knowledge than those [the strong] who have strength (*mĕammeṣ-kôaḥ*)" (Prov 24:5). One of the interesting aspects of this painting is that Wisdom looks up, heavenward, whilst Hercules looks down. She is in light, whilst he is in shadow. Her gaze

---

1. All biblical and deuterocanonical translations are from the NRSV unless otherwise noted.

upwards represents a link with the divine, represented by a kind of sun god above in white. Strength looks downwards to earthly desires at the child, the crowns, and other jewels that lie below (Fig. 12.1).

As we look back to one of the earliest personifications of Wisdom as a woman in the book of Proverbs, Veronese's image guides us into the text. Our first introduction to the idea of a female figure of Wisdom is in Prov 1:20-33 where Wisdom cries out at the entrance to the city gates and in street and square to all who need to hear her call. Wisdom is often likened to a prophetic figure in that much of her speech is a warning to those who refuse her call and do not listen. But "those who listen to me will be secure and will live at ease, without dread of disaster" (Prov 1:33). This is not a full personification, yet in Prov 3:13-20 we have a third-person description of this elusive woman: she is more precious than gold or jewels; "long life is in her right hand and in her left hand are riches and honour"; her paths represent peace; and she is "a tree of life" for those who grasp her. She becomes more and more attractive. Not only is she the way to riches and honour; she is the path to long life—and perhaps even more if the imagery of the "tree of life" represents eternity (cf. Gen 3:22). The climax then follows, "The LORD by wisdom founded (lit., made) the earth" (v. 19). Wisdom becomes part of the creative act of God, the means by which the earth was made. Indeed, her very qualities of understanding and knowledge are linked to the creative acts that we know from Genesis 1 (Prov 3:20). A warning is then given: do not let these escape (v. 21)! Hold on to these qualities "and they will be life for your soul and adornment for your neck."[2] This is the path to follow, the secure path of Wisdom.

Two aspects of Wisdom are immediately apparent in these two texts from Proverbs. First, Wisdom is offering all kinds of wonderful things; in fact, she herself is on offer to all who will hear her words. Second, Wisdom is somehow the agent of God in creation with an essential relationship to the divine. How do these two ideas sit together? I suggest that this tension is what characterizes Wisdom's portrayal both in its biblical manifestations and also beyond, in the reception history of Wisdom.

---

2. This picture resonates with that of the equivalent Egyptian figure of *ma'at*, portrayed as a goddess with ankh and garland.

Figure 12.1. Paolo Veronese, *Allegory of Wisdom and Strength*, ca. 1565. Oil on canvas. 214.6 x 167 cm. The Frick Collection, New York, Henry Clay Frick Bequest. Photo Credit: The Frick Collection, New York

Proverbs 8 contains the fullest passage on Wisdom's unique identity. Here, Wisdom is no longer described in the third person; rather, she speaks in the first person. The chapter opens with a description of her, again, as an ideal woman. She stands at the gates of the town calling to those who are simple to "learn prudence and acquire intelligence" (8:5). She needs to be heard—Wisdom's words are those of truth and better than all precious things. She is the principle of truth by which kings reign, and she rewards those who "love" her with riches and honour. She is associated, then, with justice, truth, wealth, and abundance. Wisdom is opposed to everything evil.

As in Prov 3:19, there is a sudden shift in the second half of Prov 8. Wisdom's role changes from one who calls humans to follow her path to one who participates in creation. She is present with God in the creation of the world, "rejoicing in God's inhabited world and delighting in the human race" (8:31). She is "created" or "acquired" (*qānâ*) by God at the very beginning, before the beginning of the created earth as we know it (v. 22). This is a surprising shift, and it is the opportunity for a hymn to the creative acts of God, which mentions the depths, water, mountains, hills, earth, and fields. Wisdom watches as God draws a circle on the face of the deep, divides the firmament, limits the sea, and marks out the earth. Her reaction to the creation and to God is one of delight and wonder. She is Wisdom, the principle of rationality and order in the world, as revealed by the creation itself and as manifested in human activity and society. She is the principle of sound judgement and sagacious dealings. Wisdom is the quest for knowledge. She is the path of truth and "life" in the fullest sense.

Here again, two aspects of Wisdom appear. Wisdom is on offer to any who wish to follow her path; she is a gift to those who wish to take up the offer. Yet Wisdom is linked to the creative work of God "at the beginning" (Prov 8:22). She is at once fully accessible to humans as God's representative as well as a means through which God effects creation, which surely can only be fully known to God. She represents both openness and hiddenness, reflecting the tension that can be found in the wisdom quest itself. On the one hand, wise men and women seek to gain knowledge of the world whose many wonders are open to scientific enquiry; on the other hand, ultimate knowledge still resides with God alone. There are hidden secrets that are not so readily on offer to humans, including how God not only created but also sustains and interacts with the world.

Before turning to the history of interpretation of the Wisdom figure, I wish to consider another text that is not usually brought into this frame: Job 28, often called the "hymn to wisdom." This text emphasizes the hiddenness of wisdom rather than its accessibility. As Balentine writes, "In a remarkable reversal of this image [Prov 8:17 and wisdom's accessibility], Job 28 personifies the Deep (v. 14a), the Sea (v. 14b), Destruction, and Death (v. 22) and has each one declare that they have no idea where wisdom can be found."[3] The poem begins with mining imagery, describing the processes by which precious jewels and stones are extracted from the earth. The refining and smelting processes exemplify human ingenuity—although one wonders if this is human skill or human avarice. Humans search intently, overturning mountains and cleaving rocks (vv. 3, 9-11). There seems to be no limit to their desire for these treasures. Then, unexpectedly, comes the poem's refrain: "Where shall wisdom be found?" (vv. 12, 20). Despite these great efforts, humans cannot find their way to wisdom—she is elusive.[4] "Where is the place of understanding?" (vv. 12, 20). There is *no* place, not even in the deepest recesses of earth, sea, or underworld (vv. 14, 22).

Wisdom's worth is then described in terms echoing the search for jewels and riches in the first part of the poem: her price is more than gold, onyx, sapphire, coral, crystal, or pearls (vv. 15-19). This is the same language of Prov 8 in which Wisdom's worth also exceeds fine jewels; yet, there, she offers her wares to all (8:17). In contrast, Job 28 depicts wisdom as elusive and beyond the greatest efforts of the miners. "Where then does wisdom come from?" asks the poem again (v. 20). Verse 23 provides the answer, "God understands the way to it, and he knows its place." God sees all, as he did when he created the world. All that humans can do is "fear God" (v. 28) and try to live a moral life. Once again, we are brought to the divine side of the wisdom conundrum: wisdom is hidden such that only God can find her, and only God has full knowledge and understanding.

---

3. Samuel E. Balentine, *Wisdom Literature*, CBS (Nashville: Abingdon, 2018), 55.

4. A hint at personification emerges here.

This elusive Wisdom is best sought by modelling God's interaction with Wisdom in creation. As Balentine writes, "Wisdom is not found in a spatial place. It comes from creatively interacting with the world, that is, from weighing, measuring, setting limits, and charting courses that offer the best possibilities for the world to become all that God intends."[5] Paul S. Fiddes adds, "Like the practical wisdom of the wise, God's wisdom as Creator is a matter of observing and handling the world."[6] Fiddes suggests that the answer to the question "Where can wisdom be found?" (Job 28:12, 20) is that "wisdom is not found in any particular place, but lies in knowing every place."[7]

So we have two models—Wisdom as openly available to humanity and yet closely bound to the divine Creator, and Wisdom as hidden from all except the Creator who, nonetheless, used her to create the world and set up its order. Running through both passages is a further contrast between Wisdom in creation, delighting in God's acts, and Wisdom as communicated word bringing a message to humans. The contrast is reflected in Wisdom as a gift to humans, on the one hand, and Wisdom as something to be sought and desired above all else, on the other, by the use of observation, skill, or attainment. We will see how these opposites play out in a selection of ideas from the history of interpretation.

Early on within the wisdom tradition itself, in Sirach, the Wisdom figure became reified as Torah. Gerhard von Rad famously wrote of this development:

> the complete identification of wisdom with the Torah . . . has to be regarded as simply a theological conclusion already latent in principle in Prov. I–IX and now come to maturity. But in it the theological concept of wisdom attained such a degree of clarification as to allow the wisdom teaching to draft a tremendous scheme of world history and saving history: wisdom was created by [YHWH] before all creation, she came forth from his mouth

---

5. Balentine, *Wisdom Literature*, 56.

6. Paul S. Fiddes, "Ancient and Modern Wisdom: The Intersection of Clinical and Theological Understanding of Health," in *Wisdom, Science, and the Scriptures: Essays in Honour of Ernest Lucas*, ed. Stephen Finamore and John Weaver (Oxford: Centre for Baptist History and Heritage, 2012), 83.

7. Ibid.

(Ecclesiasticus I.4, XXIV. 3). All Creation with all the nations was open before her, and she had searched for a home on earth among men [*sic*]. But this first attempt to find a habitation among men failed, God then assigned her a resting-place in Israel, and there, in the form of the Torah, 'the Book of the Covenant of God,' she took root and grew up into a magnificent tree (Ecclesiasticus XXIV. 12–23).[8]

This was a masterstroke—the availability of Wisdom as a gift was still stressed, but only to those who feared God and kept the Torah. The universality of the appeal was lost. Sirach's presentation also had the advantage of linking Torah with God's creation—Torah was now preexistent, God's delight, and the communicated word of God.

Thus in Sir 24, the most famous passage describing Woman Wisdom, a line is drawn from the primeval order to the specific revelation of YHWH to Israel. She is described as coming out of "the mouth of the most High" (v. 3) and of covering "the earth as a cloud," a phrase that has overtones of Moses in the cloud in Exod 24:15-18. She is described as dwelling in high places with a cloudy pillar as a throne (Sir 24:4), which almost reads as an answer to Job 28's question, "Where shall wisdom be found?" She is described as compassing "the circuit of heaven" and walking "in the bottom of the deep" (Sir 24:5); Wisdom inhabits the entire world—sea, earth, and "every people and nation" (v. 6). She is thus on a higher cosmic plane than previously described, seeming more like an angel of the heavenly council (cf. the Satan in Job) than the created being of Prov 8.

The quest for a dwelling place leads Wisdom to reside in Israel, within the temple in Jerusalem (Sir 24:8-11). This imagery reflects the journey of the ark of the covenant, which also took time to find its resting place in Jerusalem. Later in the same chapter (Sir 24:23), the author makes it explicit that Wisdom is available to Israel: "All these things are the book of the covenant of the most high God, even the law which Moses commanded for an heritage unto the congregations of Jacob." Although once dwelling among other nations, Wisdom is now essentially hidden from them. Only God knows her thoroughly (cf. Sir 1:1-10). The gift of Wisdom is a more specific

---

8. Gerhard von Rad, *Old Testament Theology*, trans. D. M. G. Stalker, 2 vols. (Edinburgh: Oliver & Boyd, 1962), 1:445.

one, nonetheless combining all the benefits associated with Woman Wisdom in Proverbs—honour, riches, knowledge, and so on. The seeking and desiring from the human side are also stressed. Sirach 24:13-17 likens her to various trees such as cypress, cedar, plane, turpentine, palm, and olive, and to a rose bush and a vine. She is described in lush terms as sweet smelling and fruitful, which is reminiscent of the lush imagery in Song of Songs.

In Sirach, there is a kind of eroticism about Wisdom's appeal. Knut Heim, in fact, finds "male stalking" of Wisdom in Sir 14:22-24. In these verses, the man is described as "pursuing [Wisdom] like a hunter, and lying in wait on her paths; who peers through her windows and listens at her doors; who camps near her house and fastens his tent peg to her walls." Heim writes, "Surprisingly this striking presentation of a rather intrusive kind of male pursuit of a female figure has rarely caused offence."[9] He attributes this to the general scholarly consensus that Wisdom was merely a literary figure of speech even in these early Jewish circles that Sirach represents. I am not sure that I entirely agree with Heim; elsewhere in Sirach the quest is more prayerful (51:13-30), although much of the same language of longing is used. Furthermore, we are already familiar from Proverbs with the language of hunting, snaring, seeking, and finding Wisdom (Prov 7:23). Likewise, if we look at another work attributed to Solomon, Song of Songs, we find a similar reference to flowers, trees, and scents to describe the altered perceptions of the two lovers and the sensuality of the love shared between them, which also involves elements of chasing and seeking. These images connect with a desire for the law as found in Deuteronomy, shown in the binding on the hands (Deut 6:8; 11:18; Prov 3:3; 7:3). Ardent, youthful pursuit and the attainment of Wisdom who "came to me in her beauty" is known, too, from a Psalms Scroll in Qumran cave 11 (11Q5:14), suggesting that it is a widely used motif. We might just note here the revealed bosom in Veronese's painting, a hint perhaps of Wisdom's erotic appeal, or maybe of a link with ideas of motherhood as symbolized by the child in the painting.

---

9. Knut Heim, "Personified Wisdom in Ancient Judaism," in *Wisdom, Science and the Scriptures*, 57.

In Jewish circles, then, it is clear that Wisdom and Torah become one. We find the same link made in another Jewish work, Baruch 3–4. Here, Wisdom finds a dwelling place in Israel amongst the people (3:37) so that some outside the Torah group are denied wisdom. Similar themes are apparent in Job 28 (cf. Deut. 30:12-14) and Sir 24. In Bar 3:30-31 we read of Wisdom, "Who has gone over the sea, and found her, and will buy her for pure gold? No one knows the way to her." Job 28:14 similarly states, "The deep says, 'It is not in me,' and the sea says, 'It is not with me.'" Again, it is only God, the creator, who knows her thoroughly. In Baruch, Wisdom is portrayed as a specific gift to Jacob/Israel through an invitation to remain faithful to the Torah, "the book of the commandments of God" (4:1), which is the path of Wisdom. Wisdom is still hidden—known only in her fullness to God as part of the creative (and sustaining) act; yet she is on offer to those who love God and follow his communicated word—the law and the commandments.

In the Wisdom of Solomon, a Jewish text from the first century BCE, we find a definite progression in the concept of Wisdom.[10] Wis 7:25 proclaims, "For she [Wisdom] is a breath of the power of God, and a pure emanation of the glory of the Almighty." Here, Woman Wisdom is hypostatized rather than merely personified. W. O. E. Oesterley and G. H. Box define "hypostasis" as "a quasi-personification of certain attributes proper to God, occupying an intermediate position between personalities and abstract beings."[11] Wisdom's relationship to God is highlighted here: she is the manifestation of God to humans, an emanation of divine attributes. In Wis 7:22 we read, "for wisdom, the fashioner of all things, taught me. There is in her a spirit that is intelligent, holy, unique, manifold, subtle, mobile, clear, unpolluted, distinct, invulnerable, loving the good, keen, irresistible." She is the orderer and creator of all things (Wis 8:1, 6). She is the teacher of virtues such as self-control and

---

10. This text was probably influenced by Greek ideas and may reflect the attempt to counter an Isis cult prevalent in Alexandria at the time (James M. Reese, *Hellenistic Influence on the Book of Wisdom and Its Consequences*, Analecta Biblica 41 [Rome: Biblical Institute Press, 1970]).

11. W. O. E. Oesterley and G. H. Box, *The Religion and Worship of the Synagogue*, 2nd ed. (London: Isaac Pitman, 1911), 169.

justice (Wis 8:7) and the supplier of all instruction (Wis 7:17-22), including information on the natural sciences. Von Rad describes this portrayal as "a mythical, speculative deification of wisdom."[12] In Wis 7:22–8:2, the Wisdom poem begins with a cosmological description of Wisdom's relationship to God. She is active in creation and superior to all created things in her ordering role.

Wisdom is there to teach her followers to respond to her, and this the author does: "I loved her and sought her from my youth" (Wis 8:2). Wisdom of Solomon 8:3-16 then describes what wisdom can give to those who respond to her: knowledge, riches, understanding, righteousness, experience. Her benefits cannot be surpassed. We find erotic language here, too, in terms of love and desire: "I loved her more than health and beauty" (Wis 7:10), and "I desired to take her for my bride and became enamored of her beauty" (Wis 8:2). The link with Torah is still clear: "love of her is the keeping of her laws, and giving heed to her laws is assurance of immortality" (Wis 6:18). Yet another step is made—a link with immortality. Wisdom bestows even greater gifts; she is an attribute of God himself, his creative agent, his very word of command.

Let us turn now to the more widely known Christian emphasis on Woman Wisdom. As Horbury writes, "This series . . . shows a continuous preoccupation with this theme, which provides a context for the importance of the figure of wisdom in Philo, the synoptic tradition, and the gnostic Christian myths of Sophia."[13] The New Testament makes the expected alignment of Wisdom with Christ, but not as frequently as we might have thought. The most famous passage is the prologue to John's Gospel where those who receive "the true light" (John 1:9) can "become children of God" (John 1:12). This passage echoes the descriptions of both Wisdom and the Torah as "the light" (cf. Gen 1:3; Wis 7:26, 29), but, here, the designator "the Word" is used, which refers to Jesus Christ.[14] The

---

12. Gerhard von Rad, *Wisdom in Israel* (London: SCM, 1972), 170.

13. William Horbury, "The Books of Solomon in Ancient Mysticism," in *Reading Texts, Seeking Wisdom: Scripture and Theology*, ed. David F. Ford and Graham Stanton (London: SCM, 2003), 197.

14. Cf. Acts Thom. 6:4, "The maiden is the daughter of light" (Julian V. Hills, ed., *The Acts of Thomas*, Early Christian Apocrypha, vol. 2, trans. Harold W.

identification of Wisdom with Word is clear, as is the influence of the Wisdom of Solomon in identifying Wisdom as a part of God, virtually synonymous with God. The Word was "in the beginning with God," echoing the idea of Woman Wisdom's role in creation and alluding to Genesis 1. Thus "the Word was with God" just as Wisdom, the first of God's creative acts, was "beside God" (Prov 8:30). But John develops the idea further: "the Word was God." We find, then, similar emphases as in Jewish tradition—here, the Word, like Wisdom, is for all. The Word is a gift of God to humanity and, again, had a key role in the creation of the world, but it is for those who follow Christ.

This aspect is brought out in another New Testament text, Col 1:15-20. Morna Hooker summarizes the message of this passage:

> Christ is the image of the invisible God, with him before all things began, the agent of creation, by whom, through whom and for whom all things have been created. In him the fullness of God was pleased to dwell and was pleased, through him, to reconcile all things to him through his death. Christ, not the Torah is now understood to be the supreme revelation of God's will or purpose, the fullest expression of his word or wisdom.[15]

Wisdom and understanding are gifts on offer to those "in Christ." Creation and redemption are thus held together: Christ is the agent of creation (cf. 1 Cor 8:46) and the source of water (1 Cor 10:1-5). He is also "the firstborn from the dead" (Col 1:18), echoing Wisdom of Solomon's promise of immortality. Taking the theme one step further, Col 1:18 proclaims Christ as the "head of the body, the church."

A fascinating stage in Christian interpretation of the Wisdom figure occurred in the fourth century CE when Arians used Prov 8:22 as a proof text for the creation of the Son in the Arian controversy.[16]

Attridge [Salem: Polebridge, 2010], 20).

15. Morna D. Hooker, "Where is wisdom to be found?: Col 1:15–20 (I)," in *Reading Texts, Seeking Wisdom: Scripture and Theology*, ed. David F Ford and Graham Stanton (London: SCM, 2003), 123.

16. For an excellent overview see Rowan Williams, *Arius: Heresy & Tradition* (Grand Rapids: Eerdmans, 2002).

The word *qānâ* came under special discussion regarding whether it should be translated as "created" or "acquired/possessed." The answer to this conundrum regarding Woman Wisdom was directly related to the question of the relationship between the Father and the Son. Was the Son essentially separate as one who was "created" by God? Or was the Son preexistent and cosmic? Interpreters of Prov 8 usually see Wisdom as some part of the created world, even though she clearly anticipates the physical realities of it. By the time of Wisdom of Solomon, though, she was depicted as the right arm of God the Creator, both preexistent and cosmic.

Athenagorus (*Legatio* 10.3–4) used both Prov 8:22 and Wis 7:25 in synthesis to argue that the Son of God is both the eternal Logos and the first begotten.[17] Theophilus of Antioch (*Ad Autolycum* 2.10) put it in a particularly colourful way: "Therefore God having his own Logos innate in his own bowels [cf. Ps 109:3], generated him together with his own Sophia, *vomiting* him *forth* [Ps 44:2] before everything else. He used this Logos as his servant in the things created by him, and through him he made all things [cf. John 1:4]."[18] Theophilus describes the Logos using intertextual links with different parts of Scripture:

> It was he, *Spirit of God* [Gen 1:2] and *Beginning* [Gen 1:1] and *Sophia* [Prov 8:22] and *Power of the Most High* [Luke 1:35] who came down into the prophets and spoke about the creation of the world and all the rest [cf. II.9]. For the prophets did not exist when the world came into existence; there were the Sophia of God which is in him and his holy Logos who is always present with him.[19]

Frances Young comments on this emergent intertextuality: "This approach generated intertextuality—collages of texts being built up to create a picture of this pre-existent creating Power of God, with

---

17. William R. Schoedel, ed. and trans., *Athenagoras: Legatio and De Resurrectione* (Oxford: Clarendon, 1972), 23.

18. Henry Chadwick, ed., *Theophilus of Antioch: Ad Autolycum*, trans. Robert M. Grant (Oxford: Clarendon, 1970), 39.

19. Ibid.

whom God conversed when he said 'Let *us* make' (Gen 1)."[20] One of the important emphases, taken from both Prov 8:22 and Gen 1:1, was that of "beginning," referring to the creative presence, energy, and actions. Wisdom says, "The Lord established me as the beginning of his ways for the creation of his works" (LXX). Athanasius in *Contra Arianos* devotes the bulk of book 2 to Prov 8 with the presumption that "the text belongs to Scripture" as having an "overarching 'mind'"[21]—the true meaning of texts was just waiting to be discovered. Like Wisdom, Christ was preexistent and cosmic, and so this was a veiled reference to Christ's incarnation.

So the aspects of the figure of Wisdom identified at the start— that she is both on offer (and offering many gifts) and an essential part of the creative process—can still be seen in these later developments, even though we seem to have come a long way from the rather simple picture in Prov 8. Wisdom's availability to all humanity is a feature that is somehow lost through both the identification with Torah and with Christ, although identifying both with the creative order itself maintains a universal appeal. Wisdom in creation is a consistent aspect of all these portrayals, and yet something of the delight that is conveyed in Prov 8 is lost in subsequent reflection. Wisdom carries a message from God to humanity, whether that be through law and commandment or through the incarnation of Christ. She is certainly hidden in part from humanity and only fully known to God, even becoming an essence of the divine in later thought; and yet she is desired by all who seek her, avidly and lovingly and in relation to study and reflection on the word of Scripture that reveals her. Woman Wisdom is indeed a rich and multifaceted figure. I wonder if Veronese realized what depths he was plumbing when he painted his famous picture!

---

20. Frances Young, "Proverbs 8 in Interpretation (2): Wisdom Personified," in *Reading Texts, Seeking Wisdom*, ed. Ford and Stanton, 105. See Justin Martyr, *Dialogue with Trypho*, 61–62 for this connection (Michael Slusser, ed., *Justin Martyr: Dialogue with Trypho*, Selections from the Fathers of the Church, vol. 3, trans. Thomas B. Falls [Washington, D.C.: Catholic University of America Press, 2003], 93–96).

21. Young, "Proverbs 8 in Interpretation (2): Wisdom Personified," 111.

Bibliography

Balentine, Samuel E. *Wisdom Literature*. CBS. Nashville: Abingdon, 2018.

Chadwick, Henry, ed. *Theophilus of Antioch: Ad Autolycum*. Translated by Robert M. Grant. Oxford: Clarendon Press, 1970.

Fiddes, Paul S. "Ancient and Modern Wisdom: The Intersection of Clinical and Theological Understanding of Health." Pages 75–98 in *Wisdom, Science, and the Scriptures: Essays in Honour of Ernest Lucas*. Edited by Stephen Finamore and John Weaver. Oxford: Centre for Baptist History and Heritage, 2012.

Ford, David F., and Graham Stanton. *Reading Texts, Seeking Wisdom: Scripture and Theology*. London: SCM, 2003.

Heim, Knut. "Personified Wisdom in ancient Judaism." Pages 56–72 in *Wisdom, Science and the Scriptures: Essays in Honour of Ernest Lucas*, ed. S. Finamore and John Weaver. Oxford: Centre for Baptist History and Heritage, 2012.

Hills, Julian V. *The Acts of Thomas*. Vol. 2 of Early Christian Apocrypha. Translated by Harold W. Attridge. Salem: Polebridge, 2010.

Hooker, Morna D. "Where is wisdom to be found?: Col 1:15–20 (I)." Pages 116–28 in *Reading Texts, Seeking Wisdom*, ed. Ford and Stanton.

Horbury, William. "The Books of Solomon in Ancient Mysticism." Pages 185–201 in *Reading Texts, Seeking Wisdom*, ed. Ford and Stanton.

Oesterley, W. O. E., and Box, G. H. *The Religion and Worship of the Synagogue*. 2nd ed. London: Isaac Pitman, 1911.

Rad, Gerhard von. *Old Testament Theology*. Translated by D. M. G. Stalker, 2 vols. Edinburgh: Oliver & Boyd, 1962.

———. *Wisdom in Israel*. London: SCM, 1972.

Reese, James M. *Hellenistic Influence on the Book of Wisdom and Its Consequences*. Analecta Biblica 41. Rome: Biblical Institute Press, 1970.

Schoedel, William R., ed. and trans. *Athenagoras: Legatio and De Resurrectione.* Oxford: Clarendon, 1972.

Slusser, Michael, ed. *Justin Martyr: Dialogue with Trypho.* Vol. 3 of Selections from the Fathers of the Church. Translated by Thomas B. Falls. Washington, D.C.: Catholic University of America Press, 2003.

Williams, Rowan. *Arius: Heresy & Tradition.* Grand Rapids: Eerdmans, 2002.

Young, Frances. "Proverbs 8 in Interpretation (2): Wisdom Personified." Pages 102–15 in *Reading Texts, Seeking Wisdom*, ed. Ford and Stanton.

Sacred Recitation as Commentary in Ben Sira's Praise of the Ancestors

Samuel L. Adams

It is a privilege to dedicate this essay to Samuel E. Balentine, with whom I have been a colleague at Union Presbyterian Seminary since 2006. He is a creative and productive scholar, and I have learned much from his prolific output and insightful lectures.

Introduction

The Praise of the Ancestors in the closing chapters (44–50) of the book of Ben Sira (or Sirach) provides a window into the early reception history of Second Temple Judea, at least from the perspective of a second-century BCE scribal-sage.[1] The author presents a litany of individuals from Israel's past whose memorable, righteous (in

---

1. The grandson's prologue to the instruction mentions Ptolemy VII Euergetes (146–117 BCE), and if we account for approximately two generations, the period in which Ben Sira had his career and wrote this instruction (early second century BCE) is not in dispute. There is no explicit awareness of the punitive actions of Antiochus IV Epiphanes (175–164 BCE) against Judea. Moreover, the glowing praise of Simon II (219–196 BCE) in 50:1-21 indicates Ben Sira's affinity for the

most cases) deeds represent his understanding of what it means to be a person of valor. These descriptions also seem to reflect popular beliefs about various figures, such as the colorful, lengthy recall of the Elijah legends in Sir 48:1-16. The attention that Elijah receives indicates the popularity of the narratives surrounding this "man of God" during the Second Temple period and beyond (cf. Mal 4:5-6; 1 Mac 2:58; Matt 16:14). We must also allow that the eclectic list of heroes indicates certain preferences of this particular author, both in terms of personal favorites and also for his own strategic reasons.

One of the more noteworthy features of the Praise of the Ancestors is the detailed attention given to priestly figures from Israel's past and Ben Sira's present. The author provides a much lengthier description of Aaron's deeds than Moses'; the latter figure gets five and a half verses (Sir 45:1b-5), while the career of Aaron spans from Sir 45:6-22. The intricate priestly terminology concerning Aaron (e.g., 45:8: "He [God] clothed him in perfect splendor . . . the linen undergarments, the long robe, and the ephod") is significant in any text, but this type of cultic language seems remarkable for an Israelite/Judean wisdom tradition that had long avoided explicit attention to such topics.[2] Moreover, laudatory statements about Aaron are bookended by parallel treatment of the high priest Simon II (Sir 50:1-22), a contemporary of Ben Sira and a member of the Aaronic line. The tribute to Simon at the end of this section further underscores the importance of priests for this author and his instructional framework.

The question then becomes why Ben Sira offers such specific and lengthy praise of priestly figures. The vivid paean to Simon demonstrates the author's respect for this individual, his office, and longstanding cultic traditions. Perhaps this means Ben Sira himself was a priest or came from a priestly family. This discussion will maintain that this is not the case, and efforts to ascribe a priestly background to Ben Sira miss the point of these specific descriptions. It is

---

priesthood and suggests that the author and this high priest were at least near contemporaries, even if this section was written after Simon's death.

2. Proverbs and Ecclesiastes are for the most part lacking in priestly terminology, but the same is not true of the book of Job. See Barry R. Huff, "Dipped in Filth and Clothed in Glory: Job's Transformation of Priestly Terms, Themes, Texts, and Theologies" (PhD diss., Union Presbyterian Seminary, 2017).

likely that Ben Sira includes such content because of his membership in the "retainer class" that trained scribes, educated elite members of Judean society, and worked with the priestly institutions of their day. Because this author's livelihood depended on positive relationships with elite classes, including priestly families, it made strategic sense for him to highlight his support for cultic figures and customs.[3]

Yet there are also more substantive reasons for this priestly preoccupation in Sirach that relate to reception history and shifts in the wisdom tradition. In the book of Sirach, Torah and the wisdom tradition have become intertwined in a manner that had not occurred in earlier instructions. The commandments are cited in this text as sources of authority in a way that does not occur in Proverbs or other antecedent instructions. Moreover, the Praise of the Ancestors offers some of the earliest commentary on cultic rules and narratives and therefore constitutes vital reception history.[4] The legacies of Aaron, Simon, and other priestly figures represent part of the essential past for this author, and they are vital exemplars of famous ancestors and recent leaders. Because the Torah is a fundamental guidepost for virtuous living, leaders of worship and other priestly rites deserve special commendation in Ben Sira's framework. Cultural traditions are never static, and this lengthy praise indicates an evolving, more expansive understanding of wisdom than what one finds in Proverbs and Qoheleth. As Samuel E. Balentine explains, "Ben Sira introduces the Law into Israel's wisdom tradition in an unprecedented way."[5] When considering this association of law and wisdom, priestly elements are an intrinsic part of the Torah, and Ben Sira pays tribute to this essential aspect.

---

3. On Ben Sira as a member of the retainer class, see Richard Horsley and Patrick Tiller, "Ben Sira and the Sociology of the Second Temple," in *Second Temple Studies III: Studies in Politics, Class, and Material Culture*, ed. Philip R. Davies and John M. Halligan, JSOTSup 340 (London: Sheffield Academic, 2002), 74–108.

4. Ben Sira appeals to "the Torah" and the commandments as sources of authority throughout this instruction (e.g., Sir 24:23). References to "Torah" and "the commandments" almost certainly do not mean the final form of the Pentateuch as we know it today, but they do suggest an authoritative tradition.

5. Samuel E. Balentine, *Wisdom Literature*, CBS (Nashville: Abingdon, 2018), 114.

Consequently, Ben Sira's interest in Aaron and his line is not incidental for his project. In exploring why Aaron (and Simon) get such disproportionate attention in the Praise of the Ancestors, a primary reason is that they represent the "priestly kingdom" and "royal nation" envisioned in antecedent texts (Exod 19:6), a vision that was clearly operative for certain believers in the late Second Temple period. Samuel E. Balentine has written eloquently on this vision for worship in the Torah, and we find it vividly represented in a Second Temple wisdom text. Through rituals, justice-seeking (especially with economics), and other requirements, the Torah provides a somewhat countercultural model that Ben Sira clearly understands to be a repository of wisdom.[6] While not a polemicist concerning cultic or financial matters, this author's instructional framework involves an affinity for the priesthood that is not just strategic but representative of his apparent belief in the holiness of those who adhere to Israel's cultic traditions *and* concern themselves with its details, namely the priests. The following discussion will explore the import of this focus and how priestly figures and terminology fit into the Praise of the Ancestors.

Content of the Praise of the Ancestors

Before proceeding with a deeper probe into priestly terms and figures in this section, we should first examine the content of the Praise of the Ancestors and how it should be classified generically. These chapters cover a range of figures, including priests, prophets, and other heroes from the past. The introductory section in 44:1-15 explains that the succeeding recitation will praise "godly men" (v. 10: there are no women in this section). These include rulers, counselors (e.g., Nathan), prophets, and sages (vv. 3-4), along with "those who composed musical tunes" (v. 5), in an obvious reference to David.[7] It seems peculiar that the author does not highlight the priestly office in this introductory section, especially since he devotes considerable

---

6. For more on the countercultural vision, see Samuel E. Balentine, *The Torah's Vision of Worship*, OBT (Minneapolis: Fortress, 1999).

7. Patrick W. Skehan and Alexander A. Di Lella, *The Wisdom of Ben Sira*, AB 39 (New York: Doubleday, 1987), 500, argue that 44:3-6 cites twelve classes of individuals, a sacred number in Israelite tradition.

attention to Aaron and Simon (among others) in the actual praise. Perhaps this is because the priestly office transcends the other categories that Ben Sira mentions. Since the priests are the guardians of cultic traditions and usually come from particular families, they have special status (see below for further discussion).

In terms of content, the list seems to be eclectic and somewhat random, especially when compared with the relative significance of various authors and figures in the Hebrew Bible. In addition to the priority of Aaron over Moses, major prophets like Isaiah (Sir 48:23), Jeremiah (49:6), and Ezekiel (49:8) receive brief descriptions, and in a surprising move Ben Sira never cites Ezra as one of his "famous men."[8] He chooses Caleb as a figure worthy of special commendation (cf. 1 Macc 2:56) but never mentions Samson. Zerubbabel appears in the list, but the vast majority of prophetic figures (i.e., the ones in the Book of the Twelve) do not receive individual acclaim. Ben Sira does not focus on specific revelatory events, such as the theophany at Sinai, but on a list of well-known characters from Israel's past. The heroes usually appear in chronological order, but not always (e.g., Sir 49:14-16). There is not an obvious guiding principle or thread that ties these various figures together other than their enduring fame and integral role in the emerging history of ancient Israel. The author never clarifies how certain "godly men" merited inclusion, while others did not. Consequently, it is necessary to find an alternative explanation(s) for the focus on priests.

Genre of Sirach 44–50

The generic classification of the Praise of the Ancestors remains a topic of significant debate and can only receive brief attention here. When comparing these chapters to earlier material, one sees that historical recitation occurs throughout the Hebrew Bible (e.g, Deut 1–3; Josh 24), but these speeches usually recount the power and beneficence

---

8. The most likely explanation for this omission is that traditions involving Ezra were still developing, and he was not yet the figure of renown in the late Second Temple period that modern scholarship often assumes him to be. See Samuel L. Adams, "Where Is Ezra? Ben Sira's Surprising Omission and the Selective Presentation in the Praise of the Ancestors," in *The Pursuit of Wisdom and Human Flourishing: The Book of Sirach and Its Contexts*, ed. Samuel L. Adams, Greg Schmidt Goering, and Matthew J. Goff, JSJSup (Leiden: Brill, forthcoming).

of the Deity rather than individuals. There are no lengthy sections in the Hebrew Bible that specifically praise human beings in the manner of Sir 44–50. Such content does occur, however, in 1 Macc 2:51-60, 4 Macc 16:20-23, 18:11-19, and in Heb 11 from the New Testament.[9] In a survey of these various passages, Abraham, David, and Elijah appear frequently in these retrospective lists, underscoring their importance in the collective memory of Jewish believers in the Second Temple period (but these other lists do not contain the same level of engagement with priestly figures). These examples from other texts also demonstrate the popularity of "hero lists" as expressions of faithfulness, bravery, and/or fame.

In searching for antecedents for this type of praise, Greek literary forms offer more convincing models than anything in the Hebrew Bible or related literature from Judea. Suggestions have included Hellenistic biography, especially of the Peripatetic variety, the epic poem, and a litany of "examples" drawn from history (*Beispielsrehen*).[10] These possibilities have not generated much enthusiasm among scholars, since Sir 44–50 does not particularly conform to the generic features of these categories. A more convincing and closer parallel would be the Greek encomium, where famous figures receive glowing praise because of their virtue and strength. They accomplish unique and unprecedented feats in the eyes of the writer and therefore deserve special commendation. The form-critical components of the encomium are fairly consistent, and they include a recognition of ancestors (*genos*) and recitation of their deeds (*praxeis*). A helpful example is the praise of Xenophon of Corinth and his family in various athletic contests:

---

9. John J. Collins, *Jewish Wisdom in the Hellenistic Age* (Louisville: Westminster John Knox, 1997), 98.

10. For the suggestion of Hellenistic biography, see Thierry Maertens, *L'Éloge des Pères: Ecclésiastique XLIV–L* (Bruges: Abbaye de Saint-André, 1956). On the Praise of the Ancestors as a type of epic poem, see Burton L. Mack, *Wisdom and the Hebrew Epic: Ben Sira's Hymn in Praise of the Fathers* (Chicago: University of Chicago Press, 1986). For a review of the scholarship and generic possibilities, see Thomas R. Lee, *Studies in the Form of Sirach 44–50*, SBLDS 75 (Atlanta: Scholars Press, 1975), 29–79.

He hath thus attained what no mortal man ever yet attained before. (Ol. 13.30–31)

... for these hundred years, no city hath given birth to a man more munificent in heart, more ungrudging in hand, than Theron. (Ol. 2.93–95)[11]

It is an open question as to whether all of these components are present in the Praise of the Ancestors.[12] Lee argues that this entire section of Sirach in effect functions as an encomium to Simon, because the author emphasizes the priests Aaron and Phinehas, the cultic functions of political figures (Joshua, Samuel, David, Solomon, Josiah), and the engineering feats of Simon along with those of predecessors like Solomon, Hezekiah, Zerubbabel/Joshua, and Nehemiah. According to Lee, "All of these fathers—priests, military heroes, kings, governors—are for Sirach types of the high priest."[13]

Lee is certainly correct that Ben Sira emphasizes priestly figures and their careers. Moreover, his argument that the Praise of the Ancestors should be read as an encomium works better than any of the other suggestions. Yet it is questionable whether the entirety of these tributes can be read *solely* as an encomium to Simon. There are too many other figures in this section who are not priests (Elijah, Joshua, son of Nun, Nathan, etc.) to depict the entirety of chapters 44–50 as focused exclusively on Simon. While eclectic and uneven in his recounting, Ben Sira's persistent fascination with priestly terms and figures requires further explanation.

Was Ben Sira a Priest?

In seeking to explain this feature of the Praise of the Ancestors, some commentators have speculated that Ben Sira was himself a

---

11. Lee, *Studies in the Form of Sirach 44–50*, 117, offers background on this passage.

12. The components of Sir 44–50 are as follows, according to Lee's schema: *Prooemium* (prologue) in Sir 44:1-15; *genos* (ancestors of the person being praised) in 44:16–49:16; *praxeis* (tribute to and accomplishments of the actual person) in 50:1-21; epilogue in 50:22-24.

13. Lee, *Studies in the Form of Sirach 44–50*, 213.

priest.[14] This sapiential author has clear respect for priestly institutions, particularly cultic leaders, and he alludes to biblical verses that glorify priests. His positive appraisal is discernible in several passages beyond the Praise of the Ancestors, particularly the discussion of proper sacrifices in 34:21–35:13 and also in 7:29-31, which sanctifies the priestly office: "With all your soul fear the Lord, and revere his priests" (v. 29). The parallelism here closely ties "fear of the Lord" with respect for the priestly office past and present. Because of his adherence to the Torah and respect for priestly institutions, Ben Sira requires his listeners to "honor the priest, and give him his portion, as you have been commanded" (v. 31). There is ample precedent in the Hebrew Bible for giving to the priest a generous allowance, but earlier instructions had not devoted the attention to this requirement that Ben Sira does.[15]

Along with the Torah stipulations that he clearly endorses, such language probably has a strategic element. As a scribal-sage and a member of the "retainer class," this author had to cultivate relationships with priests and other elite officials in order to maintain his status and livelihood.[16] Earlier sages had negotiated a royal patronage

---

14. Helge Stadelmann, *Ben Sira als Schriftgelehrter: Eine Untersuchung zum Berufsbild des vor-makkabäischen Sōfēr unter Berücksichtigung seines Verhältnisses zu Priester-, Propheten- und Weisheitslehrertum*, WUNT 2 (Tübingen: Mohr, 1981), claims that Ben Sira was actually a priest, since he functioned as a scribe and educator after the exile in a manner similar to Ezra. Stadelmann's theory has not attracted consensus, but see Saul Olyan, "Ben Sira's Relationship to the Priesthood," *HTR* 80 (1987): 261–86, who claims that Ben Sira's regard for the priesthood is central to his overall project, especially the language in Sir 7:29-31. Moreover, Olyan argues that the model for Ben Sira's understanding is not an exclusive (Zadokite) understanding or a pan-Levitical framework but rather a pro-Aaronid "P" perspective. See below for further discussion.

15. For the antecedent passages, see Exod 29:27; Lev 7:31-34; Deut 18:3.

16. Along with other scholars, Benjamin G. Wright, "'Fear the Lord and Honor the Priest': Ben Sira as Defender of the Jerusalem Priesthood," in *The Book of Ben Sira in Modern Research: Proceedings of the First International Ben Sira Conference, 28-31 July 1996, Soesterberg, Netherlands*, ed. Pancratius C. Beentjes, BZAW 255 (Berlin: de Gruyter, 1997), 195–96, finds a hierarchy in Sirach, where the author is part of the "retainer class" of educated "scribe-sages" who served the priestly elite and other powerful individuals (including Greek officials). Deference to the priesthood becomes a necessary strategic decision.

system and a bureaucracy that deferred to the king and his coterie of advisers as guarantors of the administrative hierarchy (e.g., Prov 25:1). In the face of exile and permanent colonial presence in the region, those in Judea during the Second Temple period had different structures to address. Cultic leaders, particularly the high priest and his officials, had more influence over the larger culture, including some control over the ability of scribal-sages to disseminate their instructional discourse.

Yet even with this strategic language, the content of the instruction does not indicate that Ben Sira was himself a priest or that he came from a priestly family. There is no indication of a priestly status in the Praise of the Ancestors or earlier sections of the book. If this author were a priest, it would stand to reason that the grandson would mention it in the prologue, but there is no such acknowledgment. Moreover, the vast majority of the content is traditional instructional discourse in the mold of Proverbs and other ancient wisdom texts. The sections on priestly matters, while innovative for a wisdom text, are relatively few in number. Moreover, the language in chapter 7 occurs in a lengthy unit on respect for different categories of people, including parents (7:27-28), priests (vv. 29-31), and those with various challenges (vv. 32-35). The next section encourages common sense with a variety of types (8:1-19). As a result, this discussion of priests constitutes just one element in a diverse list. Similarly, in the section on sacrifices, topics such as concern for the poor (34:24-25) and virtuous behavior (35:5) are familiar tropes for instructional discourse. These references to priests reflect sincere engagement with the Torah but should not necessarily lead one to assign priestly status to Ben Sira. One might compare this instruction with *Jubilees* (late second century BCE), which deals extensively with priestly concerns. Sirach does not reflect the same type of halakhic engagement with priestly matters that one finds in *Jubilees*, however. Ben Sira's respect for cultic institutions is an indicator of his membership in the "retainer class" and his sincere allegiance to Mosaic traditions, yet there is no real indication that he himself was a priest.

Aaron, Phinehas, and Simon in the Praise of the Ancestors

When we turn to the priestly figures in the Praise of the Ancestors, we see that Aaron has a more prominent role than any figure in this section, with the exception of Simon, and his authority rivals or even supersedes that of Moses. In deference to Aaron, it is a noteworthy feature that the priestly aspect of Moses' mission receives no mention in this section.[17] Ben Sira declares that the Deity gave Aaron "the priesthood of the people" (Sir 44:6) and a crown inscribed with "holiness" (v. 12). When ordained by Moses, Aaron received special status:

> He chose him out of all the living
>   to offer sacrifice to the Lord,
> incense and a pleasing odor as a memorial portion,
>   to make atonement for the people (Heb. "all of the Israelites").
> In his commandments he gave him
>   authority and statutes and judgments,
> to teach Jacob the testimonies,
>   and to enlighten Israel with his law. (Sir 45:16-17)

In addition to investing Aaron with the accoutrements of holiness (Sir 45:8-12), God (through Moses) endowed Aaron with the task of offering sacrifices, the critical role of "making atonement" (Heb. *lekapper*) for the people and instructing the nation in Torah. This last aspect of Aaron and his vocation finds its basis in Deut 33:10 and Moses' blessing to Levi: "They teach Jacob your ordinances, and Israel your law."[18]

Based on this passage and subsequent ones, it seems clear that Ben Sira views Aaron as perhaps the central figure in setting a template for subsequent believers and preserving the tradition. The intricate recall attests to this author's clear affinity for Aaron and his allegiance

---

17. Olyan, "Ben Sira's Relationship to the Priesthood," 267, points out that the Priestly (P) genealogy of Levi in Exod 6:16-25 does not include Moses.

18. John J. Collins, *The Scepter and the Star: The Messiahs of the Dead Sea Scrolls and Other Ancient Literature* (New York: Doubleday, 1995), 88–89, notes a similar teaching role for the eschatological high priest in 4Q541 (4QAaron A) from the Dead Sea Scrolls corpus.

to priestly authority. Aaron receives more attention than Abraham, Moses, or David, and he represents the obvious model for Simon and other high priests to follow. For Ben Sira, it is Aaron who is the primary lawgiver in the Praise of the Ancestors, not Moses (contrast Philo's *De Vita Moses* 1.155–158).

Commentators have long noticed the absence of Zadokite language in this section on Aaron. There are no references to Zadok or the sons of Zadok. The descendants of Zadok and his line are seen in some passages as the pure and legitimate successors in the lineage (e.g., Ezek 40:46, where only the Zadokites can minister in the newly reconstructed temple). Saul Olyan argues that a protest against Zadok is implicit in the non-mention of this figure in the Praise of the Ancestors: this text supports a "pan-Aaronid" framework rather than the exclusivism of the Zadokite line (as reflected in the addition of Sir 51:12i).[19] Yet arguments from silence are rarely sufficient evidence for finding a polemic in an ancient text, and this is a venturesome argument. While it is perplexing that Simon II's Zadokite lineage is not mentioned in this section, the most we can reasonably say about this issue is that Ben Sira offers a lengthy tribute to Aaron and bookends this section with similar praise of Simon.

Ben Sira next commends the priestly figure of Phinehas, who shows great "zeal" in Num 25:7-13 by violently purging idolatry from the midst of the wandering Israelites (the Baal Peor episode). While Ben Sira praises this figure's enthusiasm, he skips the grim violence in which Phinehas engages and makes a more generic reference to his "zeal" and willingness to "make atonement for Israel" (Sir 45:23). We should note the similar priestly terminology that the author used in reference to Aaron. In his discussion of Phinehas, Ben Sira distinguishes the covenant with David and the one with Aaron, and there are strong indicators that the priestly line is superior to the royal one. Aaron, Phinehas, and their successors have the "dignity of the priesthood forever" (v. 24), and the line always runs through Aaron (v. 25). This section concludes with a stirring benediction (45:26), and the only other declaration of this type occurs at the end of the encomium to Simon (Sir 50:22-24). The use of a benediction at the end of these two sections is hardly coincidental; it attests to Ben Sira's

---

19. Olyan, "Ben Sira's Relationship to the Priesthood," 285.

enduring respect for priests and their networks and his reverence for the lineage that traces back to Aaron.[20]

The Praise of the Ancestors concludes with a vivid tribute to Simon that draws upon the encomium of Hellenistic literature. According to the paen to Simon, this figure made key architectural improvements to the temple (Sir 50:1-3) and other infrastructure advances (v. 4) that live into the models of earlier history and indicate actual historical events.[21] What most distinguishes Simon in this section is his splendor as a priest: "When he put on his glorious robe and clothed himself in perfect splendor, when he went up to the holy altar, he made the court of the sanctuary glorious" (v. 11). The ties to Aaron in this section are obvious, as Simon is flanked by priestly attendants in his presentation of the offerings: these sons of Aaron "in their splendor held the Lord's offering in their hands before the whole congregation of Israel" (v. 13). Simon's majesty and preeminence over this glorious celebration, which includes singers and elaborate offerings, are clearly apparent in this section. There is a comparable passage in the *Letter of Aristeas*, where the author describes the majesty of the high priest in laudatory, almost superhuman terms (96–99).

In addition to praising Simon as the legitimate successor to Aaron, there are additional reasons for this descriptive praise. Ben Sira reveres the temple as a place of worship *and* a source of knowledge, as evidenced by his earlier association of the Wisdom figure and the temple in the middle of the instruction (e.g., Sir 24:10, where he refers to the temple as a "holy tent").[22] It could also be the case that he exalts Simon as "the full moon at the festal season" (Sir 50:6) to refute rival groups who followed the solar calendar, such as those responsible for *1 Enoch* (especially the Book of the

---

20. Collins, *Jewish Wisdom in the Hellenistic Age*, 102.

21. The background for this activity around the temple is Judean aid for the Syrian ruler, Antiochus III, in his campaigns against an Egypt garrison. In exchange for this assistance, Antiochus provided resources for temple renovations (see *Ant.* 12.129–153). Ben Sira devotes his praise to Simon rather than wading into these historical details about a political alliance.

22. Wright, "'Fear the Lord and Honor the Priest,'" 189–222.

Watchers) and *Aramaic Levi*.²³ As many commentators have argued, Ben Sira was clearly aware of the Enochic traditions involving calendrical matters, priestly institutions, and eschatological proposals, and he sought to refute them.²⁴ Yet the baseline reason for his praise seems to be an allegiance to priestly traditions in the Torah. This section reflects Ben Sira's clear devotion to the priestly institutions as described in the Torah, including and especially the priestly office. The ceremonial aspects of Simon's work are of great importance to Ben Sira as a manifestation of Torah and Jewish identity.

Conclusion

The Praise of the Ancestors in Sir 44–50 involves selective recitation, modeled in part on the Greek encomium, that describes and exalts figures from Israel's past and present. When compared with earlier instructions, this is a pioneering move for a sapiential text, though we have other examples of this retrospective praise in the late Second Temple period (e.g., 1 Macc 2:51-60). In a real sense, this section of the instruction constitutes reception history because it offers a snapshot of how certain figures from the past were being remembered, recast, minimized, or ignored altogether. There seems to be a great deal of subjectivity, as is usually the case when interpreting earlier traditions. In a great many cases, the attention in these chapters to a particular figure does not correlate with his prominence in the Hebrew Bible, and we have already mentioned the complete absence of women in the praise.

One of the distinguishing features of these chapters is the lengthy praise dedicated to priestly figures and the intricate, vivid detail in which they are described. Many reasons have been offered to explain this aspect of Sirach, including the author's need to cultivate healthy relationships with priests in order to prosper, his devotion to Aaron and his lineage, and perhaps an implicit polemic against those who opposed the official cultic structures of his day. Many of these

---

23. Ibid., 207.

24. For background on Ben Sira's response to the Enochic traditions, see Randal A. Argall, *1 Enoch and Sirach: A Comparative Literary and Conceptual Analysis of the Themes of Revelation, Creation, and Judgment.* SBLEJL 8. (Atlanta: Scholars Press, 1995).

arguments have merit and shed insight on this striking feature of the instruction. Yet there is perhaps a much more basic reason for this aspect of the Praise of the Ancestors. Ben Sira venerated Aaron and his descendants, including Simon, as the recipients and purveyors of what was commanded in the Torah. This sapiential author had an affinity for and clear allegiance to cultic practices and priestly traditions, and he repeatedly emphasizes the Torah as an essential component of wisdom. In his scholarship, Samuel Balentine has shown that the Torah's vision for worship was complex and that it extended and developed among successive generations after the exile. Ben Sira perpetuated these traditions by connecting Torah and wisdom, and also giving sustained attention to priestly figures. This feature of the instruction seems to represent not only strategic inclusion but also sincere and faithful recitation. The Praise of the Ancestors demonstrates that reception history can be an innovative process, and the modern generic categories we create do not necessarily reflect the complexity of the ancient sources.

Bibliography

Adams, Samuel L. "Where Is Ezra? Ben Sira's Surprising Omission and the Selective Presentation in the Praise of the Ancestors." In *The Pursuit of Wisdom and Human Flourishing: The Book of Sirach and Its Contexts*. Edited by Samuel L. Adams, Greg Schmidt Goering, and Matthew J. Goff. JSJSup. Leiden: Brill, forthcoming.

Argall, Randal A. *1 Enoch and Sirach: A Comparative Literary and Conceptual Analysis of the Themes of Revelation, Creation, and Judgment*. SBLEJL 8. Atlanta: Scholars Press, 1995.

Balentine, Samuel E. *Wisdom Literature*. CBS. Nashville: Abingdon, 2018.

———. *The Torah's Vision of Worship*. OBT. Minneapolis: Fortress, 1999.

Collins, John J. *Jewish Wisdom in the Hellenistic Age*. Louisville: Westminster John Knox, 1997.

———. *The Scepter and the Star: The Messiahs of the Dead Sea Scrolls and Other Ancient Literature*. New York: Doubleday, 1995.

Horsley, Richard, and Patrick Tiller. "Ben Sira and the Sociology of the Second Temple." Pages 74–108 in *Second Temple Studies III: Studies in Politics, Class, and Material Culture*. Edited by Philip R. Davies and John M. Halligan. JSOTSup 340. London: Sheffield Academic, 2002.

Huff, Barry R. "Dipped in Filth and Clothed in Glory: Job's Transformation of Priestly Terms, Themes, Texts, and Theologies." PhD diss., Union Presbyterian Seminary, 2017.

Lee, Thomas R. *Studies in the Form of Sirach 44–50*. SBLDS 75. Atlanta: Scholars Press, 1975.

Mack, Burton L. *Wisdom and the Hebrew Epic: Ben Sira's Hymn in Praise of the Fathers*. Chicago: University of Chicago Press, 1986.

Maertens, Thierry. *L'Éloge des Pères: Ecclésiastique XLIV–L*. Bruges: Abbaye de Saint-André, 1956.

Olyan, Saul. "Ben Sira's Relationship to the Priesthood." *HTR* 80 (1987): 261–86.

Skehan, Patrick W., and Alexander A. Di Lella. *The Wisdom of Ben Sira*. AB 39. New York: Doubleday, 1987.

Stadelmann, Helge. *Ben Sira als Schriftgelehrter: Eine Untersuchung zum Berufsbild des vor-makkabäischen Sōfēr unter Berücksichtigung seines Verhältnisses zu Priester-, Propheten- und Weisheitslehrertum*. WUNT 2. Tübingen: Mohr, 1981.

Wright, Benjamin G. "'Fear the Lord and Honor the Priest': Ben Sira as Defender of the Jerusalem Priesthood." Pages 189–222 in *The Book of Ben Sira in Modern Research: Proceedings of the First International Ben Sira Conference, 28-31 July 1996, Soesterberg, Netherlands*. Edited by Pancratius C. Beentjes. BZAW 255. Berlin: de Gruyter, 1997.

14

Job the Priest
From Scripture to Sculpture

Barry R. Huff

It is an honor and a joy to dedicate this essay to my dissertation adviser and friend, Samuel E. Balentine, whose groundbreaking scholarship and enlightening conversations illumined my research of priestly themes in both the book of Job and its reception history. In multiple publications, Sam brilliantly analyzes artistic depictions of Job as a priest and the theological implications of connections between Job and the Torah's priestly traditions.[1] I deeply appreciate Sam's consummate scholarship, sterling character, gracious mentoring, insightful guidance, and inspiring encouragement to research priestly depictions of Job in Scripture and sculpture.

Flame in hand, an innovative sculpture of Job drew more than 20,000 pilgrims per year to a parish church in Wezemaal, Belgium, between 1495 and 1520 (Fig. 14.1).[2] This short sculpture is displayed at an

---

1. Samuel E. Balentine, "Job as Priest to the Priests," *ExAud* 18 (2002): 30–31, 49–50; idem, *Job*, SHBC (Macon, GA: Smyth & Helwys, 2006), 446, 481–87; idem, "Job and the Priests: 'He Leads Priests Away Stripped' (Job 12:19)," in *Reading Job Intertextually*, ed. Katharine Dell and Will Kynes, LHBOTS 574 (New York: Bloomsbury, 2013), 51–52; idem, *Have You Considered My Servant Job?: Understanding the Biblical Archetype of Patience*, Studies on Personalities of the Old Testament (Columbia: University of South Carolina Press, 2015), 43–44.

2. Historian Bart Minnen shared these pilgrimage numbers in an email on 5 June 2011 titled "In-depth study on the St Martin's Church of Wezemaal (Belgium) & the devotion to St Job, 1000–2000." I am grateful to Bart

elevated height so that Job glances downward from his throne toward pilgrims.³ Gold leaf covers the sculpture's wood surface and enhances the grandeur of Job's robe and turban. The deep red of the flame draws the viewer's eyes to the fire rising directly from Job's left hand, carved from the same piece of wood as if Job and the flame were one. Four painted words, "GODT GAF GODT NAMP" ("God gave, God took") (Job 1:21), appear in a book held in Job's right hand.⁴ Remarkably, this sculpture has remained in the main edifice of St. Martin's Church for six centuries, attracting pilgrims in search of healing and inspiration. Following mass on the Feast of Job, this sculpture would be carried in procession.⁵ Today, the Brotherhood of

---

Minnen, art historian Ingrid Geelen of the Royal Institute for Cultural Heritage (KIK-IRPA), and Reverend Michel Tilleman—Pastor Emeritus of St. Martin's Church in Wezemaal, Belgium—for providing valuable insights during our meeting at this church on 27 February 2008 and through our correspondence and their contributions to Bart Minnen, ed., *Den Heyligen Sant al in Brabant: De Sint-Martinuskerk van Wezemaal en de Cultus van Sint-Job 1000–2000*, 2 vols. (Averbode: Altiora, 2011).

3. This sculpture is 70 cm. tall. Ingrid Geelen conveyed this helpful detail in an email on 15 January 2020.

4. KIK-IRPA, "Sint-Job, Kerk Sint-Martinus [Wezemaal], 4411," BALaT, http://balat.kikirpa.be/object/4411. I appreciate Ingrid Geelen, Heidi Hornik, and Amy Torbert sharing insights on polychromy as well as Amy Torbert highlighting the potential significance of the flame and Job's hand being carved from one piece of wood.

5. The first record of pilgrims coming to Wezemaal to venerate Job dates to 1437, and the devotion to Saint Job in Wezemaal likely began between 1377 and 1437. Bart Minnen, "Le Culte de Sint Job à Wezemaal aux XVᵉ et XVIᵉ Siècles," in *Congrès d'Ottignies-Louvain-La-Neuve: 26, 27 et 28 Août 2004: Actes des VIIᵉ Congrès de l'Association des Cercles Francophones d'Histoire et d'Archéologie de Belgique (AFCHAB) et LIVᵉ Congrès de la Fédération des Cercles d'Archéologie et d'Histoire de Belgique* (Brussels: Safran, 2007), 604, 608; Bart Minnen, "De Sint-Martinuskerk van Wezemaal en de cultus van Sint-Job 1000–2000," in *Den Heyligen Sant al in Brabant: De Sint-Martinuskerk van Wezemaal en de Cultus van Sint-Job 1000–2000*, ed. Bart Minnen (Averbode: Altiora, 2011), 1:39; Ingrid Geelen and Anna Bergmans, "Beeldenpracht in een middeleeuwse dorpskerk," in *Den Heyligen Sant al in Brabant*, ed. Minnen, 2:116.

Figure 14.1. *Sint-Job (Saint Job)*, ca. 1390–1430. Polychromed wooden sculpture. 70 cm. tall. Kerk Sint-Martinus, Wezemaal, Belgium. Photo Credit: KIK-IRPA, Brussels.

Job, formed in 1878,⁶ still gathers annually at this church in May to celebrate the Feast of Job, pray, and give an offering in honor of Job.⁷

What has attracted pilgrims for more than half a millennium to this sculpture of Job? What inspired its sculptor to break from artistic convention and depict Job not naked on a dung heap but enthroned in regal attire? What is the significance of and inspiration behind the flame in the hand of several depictions of Job in this era? What led Samuel Terrien to identify this and other sculptures in Belgium, Luxembourg, and the Netherlands as "Saint Job the Priest," and is this identification accurate?⁸ What light can priestly themes in the book of Job shed on priestly iconography in sculptures of Job, and vice versa? What are the theological implications of priestly themes in Joban texts and visual art?

This essay explores these questions, centering on one church's illuminating contributions to the rich reception history of Job and on the recurring motif of a flame in the hand of Job. This iconography unites this statue of Job in Wezemaal with two early sixteenth-century examples: a Job sculpture in Museum Mayer van den Bergh (Fig. 14.2) where the flame emerges from a chalice, and the Passion Altarpiece at Nordingra (Fig. 14.3).⁹ The multivalence of this imagery—including the juxtaposition not only of Job and the crucifixion of Jesus in the Passion Altarpiece at Nordingra but also of sculptures of Job the priest (see Fig. 14.1) and Job the sufferer in St. Martin's Church in Wezemaal—resonates with the book of Job's

---

6. Minnen, "Sint-Martinuskerk," 1:337.

7. These insights about the Brotherhood of Job are based on helpful comments by Father Michel Tilleman in our conversation on 27 February 2008 at St. Martin's Church in Wezemaal. While this organization is named the Brotherhood of Job, the book of Job itself ends with the protagonist surpassing the rights granted to women in the Torah by giving his daughters an inheritance along with his sons (Job 42:14-15; cf. Num 27:1-11).

8. Samuel Terrien, *The Iconography of Job Through the Centuries: Artists as Biblical Interpreters* (University Park, PA: Pennsylvania State University Press, 1996), 149–51.

9. For additional depictions of Job holding a flame, created from around the late fourteenth century to the early sixteenth century, see Geelen and Bergmans, "Beeldenpracht," 2:121–24.

nuanced engagement with and transformation of the Torah's priestly themes and theologies.

Sculptures of Job in Belgium exemplify Balentine's conclusion that every layer of interpretation of Job "is a witness to historical and cultural contingencies that shape both academic and ordinary apprehensions of the text."[10] The historical contingency of a syphilis epidemic heightened the sculptures' relevance as diseased pilgrims saw in Job a Christlike model of faithful endurance through the fire of suffering. Balentine further observes that each layer of interpretation "is a reminder that critical analysis of what the text means to contemporary readers is at least as important as what it meant to its presumptive first readers and hearers."[11] Additionally, more recent layers, like the Testament of Job and Gregory the Great's *Moralia in Job*, may be more relevant than the original layer of the book of Job to the design and interpretation of the sculpture of an enthroned Job in Wezemaal. Through his concept of "visual exegesis," art historian Paolo Berdini argues that what the artist visualizes is not the biblical text itself but rather an expansion of the text based on the artist's reading of the text in light of the artist's interests, sources, and contexts.[12] While the names of the artists who created the sculptures in this essay are unknown, an analysis of these sculptures in light of the social, religious, and historical contexts in which they were created and displayed, and especially in light of the reception history of Job in those eras, can illumine our understanding of them.[13]

Biblical scholarship has often overlooked many of the intertextual, thematic, theological, and especially lexical connections between

---

10. Balentine, *Have You Considered*, 11.

11. Ibid.

12. Paolo Berdini, *The Religious Art of Jacopo Bassano: Painting as Visual Exegesis* (Cambridge: Cambridge University Press, 1997), xi, 35; Heidi J. Hornik and Mikeal C. Parsons, *Illuminating Luke: The Infancy Narrative in Italian Renaissance Painting* (Harrisburg: Trinity Press International, 2003), 6–7; Martin O'Kane, *Painting the Text: The Artist as Biblical Interpreter* (Sheffield: Sheffield Phoenix, 2007), 36, 41–43.

13. Hornik and Parsons, *Illuminating Luke*, 6–8; cf. J. Cheryl Exum and Ela Natu, "Introduction," in *Between the Text and the Canvas: The Bible and Art in Dialogue*, ed. J. Cheryl Exum and Ela Natu (Sheffield: Sheffield Phoenix, 2007), 2; O'Kane, *Painting the Text*, 46.

Figure 14.2. *Job op de Mesthoop (Job on the Dung Heap)*, 1510–1520. Wooden sculpture. 79.5 cm. tall. Museum Mayer van den Bergh, Antwerp, Belgium. Photo Credit: KIK-IRPA, Brussels.

Figure 14.3. Bernard Van Orley, *Retable de la Passion (Passion Altarpiece)*, detail, 1500–1510. Oil on oak. Church, Nordingra, Sweden. Photo Credit: KIK-IRPA, Brussels.

Job and the Torah's priestly corpus.[14] Yet the reception history of Job includes numerous examples of artists, authors,[15] priests, and pilgrims drawing connections between Job and priestly themes.[16] Artists discerned connections between Job and priestly themes centuries before biblical scholars. Over the past several decades, a small number of biblical scholars have begun to highlight these

---

14. The Torah's priestly corpus includes texts like the following: Gen 1:1–2:4a; Exod 25–30; 35–40; Leviticus; Num 1:1–10:28.

15. A fourth-century CE text, *Apostolical Constitutions*, identifies Job as a priest. See Lawrence L. Besserman, *The Legend of Job in the Middle Ages* (Cambridge: Harvard University Press, 1979), 167.

16. Cf. Bart Minnen, ed., *Den Heyligen Sant al in Brabant*; Balentine, *Have You Considered*, xiv–xv, 22–23, 43–44, 210–13; Balentine, "Job as Priest to the Priests"; Samuel Terrien, *Iconography of Job*, 149–51.

connections.[17] Yet much of the priestly imagery in Job depicted by artists has not been adequately addressed in biblical scholarship. Job scholars have much to learn from this rich reception history, and an increased emphasis by biblical scholars on under-appreciated priestly themes in Job would enrich art historians' analysis of the elusive priestly iconography in Joban sculptures.

The Fire of Job: Its Source and Significance

The most overt connection between Job and the Torah's priestly themes is the central role that burnt offerings play in the prose tale of Job and in Leviticus. Burnt offerings epitomize Job's piety in the book's prologue as he offers burnt offerings for his children and in the epilogue as he receives his friends' burnt offerings and prays for his friends (Job 1:5; 42:8). This is the most likely biblical foundation for the flame in the left hand of the oldest Job sculpture in Wezemaal (see Fig. 14.1), reinforced by the biblical text in Job's right hand since this text and burnt offerings both appear in the prologue of Job. Because the burnt offering is the only sacrifice in Leviticus in which the entire animal, except for the hide (Lev 7:8), is wholly consumed by fire and completely offered as a gift to God, James W. Watts concludes that the burnt offering is the sacrifice that represents

---

17. In addition to the works by Balentine cited above, see Leo G. Perdue, *Wisdom and Cult: A Critical Analysis of the Views of Cult in the Wisdom Literatures of Israel and the Ancient Near East*, SBLDS 30 (Missoula, MT: Scholars Press, 1977); Israel Knohl, *The Sanctuary of Silence: The Priestly Torah and the Holiness School* (Minneapolis: Fortress, 1995), 165–67; Mary Douglas, *Leviticus as Literature* (Oxford: Oxford University Press, 1999), 205–12, 247–51; William Scott Green, "Stretching the Covenant: Job and Judaism," *RevExp* 99 (2002): 574–77; Konrad Schmid, "Innerbiblische Schriftdiskussion im Hiobbuch," in *Das Buch Hiob und seine Interpretationen: Beiträge zum Hiob-Symposium auf dem Monte Verità vom 14–19 August 2005*, ed. Thomas Krüger, Manfred Oeming, Konrad Schmid, and Christoph Uehlinger, ATANT 88 (Zürich: Theologischer Verlag Zürich, 2007), 241–63; Konrad Schmid, "The Authors of Job and Their Historical and Social Setting," in *Scribes, Sages, and Seers: The Sage in the Eastern Mediterranean World*, ed. Leo G. Perdue, FRLANT 219 (Göttingen: Vandenhoeck & Ruprecht, 2008), 145–53; Barry R. Huff, "Dipped in Filth and Clothed in Glory: Job's Transformation of Priestly Terms, Themes, Texts, and Theologies" (PhD diss., Union Presbyterian Seminary, 2017).

"the purist form of divine service."[18] The LXX and Testament of Job amplify sacrificing as Job's defining religious act by stating that Job's children feast daily, thereby implying that Job offers burnt offerings daily for his children in case they sinned (T. Job 15:1-9).[19] The Testament of Job goes even further by specifying the enormous number of animals that Job would sacrifice: "300 doves, 50 goat's kids, and 12 sheep" (15:4).[20]

The Testament of Job, likely written in the first century BCE or CE,[21] describes Job witnessing burnt offerings brought to the temple of Satan's idol and Job choosing to destroy it, even though the divine voice out of the flame warns Job that doing so will result in the loss of his children and health (2:2–3:3).[22] The Testament of Job's depiction of Job sitting on a dung heap (T. Job 20:7; 21:1; 28:8) is echoed in many sculptures of Job in Belgium around the time of this sculpture, and its description of Job as a king may be reflected in the regal attire of the enthroned Job in this sculpture (T. Job 28:7). Therefore, it is possible that the flame in Job's hand is also informed by the Testament of Job's depiction of Job as daily sacrificing and willingly losing everything in order to prevent burnt offerings from being brought to the temple of Satan's idol. The prevalence of burnt offerings in the biblical prose tale of Job, their amplification in the Testament of Job, and the direct linkage between these texts and other features in this and contemporaneous sculptures of Job in Brabant bolster the likelihood that the flame in Job's hand represents burnt offerings.

---

18. James W. Watts, *Ritual and Rhetoric in Leviticus: From Sacrifice to Scripture* (Cambridge: Cambridge University Press, 2007), 71. Cf. Huff, "Dipped in Filth and Clothed in Glory," 65.

19. Harold W. Attridge, "Testament of Job," in *Outside the Bible: Ancient Jewish Writings Related to Scripture*, ed. Louis H. Feldman, James L. Kugel, and Lawrence H. Schiffman (Philadelphia: Jewish Publication Society, 2013), 2:1879.

20. Ibid., 2:1879–80.

21. Susan Docherty, *The Jewish Pseudepigrapha: An Introduction to the Literature of the Second Temple Period* (Minneapolis: Fortress, 2015), 101; Attridge, "Testament of Job," 2:1872.

22. R. P. Spittler, "Testament of Job: A New Translation and Introduction," *OTP* 1:840. Cf. Balentine, *Have You Considered*, 55–56.

While the identity of the artist who created this unique wood sculpture is unknown, Ingrid Geelen and Anna Bergmans conclude that the sculpture was likely created in a Brabantine workshop and that its sophisticated symbolism may have been inspired by the Norbertines of Averbode, who would have been familiar with Gregory the Great's *Moralia in Job*.[23] Due to the significant influence throughout the Middle Ages of Gregory the Great's late sixth-century magnum opus, *Moralia in Job*, one must consider references to fire in *Moralia in Job* when interpreting the sculptor's "visual exegesis."[24]

Describing burnt offerings as a holocaust, Gregory the Great metaphorically interprets Job's burnt offerings in Job 1:5 as intense prayer that purifies each virtue, proclaiming, "a holocaust is a sacrifice that is totally consumed. Therefore the offering of a holocaust means to burn the mind completely with the fire of compunction, so that the heart may burn on the altar of love and consume its impure thoughts, as though they were the sins of its own family."[25] Similar themes emerge in Gregory the Great's commentary on Job 23:10:

> *He tries me like gold that passes through fire.* Gold in the furnace reaches the brightness of its nature when it loses its dross. So like gold that passes through fire, the souls of the just are tried; by the burning action of trials their vices are removed and their merits increase. . . . it was not on account of any vices that had to be purged that [Job] was permitted to be tried, but his gold was purified in the fire in order that his merits might increase.[26]

---

23. Geelen and Bergmans, "Beeldenpracht," 2:125. I appreciate Ingrid Geelen's helpful comments to me on 15 January 2020, clarifying that, while the sculpture's symbolism was likely inspired by the Norbertines of Averbode, the sculpture itself was not necessarily carved in the Averbode Abbey.

24. Cf. Paolo Berdini, *The Religious Art of Jacopo Bassano*, xi; Mark Del-Cogliano, introduction to *Moral Reflections on the Book of Job: Volume 1, Preface and Books 1–5*, by Gregory the Great, trans. Brian Kerns, Cistercian Studies 249 (Collegeville, MN: Liturgical Press, 2014), 26–27; Balentine, *Have You Considered*, 34, 92.

25. Gregory the Great, *Moral Reflections on the Book of Job, Volume 1*, trans. Kerns, 107.

26. Gregory the Great, *Moral Reflections on the Book of Job: Volume 3, Books 11–16*, trans. Brian Kerns, Cistercian Studies 249 (Collegeville, MN: Liturgical Press, 2016), 293.

Thus, burnt offerings and fire in *Moralia in Job* signify the purification of thought and virtue through suffering that results in the gold of character shining forth. The union of the flame and Job's left hand, carved from a single piece of wood, in the Wezemaal sculpture reinforces this symbolism. The protagonist who consistently sacrifices for his children becomes a sacrifice himself (cf. Job 16:13), purified through fire.

The motif of Job holding a flame in art in Brabant from the late fourteenth century through the early sixteenth century captures the central priestly theme of Job's burnt offerings from the Joban prologue and the Testament of Job. Through the lens of Gregory the Great's interpretation, this motif speaks with new relevance to the lives of all believers, beckoning them, like Job, to persevere through the fire of suffering that burns away the dross of impurity so that the gold of virtue can radiate. Although this sculpture was created ca. 1390–1430,[27] the flame's potential message of purification by fire and endurance through suffering likely helped draw the thousands of pilgrims who traveled to it a century later during the height of the syphilis epidemic. A sermon by Pierre de Radis that was printed in 1514 describes syphilis as Job's malady, highlights Job's patience while suffering from disease, encourages pilgrimage to the Job sculpture in Wezemaal, and attributes the regaining of bodily health of many people at Wezemaal to Job's invocation.[28] A 1625 litany by Wezemaal Pastor Bergans reinforces Gregory the Great's interpretation

---

27. KIK-IRPA's database dates this sculpture to ca. 1400–1430 at the web page "Sint-Job, Kerk Sint-Martinus [Wezemaal], 4411," BALaT, http://balat.kikirpa.be/object/4411. Agnès Ballestrem and Robert Didier argue for an earlier date in the second half of the fourteenth century based on stylistic factors. See Agnès Ballestrem and Robert Didier, "Le Calvaire, la Madeleine et le Job de Wezemaal: Un Groupe de Sculptures Gothiques Polychromes," *Bulletin de l'Institut Royal du Patrimoine Artistique = Bulletin van het Koninklijk Instituut voor het Kunstpatrimonium* 7 (1964): 140. Geelen and Bergmans posit a date for this sculpture around 1400 or even during the last decade of the fourteenth century (Geelen and Bergmans, "Beeldenpracht," 2:119).

28. Minnen notes that an alternative spelling, Badis, is also attested (Minnen, "Le Culte de Sint Job," 603).

of fire imagery in Job, praising Job as a forerunner of Christ, gold tested and refined in fire.[29]

The gilded robe and turban on this polychromed sculpture enhance its sacredness.[30] Furthermore, they resonate with Gregory the Great's description of gold passing through the fire and with Job's portrayal of his justice as "a robe (*měʿîl*) and a turban (*ṣānîp*)" (Job 29:14). The term *ṣānîp* ("turban") describes the wardrobe of only one other person in the Hebrew Bible, the high priest Joshua in Zech 3:5, giving Job's regalia a priestly dimension in Job 29:14.[31] Furthermore, *měʿîl* ("robe") describes the high priest's robe in Exodus (Exod 28:4, 31, 34; 29:5; 39:22-26).[32] Balentine identifies the robe on this sculpture as priestly and notes that the book with an inscription from Job 1:21, which blesses God's name, is held in the sculpture's right hand, "the priestly 'blessing hand.'"[33] While Samuel Terrien discerns a priestly dimension in the cap on the oldest Job sculpture in Wezemaal, which he asserts "vaguely resembles a Phyrgian cap, the ancient headgear of the god Mithras,"[34] Ingrid Geelen and Bart Minnen challenge this conclusion in light of the similar caps used on other sculptures in the region during this era simply to designate Old Testament characters.[35]

Job and Jesus: Priestly Symbolism beyond Wezemaal Sculptures

The flame motif from the oldest sculpture of Job in Wezemaal (see Fig. 14.1) also appears in an oak sculpture of Job at Museum Mayer van den Bergh. This sculpture sits 79.5 cm. tall and dates from

---

29. Geelen and Bergmans, "Beeldenpracht," 2:122–23.

30. Ibid., 2:120.

31. Balentine, "Job as Priest to the Priests," 37–38; Balentine, "Job and the Priests," 49–50.

32. Huff, "Dipped in Filth and Clothed in Glory," 45–47.

33. Balentine, "Job as Priest to the Priests," 31.

34. Terrien, *Iconography of Job*, 149.

35. Ingrid Geelen and Bart Minnen provided this helpful context during our conversation at St. Martin's Church in Wezemaal on 27 February 2008 and in my conversation with Ingrid at KIK-IRPA on 28 February 2008.

1510–1520 (see Fig. 14.2).[36] Here Job lacks a throne and robe, yet he holds a more explicit priestly symbol. The flame reappears in Job's left hand, but now, rather than holding the flame directly, the flame emerges from a chalice.[37] Priestly symbols for sacrifice from Judaism and Christianity unite in Job's left hand through the presence of this Jewish symbol for burnt offerings in the Christian chalice held by a priest during the Eucharist.[38] C. L. Seow insightfully interprets this fiery chalice as alluding to "the cup (Vulgate: *calix*) of divine wrath" drunk by the suffering servant (Isa 51:17, Vulgate), noting that drinking from this cup represents devastation (Jer 25:15-29; cf. Matt 26:39) and that God taking away this cup represents restoration (Isa 51:22; cf. Job 1:21).[39] Flames from the chalice connect to the upper rib of the Job sculpture at Museum Mayer van den Bergh. While this may be merely a structural design "to assure the stability of the chalice,"[40] Terrien concludes, "From the cup of sacramental blood emerge flames that have burned a gaping wound at the very heart of the Christ-like priest."[41]

The flame imagery also reappears in Job's hand in the Passion Altarpiece at Nordingra (see Fig. 14.3), which juxtaposes Job and the crucifixion of Jesus. This altarpiece of the Passion was painted

---

36. KIK-IRPA, "Job op de Mesthoop, Museum Mayer van den Bergh," BALaT, http://balat.kikirpa.be/object/138202.

37. A sculpture of Job from the first half of the sixteenth century at the Musée d'Art Religieux et d'Art Mosan in Liège, Belgium, also depicts Job holding a chalice from which emerges a flame. Behind the flame on Job's left shoulder sits a small figure, likely Satan, whispering in Job's ear. Job stands and wears a robe decorated with crosses. The robe does not cover Job's left leg, which is covered in sores. (Geelen and Bergmans, "Beeldenpracht," 2:124).

38. Cf. Balentine, "Job as Priest to the Priests," 31; Balentine, "Job and the Priests," 51.

39. I am grateful to C. L. Seow for shedding new light for me on Joban sculptures through his helpful comments and magnificent essay, "Job in Christian Visual Art: From Late Antiquity to 1700," in *The Many Faces of Job, I: From Antiquity to the Early Modern Period*, ed. C. L. Seow, Handbooks on the Bible and its Reception (Berlin: de Gruyter, forthcoming).

40. Ingrid Geelen conveyed this structural detail in an email on 10 March 2008.

41. Terrien, *Iconography of Job*, 149.

in oil on oak by Bernard Van Orley ca. 1500–1510 in Brussels.[42] A flame emerges directly from the hand of a robed Job in the Passion Altarpiece at Nordingra; this time, though, the flame is in Job's right hand while Job's left hand holds an inscription of Job 1:21. When the altarpiece is closed, one sees several religious scenes and characters, including Job at the top (Fig. 14.4). When the altarpiece is open, one sees the crucifixion of Jesus (Fig. 14.5). Thus, the Passion Altarpiece at Nordingra suggests a possible priestly profile of Job not only through the flame but also through the juxtaposition of Job with the atoning sacrifice of Jesus.

Sacred objects at St. Martin's Church in Wezemaal also juxtapose the suffering of Job and the crucifixion of Jesus, exemplifying Gregory the Great's description of Job as the precursor to Christ's suffering.[43] At the top of a solar, cylinder monstrance (Fig. 14.6), which held the consecrated Host, is a crucified Jesus, and immediately below the crucifix is Job (Fig. 14.7). This silver monstrance juxtaposing the faithful suffering of Job and Jesus was created by goldsmith Jan Wynants in Leuven between 1601 and 1650,[44] around the time of Wezemaal Pastor Bergans's 1635 litany praising Job as a forerunner of Christ.[45] This monstrance resonates with Balentine's conclusion: "In the rich and variegated history of Joban interpretation, Job is the model for the priest who offers to the sick of heart and wounded of faith what Terrien aptly describes as 'a sacramental Communion with the crucified and risen Lord.'"[46]

---

42. KIK-IRPA, "Retable de la Passion, Nordingra," BALaT, http://balat.kikirpa.be/object/40001382.

43. Minnen, "Sint-Martinuskerk," 1:41.

44. KIK-IRPA, "Cilindermonstrans, Kerk Sint-Martinus [Wezemaal]," BALaT, http://balat.kikirpa.be/object/4298.

45. Geelen and Bergmans, "Beeldenpracht," 2:122–24. Over two centuries later, a brass crucifix was created by goldsmith Raeymaeckers in 1861 featuring two biblical characters, Job at the base sitting with diseased skin on the dung heap and Jesus crucified at the top. See KIK-IRPA, "Kruisbeeld, Kerk Sint-Martinus [Wezemaal]," BALaT, http://balat.kikirpa.be/object/4294.

46. Balentine, "Job as Priest to the Priests," 31.

Figure 14.4. Bernard Van Orley, *Retable de la Passion (Passion Altarpiece)*, closed, 1500–1510. Oil on oak. Church, Nordingra, Sweden. Photo Credit: KIK-IRPA, Brussels.

Theological Conclusions from a Dialogue of Job Sculptures: Priestly Ministry from and to the Ash Heap

In the Wezemaal sculpture of Job enthroned (see Fig. 14.1), the sculpture's right hand holds a book displaying the message, "GODT GAF, GODT NAMP" ("God gave, God took").[47] Job proclaims these words at the close of the opening chapter of the book of Job after learning of the loss of his animals and children (Job 1:21). The biblical text depicts the protagonist tearing his robe, shaving his head, falling to the ground, and proclaiming that nakedness accompanies birth and death before voicing this message (Job 1:20-21). In contrast, the sculpture depicts Job clothed in robes, wearing a cap,

---

47. During our 27 February 2008 conversation at Saint Martin's Church in Wezemaal, Bart Minnen conveyed that this sculpture's right hand was replaced.

Figure 14.5. Bernard Van Orley, *Retable de la Passion (Passion Altarpiece)*, open, 1500–1510. Oil on oak. 185 x 221 x 20.5 cm. Church, Nordingra, Sweden. Photo Credit: KIK-IRPA, Brussels.

enthroned, and holding this message. Might this sculpture hint that even while physically on the ground with his robe in tatters, Job still exemplifies royalty? Even while labeled unclean, he still embodies the holiness of a priest. The prologue depicts Job as inflicted with *šĕḥîn* (Job 2:7), a skin disease that makes one ritually unclean and in need of priestly purification rituals before one can rejoin the community according to Lev 13–14.[48] Yet, in the book's epilogue, Job serves as a priest for his friends without being officially recognized as purified from his skin disease (Job 42:8-9; cf. Lev 14:2-3).

Job is a priest who persevered through skin disease and loss, who exemplified holiness while ritually unclean, and who understands the struggles of those to whom he is ministering. His journey and example spoke to the thousands of pilgrims suffering from syphilis

---

48. Cf. Balentine, "Job as Priest to the Priests," 31, 36.

Figure 14.6. Jan Wynants, *Cilindermonstrans (Cylinder Monstrance)*, 1601–1650. Silver. 64 cm. tall. Kerk Sint-Martinus, Wezemaal, Belgium. Photo Credit: KIK-IRPA, Brussels

Figure 14.7. Jan Wynants, *Cilindermonstrans (Cylinder Monstrance)*, detail, 1601–1650. Kerk Sint-Martinus, Wezemaal, Belgium. Photo Credit: KIK-IRPA, Brussels.

who flocked to Wezemaal in the late fifteenth and early sixteenth centuries yearning for healing and inspired by Job's model of resilient faith throughout ongoing suffering. A fence was erected around this sculpture to protect it from the crowds. Visible on the outside of the church's south wall are vertical scratch marks carved by pilgrims desperate to have a piece of this sacred sanctuary where Job sat enthroned (Fig. 14.8).[49] Carrying the text that symbolizes the steadfastness of his faith despite losing everything and the flame that conveys his complete devotion to God and purification by fire, this sculpture has inspired pilgrims for centuries as a model of faith that perseveres through the fire of suffering and emerges stronger from it.

Upon entering St. Martin's Church in Wezemaal today and following in the footsteps that pilgrims have trod for centuries, one sees two strikingly different sculptures of Job standing near the entrance. To the right is the enthroned Job, clothed in robes and flame in hand. To the left, near a stone sculpture of Mary Magdalene, is a stone sculpture of Job (Fig. 14.9).[50] This life-size Job, with robes removed and ribs exposed, sits on a dung heap rather than a throne. Job glances downward, a somber expression on his face. Because this sculpture was created ca. 1500 and the syphilis outbreak began in 1495, this sculpture of a diseased Job on a dung heap likely provided for diseased pilgrims flocking to Wezemaal a depiction of Job—a patron saint of syphilis sufferers—that resonated with their struggles and inspired them to persevere.[51] Furthermore, this stone sculpture

---

49. Ibid.; Minnen, "Le Culte de Sint Job," 608; KIK-IRPA, "Snijsporen op Gevelsteen, Kerk Sint-Martinus [Wezemaal]," BALaT, http://balat.kikirpa.be/object/150854.

50. KIK-IRPA, "Sint-Job, Kerk Sint-Martinus [Wezemaal], 4415," BALaT, http://balat.kikirpa.be/object/4415. In her 15 January 2020 comments on this essay, Ingrid Geelen notes that the BALaT database should date this sculpture to 1490–1510. She dates it to the beginning of the sixteenth century or around 1500. Ballestrem and Didier also date this sculpture to the beginning of the sixteenth century ("Le Calvaire, la Madeleine et le Job de Wezemaal," 146).

51. Minnen notes that, since syphilis struck separate individuals and was a disease that individuals suffered with for years, it became known as the disease of St. Job. Job emerged as a patron saint of syphilis sufferers beginning in the late fifteenth century and continuing into the sixteenth century (Minnen, "Sint-Martinuskerk," 1:40–42, 62–63).

Figure 14.8. *Snijsporen op Gevelsteen (Cut Marks on Brick)*, ca. 1401–1500. Kerk Sint-Martinus, Wezemaal, Belgium. Photo Credit: KIK-IRPA, Brussels.

of Job resembles the popular theme in the late fifteenth century of Christ sitting nearly naked on a stone awaiting crucifixion.[52] The suffering Job's prayer for his accusers prefigures the crucified Jesus' prayer for his executioners (Job 42:8-10; Luke 23:34),[53] and the iconography of Job parallels that of Jesus.[54]

The placement of both sculptures of Job on different sides when one enters the main edifice of the Church of Saint Martin holds in dialogue and tension two important dimensions of the biblical Job. While these sculptures at the entrance to the church are drawn from

---

52. Geelen and Bergmans, "Beeldenpracht," 2:131. Ballestrem and Didier compare Job's attitude in this sculpture to Christ's attitude at Calvary ("Le Calvaire, la Madeleine et le Job de Wezemaal," 140).

53. Balentine, *Job*, 711.

54. G. Von der Osten asserts that "the iconography of Job was in fact the origin of the closely related type of the Christ in Distress. . . . Job in Distress becomes the Christ in Distress" ("Job and Christ: The Development of a Devotional Image," *Journal of the Warburg and Courtauld Institutes* 16 [1953]: 156).

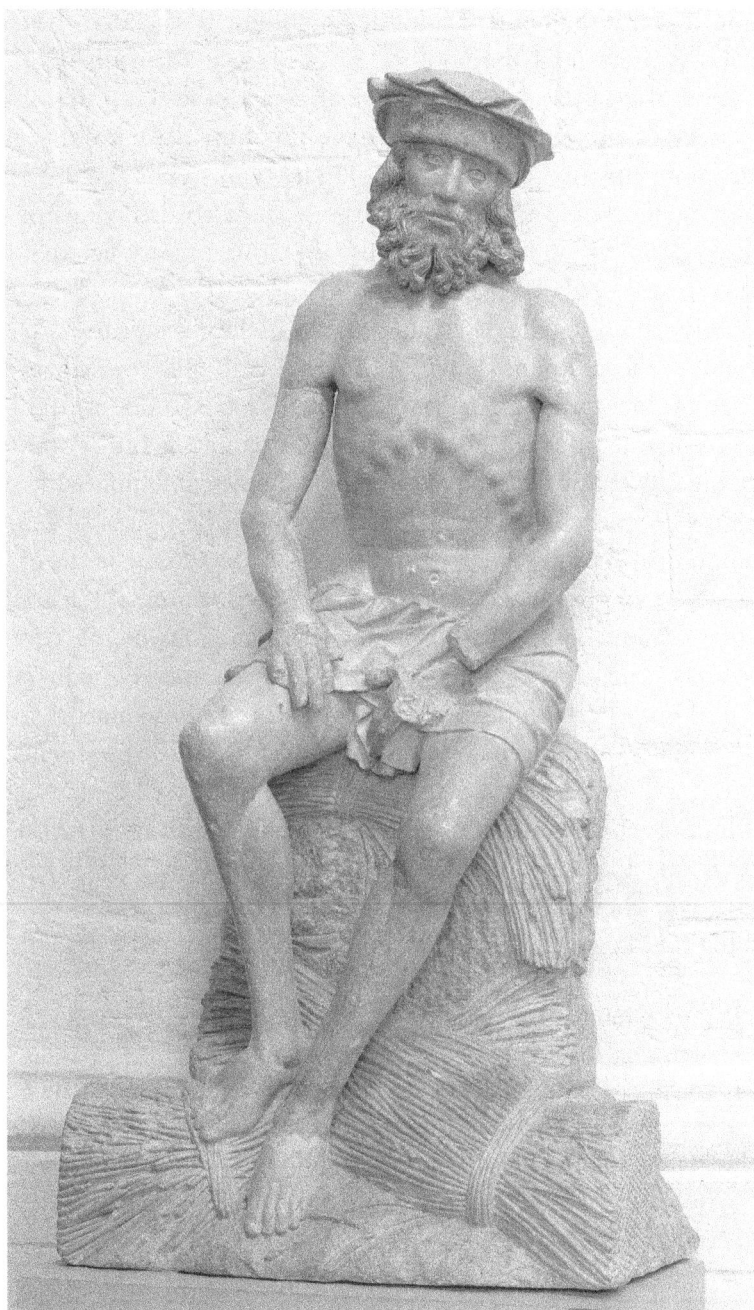

Figure 14.9. *Sint-Job (Saint Job)*, ca. 1500. Stone. 177 x 87 x 43 cm. Kerk Sint-Martinus, Wezemaal, Belgium. Photo Credit: KIK-IRPA, Brussels.

the prologue of the book of Job, they highlight aspects that the close of Job's speeches and the book's epilogue also hold in dialogue. At the close of his speeches, while appearing like the sculpture of Job on a dung heap, the protagonist envisions himself in royal regalia as he confronts God (Job 31:35-37). The book's epilogue opens by depicting Job accepting burnt offerings from and praying for his accusers (Job 42:7-9). Yet it is only after this priestly act that the biblical text describes Job's restoration (Job 42:10-13).

Only through the dialogue of these Job sculptures do we encounter the moment depicted in the Joban epilogue, where the ostracized Job rather than the enthroned Job should be the one performing the priestly act and holding the flame of a burnt offering. Flipping the levitical script, it is the protagonist inflicted with skin disease who, rather than being examined by a priest (Lev 14:2-3), is appointed by God to serve as a priest (Job 42:8-9). Some of the oldest badges sold to pilgrims in Wezemaal capture this moment as well as features of both sculptures through their depictions of Job covered in sores, sitting on a dung heap, yet holding a flame.[55] The juxtaposition of these Job sculptures reminds visitors to Wezemaal that the ideal priest is one who has sat on a dung heap, whose experience of suffering informs empathetic ministry. Balentine observes that Leviticus links the ordination ceremony for priests (Lev 8:22-30) with the restoration ritual for those healed of skin disease (Lev 14:1-32) as the sole rituals where a priest daubs blood on the right earlobe, thumb, and big toe (Lev 8:23-24; 14:14). He insightfully questions,

> Is it the case, perhaps, that only those who have traveled the life-scarring road from being condemned and ridiculed to being restored and embraced can really know what it means to be a priest to the afflicted? Is it the case, perhaps, that priests who stand inside the rituals that bind a fragile world to a holy God are most

---

55. These pilgrim badges predate 1473 and resonate with the later Job sculpture at Museum Mayer van den Bergh (1510–1520) by portraying Job giving a miraculous coin, holding a flame, and sitting on a dung heap (Minnen, "Sint-Martinuskerk," 1:48–49, 333; Geelen and Bergmans, "Beeldenpracht," 2:123–24).

attuned to their tasks when they know themselves vulnerable to the wounds of this world?[56]

Like the daubing rituals in Leviticus, the sculptures of Job in St. Martin's Church in Wezemaal unite priests and those who have experienced skin disease. Both sculptures reflect vital aspects of Job's journey and identity: Job the priest and Job on the ash heap in need of a priest.[57]

In isolation, neither sculpture tells the whole story, but together they remind priests that ministry must be grounded in compassion for and understanding of the life experience of those who are suffering. Together they remind pilgrims that those the world sees as unclean and ostracized are viewed instead by God as holy and worthy to serve the Almighty. Together they bring hope for divine restoration to those who have suffered loss (Job 1:21).[58] Together they echo the book of Job's nuanced engagement with, challenge to, and transformation of the Torah's priestly tradition. Together they comfort the afflicted and inspire outcasts, from the height of a sixteenth-century syphilis epidemic in Europe to today.

For over six centuries, St. Martin's Church in Wezemaal has celebrated the Feast of Saint Job. During this celebration in recent years, the liturgy includes intercessions to Job, who overcame suffering, to provide support to those whose bodies are marked with disease. Facing the sculpture of the enthroned Job, the Brotherhood of Job also prays for Job, who was misjudged and abandoned, to embrace those in broken relationships and to be a model for the marginalized.[59]

From the book of Job to the Brotherhood of Job and from Scripture to sculpture, Job attunes priests to the voices of sufferers and serves sufferers as a priest whose bleeding footsteps we may follow. In

---

56. Balentine, "Job as Priest to the Priests," 49.

57. Cf. ibid., 31, 36, 38.

58. Cf. Seow's inspiring interpretation of Job 1:21 in the context of the flame imagery in Joban sculptures (Seow, "Job in Christian Visual Art").

59. These insights are drawn primarily from Michel Coune, "Sint-Job—Wezemaal" (brochure, Tremelo: Druk Eraly), and secondarily from my conversation at St. Martin's Church in Wezemaal on 27 February 2008 with the parish priest, Father Michel Tilleman.

those moments when we are clawing the walls, when we are yearning for health and holiness, when we are sitting on the ash heap, when we are labeled unclean and longing for dignity, we can see in the juxtaposition of the Wezemaal sculptures of Job a model of solidarity in our suffering, resilience in the face of tragedy, faith forged in the fire, and royal holiness embodied even by those labeled unclean.[60]

Bibliography

Attridge, Harold W. "Testament of Job." Pages 1872–99 in vol. 2 of *Outside the Bible: Ancient Jewish Writings Related to Scripture*. Edited by Louis H. Feldman, James L. Kugel, and Lawrence H. Schiffman. Philadelphia: Jewish Publication Society, 2013.

Balentine, Samuel E. *Have You Considered My Servant Job?: Understanding the Biblical Archetype of Patience*. Studies on Personalities of the Old Testament. Columbia: University of South Carolina Press, 2015.

———. *Job*. SHBC. Macon, GA: Smyth & Helwys, 2006.

———. "Job and the Priests: 'He Leads Priests Away Stripped' (Job 12:19)." Pages 42–53 in *Reading Job Intertextually*. Edited

---

60. I deeply appreciate the numerous individuals and organizations whose helpful guidance and gracious support made this essay possible. Samuel E. Balentine inspired, encouraged, facilitated, and guided my research on this topic. Bart Minnen, Ingrid Geelen, and Father Michel Tilleman shared important insights in our conversations and correspondence. Colin Campbell, Jover Christianson, Kat Collins Booth, Katherine Hynd, and especially Erik Mack assisted with translating sections of these volumes and other Dutch, Italian, and French sources related to my research for this essay. KIK-IRPA, The Royal Institute for Cultural Heritage in Brussels, granted permission to use the photos in this essay, and its staff, including Ingrid Geelen, thoughtfully supported my research in their superb collections. Grants from Principia College's Faculty Research Fund, Dorothy D. Moller Research Fellowship, and Humanities Division paid for translation and permission expenses. The Bible and Visual Art Section shared helpful feedback when I presented this essay at the 2019 Annual Meeting of the Society of Biblical Literature in San Diego. The section's Co-Chair, Heidi Hornik, as well as Amy Torbert of the Saint Louis Art Museum, Ingrid Geelen, C. L. Seow, Patricia Vesely, and Ann Torbert all provided insightful comments on a draft of this essay, strengthening it with their expertise.

by Katharine Dell and Will Kynes, LHBOTS 574. New York: Bloomsbury, 2013.

———. "Job as Priest to the Priests." *ExAud* 18 (2002): 30–31.

Ballestrem, Agnès, and Robert Didier. "Le Calvaire, la Madeleine et le Job de Wezemaal: Un Groupe de Sculptures Gothiques Polychromes." *Bulletin de l'Institut Royal du Patrimoine Artistique =Bulletin van het Koninklijk Instituut voor het Kunstpatrimonium 7* (1964): 133–52.

Berdini, Paolo. *The Religious Art of Jacopo Bassano: Painting as Visual Exegesis.* Cambridge: Cambridge University Press, 1997.

Besserman, Lawrence L. *The Legend of Job in the Middle Ages.* Cambridge: Harvard University Press, 1979.

Coune, Michel. "Sint-Job—Wezemaal." Brochure. Tremelo: Druk Eraly.

de Coo, Jozef. *Museum Mayer van den Bergh: Catalogus 2.* Antwerp: Drukkerijen Govaerts, 1969.

DelCogliano, Mark. Introduction to *Moral Reflections on the Book of Job: Volume 1, Preface and Books 1–5*, by Gregory the Great. Translated by Brian Kerns. Cistercian Studies 249. Collegeville, MN: Liturgical Press, 2014.

Docherty, Susan. *The Jewish Pseudepigrapha: An Introduction to the Literature of the Second Temple Period.* Minneapolis: Fortress, 2015.

Douglas, Mary. *Leviticus as Literature.* Oxford: Oxford University Press, 1999.

Exum, J. Cheryl, and Ela Natu, eds. *Between the Text and the Canvas: The Bible and Art in Dialogue.* Sheffield: Sheffield Phoenix, 2007.

Geelen, Ingrid, and Anna Bergmans. "Beeldenpracht in een middeleeuwse dorpskerk." Pages 113–35 in vol. 2 of *Den Heyligen Sant al in Brabant: De Sint-Martinuskerk van Wezemaal en de Cultus van Sint-Job 1000–2000.* Edited by Bart Minnen. Averbode: Altiora, 2011.

Green, William Scott. "Stretching the Covenant: Job and Judaism." *RevExp* 99 (2002): 569–77.

Gregory the Great. *Moral Reflections on the Book of Job: Volume 1, Preface and Books 1–5*. Translated by Brian Kerns. Cistercian Studies 249. Collegeville, MN: Liturgical Press, 2014.

———. *Moral Reflections on the Book of Job: Volume 3, Books 11–16*. Translated by Brian Kerns. Cistercian Studies 249. Collegeville, MN: Liturgical Press, 2016.

Hornik, Heidi J., and Mikeal C. Parsons. *Illuminating Luke: The Infancy Narrative in Italian Renaissance Painting*. Harrisburg: Trinity Press International, 2003.

Huff, Barry R. "Dipped in Filth and Clothed in Glory: Job's Transformation of Priestly Terms, Themes, Texts, and Theologies." PhD diss., Union Presbyterian Seminary, 2017.

Knohl, Israel. *The Sanctuary of Silence: The Priestly Torah and the Holiness School*. Minneapolis: Fortress, 1995.

Minnen, Bart. "Le Culte de Sint Job à Wezemaal aux XVe et XVIe Siècles." Pages 603–609 in *Congrès d'Ottignies-Louvain-La-Neuve: 26, 27 et 28 Août 2004: Actes des VIIe Congrès de l'Association des Cercles Francophones d'Histoire et d'Archéologie de Belgique (AFCHAB) et LIVe Congrès de la Fédération des Cercles d'Archéologie et d'Histoire de Belgique*. Brussels: Safran, 2007.

———, ed. *Den Heyligen Sant al in Brabant: De Sint-Martinuskerk van Wezemaal en de Cultus van Sint-Job 1000–2000*. 2 vols. Averbode: Altiora, 2011.

———. "De Sint-Martinuskerk van Wezemaal en de cultus van Sint-Job 1000–2000." Pages 27–348 in vol. 1 of *Den Heyligen Sant al in Brabant: De Sint-Martinuskerk van Wezemaal en de Cultus van Sint-Job 1000–2000*. Edited by Bart Minnen. Averbode: Altiora, 2011.

O'Kane, Martin. *Painting the Text: The Artist as Biblical Interpreter*. Sheffield: Sheffield Phoenix, 2007.

Perdue, Leo G. *Wisdom and Cult: A Critical Analysis of the Views of Cult in the Wisdom Literatures of Israel and the Ancient Near East*. SBLDS 30. Missoula, MT: Scholars Press, 1977.

Schmid, Konrad. "The Authors of Job and Their Historical and Social Setting." Pages 145–53 in *Scribes, Sages, and Seers: The Sage in the Eastern Mediterranean World*. Edited by Leo G. Perdue. FRLANT 219. Göttingen: Vandenhoeck & Ruprecht, 2008.

———. "Innerbiblische Schriftdiskussion im Hiobbuch." Pages 241–63 in *Das Buch Hiob und seine Interpretationen: Beiträge zum Hiob-Symposium auf dem Monte Verità vom 14–19 August 2005*. Edited by Thomas Krüger, Manfred Oeming, Konrad Schmid, and Christoph Uehlinger. ATANT 88. Zürich: Theologischer Verlag Zürich, 2007.

Seow, C. L. "Job in Christian Visual Art: From Late Antiquity to 1700." In *The Many Faces of Job, I: From Antiquity to the Early Modern Period*. Edited by C. L. Seow. Handbooks on the Bible and its Reception. Berlin: de Gruyter, forthcoming.

Spittler, R. P. "Testament of Job: A New Translation and Introduction." *OTP* 1:829–68.

Terrien, Samuel. *The Iconography of Job Through the Centuries: Artists as Biblical Interpreters*. University Park, PA: Pennsylvania State University Press, 1996.

Von der Osten, G. "Job and Christ: The Development of a Devotional Image." *Journal of the Warburg and Courtauld Institutes* 16 (1953): 153–58.

Watts, James W. *Ritual and Rhetoric in Leviticus: From Sacrifice to Scripture*. Cambridge: Cambridge University Press, 2007.

Scripture Index

HEBREW BIBLE

GENESIS
1–11	4, 49, 59, 63, 72
1–9	70, 72
1–2	49
1:1–2:4a	333
1:1–2:3	59, 64
1	45, 46, 47, 48, 52, 60, 62, 64, 67, 68, 70, 71, 72, 220, 305, 307
1:1	306, 307
1:2	46, 64, 306
1:3	304
1:3, 6, 9, 11, 14, 20, 24, 26	47
1:4, 10, 12, 18, 21, 25	48
1:9, 11, 20, 24	49
1:11, 20-21, 24-25	49
1:21	50, 51
1:21, 26-30	50
1:22	49
1:26-31	50
1:26, 28	70
1:30	70
2–4	62
2–3	63
2:2-3	61
2:17	64
3:22	183, 296
5	60
5:1-3	67
6	62
6:5	64
6:9-13	61
6:11-13	64
6:13	49, 60, 61, 62
8:1	65
8:21	64, 188
9	68, 70, 71
9:1-17	64, 70
9:1-7	65
9:1	65
9:2	70
9:3-4	49
9:4-6	66, 67, 68, 70
9:5	67, 69
9:8-17	65
9:9-11	71
9:10	71
9:12-16	71
9:13-15	65
9:15	65
10	68
16:7	103
17	54, 66, 71
18:27	253
24:67	252, 254
25:27	21
32:22-32	21
32:22-31	20
32:30	21
37:3-4	130
37:23-24	130
37:35	252, 254
38:12	252
39	5, 127, 129
39:1	129
39:3-6	129
39:7-10	129
39:11-15	129
39:12-18	129

39:16-20	129	14:10	104	29	82
39:20	130	14:13	103	29:5	338
39:21-23	130	14:14	103, 119	29:27	318
		14:19	103	30:13	117
EXODUS		14:24	117	31	71
1:1-4	112	15:2	114	32–34	82
1:7	116	15:13	115	32:12, 14	252
1:15	116	15:20	119	32:27	96
1:19	119	16:4	119	32:32	113
1:22	114	16:15	117	33:2	103
2	79	16:18	119	33:7	117
2:3	117	16:36	117	34:19-20	81
2:16	114	17:7	119	35–40	60, 333
2:18	114	17:8	116	38:8	110
3–4	79, 80	18:11b	113	39:22-26	338
3	78	19–Num		40:15	118
3:1	103, 116	10:10	81		
3:2	119	19–24	75	**LEVITICUS**	
3:4	117	19:1	117	1:1-9	82
3:16	114	19:4	117	7:8	334
3:22	119	19:6	314	7:31-34	318
4:14	119, 182	20:1-17	118	8	82
4:20	114	21–23	114	8:22-30	348
6:7	119	21	118	8:23-24	348
6:12	117	21:6	184	13–14	342
6:20	79, 116	21:12-32	67	14:1-32	348
6:23	116	21:12-14	67	14:2-3	342, 348
9:16	117	21:15-16	67	14:14	348
10:3	119	21:28	67	17–26	75
10:14	114	23:19	117	21:1-4	83
10:19	116	23:20-24	103	25:32, 33	77
11:9	117	24:1-14	114		
12:14	118	24:1	114	**NUMBERS**	
12:37	116	24:15-18	301	1:1–10:28	333
13:2	81	25–40	75	1:1–10:10	81
13:4	117	25–31	60	3–Deut 34	76
13:13	117	25–30	109, 333	3:1	76
13:17	252	25:17	118	3:11-13	76
14	109	26:15	104	3:11	81
14:7	104	28:4	117	3:40-51	81
14:8	117	28:4, 31, 34	338	3:44-51	76
14:10-26	107	28:30	117	8	77, 82

8:5-19	81	**JOSHUA**		10:24	183
8:13-19	76	3:5	249	11	160
16–18	83	24	315	11:1-2	161
17–20	4			11:3-4	160
17–19	4	**JUDGES**		11:41	159
17–18	77, 78, 83	6	80	12:1-19	160
18	85			17–2 Kgs 9	165
18:9, 11	84	**RUTH**		21:20	171
18:12-17	85	2:10-13	254		
19	79, 85			**2 KINGS**	
19:2-10	85	**1 SAMUEL**		4:1-7	165, 167,
19:11-12	86	1:8	182		169, 170
20	4, 75, 79	4:20	182	5:1-27	166, 167,
20:1-13	77, 78	12:21	46		169, 170
20:1	78, 82, 86	15:11, 29	252	6:8-23	166, 167,
20:2-13	83, 86				169, 170
20:8	78	**2 SAMUEL**		6:24–7:20	166, 167,
20:12	4	13:39	252		169, 170
20:22-29	87			6:27	166
25:7-13	321	**1 KINGS**		7:1	167
27:1-11	330	2:33	184	7:2	167
33	109	3:9	206	18–20	162
		3:14	161	22–23	162
DEUTERONOMY		3:16-28	159	22:1–23:25	99
1–3	315	3:28	159	22:1	163
1:9-18	94	4:1-7	173	22:11	162
4:9	182	4:7-19	160	22:13	163
6:8	302	4:11, 15	160	22:19-20	163
11:18	302	4:29-34	159	23:28-30	163
17:8-20	93	4:34	159		
17:14-20	161	5:1-27	173	**1 CHRONICLES**	
18:3	318	5:12	159, 161	16:36	184
23:4	184	6:8-23	173	21:15	252
28:65	183	6:24–7:20	173		
29:4	183	8:9	160	**2 CHRONICLES**	
30:12-14	303	8:23-53	160	9:23	183
30:15	235	8:27	160	15:16	119
32:10	46	9:4-7	162		
32:33	50	10:4-8	159	**EZRA**	
33:10	320	10:8	160	4	104
34	87	10:14-25	160	7:27	183
		10:23-25	159		

NEHEMIAH		9:21	250	24:18-25	248
2:12	183	9:34-35	248	26:7-14	259
7:5	183	10:1-2	248	26:7	46
		10:2, 6-7, 17	251	26:14	256
JOB		10:3	250	27:6	244
1:1	21, 273	10:9	253	27:13-23	248
1:1, 8	272	12:2-3	248	28	8, 157, 176, 299, 303
1:4-5	273, 276	12:7	213		
1:5	243–44, 334, 336	12:13-25	259		
		12:24	46	28:1-19	176
1:8	13	13:3, 15b, 18-19	248	28:3, 9-11	299
1:15, 17	53			28:12	5, 8, 157, 158, 173, 175, 176, 179, 196
1:16, 19	53	13:6-12, 17-28	251		
1:19	262				
1:20-21	341	13:12	253		
1:21	328, 338, 339, 341, 349	13:15a	248	28:12, 20	299, 300
		13:18-19	259	28:14	303
		13:19	248	28:14, 22	299
1:22	272	13:25	248	28:15-19	299
2:3	272	14:1-5	268	28:20, 23, 28	299
2:7	53, 342	14:3	251		
2:8, 12	252	14:7-10, 18-19	248	28:23-27	176
2:10	272			28:28	176
2:11	251, 254	15:11	251	29–31	241
3:24-25	248	16:2	251	29:14	338
4:19	253	16:8, 19-21	251	29:25	251
5:9	249	16:13	337	30	175
5:17	250	16:18-19	248	30:1	250
6:4	248	19:5, 7, 25	251	30:7-8	258
6:18	46	19:13-16	248	30:19	253
6:21	248	19:18	250	30:29	258, 262
6:24	248	19:25	248	31	244, 245
6:28-29	241	21:2-26	248	31:1	244
7:11	248	21:4b	247	31:7	244
7:12	51, 248	21:34	251	31:13	250
7:13	251	23:4	248	31:23	248
7:22-23	52	23:4, 6-7	248	31:35-37	348
8:17	299	23:6-7	248	31:37	248
8:20	250	23:6	251	34:33	250
9:2-35	251	23:10	336	36:5	250
9:2-20	248	23:15-16	248	37:5	249
9:4-10	259	24:4b	258	37:14	249

38–42	248	41:3	53	98:1	249
38–41	7, 46	41:26	258, 260	101	245
38:1	250	41:33	53	104:1	218
38:2	249	42:1-6	249	104:21	257
38:3	259	42:2-3	256	106:22	249
38:16	256	42:2	257	107:40	46
38:16, 19	259	42:3	249, 254,	109:3	306
38:17	256		255, 257	119	206
38:18	256	42:6	7, 249,	119:11, 15,	
38:19	256		250, 251,	34, 67, 71	245
38:22	256		252, 261	119:18	249
38:23	259	42:6b	253	136:4	249
38:25-27	256	42:6b, 11	252	139:13	226
38:25	260	42:7-9	348	141:4	206
38:28-29	260	42:7-8	175		
38:29-41	52	42:8-10	346	**PROVERBS**	
38:39–39:30	257	42:8-9	342, 348	1–9	6,
38:39-41	260	42:8	334		200–203,
38:39	257	42:10-13	348		205–207,
38:8-11	52, 259	42:10-12	254		216,
39:2	52	42:11	251, 252,		218–19,
39:5-12	52		254		221–27
39:5-8	257	42:14-15	330	1:2	237
39:5	52	42:15-17	263	1:3	237
39:6	258, 260	52:4-7	268	1:18, 19	223
39:9-12	53			1:20-33	296
39:13-18	52	**PSALMS**		1:20-23	8, 204,
39:18	258	4:7	183		237
39:19-25	260	4:19	103	1:33	238
40–41	52	15	245	2–3	204, 224
40:4-5	254, 257	19:2-7	218	2	202, 204,
40:4	248, 253	19:7	218		206, 207,
40:6	250	37:25	239		223
40:7	259	44:2	306	2:1-10	221
40:9-14	257, 259	49:5	206	2:1-6	204, 205
40:11-12	258	71:20-21	254	2:1-2	206
40:15–41:26	257	74:13	51	2:10	183, 207,
40:15-24	52	74:14	258		223, 225
40:15	53	79:7	115	2:17	220
40:15, 16a	262	84	218	2:2	223
40:19	259, 262	86:17	254	2:2, 3, 6, 11	206
41:1-34	52	91:13	50	2:2, 10	223

2:3	206	8	8, 204, 298, 306, 307	1:13, 17	187
2:5-6	206			1:14	189
2:5	225			1:16	183, 187, 189
2:6	204, 206	8:5	223, 298		
2:6, 10	223	8:14	295	1:17	189
2:7-9	207	8:17	299	2:1	187, 189
2:7	158	8:22-36	225	2:1, 15	187
2:9	158	8:22-24	204	2:3	183
3	225	8:22	226, 298, 305, 306, 307	2:10	183
3:1, 3, 5	223			2:12	189
3:3	302			2:13	189
3:5-8	225	8:23	226	2:14	192
3:13-20	8, 296	8:30	305	2:15a	187, 189
3:16-20	225	8:31	298	2:15b	187, 189
3:18	204	8:36	223	2:16	184
3:19-20	204	9:4, 16	223	2:24-26	180
3:19	225, 298	10–29	236	2:24	189
3:20	296	10:22	238	2:26	184, 187
3:21	296	11:22	52	3:1-8	185
3:22	223	14:1	52	3:9-15	190
4	202	15:17	52	3:10-15	192
4:1-5	203	15:19	52	3:10	184, 189, 190, 191, 195, 196
4:4-5	204	17:11	52		
4:4	204	19:12	52		
4:4, 23	223	21:19	52	3:11	181, 182, 190, 195, 289
4:5	206	22:5	52		
4:20	223	22:13	52		
5:1, 13	223	24:5	295	3:11a	191
5:12	223	25:1	159, 319	3:11b	6, 181, 183, 185–86, 188–89, 191–93, 196
5:19	52	26:9	52		
6:5, 6	52	26:13	52		
6:6	213	28:15	52		
6:14, 18, 21, 32	223	30:18	249		
		30:30	52		
6:16, 26, 30, 32	223	**ECCLESIASTES**		3:11b, 14	184
				3:11c	185, 189, 191–93
7:3	302	1:1–3:10	190		
7:3, 7, 10, 25	223	1:2, 15a	187	3:12-13, 22	180
		1:4, 10	184	3:12	190, 191
7:23	223, 302	1:7-10	180	3:13	190, 191
		1:12–2:26	175	3:14	191
		1:13	184, 189	3:15	191

SCRIPTURE INDEX

3:16–12:14	190	8:17	189	49:13	254
3:16-22	192	9:1-12	193	51:3	254
3:16-18	192	9:1-3	193	51:9	51
3:16	189	9:1	187, 189, 193	51:17	339
3:17-18	187			51:22	339
3:17	187, 189, 193	9:4-6	193	59:4	46
		9:6	184	60:19	218
3:18	187, 189, 193	9:7-12	193	63:19	184
		9:7-9	180, 193	64:7	253
3:19–8:8	189, 192, 193	9:10	194	66:13-14	254
		9:11	189		
3:19-22	192	9:13	189	**JEREMIAH**	
3:19	188	10:5	189	1	80
3:22	189	10:7	189	2:20	184
4:1–8:15	192	12:5	184	4:23	46
4:1	189	12:7	185	5:15	184
4:7	189	12:13	176	9:10	258
5:13	189			9:23-24	165
5:17	184	**ISAIAH**		10:22	258
5:18-20	180	5:1-7	61	18:4, 6	253
5:18	185	10:7	182	22:13-19	163
6:1	189	12:1	254	22:13-15, 17	164
6:2	185	13:22	258	22:15-16	164
7:15	189	24:10	46	22:17	182
7:23-29	195	26:4	184	22:18-19	164
7:25	192	27:1	51, 258	25:15-29	339
7:26	187	29:16	253	31:13	254
7:27	189	29:21	46	31:15	252
7:28	195, 196	33:20	115	31:19-20	69
7:29	189	34:11	46	31:33	183
8:5, 12-13	187	34:13	258	32:40	183
8:8	188	40:1	254	36:23	163
8:9-15	192	40:17, 23	46	49:6	315
8:9	189, 192, 193	41:25	253	49:33	258
		41:29	46	51:34	51
8:9, 16	187	42:14	184	51:37	258
8:10	189	44:9	46		
8:12	192	45:9	253	**EZEKIEL**	
8:15	180, 184	45:18	46	2–3	80
8:16–9:1	192	45:19	46	7:2-6	61, 62
8:16	189, 193	49:4	46	14:22	252

18:1-9	69	7:22	303	45:8	312
28	158	7:25	303, 306	45:16-17	320
28:16-18	158	7:26, 29	304	45:23	321
29:3	51	8:1, 6	303	45:24	321
31:16	252	8:2	304	45:25	321
32:2	51	8:3-16	304	45:26	321
32:31	252	8:5-7	243	48:1-16	312
40:46	321	8:7	304	48:23	315
49:8	315	12:23–13:9	245	49:14-16	315
				50:1-22	312
JOEL		**SIRACH**		50:1-21	311, 317
2:13	252	1:1-10	301	50:1-3	322
		4:11-19	242–43	50:4	322
AMOS		6:8-13	241	50:6	322
7:3	252	7:27-28	319	50:11	322
8:2	61	7:29-31	318, 319	50:13	322
		7:32-35	319	50:22-24	317, 321
JONAH		8:1-19	319	51:12	321
3:10	252	14:22-24	302	51:13-30	302
4:2	252	24	301, 303		
		24:3	301	**BARUCH**	
MICAH		24:4	301	3–4	303
1:8	258	24:5	301	3:30-31	303
7:15	249	24:6	301	3:37	303
		24:8-11	301	4:1	303
ZECHARIAH		24:10	322		
3:5	338	24:13-17	302	**1 MACCABEES**	
		24:23	301, 313	2:58	312
MALACHI		34:21–35:13	318	2:51-60	316, 323
4:5-6	312	34:24-25	319	2:56	315
		35:5	319		
APOCRYPHA		44–50	8, 311, 315–17, 323	**1 ESDRAS**	
TOBIT				2	104
4	244	44:1-15	314, 317	**4 MACCABEES**	
		44:6	320	16:20-23	316
WISDOM		44:12	320	18:11-19	316
6:18	304	44:16–49:16	317		
7:10	304	45:1b-5	312		
7:17-22	304	45:6-22	312		
7:22–8:2	304	45:8-12	320		

NEW TESTAMENT

MATTHEW
2:12	119
11:25-30	174
11:25a	174
11:25b-27	174
11:29	174
16:14	312
16:25	22
26:39	339

LUKE
1:35	306
12:13-21	161
12:20	161
12:27	161
19:42	166
23:34	346

JOHN
1:4	306
1:9	304
1:12	304
17:6-21	94
18:33-37	94

ROMANS
1:21-23	245
8:28	54
13	93

1 CORINTHIANS
1:25	174
2:14	273
8:46	305
10:1-5	305

2 CORINTHIANS
3:6	273

GALATIANS
4:24	207

COLOSSIANS
1:15-20	305
1:18	305

HEBREWS
10:6	274
11	316

1 PETER
5:1-11	94

Samuel E. Balentine

Advance Praise for
Seeking Wisdom's Depths and Torah's Heights

"This impressive collection of papers on Torah and wisdom, in honour of Samuel E. Balentine, offers a veritable cornucopia of lexical, theological, ethical, and epistemological readings of Scripture, as well as engaging with biblical texts expressed through sculpture, dance, visual arts and even quantum physics. Sam is well known not only for his prolific publications but also for the influence he has had on students and colleagues worldwide: this Festschrift is a worthy testimony to both aspects of his legacy."

—*Sue Gillingham*
Emeritus Professor of the Hebrew Bible
University of Oxford

"This volume admirably reflects Samuel Balentine's breadth of mind, depth of insight, height of character, and length of influence in biblical studies. It draws together established leading scholars in the field with exciting younger voices, who incorporate insight ranging from quantum mechanics and psychology to art history and ballet into careful literary analysis and creative theological and ethical exposition of the biblical text with the openness and curiosity that makes Balentine's work so captivating. The focus on Torah and wisdom furthers his important contributions to bridging the externally imposed categorical breach between them."

—*Will Kynes*
Associate Professor of Biblical Studies
Samford University

"Rich with exegetical insights, this volume makes provocative forays into terrain long scouted with perspicacity by Sam Balentine. In these pages, creation is explored as wild, as ruined, as generative of moral yearning and spiritual awe. Here are musings on the art of translation and visual exegesis, on clashing epistemologies and formation of the ethical imagination, on fearlessness and fragility as dimensions of life in community, and more. Highly recommended!"

—*Carolyn J. Sharp*
Professor of Homiletics
Yale Divinity School

"The only thing richer than a book by Samuel E. Balentine (though this might be debated) is a volume in honor of this one-of-a-kind scholar, teacher, and theologian. The present collection, authored by leading scholars focused on Torah and wisdom, is a worthy tribute to Balentine's innovations in theological and ethical interpretation, performed in interdisciplinary modes, with consistent attention paid to the history of reception. Echoing God's words in Job, one of the contributors asks, 'Have you considered my servant, Sam?' This book helps one do just that—and not just Sam, also his God and his beloved Scripture. A perfect trifecta!"

—Brent A. Strawn
Professor of Old Testament and Professor of Law
Duke University

"This volume is a stunning tribute to Samuel E. Balentine, a scholar and teacher beloved for his curiosity and creativity, his penetrating engagement with biblical texts and their theological-ethical implications, and his wise, generous collegiality. Inspired by and reflective of Sam's expansive interests and deep scholarly commitments, these essays that celebrate and demonstrate without question Sam's significant and enduring impact on biblical studies."

—Christine Roy Yoder
J. McDowell Richards Professor of Biblical Interpretation
Columbia Theological Seminary